Venice

The gorgeous and wonderful reality of Venice is beyond the
fancy of the wildest dreamer. Opium couldn't build such a
place, and enchantment couldn't shadow it forth in a vision.

... but Venice is above, beyond, out of reach of coming
near, the imagination of man. It has never been rated
high enough. It is a thing you would shed tears to see...

Charles Dickens
The Letters of Charles Dickens

Travel Publications

38 Clarendon Road - WATFORD Herts WD1 1SX - U.K.
Tel. (01923) 415 000
www.michelin-travel.com
TheGreenGuide-uk@uk.michelin.com

Manufacture française des pneumatiques Michelin

Société en commandite par actions au capital de 2 000 000 000 de francs
Place des Carmes-Déchaux – 63 Clermont-Ferrand (France)
R.C.S. Clermont-Fd B 855 200 507

© *Michelin et Cie, propriétaires-éditeurs, 2000*
Dépôt légal Août 2000 – ISBN 2-06-000052-1 – ISSN 0763-1383
Printed in France 11-00/2.2

Controllato ai sensi della Legge 02.02.1960 N. 68.
Nulla Osta alla diffusione N. 376 in data 01/09/2000.

Compograveur : APS-CHROMOSTYLE, Tours
Imprimeur-Brocheur : IME, Baumes-les-Dames
Maquette de couverture extérieure : Agence Carré Noir à Paris 17ᵉ

THE GREEN GUIDE:
The Spirit of Discovery

The exhilaration of new horizons, the fun of seeing the world, the excitement of discovery: this is what we seek to share with you. To help you make the most of your travel experience, we offer first-hand knowledge and turn a discerning eye on places to visit.

This wealth of information gives you the expertise to plan your own enriching adventure. With THE GREEN GUIDE showing you the way, you can explore new destinations with confidence or rediscover old ones.

Leisure time spent with THE GREEN GUIDE is also a time for refreshing your spirit and enjoying yourself.

So turn the page and open a window on the world. Join THE GREEN GUIDE in the spirit of discovery.

Contents

A gondola laden with fruit
and vegetables

Brightly coloured houses
in Burano

Portrait of Doge Leonardo Loredan
by Carpaccio (Bergamo, Accademia Carrara)

A typical
Venetian scene

Maps and plans

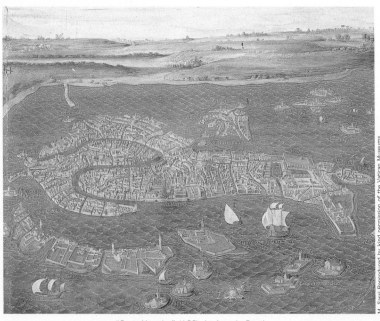

"Carte Venetiae" (16C), by Ignazio Danti
(Galeria delle Carte Geografiche, Musei Vaticani)

M. Sarri-Reproduced by kind permission of the Vatican Museums

Route planning made simple

Plan your route with the assistance of our web site www.michelin-travel.com; the site also provides information on the full range of Michelin maps and travel publications.

LIST OF MAPS AND PLANS

Thematic plans

Plans of churches

Plans of museums and palazzi

Using this guide

● The summary maps on *pp* 7-11 are designed to assist at the planning stage: the first map shows the **Venetian lagoon**, whereas the **Map of principal sights** identifies the major attractions located within Venice proper. Both of these maps offer a bird's eye view of the city with its main churches, museums and *palazzi*. A detailed **street map** can be found on *p* 14, running from 2 to 11. The plan on *pp* 24-25 shows the various *vaporetto* routes and their respective stops along the canals and river banks.

● It is worth reading the **Introduction** before setting out as it gives background information on the history of the city, its art and architecture, and many aspects of traditional culture.

● The central section of the guide describes the **Sights** of Venice, listed in alphabetical order, followed by chapters on the outlying islands and the Brenta Valley. Every section features a choice of **Travellers' addresses** with recommendations for local cafés, restaurants, *pizzerie* or *bacari*, as well as some practical information.

● The blue clock symbol ⊙ placed after a sight name indicates that the **Admission times and charges** for that sight are to be found in the **Practical information** section of the guide, in the order of the sight's appearance in the guide.

● The **Practical information** section at the end of the guide also contains advice on planning your trip, accommodation, travelling in and around Venice, general tourist information, further reading, a calendar of traditional events and a glossary.

● The pink boxes in the guide contain anecdotes, legends, interesting and unusual facts or further details regarding information given in the main text.

● We greatly appreciate comments and suggestions from our readers. Contact us at:
Michelin Travel Publications, 38 Clarendon Road, Watford WD1 1SX, UK.
☎ 01923 415 000
Fax 01923 415 250
thegreenguide-uk@uk.michelin.com
www.michelin-travel.com

D. Zane

Key

	Sight	Seaside Resort	Winter Sports Resort	Spa
Worth a journey	★★★	⚲⚲⚲	✳✳✳	♨♨♨
Worth a detour	★★	⚲⚲	✳✳	♨♨
Interesting	★	⚲	✳	♨

Tourism

⊙ Admission Times and Charges listed at the end of the guide

▶▶ Visit if time permits

●━━▭ Sightseeing route with departure point indicated

AZ B Map co-ordinates locating sights

♙♦♙♦ Ecclesiastical building

🛈 Tourist information

▨ ☗ Synagogue – Mosque

⤫ ⁛ Historic house, castle – Ruins

▭ Building (with main entrance)

◡ ✿ Dam – Factory or power station

■ Statue, small building

☆ ∩ Fort – Cave

† Wayside cross

⊤⊤ Prehistoric site

◎ Fountain

▼ Ⱳ Viewing table – View

━●━■▸ Fortified walls – Tower – Gate

▲ Miscellaneous sight

Recreation

🏇 Racecourse

🏃 Waymarked footpath

⛸ Skating rink

◆ Outdoor leisure park/centre

≋ ⊠ Outdoor, indoor swimming pool

🎿 Theme/Amusement park

⟁ Marina, moorings

ⵛ Wildlife/Safari park, zoo

⛰ Mountain refuge hut

❀ Gardens, park, arboretum

◻━■━■━◻ Overhead cable-car

☯ Aviary, bird sanctuary

🚂 Tourist or steam railway

Additional symbols

═ ═ Motorway (unclassified)

◉ ◎ Post office – Telephone centre

❶ ❶ Junction: complete, limited

✉ Covered market

▭ ═ Pedestrian street

•⋌• Barracks

I═══I Unsuitable for traffic, street subject to restrictions

△ Swing bridge

⊏⊐ ---- Steps – Footpath

◡ ✕ Quarry – Mine

🚃 🚐 Railway – Coach station

Ⓑ Ⓕ Ferry (river and lake crossings)

◻+++++◻ Funicular – Rack-railway

⛴ Ferry services: Passengers and cars

━━ ⓜ Tram – Metro, Underground

⛵ Foot passengers only

Bert (R.)... Main shopping street

③ Access route number common to MICHELIN maps and town plans

Abbreviations and special symbols

H Town hall (Municipio)

T Theatre (Teatro)

J Law courts (Palazzo di Giustizia)

U University (Università)

M Museum (Museo)

ⓐ Hotel

P Local authority offices (Prefettura)

🏛 Palace, villa

POL. Police station (Polizia) (in large towns: Questura)

8 EX Map number and grid reference locating sights on maps **2** - **11**

Ven. Ang. 1bis

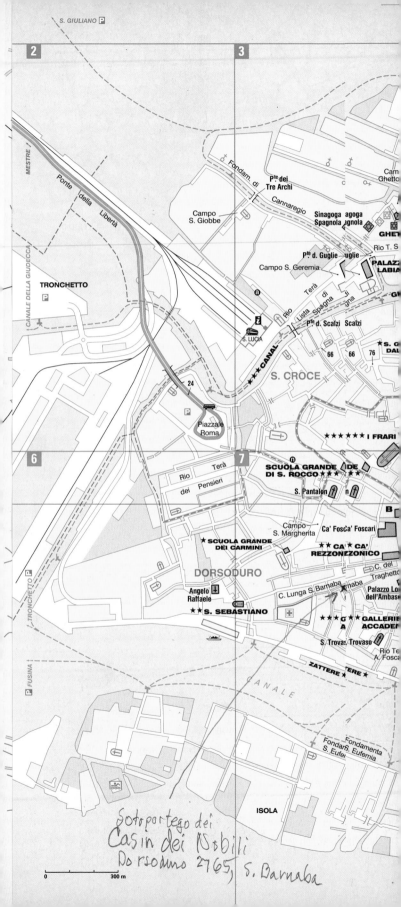

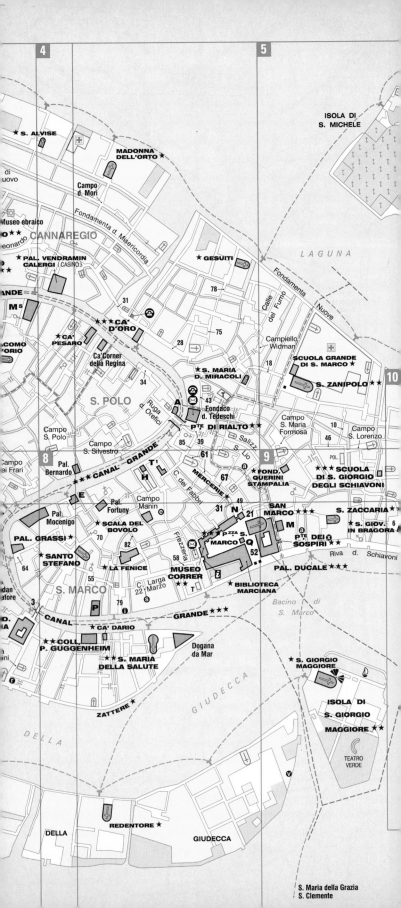

PRINCIPAL SIGHTS

★★★ **Highly recommended**

★★ **Recommended**

★ **Interesting**

MURANO ★★
TORCELLO ★★
BURANO ★★
S. FRANCESCO
D. DESERTO ★
S. Erasmo

S. POLO   Name and boundaries of quarter (sestiere)

Vaporetto line and stop

2   Map number

Accademia (Ponte dell')	3	S. Maurizio (Campo)	55
Bandiera e Moro (Campo)	6	San Moisé (Salizzada)	58
Capello (Ramo)	10	San Salvador (Merceria)	61
Gallina, Giacinto (Calle larga)	18	San Samuele (Campo)	64
Leoncini (Piazzetta dei)	21	San Simeon Profeta (Campo)	66
Libertà (Ponte della)	24	San Zulian (Merceria)	67
Nuova (Strada)	28	Sant'Angelo (Campo)	70
Orologio (Merceria dell')	31	Santi Apostoli (Rio Terà dei)	75
Pescaria (Campo della)	34	Sauro Nazario (Campo)	76
San Bartolomeo (Campo)	39	Seriman (Salizzada)	78
San Giovanni Crisostomo (Salizzada)	43	Traghetto (Campo del)	79
San Lorenzo (Calle larga)	46	Verona (Calle della)	82
San Marco (Calle larga)	49	2 Aprile (Via)	85
San Marco (Piazzetta)	52		

A   Palazzo dei Camerlenghi

B   Palazzo Balbi (Pal. della Regione)

E   Palazzo Lando Corner Spinelli

H   Palazzo Loredan (Municipio)

M   Museo diocesano di arte sacra

M⁵   Fondaco dei Turchi (Museo di storia naturale)

N   Torre dell'Orologio

P   Pal. Corner della Ca' Granda (Prefettura)

Q   Campanile

T¹   Teatro Goldoni

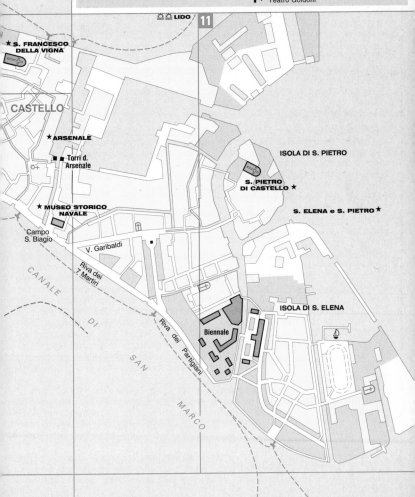

The Venetians

Even though the number of visitors in Venice far exceeds her resident population, it is the Venetians who, indifferent to the problems posed by the site, have created the city of their dreams from the mud of the lagoon and cultivated a historical and artistic heritage second to none.

To describe the countless faces of Venice and ignore the particular personality of her citizens who breathe life and colour into the city would therefore not merely be incomplete, but false: it would sustain the unfortunate, commonly held view of the place as a museum to which one makes a cursory visit, or as a monument to be considered as one might study a dead language. To refute this adage, take a stroll down to Campo della Pescaria, visit the Cannaregio district, linger in a bar in Campo San Luca over a glass of wine, or idle away a moment on a bench in Campo San Giacomo dall'Orio to eavesdrop on a nearby conversation; even doing the shopping around Sant'Elena will provide a glimpse of the living spirit of Venice. As is the case with any other place, the best impressions of Venice are gleaned away from the obvious tourist traps.

The average Venetian is an unpredictable character. He may be both charming and astute – a quality sharpened by an age-old affinity for business – he may appear effusively genial in addressing you in Italian and suspiciously distant when reverting to his native dialect.

The split personality of Venice – If setting out to explore the tourist's Venice, the way is clearly signed at every step by shopkeepers standing in doorways, enticing menus at a competitive "fixed price", corn-sellers proffering grain to attract the pigeons for that classic but kitsch photo... This doubtless makes for one snapshot of Venice but such a superficial veneer cannot do justice to the multiplicity of impressions to be gained.

Each and every person must formulate their own individual opinion of Venice: it may be a highly personal response to the unique atmosphere of this enchanting city; it may be one tainted by bad weather. To stereotype the flavour of Venice would be detrimental to the magic of the place and offensive to her proud inhabitants.

Just outside the tourist mainstream, a local resident is often ready to regale the visitor with intriguing anecdotes; the long-serving employee at some sumptuous palace will enjoy sharing its enthralling history with whoever gives him the chance; the parish priest, in his sacristy, is forever happy to unlock secret doors to hidden treasures in his custody. Theirs is "the" Venetian personality too complex to be defined but too colourful to be ignored.

Venetian idiosyncrasy – The Venetian is born with a **positive** outlook on life that is maintained by an **imperturbable** nature in which emotional involvement is tempered, in a very gentlemanly manner, by a certain indifference to anything that lies beyond the lagoon. This leads him to a noticeably predisposed state of tolerance an innate quality acquired from a knowledge of different peoples distilled over the centuries. The blend of an almost Anglo-Saxon aplomb with boundless and all-embracing curiosity renders this personality even more fascinating.

Yet perhaps the attribute that most readily springs to mind, indeed to the ear, is the pleasure the Venetian derives from gossiping, a pastime that delights all the more given the subtle sense of humour with which all Venetians are naturally and happily endowed, regardless of age, intellect or social class.

Jocular **chatter** is always conducted in dialect to allow quips and puns to spark and scintillate to full effect. It fills the bars and cafés, the shops and markets, but most of all the streets and squares, exchanged in passing or during a pause which the Venetians take pleasure in granting themselves at every opportunity. Unlike citizens of other cities, the Venetian is a wholly sociable creature, revelling in the advantages of sharing his environment with like-minded people who draw the calm and philosophical conclusion that only the truly essential priorities of life are worth worrying about thereby regarding the inconveniences of existence as relative. With a clear conscience and light heart, the Venetian walks with a **purposeful stride**: it is clear when he is on his way somewhere, moving at a sustained speed, whether empty handed or earnestly pushing awkward carts up and over the bridges, heralded by a spritely *"atansion!"* from behind.

It is rare to meet an **ill-intentioned person** in Venice, partly because the very structure of the city impedes criminal designs: where would you escape to? This underpins the genuinely happy atmosphere of the place, savoured in full by its contented residents, treasured by its temporary inhabitants and enjoyed by tourists who are able to roam the city at any time of the day or night.

"So much has been said and written about Venice already that I do not want to describe it too minutely. I shall only give my immediate impression. What strikes me most is again the people in their sheer mass and instinctive existence."

Goethe – Italian Journey – *29 September 1786*

Street index

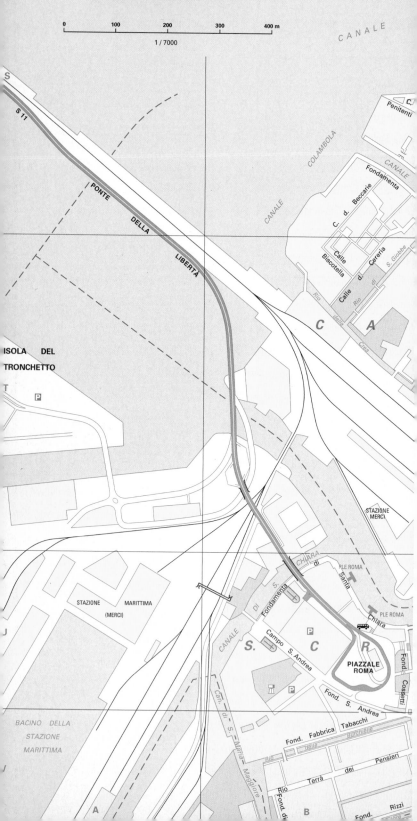

2

VENEZIA

0   100   200   300   400 m

1 / 7000

CANALE

S

S 11

PONTE DELLA LIBERTÀ

C. Penitenti

COLAMBOLA

CANALE

Fondamenta

C. d. Beccarie

CANALE

C. d.

Calle Biscotella

Calle di Cereria

S. Giobbe

Rio di

Rio delle

Cros

C

A

ISOLA DEL TRONCHETTO

T

P

STAZIONE MERCI

CHIARA di

PLE ROMA

S. Santa

STAZIONE MARITTIMA (MERCI)

S. Fondamenta

Chiara

PLE ROMA

CANALE DI

S.

Campo S. Andrea

C

P

P

R

PIAZZALE ROMA

Fond. Cossetti

Fond. S. Andrea

BACINO DELLA STAZIONE MARITTIMA

Can. di S. Maria Maggiore

Fond. Fabbrica Tabacchi

Burchiella

della

Rio

Terrà

dei Pensieri

Rio Fond. di

Fond. Rizzi

A   B

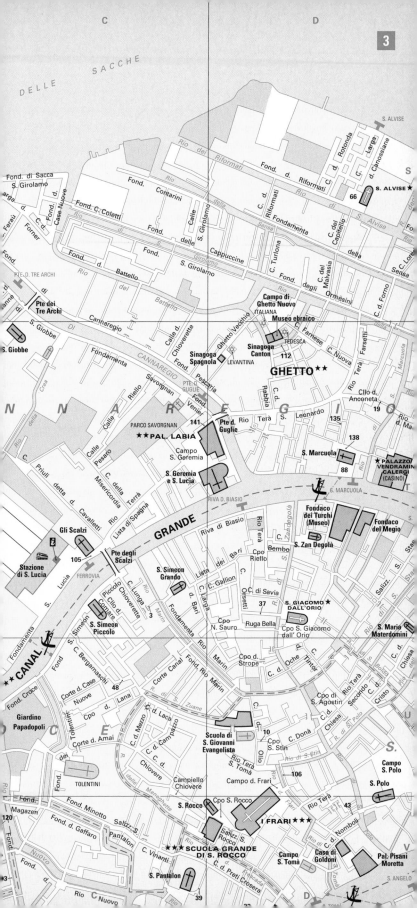

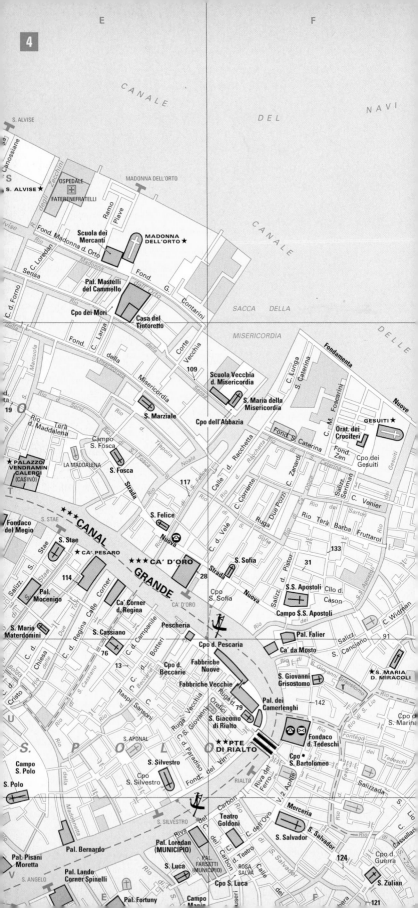

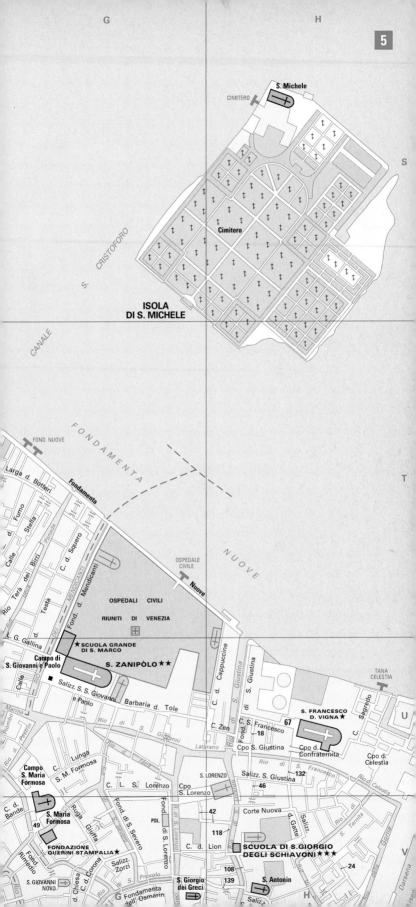

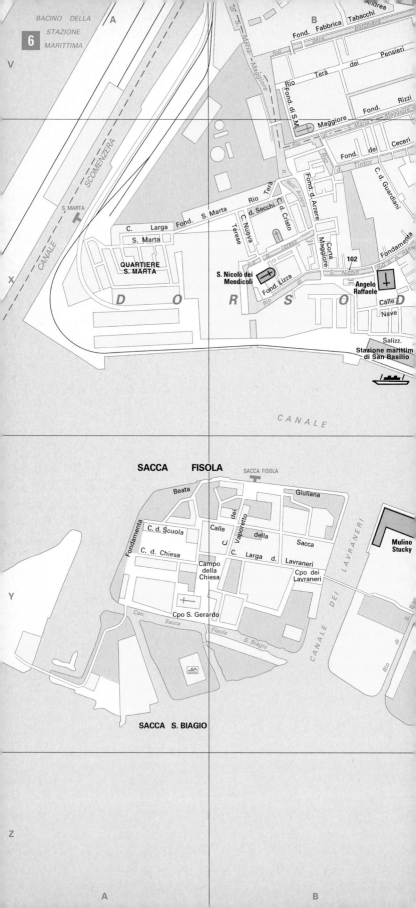

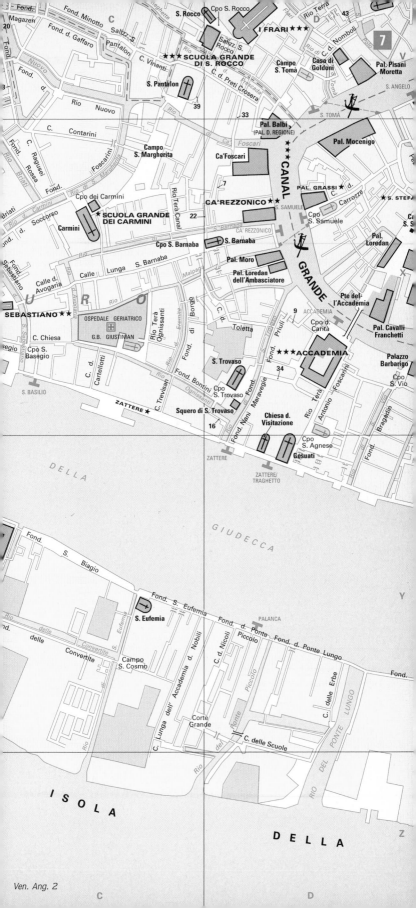

Pal. Pisani
Moretta
S. ANGELO

Pal. Bernardo

Macchinetta

E

Pal. Lando
Corner Spinelli

Pal. Fortuny

Oratorio del-
l'Annunciata

C. del Pestrin

C. del
Spezier

15

Cpo
S. Angelo

★ S. STEFANO

Campo
S. Stefano

27

Pal.
Loredan

Campo
S. Maurizio

Pal. Morosini

Pal. Pisani

Pal. Corner
della
Ca'Granda
(PREFETTURA)

Pal. Cavalli
Franchetti

Pal. Loredan

S. Luca

PAL.
FARSETTI
(MUNICIPIO)

C. d. Carbon

Riva del Carbon

S. SILVESTRO

Teatro
Goldoni

C. dell'Ovo

Mercerie

S. Salvador

S. Salvador

Cpo d.
Guerra

124

Cassell

C. d. Teatro

ROSA
SALVA

Cpo S. Luca

Campo
Manin

C. d. Fuseri

C. d. Mandola

Cortesia

★ SCALA DEL
BOVOLO

Pal. Duodo

Ateneo
Veneto

Cpo
S. Fantin

S. Fantin

Verona

C. d. Verona

C. d. Veste

★ TEATRO
LA FENICE

C. Larga 22 Marzo

C. d. Maurizio

Cpo S. M.
Zobenigo

25

PAL. GRITTI

S. M. DEL GIGLIO

C. d. Fabbri

C. Fiubera

121

Torre dell'-
l'Orologio

126

Procuratie
Vecchie

★★★
BASILICA

CAMPANILE

PZZA S. MARCO ★★★

★★ MUSEO
CORRER

Frezzeria

Barcaroli

Frezzeria

144

Rio di S. Moisè

S. Moisè

C. Vallaresso

TEATRO
RIDOTTO

Procuratie Nuove

Giardini
Reali

Museo
archeologico

BIBLIOTECA
MARCIANA

n

S. MARCO

S. M A R C

O

S M A R C O

Pal.
Barbarigo

Palazzo
Barbarigo

Cpo
S. Vio

COLL. P. GUGGENHEIM ★★
(Pal. Venier
dei Leoni)

★ CA' DARIO

Pal. Salviati

Calle
Bastion

C. Abazia

40

45

R. Terà S. Vio

C. d. Bragadin

Fond.

Fond.

C. d. Monastero

Scuola Monastero

SPIRITO
SANTO

C. d.

ZATTERE ★

★★★ CANAL

GRANDE

SALUTE

Fond. Dogana
alla Salute

Cpo d. Salute

Dogana
da Mar

S. MARIA
DELLA SALUTE ★★

R. Terà ai Saloni

C A N A L E

D E L L A

G I U D E C C A

Y

Fond.

S. Giacomo

REDENTORE

S. Giacomo

Calle S.

Calle

REDENTORE ★

Calle

d.

Fond.

Croce

della

Croce

della

Rio della

Croce

della

Squero

Croce

ZITELLE

Fond. d. Zitelle

Zitell

Calle

Calle

dello

Calle

Michelangelo

Z

G I U D E C C A

E

F

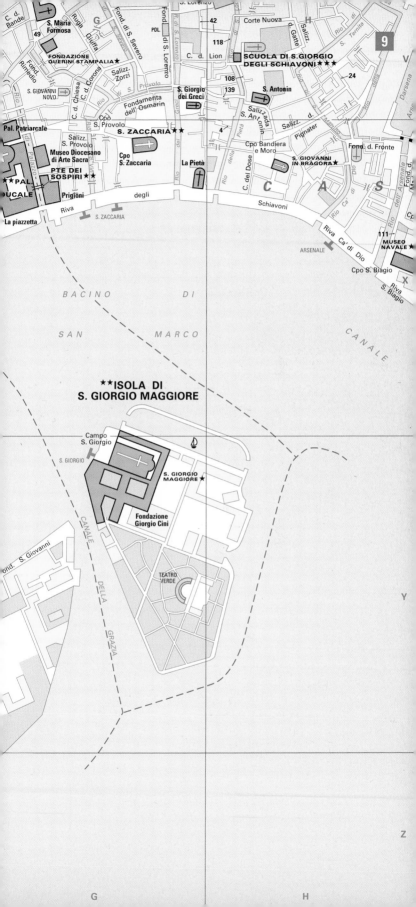

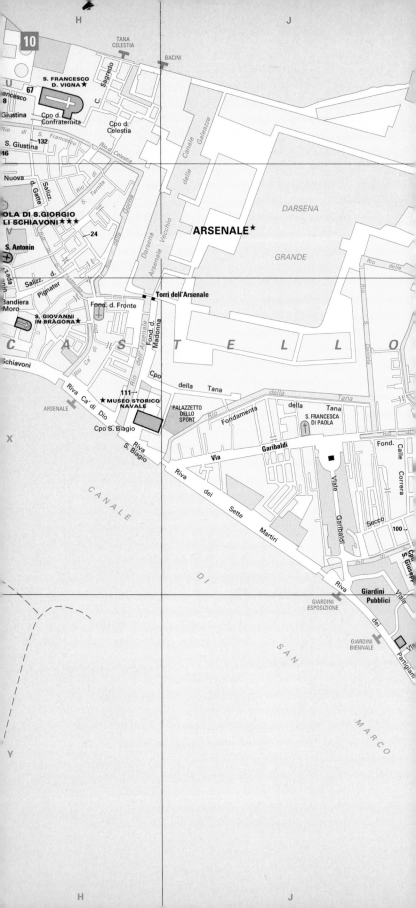

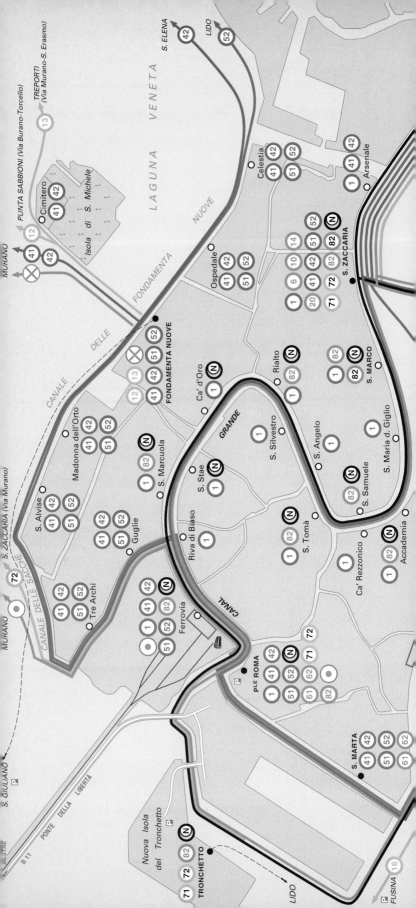

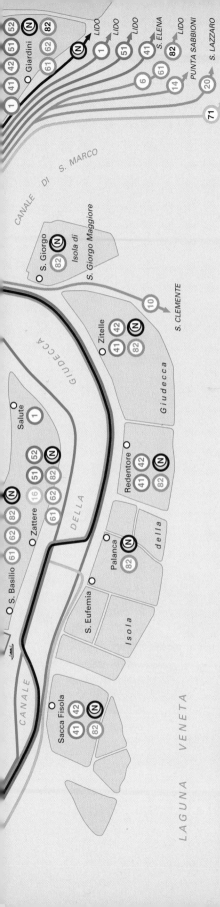

NB: line numbers and routes, although correct at the time of going to press, are subject to change.

VAPORETTO

NORMAL SERVICES

■ Circular "Giracitta" services

(1) PIAZZALE ROMA - Rialto - S. Marco - *LIDO*

(6) S. ZACCARIA - *LIDO*

(10) S. ZACCARIA - la Grazia - *S. CLEMENTE*

(12) FONDAMENTA NUOVE - Murano - PUNTA *SABBIONI*

(13) FONDAMENTA NUOVE - Murano - S. Erasmo - *TREPORTI*

(14) S. ZACCARIA - Lido - *PUNTA SABBIONI*

(16) ZATTERE - *FUSINA*

(20) S. ZACCARIA - S. Servolo - *S. LAZZARO*

(41) ■ S. ZACCARIA - S. Elena - Murano - Ferrovia - *S. ZACCARIA*

(42) ■ S. ZACCARIA - Ferrovia - Murano - S-Elena - *S. ZACCARIA*

(51) ■ S. ZACCARIA - Lido - Fondamenta Nuove - Ferrovia - *S. ZACCARIA*

(52) ■ S. ZACCARIA - Ferrovia - Fondamenta Nuove - Lido - *S. ZACCARIA*

(61) ■ PIAZZALE ROMA - Giardini - S. Elena - *LIDO*

(62) ■ LIDO - S. Elena - Giardini - *PIAZZALE ROMA*

(82) S. MARCO - Tronchetto - *S. ZACCARIA*

HIGH SEASON ONLY

(71) S. ZACCARIA - Murano - *TRONCHETTO*

(72) TRONCHETTO - Murano - *S. ZACCARIA*

(82) S. MARCO - S. Zaccaria - *LIDO*

OTHER SERVICES

Murano direct service
PIAZZALE ROMA - Ferrovia - Murano - Ferrovia - *PIAZZALE ROMA*

⊙ Murano shuttle service
FONDAMENTA NUOVE - Colonna - *VENIER*

⊗

(N) Night service
LIDO - S. Zaccaria - Rialto - Ferrovia - Tronchetto - S. Giorgio - *S. ZACCARIA*

0   600 m

Introduction

The Venetian lagoon

The Venetian lagoon extends over an area of 550km²/213sq mi, making it the largest in Italy. It was formed at the end of the Ice Age by the convergence of flooded rivers, swollen by melted snow from the Alps and Apennines.

Today it provides a natural and complex habitat to wetland flora and fauna between the Cavallino coast to the northeast and the Lido and Chioggia to the southwest. Water levels are maintained by the sea: its tides constitute both an ever-present threat to the delicate make-up of the Venetian lagoon while also providing its regular safeguard from stagnation. The sea merges with the canals' fresh water through three channels (*bocche di porto*) by the Lido, at Chioggia and Malamocco, where dikes were installed during the 19C and 20C.

The mainland reaches out a finger towards Venice, and the gap is spanned by the **Ponte della Libertà** (Bridge of Liberty). Otherwise, the coast's ominous profile cast in reflection across the lagoon is that of industrial developments at Mestre and Porto Marghera. These have grown around the ageless waters of the Brenta Naviglio which, having run among Palladian villas, flows peacefully into the lagoon at Malcontenta. Other buildings betray the affluence of tourism: the modern Tessera airport and the prettified Jesolo beach huts along the sandy beach stretch as far as Punta Sabbioni. In summer, crowds drawn through a tree-lined avenue to this natural "barrier" punctuated by the Lido di Jesolo, Cavallino, Ca' Savio, Treporti and Punta Sabbioni, are swollen by large numbers of camp sites and the proliferation of other forms of accommodation and, naturally, day-trippers from Venice which can be reached by *vaporetto* from Punta Sabbioni and Treporti.

A few lagoon terms

Bacino scolante: earth that carries rainwater and river-water into the lagoon.

Barene: small sandbanks with hardly any relief which can be seen protruding from the water and which are immersed at high tide.

Bricole: groups of wooden masts roped together which mark out canals fit for navigation.

Ghebi: tiny canals which meander their way across the sandbanks.

Punto zero: standard reference for measuring the water level in the lagoon. It is established by the Punta dell Salute tide gauge. The levels communicated by Punta della Salute are usually 23cm/9.3in higher than the average sea level.

Valli da pesca: dyked stretches of the lagoon set aside for fishing.

Velme: small strips of land which, unlike the *barene*, can only be seen at low tide, when they appear on the surface.

An age-old problem

In the 12C, Europe enjoyed a long period of mild weather followed by a noticeable rise in temperature; then came torrential rains that caused high tides and flooding. The River Brenta broke its banks and water flooded a large part of the lagoon, depositing silt, mud and detritus. Malaria broke out. The Republic of Venice tried to defend itself by placing palisades along the coast, diverting the course of the rivers and building great dykes, but the lagoon continued to pose a threat. Over the ensuing centuries (15-17C), major drainage programmes were implemented that affected the Brenta, Piave, Livenza and Sile rivers. In 1896 the operation aimed at diverting the waters of the Brenta was finally completed, channelling them into the mouth of the Bacchiglione. Despite these measures, as water levels continue to rise and fall, the sand deposited in the lagoon by the rivers is buffeted back inland by the sea and the wind. Thus the sandbanks are formed and strengthened. All the while, caught between marine erosion and the rebuilding action of the rivers, the fate of Venice itself is at stake: after more than 1000 years of existence, it is slowly sinking.

Understanding the nature of the lagoon – The Venetian lagoon can be likened to a sophisticated system that has achieved a subtle balance between excessive **sedimentation** (leading to the emergence of "new" land) and **erosion** (in which the deposits carried by the sea and rivers are so scarce that a stretch of lagoon can turn into a stretch of sea). This is precisely the risk which is currently threatening the lagoon. About one quarter of the lagoon surface is rendered unnavigable by the existence of sandbanks or *barene*. Their importance is capital: they encourage the proliferation of a great many animal and vegetal species while at the same time attracting sediments that might otherwise be scattered in the water, contributing to reducing the swell.

About 4000ha/15sq mi are taken up by the large inhabited islands and smaller deserted ones leaving another 40 000ha/155sq mi occupied by water.

Anyone surprised at seeing how shallow a Venetian canal may be when drained of its water (from an average of 1-2m/3-7ft to a maximum depth of 8-10m/26-33ft) will understand why the seabed of the open lagoon is often exposed at low tide. Despite

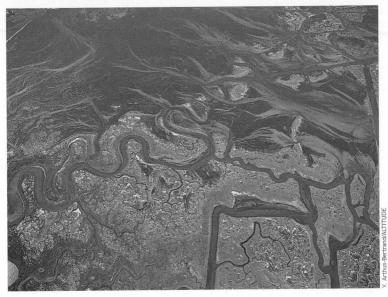

The lagoon, a network of waterways

this lack of depth which gives the lagoon its millpond appearance, a complex network of crisscrossed channels maintain currents and easy movement. Navigable areas are marked by lone wooden posts or groups of poles roped together, known as *bricole*. The deepest channels are those nearest the mouths of the ports, and as the distance from the sea increases, these rivulets become shallower and narrower *(ghebi)*, dwindling across the sandbanks before disappearing into *chiari*, basins where salt water and rainwater mingle.

Tides

Life-blood of the lagoon – Tidal changes occur every six hours, fluctuating between two high points per day. Low atmospheric pressure, and the sirocco and bora winds are known to accentuate high tide, whereas high atmospheric pressure and northwesterly winds tend to bring on a low tide. In this case, some of the rivers may dry up. Sea water is thereby drawn into the lagoon through the three ports, flushing "new" water in and "old" water out – assisted by a current from the rivers on the opposite side. Parts affected by these tides are thereby known as the "living" lagoon, whereas sections little affected by this life-line are referred to as the "dead" lagoon. These outlying parts tend towards marsh, channelled with canals, *ghebi* between fishing banks and dyked lakes built by and for the fishing industry.

The tide, destroyer of the lagoon – The health of the lagoon is totally dependent upon the influx of "new" water brought by the tides: however, the inflow of fresh water provided by the rivers that once maintained saline levels has been greatly reduced as the rivers have progressively been diverted. This has also reduced the strength of current across the lagoon and allowed vast quantities of polluting material to be deposited.

In the 20C the problem has been exacerbated by the growth of industrial sites around Mestre and Porto Maghera accommodating petrol-tankers with obvious implications on the environment of the lagoon. The reduction in oxygenated water flowing through the canals of Venice is gradually eroding the ability of plant and marine life to survive. Only those organisms with short life-cycles have had time to adapt, and so quantities of macro-algae *(ulva rigida)* and insects (mosquitoes and the like) have increased at a fantastic rate.

Why do tides occur?

Gravitational forces caused by the earth's rotation around the sun and its relation to the moon are responsible for the movement of the tides; it is the moon, however, being nearer the earth, that exerts the greater force as regards changes in liquid levels and therefore the movement of water in the oceans and seas.

The strength of this force is also affected by air pressure and winds. In the case of Venice, the greatest floods have always followed major sirocco storms.

When the moon passes over the meridian of an area, it causes a high tide; when it is at 90 to that meridian, it produces a low tide. When the earth, moon and sun are all in alignment, the tide reaches its maximum levels.

Tidal flooding – The tide along these coasts can fluctuate wildly; for it to be classified as tidal flooding its level has to reach or exceed 1.10m/3ft 6in. The last such occurrence happened on 4 November 1966 when consequences were felt way beyond the shores of Venice – the Arno overflowed in Florence with tragic results. That year an alarming prediction was rumoured that Venice might possibly disappear – fortunately, radical action against further subsidence, including the closure of artesian wells on the mainland (1975), have proved the prophecy false. Plans for natural gas exploration 12 nautical miles off Chioggia are presently under review pending a feasibility study of environmental consequences (1995).

Similar crises of this kind are documented as far back as 589. Contemporary personal accounts are terrifying. **Paolo Diacono** (c 720-799) wrote of the first flood tide: *"non in terra neque in aqua sumus viventes"* (neither on earth nor in water were we alive). Records from 1410 state that *"almost one thousand people coming from the fair at Mestre and other places drowned"*.

Since the 17C the water level of the Venetian lagoon has dropped by 60cm/24in. In past centuries, once every five years, the tide would rise above the damp-proof foundations made of Istrian stone that were built to protect the houses against salt deposits. Nowadays, in the lower areas, these foundations are immersed in water more than 40 times in a single year and the buildings can do very little to stall the degradation process.

Venice victim of the tides – On 4 November 1966 the mareograph at Punta della Salute registered an exceptionally high tide of 1.94m/6ft. Medium to high tides usually reach a level of around 70cm/28in, flooding the Piazza San Marco with water and with a further 30cm/12in, even narrow alley streets would be inundated. Between December and February the city can be the scene of very low tides indeed, estimated at less than 90cm/36in.

At the end of the 18C, when the first part of the Riva degli Schiavoni promenade was completed, Venetian magistrates ordered that the letter "C" be engraved on the city houses and their foundations. The letter was to indicate the average level of the highest-known tides. However, today it is difficult to spot these inscriptions since most of them are located under the level of the sea.

Life-forms

The lagoon comprises a vast and rich habitat for fauna and flora, part of which may even be glimpsed from the *vaporetto* between Venice and Burano or from a car driving through the section enclosed by the Cavallino coast. The best way, however, to appreciate the extent of vegetation and animal life thriving in this "watery plain" is to explore the sandbanks by boat.

Lagoon environment – The waters of the lagoon vary in salt concentration depending on their proximity to the river outlets, where the water is almost fresh. In the middle they tend to be brackish whereas, near the ports, where the tides inject sea water, they are far saltier. At the same time, areas around the river deltas tend to be muddy, whereas by the port mouths the lagoon bed is sandy.

A marine haven

A *bricola* is rather like a crowded apartment-block. Its external surface seems literally corroded by crustaceans, whereas within, bivalvular molluscs called *teredini* have taken up residence.

Closest to the surface and buffeted by the tides, live crustaceans *(balani)* and green algae. Below, in calmer currents live mussels *(mitili)*, whereas the submerged part is the kingdom of the sponges, the tube-shaped *ascidie* and the *hydrozoans*.

Fauna – At the lower end of the food chain, different types of **molluscs** breed successfully on the wooden piles or *bricole*.

The principal category is undoubtedly that of the **fish kingdom**, which has defined both the very character of the lagoon with its distinctive collection in shoals around sandbanks, and the interaction of man with this environment as he seeks to exploit such rich resources.

Crab and **shrimp** are central to the fishing industry and to Venetian cuisine. From a boat it soon becomes obvious where the fishing banks are situated as these attract various species of aquatic birds: wild duck (mallard and teal), tens of thousands of coots, herons and marsh harriers. Besides the common sparrows, swallows and blackbirds, the Venetian lagoon is visited by special migratory birds, often with highly-coloured plumage.

Kingfisher

Cormorant

Coot

Black-winged stilt

Grey heron

Little egret

Illustrations: M. Dewynter (Kingfisher, Grey heron); R. Corbel (Coot, Black-winged stilt, Little egret)

31

It is perhaps their beauty, strangeness and cleverness that is most fascinating: the black-whiskered bearded tit clings to the reeds; the reed warbler builds a floating nest between four reeds, that rises and falls with the tide; the kingfisher dives acrobatically while the moorhen nods her head in time to the rhythm of her strokes; little grebe pop out of the water only to dive quickly and silently below the surface again and emerge where least expected.

The very rich bird life of the lagoon also includes the cormorant, the inevitable sea-gull and the sea swallow whose whirling wings and V-shaped tail allow it to swoop effortlessly time and again; the little egret, recognisable by its elegant carriage and startlingly white feathers with which ladies adorned themselves at the beginning of the 20C. Even more beautiful is the black-winged stilt whose somber wings contrast with its white body and the red of its long legs; its thin, distinguished beak adds a touch of refinement.

Elegance seems to be a trait shared by all the birds of the lagoon, among which the mute swan must reign supreme.

There are numerous marsh harriers and hen harriers among the birds of prey.

Among the mammals the rodent provides a somewhat harmful presence. The rat, the so-called *pantagena*, is at home anywhere, on the city squares as well as in rubbish dumps and attics.

Fishing areas

Known as *valli da pesca*, these stretches of the lagoon are used for fishing, taking into consideration the migratory movements of the fish. Because they have been dyked, they are not exposed to the ebbing of the water.

During the spring season, the fish (mainly eel, sea bass and gilt-head bream) congregate in the lagoon, attracted by the rich organic vegetation brought along by rivers and mountain waters after the thaw.

During the winter season, when weather conditions are especially harsh, the fish try to swim back towards the sea but on reaching the *chiaveghe* (structures with bulkheads built to regulate the flow of the sea water), they are caught and sorted by traditional methods. Among the various nets used for fishing, two in particular stand out: the *bilancione*, a huge trawlnet suspended from four tall piers and the *cogolo*, a cylindrical net consisting of several parts, ending in a cone.

Flora – The sandbanks are abundantly cloaked in vegetation: glasswort, sea lavender and asters turn the mounds first green, then red, then blue, then grey. Rooted in the water are various reeds and rushes with long stalks and spiky flowers. On the beaches grow convolvulus with shiny dark-green leaves and pink flowers, and sea rocket with its violet blooms.

On the first dunes of shifting sands grows couch grass, a perennial member of the grass family, whereas further back, tufts of coarse grass sprout among the spurges with long stalks of small lancet-like leaves and flowers with yellowish bracts. Tall bushy *gramineae (erianthus ravennae)* are also widely found.

Shrubs and trees grow beyond the dunes: along the Romea highway, south of Chioggia, between Santa Anna and Cavanella d'Adige, is the Bosco Nordio (Nordio Wood) of evergreen oaks. Even the market gardens form part of the vegetation of the lagoon, especially in the south at Chioggia, where red chicory *(radicchio)* is grown, highly-prized but not as famous as the *radicchio* of Treviso.

Venice in peril

Flooding – The *Centro Previsioni e Segnalazioni Maree* provides warnings of impending danger and information on forecasts and tide tables. Tidal flooding tends to occur between April and September, and forecast warnings are issued about 48 hours in advance. Details are published in the *Gazzettino* and posted up on the landing stages of the *vaporetti*. Should the level threaten to exceed 1.10m/3ft 7in, 16 sirens sound five times for ten seconds each time, three or four hours in advance of the high point.

Should high tide not exceed 1.20m/3ft 11in, the **AMAV** (Azienda Multiservizio Ambientale Venezia) sees to the laying of footbridges along prescribed routes. However, if the water level goes above this limit, then footbridges can become dangerous because they start to float. In the case of tidal flooding, the AMAV is unable to maintain its principal function which is rubbish collection, because its boats are no longer able to pass under the bridges: it is therefore made responsible for laying down emergency footbridges. Meanwhile, the Venetian Municipality requests the population to just hang on to their household waste! In case of a generalised flooding emergency, call the **Centro Maree** ☎ 041/52 06 344 - 52 07 722 *(answerphone)*.

Today's concerns – In the past, land and water were clearly separated, with the lagoon acting as a link between the two, drawing on both to produce life and movement. However, the presence of factories, farms and areas inhabited by man have

Coping with flooding in the Piazzetta

gradually changed the face of the *gronda*, in other words, the sloped land licking at the lagoon shores. Today, the lagoon has reached a sort of "standstill": it takes two weeks for waste material to leave the lagoon and end up in the open sea. Every year more than 1 million m^3/35.3 million cu ft of solid matter is lost. Erosion, the sediments lost in the water and the rising level of the sea all contribute to lowering the lagoon depths. This phenomenon is threatening the sandbanks known as *barene*, which are doomed to disappear by the year 2050 if drastic action is not taken to remedy the situation.

Water fluctuations and land subsidence – Variations in the level of the water are referred to as *"eustatismo"*: in the course of the last century this phenomenon caused the waters of Venice to rise by 8cm/3.2in. This has led to dire consequences, aggravated by the effects of local subsidence, causing the land to drop, representing around 15cm/6.2in for the same period. Therefore, the city of Venice has "sunk" by around 23cm/9.2in since the end of the 19C.

Erosion – Erosion is the result of a number of factors: higher water levels, subsidence, digging for artificial canals and the swell, which slowly increases while the seabed slumps and the sandbanks dwindle.

Pollution – Finally, to crown this somewhat pessimistic picture, we have pollution, responsible of the destruction of phanerogamic flora, invaluable seawater plants whose roots serve to prevent erosion and stabilize the seabed. Water pollution has also killed the algae and other marine varieties which once thrived on sandbanks and mudflats and which are no longer able to attract sediments.

Tackling the problem – The risk of losing Venice through both tides and progressive depopulation is so great that the Italian State has declared the salvation of the city to be a question of "pre-eminent national interest". The residents of Venice appear to be particularly concerned about high-to-medium tides, which cause the city to be flooded. Consequently, a number of

What is an insula?

In the lagoon city, an *insula* is a tiny piece of territory which is circumscribed by a river or a canal. These *insule* are therefore linked to each other by a network of bridges. A small cluster of them is said to form a *sestiere*, one of Venice's six administrative divisions.

projects currently being examined or implemented are aimed at making these inhabited areas far safer. It is a highly delicate and complex situation: the town of Venice and the myriad islands are home to many buildings, monuments and works of art which cohabit in perfect harmony but, technically speaking, require different forms of intervention. On the San Marco and Tolentini islands, the stability of paved streets, bridges and houses was meticulously checked, as well as that of underground passages and sewage drains. In the lower sections, the paving has been raised (as is clearly visible on Campo San Zanipòlo) and the shores of the lagoon consolidated to cope more efficiently against tides below 100cm/40in (120cm/48in in Chioggia).

There is a project to deal with exceptionally high tides by placing mobile barriers at the three entrances to the port. A prototype of this system, the Mo.S.E. (Experimental Electronic Module) comprises a huge mobile sluice-gate devised to regulate the movement of the tides. It was tested along the Canale di Treporti facing the Lido from 1988 to 1992. It is thought that the final project would need to provide 79 of these sluice-gates.

Sluice-gates

These ambitious structures should be placed side by side to form a floating barrier linked to the seabed, rising and falling with the movement of the waves. Each gate, 20-30m/66-98ft long, 20m/66ft wide and 3-5m/10-16ft thick, contains compressed air controlled by valves, which enables the gate to be lowered.

In the Experimental Centre for Hydraulic Models, at Voltabarozzo, near Padua, a simulated mock-up of the lagoon area allows study to be carried out into projects for the harbour mouths, the safeguarding of the coastal region and of the jetties.

In the meantime, reconstruction of the coastal region of Cavallino and Pellestrina is being carried out. The coastal area has been consolidated with 2 million m³/70.6 million cu ft of sand taken from the sea. These deposits were also used to reinforce sandbanks, which play a crucial role as they combat the swell and local winds, while at the same time protecting the environment. In an attempt to increase their stability, these coastal dunes have been planted with *ammofila*, a special variety of grass that thrives on sandy soil.

The north pier at Chioggia has been strengthened, 50km/31mi of canals have been dredged and the sediment obtained through this operation served to rebuild 300ha/740 acres of sandbanks.

Further operations currently under way involve cleaning up the lagoon waters, gathering the macroalgae and salvaging the smaller islands such as Lazzaretto Vecchio. The **Consorzio Venezia Nuova** is responsible for all this research and for the implementation of future developments.

The restoration of sandbanks is achieved by fencing off a stretch of the lagoon with wooden masts; a large canvas sheet is then fixed to the poles and laid down over the sea depths. Into this artificial basin are poured sediments as well as water, which is then filtered by the canvas.

The art world fights to save Venice – In 1966, the year in which record water levels were registered in Venice, UNESCO stressed the urgency of the fight to save this beautiful city and her lagoon. A number of organisations and committees, both public and private, were set up to salvage and restore Venice's cultural heritage, namely the **Ufficio per la Salvaguardia di Venezia**.

The Head of the Monuments and Fine Arts Department is involved in the technical aspects of this undertaking, while UNESCO oversees the allocation of funds raised by several private committees. Every year an estimated 2 billion lira are spent on rescue operations aimed at preserving the architectural, historical and artistic treasures of the city, as well as on scholarships for artisans and research. Each of these committees is directly concerned with a specific project on a regular basis. Among the many organisations dedicated to saving Venice, the most important are **The Venice in Peril Fund** (Great Britain), **Save Venice** (United States), **Comité Français pour la Sauvegarde de Venise** (France) and **Venedig Lebt** (Austria).

"The interaction of tides and earth, followed by the gradual fall in the level of the primaeval ocean, formed an extensive tract of swampland at the extreme end of the Adriatic, which was covered at high tide but partly exposed at low."

Goethe

To best enjoy the major tourist attractions, which draw big crowds, try to avoid visiting at the peak periods of the day or year.

Unique to Venice

The inhospitable nature of the lagoon, from which Venice sprung up as if by magic, has demanded of the Venetians an extraordinary ability to adjust to a particular lifestyle implemented through a rare spirit of initiative. To combat the waters, either too high or too low, and to make their way around the myriad islands, the Venetians built the gondola and hundreds of bridges; they also planted thousands of poles.

The Gondola – No-one knows exactly when the gondola was invented: the word *gundula* appears as early back as 1094 in a decree of Doge Vitale Falier although the reference relates to a massive boat equipped with a large crew of rowers – a far cry from the gondola we know today.

In the 14C, small boats covered with a central canopy bore metal decorations on the prow and stern. At the end of the century the vessel began to be made longer and lighter, the prow and stern were raised and the *felze* or cabin was added, affording shelter in bad weather. Some had decorated prows. Others were painted in bright colours and decked with satin, silk and gleaming brass. On the prow and stern stood painted cherubs bearing the coat of arms of the family to which the gondola belonged.

> **Distinguishing between canals and rivers**
>
> Although all Venetian waterways tend to be called canals, there exist only three real canals in the city: Canal Grande, Canale della Giudecca and Canale di Cannaregio. Canals, which are wider, are tributaries of the lagoon, whereas the narrow rivers *(rii)* can be compared to streets: they are not linked to the sea and wend their way across the city along a sinuous, meandering course. The only exception is the Cannaregio *sestiere*, a fact clearly visible on any plan of Venice.

From the 16C, boats were toned down by being painted black: a colour we might judge to be rather funereal, but in Venice red, not black, is the colour of mourning. Today the gondola is about 11m/36ft long, 1.42m/4ft wide and comprises altogether 280 pieces of wood.

Whittling a new gondola

Building a gondola – The shipyards where gondolas are built and repaired are called **squeri**. At one time, each of these was allocated primarily to a family from Cadore, the wooden galleried constructions resembling alpine houses *(see ACCADEMIA - Squero di San Trovaso)*.

The **ferro**, a sabre-toothed projection made of iron placed at the prow and stern, is without doubt the most crucial element of the gondola: implemented initially as a fender to safeguard against knocks, today it serves as a counter-weight to the gondoliere, and is used to align the boat around hazards in the narrowest passages. The curved fin is said to echo the dogal *corno* and to symbolise its power over the six *sestieri* or divisions of the city represented by the six serrations. The tooth that "guards" over the gondola itself is the Giudecca.

The *paline*

The **forcola** or rowlock, is an intricate piece of carving hewn from walnut wood, designed as a pivot that allows the oar maximum mobility. The oar is made of well-seasoned beechwood. But perhaps only the most observant will notice the two bronze sea-horses cleating the cords of the seats.

"... a Venetian gondola? That singular conveyance, came down unchanged from ballad times, black as nothing else on earth except a coffin – what pictures it calls up of lawless, silent adventures in the slashing night; or even more, what visions of death itself, the bier and solemn rites and last soundless voyage! And has anyone remarked that the seat in such a bark, the arm-chair lacquered in coffin-black, and dully black-upholstered, is the softest, most luxurious, most relaxing seat in the world?"

Thomas Mann – Death in Venice

Paline, dame and bricole – Whether travelling by gondola, *vaporetto* or boat, there is always the risk of running aground. Navigable channels are identified by means of **bricole** – a series of large poles *(pali)* roped together, whereas the entrance to a canal or a junction is indicated by **dame** which are smaller poles than the *bricole*.
The **paline** are those thin individual poles that project from the water at odd intervals to which private craft are tethered. They are particularly evocative if painted with coloured swirling stripes, outside some fine building to mark the landing stage of some patrician family in days of yore.

The bridges – Among the hundreds of Venetian bridges crossed to the sound of laughter and merriment during the tussles of *su e zo per i ponti* meaning "up and down the bridges" *(see Practical Information: Calendar of events)*, there are several like the Ponte Chiodo *(see CA' D'ORO)* without railings or parapet, where rival factions such as the Castellani and Nicolotti faced each other during "fist fights" *(see I CARMINI)*. Projects for bridges with three arches met with less success *(see GHETTO)*.

Draining the rivers

Tourists acquainted with Venice will undoubtedly have witnessed a familiar scene in which the local authorities undertake to dry out the city rivers. This operation is aimed at both cleansing the water and restoring the bridges. It is only then that one realises how deep the waters run and how hollowed out the river bed is. It is also extremely dark and malodorous since it tends to collect wastage as well as any objects that fall into the water by accident.
Documents relating to this practice can be traced back to the late 13C and the early 14C. It is established that these dredging operations have been carried out regularly since the 15C to renew the water and facilitate navigation. The two main bodies in charge of implementing these schemes are the Magistratura del Piovego and the Savi alle Acque.

"The bathing, on a calm day, must be the worst in Europe: water like hot saliva, cigar-ends floating into one's mouth, and shoals of jelly-fish."

Robert Byron - The Road to Oxiana, 1937

Over a thousand years of glory

Legendary beginnings

It seems reasonable to turn to Homer when tracing the very ancient and uncertain origins of the Venetians. In the Iliad *(BkII, v852)* we see them arriving from Paflagonia to aid Priam. They were called the Enetii. Having abandoned their native land, these people arrived in the territory occupied by the Eugeneans whom they put to flight. They founded the future Altino from where they left for Torcello.

1000-700 B.C.	The Venetian civilisation known as *"atestino"* was founded around the city of Este.
530 B.C.	The Etruscan colony of Spina was founded.
181 B.C.	The colony of Aquileia was founded.
568	First dated documentation regarding the port of Altino.
400 A.D.	From Padua, Altino, Concordia Sagittaria, Aquileia and Oderzo, the future inhabitants of Venice visited the lagoon solely for its provisions of salt and fish. In the 6C Cassiodoro (c 490-583) requested these watermen, fishermen and salt-workers to help supply Ravenna.
568	The Lombards descended into Italy. The Roman-Byzantine province of Venetia was gradually conquered.
639	Oderzo, the capital of Venetia, fell. The Byzantine governor moved to Cittanova which took the name **Heracleia**, from Emperor Heraclius. The Church of Santa Maria Assunta was built on the Island of Torcello.
697	**Paoluccio Anafesto** was named the first doge.
742	The ducal seat was transferred from Cittanova to Malamocco.
775	Olivolo, the present-day San Pietro di Castello, became a bishop's see. It was accountable to the patriarchate of Gradi until 1451, when Lorenzo Giustinian was appointed First Patriarch of Venice.
810	Pepin, son of Charlemagne, was defeated after an attempted invasion of Dalmatia and the lagoon. Many inhabitants of the lagoon moved to the Realtine Islands where the dogate was established. In 811 **Agnello Partecipazio** or "Particiaco" was elected doge. **Venice was born.**

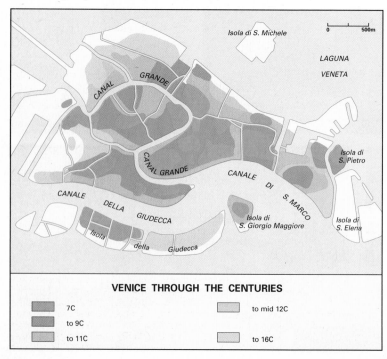

VENICE THROUGH THE CENTURIES

7C
to 9C
to 11C
to mid 12C
to 16C

During the 9C, when the dogeship was transferred, and for the three following centuries, Venice was made up of dozens of islands; however, the city was considerably smaller than it is today because most of the land was below sea level.

The independent city, ruler of the Adriatic

814	With the **Pax Nicephori** (Treaty of Nicephorus), Charlemagne ceded his claims to the lagoon, and Venice guaranteed her neutrality throughout the political struggles that were to rage in Italy during the eras of feudalism and the inter-city state rivalry.
828	The body of St Mark was stolen from Alexandria in Egypt and brought to Venice where work began on the construction of the first basilica the following year.
829	In his will Doge Giustiniano Particiaco called for the construction of **San Marco**, which was to become the ducal chapel.
840	In the **Pactum Lotarii** (Peace of Lothar) the Byzantine ruler confirmed the autonomy of Venice and assured her navy the control of the seas.
946 or 948	Narentine Slav pirates carried out the legendary abduction of the maidens *(see SAN ZACCARIA)*.
976	The Venetians rebelled against the repressive **Doge Pietro Candiano IV** who chose to ignore the maritime powerbase of Venice, and instead engaged foreign troops so as to conquer territories on the mainland which would enhance his own political standing and reputation. This provoked a fierce popular revolt: fire damaged St Mark's, the Doges' palace, San Teodoro, destroying more than 300 houses, then built almost exclusively in wood. **Pietro Orseolo I** was elected doge at San Pietro di Castello.

A Witness Recounts

Seized with panic and almost suffocating, the doge, his wife and their young son sought safety by heading towards the entrance of St Mark's where, however, they were stopped by a group of noblemen. Pietro's promises to accept any compromise were of no avail.
"...Affirming that he was a most evil man and deserving of death, they shouted with fearful voices that there could be no salvation for him. They immediately surrounded him and cruelly ran him through with the points of their swords so that his immortal spirit abandoned his bodily prison in search of the retreat of the blessed". John Julius Norwich adds however that *"for what we know of Pietro Candiano IV, this happy final destination is somewhat improbable"*.

1000	After defeating the Croats and the Narentines, Venice assumed her role as ruler and protector of Dalmatia with the title *dux Dalmatinorum* (Duke of Dalmatia).
1032	The Venetians' strong spirit of independence precipitated a dislike for any government that resembled a monarchy and so, to avoid such a danger, the power of the doge was "split" between two ducal councillors, each one responsible for half of the city, with the Grand Canal as the dividing line.
11C	In the second half of the century the new Basilica of St Mark was built, modelled upon the Basilica of the Apostles at Constantinople.
1081	Venice defended Byzantium from attack by the Norman Robert Guiscard. The following year, the **Crisobollo** issued by the Byzantine Emperor, Alessio I Comneno, allowed Venetians to trade freely throughout the empire and to open shops in Constantinople without having to pay duty on their goods.
1099	Venice defeated the Pisans near Rhodes where the Venetian and Pisan fleets were taking part in the Crusades. The released Pisan prisoners undertook not to haunt the waters of Byzantium.
1104	The first nucleus of the Arsenal was created. The following year the city was ravaged by fire.
1122-1124	Under the dogeship of **Domenico Michiel**, Venice attacked and defeated the Egyptian fleet that was besieging Jaffa, taking possession of the merchant ships and their cargo of treasure trove and spices. She then went on to participate in the victorious siege of Tyre, and the sacking of Byzantine ports in the Aegean and the Adriatic. These shows of force were crucial in restoring the city's reputation and political footing enjoyed before the King of Hungary had affirmed his power in

	Dalmatia and were recognised by the predecessors of the current Byzantine Emperor, **Giovanni Comneno**, who refused to accept the fundamental independence of the city.
1143	It is known that the **Council of the Wise Men**, or *Consilium Sapientium*, was already in existence by this date. It is thought to have consisted of 35 members presided over by the doge. From this organisation was to evolve the Great Council.
1145-1153	Istria, already protected by Venice, now found herself totally subjugated as the doge was proclaimed *totius Istriæ dominator*.
1171	Emergency measures were implemented by the Eastern Empire angered by the plundering of their trade ships by Venetian, Genoese and Pisan navies. The disastrous expedition of **Doge Vitale Michiel II** whose crew was decimated by the plague, was judged very harshly by the Venetians, and led to his murder. His successor **Sebastiano Ziani** (1172) was elected under a system similar to that which later (1268) was sanctioned by law and which lasted into the following centuries. During the dogeship of Vitale Michiel II the six *sestieri* were created as subdivisions of the city, thereby facilitating the collection of taxes.

Musée du Louvre, Paris/SCALA

The Departure of the Bucintoro by Francesco Guardi (Louvre Museum)

1175	Construction of a wooden Rialto Bridge.
1177	It was in Venice that **Pope Alexander III** and **Federico Barbarossa** ended the conflict between the city states and their antagonists, the Church and the Swabian Empire. According to legend, this was the occasion that saw Alexander III donate his ring in the "Sposalizio del Mar".
1178	Eleven men were nominated to elect the 40 electors of the doge including six ducal councillors – one for each *sestieri*.
1201-1204	**Fourth Crusade**. Doge **Enrico Dandolo**, a man of extraordinary energy despite being 90 and blind, attacked **Constantinople** (1203) which succumbed decisively to a second assault the following year. The Eastern Latin Empire was formed under an emperor nominated by six Venetians and six crusader barons. Spoils and lands were divided between the emperor, who took a quarter of the empire, the barons and the Venetians. Recognition was given to the doge's lordship over "a quarter and a half of the empire".

13C	Around 1220 the **Quarantia**, a bench of 40 magistrates with judicial powers was formed as part of the Great Council.
1240	Venice besieged Ferrara thereby securing commercial control of the Po Valley.
1255	First dated documentation regarding the **Pregadi**, who were charged *(pregati)* with expressing opinions and fulfilling particular duties as members of the **Senate**. The Council of the Pregadi was appointed by the Great Council, to deal with questions of navigation and international politics, thus assuming both legislative and executive functions.
1257-1270	Venice entered into conflict with Genoa. The Venetians defeated the Genoese at Acre from where they brought the Acrean pillars now in front and to the right of the basilica. The Eastern Latin Empire fell when the Byzantine Emperor, **Michele Paleologo III**, an ally of the Genoese, took possession of Constantinople. The Genoese were subsequently bound by treaty (1270) to Louis IX of France who needed the Genoese fleet for the Crusades.
1268	New rules were drafted for the election of the doge. The Great Council had first to nominate the **Council of Forty**, charged with electing the next doge, by means of a 10-stage process of elections and drawing lots. The first doge appointed in this manner was **Lorenzo Tiepolo.**
1284	The **gold ducat** began to be minted, equal in weight and gold content to the Florentine florin which had been in circulation for 30 years (0.997g gold per 3.55g coin). The gold ducat was accepted currency until the fall of the Republic. When silver ducats were struck in 1561 the gold ducat became known as the *zecchino.*
1294-1299	Venice was once more at war with Genoa. At the **Battle of Curzola** (1298) the victorious Genoese sustained grievous losses. The treaty signed in 1299 sanctioned the Genoese dominance over the Riviera and that of the Venetians over the Adriatic.
1297	This was the year of the **Locking of the Great Council**, a reform that considerably increased the number of council members to more than 1000, as well as tightening up the system for their selection. Current as well as former members had to conform to rigorous procedures. By 1323, nomination was standardised, membership was for life and passed down the generations. Later still, the Great Council degenerated into a corps for the Venetian nobility.
1308-1313	Venice, dissatisfied with the duty levied on all the goods travelling through the Po Valley and wishing to consolidate its power over the area, attacked Ferrara. **Pope Clement V**, keen to defend his right of sovereignty over the city, issued from Avignon an **interdict** on Venice, which lasted until 1313.
1310	**Baiamonte Tiepolo**, a Venetian nobleman, tried to depose Doge Pietro Gradenigo. The revolt was suppressed with much bloodshed, and prompted the creation of a remarkable judicial body known as the **Council of Ten** whose prime function was to protect constitutional institutions. Presided over by the doge, it consisted of 10 members

El Paron de la Repubblica

The **Great Council** held a quintessential position at the heart of the Venetian Republic in that it carried out all the duties of state: not only did it pass laws, it also had the power to select the most important people in Venice. When it met in the chamber of the Doges' Palace, the doge would preside from the centre of the Tribunale or Bench of St Mark, while nobles seated upon armchairs would line the walls or fill rows of parallel benches down the length of the room.

of the Senate and six wise men. It employed the service of secret police and informers to investigate suspicious citizens and deal with denunciations and charges of libel against the State posted in the **lions' mouths**.

1321	The poet **Dante Alighieri** stayed in Venice in his capacity as ambassador to Ravenna.
1347-1348	A Venetian galley introduced the **plague** from Crimea which was to decimate the densely populated city (over 100 000 inhabitants) by three-fifths.
1350-1355	Conflict with Genoa continued. In 1350, troubled by heavy traffic which often caused serious accidents, it was established that horses should be provided with "bell-collars to warn pedestrians of their passage".

The dogeship of Marino Falier (1354-1355)

Marino Falier was 80 when he was elected doge. Irascible and resentful, his dogeship began under the worst of omens: the day he arrived in Venice, the **Bucintoro**, the grandiose dogal barge, decorated with friezes and gold carvings, could not draw alongside its mooring because of fog; secondly, on arriving on the Piazza, the doge entered the Palace by passing between the two columns where outlaws were executed; thirdly he was offended by insults about his wife scrawled on his chair by a young boy: Falier became even more viperish when he found out how lightly the culprit had been punished.

He decided to mete out punishment and exact his revenge by plotting murder on those members of the nobility whom he thought had betrayed him. The conspiracy was exposed in time. The doge was accused of treason and sentence passed for his execution. A black-draped portrait in the chamber of the Great Council, recording his unhappy rule, bears a defamatory but accurate inscription. *(see PIAZZA SAN MARCO - Palazzo Ducale)*. The story of Marino Falier has inspired both Byron and Swinburne (who both wrote works bearing the same title: *Marino Falier*), Donizetti *(Marin Falier)* and Delacroix.

1358	Dalmatia or *"Schiavonia"* was ceded to Hungary.
1378-1381	A fourth offence was mounted by the Venetians against Genoa to liberate Chioggia from Genoese and then Paduan hands.
1386	Corfu comes under Venetian rule.
1389-1420	Venice gradually gained dominion over a vast territory corresponding, more or less, to the present areas of Veneto and Friuli.

Lions' Mouths

The "lions' mouths" or "mouths of truth" were found along streets or in the walls of public buildings. These lion head masks were set with fierce expressions, the mouth carved hollow to accommodate anonymous denunciations posted to the State. These were taken into account only if two witnesses were cited.

Lion's mouth (Palazzo Ducale)

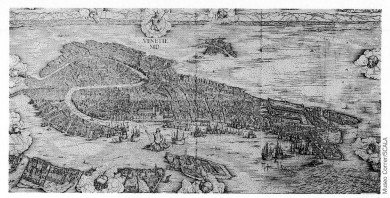

The De' Barbari map (Museo Correr)

1409	Venice regained possession of Dalmatia.
1410	Venice was badly hit by a high tide.
1424	Building was begun on the Ca' d'Oro.
1425-1454	During the dogeship of **Francesco Foscari**, by now head of an oligarchic system (since 1423 the formula had been dropped which had once required the popular approval of the new Doge: "If it is pleasing to you"), Venice was at war with the Lombards. **Carmagnola** took part in the battles and, suspected of treason, was condemned by the Council of Ten to be beheaded between the columns of the Piazzetta. After three decades of battle, Venetian territory stretched as far as the River Adda.

In 1428 Venice was devastated by an exceptionally high tide. |
1463-1479	The capture of the Venetian Argosy by the Turks was one of several humiliations to which Venice had to succumb, including the loss of Cumae and Scutari in Albania that prompted an annual levy of 10 000 ducats. This tribute was finally abolished at the death of Mehmet II.
1472	**Caterina Cornaro** married Giacomo Lusignano II, King of Cyprus, after whose death Queen Caterina was toppled by a *coup d'état. (see RIALTO).*
1490	The art of printing was introduced from Germany by **Aldo Manuzio** who set up his own printing press famed for its refined italic characters and for the intellectual nature of his books stamped with a dolphin and an anchor.
1494	Charles VIII, King of France, arrived in Italy to conquer the Kingdom of Naples. The anti-French league, of which Venice was part, failed to defeat him in the **Battle of Fornovo** the following year.
1499	The Turks attacked Lepanto. Antonio Grimani was defeated off the coast of Sapienza: in Venice he earned the epithet *"Antonio Grimani, ruin of the Christians"*. The Turks sacked Friuli. The peace treaty of 1503 sanctioned the loss of Lepanto, Modone and Corone.
1500	The **De' Barbari map** was published, providing a strangely evocative and realistic impression of the city.
1508	In order to split up Venetian territory, Julius II, Louis XII and Emperor Maximilian I formed the **League of Cambrai** in alliance with Spain, Hungary, the Duke of Savoy, the Duke of Ferrara and the Marquis of Mantua. After an initial defeat, Venice took seven years to recover her possessions as far as the Adda.
1514	The Rialto market was destroyed by fire.
1516	The Jews were segregated in the Ghetto district.

Dangerous years

1538	Andrea Doria, admiral under Emperor Charles V and a Venetian ally, was defeated at Prevesa. The Turks now controlled the seas.
1539	A secret service was set up by the **State Inquisitors**, the *Supreme Tribunale*, comprising three inquisitors: "the Red", a dogal councillor in a scarlet gown, and "the Blacks", two members of the Council of Ten. Working on information from delators, they took part in intrigue and counter-espionage.
1570	The Turks landed in Cyprus and conquered Nicosia.
1571	After the siege and fall of Famagusta, **Marcantonio Bragadin**, the Venetian governor, was flayed alive by the Turks.

Lepanto

Joined in the Holy League with the Pope and Spain, Venice confronted the Turks at Lepanto on 7 October 1571. The Christian fleet commanded by **Sebastiano Venier** comprised 202 galleys and six smaller ships, of which more than half were Venetian, whereas the Turkish fleet comprised 208 galleys and a flotilla of 63 boats. The Turks were heavily defeated: 30 000 men were killed, 80 ships sunk and 140 captured. The League lost 7600 men and 12 ships.

The Battle of Lepanto by Michieli (Palazzo Ducale)

Among the wounded Christians was **Cervantes**, author of *Don Quixote* who always considered the Battle of Lepanto the most important event not only of his life, but of all history. Cervantes believed that the injury to his left hand, which was permanently crippled, was "to the greater glory of his right one".

| 1573 | Venice signed a treaty with the Turks that clinched control over Cyprus which was abandonned and left to decline. |
| 1577 | Fire damaged much of the Doges' Palace; refurbishment is undertaken by Antonio da Ponte. |

Paradise replaces the Coronation of the Virgin

In 1365 the Chamber of the Great Council was decorated with the fresco by Guariento, (recorded 1338-1370) representing *The Coronation of the Virgin*. After the fire, it was decided to "remake Paradise as it was before". After a first competition, won by Veronese and Bassano who, however, never executed the work, a second competition was held and the commission entrusted to Tintoretto, author of the immense *Paradise*.

1587	The **Banco della Piazza**, the first public Venetian bank was set up. The second, the **Banco Giro** (or Banco del Giro), was created in 1619 *(see RIALTO)*.
1588	The Rialto Bridge was rebuilt in stone.
1593	The fortress of Palmanova was built, designed in the form of a nine-pointed star to defend the eastern borders against the Turks and Habsburgs. To commemorate the victory at the Battle of Lepanto, the foundation stone was laid down on 7 October.
1599-1604	The **Po River**, which deposits huge quantities of sediments around Chioggia, was diverted towards Goro.
1600	Once again, the city of Venice was flooded at hige tide.

Another interdict

In order to understand the rapport that existed between Venice and the Holy See, it is useful to note what the Venetians, who held themselves to be "first Venetian and then Christian", used to boldly claim: "We believe greatly in St Mark, sufficiently in God and little or less in the Pope".

The Pope did not readily accept the right to religious freedom that Venice granted the Protestants. In 1605 the denunciation before the Council of Ten of two priests, accused of various crimes, proved to be the last straw. The Pope maintained that the two should have been handed over to the ecclesiastical authorities. On the Venetian side was a Servite priest, **Paolo Sarpi**, whose arguments appeared heretical to Rome. When the Pope threatened an interdict and excommunicated Venice, the city responded: "Your excommunication we regard as nothing and we care not a fig about it".

The interdict lasted for one year. Although the relationship between Venice and the Vatican normalised, Paolo Sarpi became the victim of an assassination attempt in 1607. Recovered from his wounds and surveying the dagger that had stabbed him, he is said to have declared: "I recognise the style of the Roman Church."

1609	**Galileo Galilei** presented the telescope to the doge.
1613-1617	After raids by the **Uskoks**, pirates from Bosnia and Turkish Dalmatia protected by the Habsburgs, Venice went to war over Istria and Friuli, which resulted in the Uskoks being deported to central Croatia.
1618	Spain instigated a complex conspiracy against Venice. The Council of Ten intervened decisively as usual: one of the participants was sewn into a sack and thrown into the sea; another two were hung upside down on the gallows of the Piazzetta.
1622	**Antonio Foscarini,** the illustrious senator and ambassador to France and England, was found guilty of spying. He was condemned to death and succumbed to the usual treatment of being hung by one foot in the Piazzetta. Some time later, it was revealed that the accusations against Foscarini were false. The man who had spread these accusations was tried by the Three *(see above: 1539)* and condemned to death. Venice made public admission of her grave error. A State declaration was sent to his family and to embassies, and copies were pasted around the city.
1628-1630	Following the death of Ferdinand of Gonzaga, Mantua was claimed both by the French, led by Charles of Gonzaga-Nevers, and the Habsburgs. It was under siege from German troops when Venice intervened: the city was nevertheless lost to the French. Mantua was savagely ransacked as the plague ravaged the region, decimating the local population and Germans, before spreading to Venice. In little more than a year. the Serenessima lost 50 000 inhabitants. When at last the contagion subsided, construction was begun on the Church of Santa Maria della Salute in fulfilment of a vow.

Galileo's new invention offered many advantages... The telescope operates in such a way that ..."he who stands at a distance of nine miles will appear to us as clearly as if he were standing only one mile away. This discovery has far-reaching implications that will be of considerable benefit to all those engaged in commercial or maritime activities. Navigators will now be able to identify the masts and sails of enemy ships far sooner than they had done so in the past and we ourselves shall discover our rivals two hours before they may discover us."

The Sultan's harem and the war of Candia (Crete)

The Knights of Malta habitually committed acts of piracy of which Venice disapproved because they were detrimental to her relationship with the East. In 1644 the Knights attacked a Turkish galleon in the Aegean and captured part of the Sultan's harem. The Sultan avenged himself not by attacking Malta, but Candia – as Crete was then known by the name of its capital, convinced that the Venetians were behind this act.

The war dragged on for over 20 years, despite the Turkish fleet having suffered a naval defeat second only to Lepanto in 1656. Finally, in 1699 Captain Francesco Morosini, backed by 3 600 men, signed the surrender with which Venice lost the island.

1684-1699	Francesco Morosini, the ally of Austria and Russia, reconquered the Peloponnese peninsular, thereby acquiring the nickname "the Peloponnesian". Unfortunately, during this military operation, a Venetian mortar was fired at the Parthenon which, being used by the Turks to store their reserves of gunpowder, was severely damaged. He was elected doge in 1688. In 1699 although the former Venetian territories had not all been reclaimed, the Treaty of Carlowitz temporarily checked Turkish military campaigns.

18C and decline

Although in decline, when faced with a choice between alliance and independence, Venice once again opted for autonomy by refusing to side either with France or the Habsburgs in conflict for two centuries.

1714-1718	Venice lost the Peloponnese forever in a final battle against the Turks, sealed by the **Treaty of Passarowitz** signed in 1718. She maintained possession of Istria, Dalmatia, the Ionian islands and a few territories in Albania.
1744-1782	The *Murazzi* (protective wall around the lagoon) was built at Pellestrina and Sottomarina, 14m/46ft wide and 4.5m /14ft 8in higher than the average level of the tide. It was made with Istrian stone and pozzolana, a type of volcanic dust which has remarkable binding qualities when mixed with water, sand and lime.
1784	The Procurator **Andrea Tron**, nicknamed *el Paron* (the Leader) for his strong personality and political standing most regarded as above the doge, lamented that *"there are no shades of our old merchants among the citizens or subjects"* before the spread of *"weakness of character, overwhelming luxury, idle shows and presumptuous entertainment and vice"* in Venice.
1784-1786	These were the years of the final naval incursions. Admiral **Angelo Emo** waged battles against pirates along the North African coast.

The Libro d'Oro

The Golden Book, first drawn up in the 16C, was the register of the civil status of Venetian nobility. Specific conditions for entry had to be fulfilled. Whoever was not high-born, and thus not inscribed, could not hold a government office.

A break with tradition and the demise of the Republic

1789	The last doge to be elected, **Lodovico Manin** ironically was the first not to be born of the old Venetian nobility but of an *émigré* family from Friuli that had paid 100 000 ducats for inclusion in the **Golden Book** in 1651.
1792	The opera house re-opened as **La Fenice**. Before the decline of Venice, the city still showed consideration for its fragile lagoon. It defined a series of boundaries referred to as the "lagoon perimeter" inside which it was forbidden to carry out any activity that might endanger the natural habitat of the lake.
1797	**Napoleon** invaded Venetian territory in 1796 while pursuing his Austrian enemy and successfully ejecting it from Italy – a possession he only maintained by posting troops in Verona and controlling access to the Brenner Pass. A temporary pact was made with the Austrians at Leoben (18 April 1797). This was ratified six months later on 18 Oc-

Museo Correr/SCALA

The dogal *"corno"* (Museo Correr)

tober by the **Treaty of Campoformio** signed by Francis II, Emperor of Austria, and Napoleon Bonaparte. It confirmed that Austria renounced her claim over Belgium and Lombardy to take possession of the Veneto as far as the Adige, Friuli, Istria, Dalmatia, the Po Valley and the islands in the Adriatic: France took the Albanian coast and the Ionian islands: Venice was left with the former papal states of Romagna, Ferrara and Bologna.

Venice's fate in effect was sealed by her resistance to ally herself to Napoleon. Not only did she show no remorse when anti-French feeling was stoked by the clergy during Easter week to the point of vicious rioting in Verona (a Venetian dominion), she positively congratulated her officers for firing at a French patrol in the Adriatic and killing the French crew. Napoleon's exasperation is documented: *"I will have no more Inquisition, no more Senate. I shall be an Attila to the State of Venice"*.

Without the reassurance of Venice's recapitulation, the government would have to be seized, war would be inevitable. The Senate met for the last time on 29 April. By Friday 12 May, Napoleon's demands had to be conceded and the Great Council met for a last, very tense sitting; a provisional government was approved by an "unconstitutional" Council falling short of its quorum of 600 by 63, many members having fled to their country estates on *terra firma*. Laying down the *cufieta*, the bonnet worn by the doge under his crown, Lodovico Manin turned with dignity to his servant: *"Take it away, I will have no further use for this"*.

After the fall

1805	With the Treaty of Presburg, Napoleon formally reclaimed Venice as part of the Kingdom of Italy.
1815	The Congress of Vienna established that Venice, the Veneto and Lombardy should belong to Austria.
1821	The Italians showed unrest caused by the failed attempts to achieve unification. Anti-Austrian movements broke out.
1839-1853	Construction of the north and south dykes at Malamocco was completed.
1841	The railway bridge linking Venice to Mestre was built.
1844	The patriot founders of the secret organisation Esperia Attilio and Emilio Bandiera, together with a sympathiser Domenico Moro, were shot at Cosenza.
1847	The lawyer **Daniele Manin** and the writer **Niccolò Tommaseo** were awarded prizes by the 11th Congresso degli Scienziati.
1848	Daniele Manin was nominated President of the Republic of St Mark and began reorganising a provisional government, before leading an insurrection against the Austrians supported by Niccolò Tommaseo. Both eminent men were subsequently exiled.
1854-58	Identical iron bridges were built near the Accademia and the station.
1866	After the Prussian defeat of the Austrians at Sadowa, Venice voted to be part of a unified Italy by a majority of 674 426 to 69.
1895	The **International Biennale of Art** was founded in the gardens of the Castle; exhibition facilities were expanded through the 19C with the erection of various modern pavilions.
1902	The bell-tower of St Mark's collapsed.
1915-1918	Venice suffered several bomb attacks but her misfortunes were not caused only by the war: once again she was flooded by the rising waters.
1932	First edition of the International Film Festival.
1933	Inauguration of the Ponte Littorio, now called the Ponte della Libertà.
1953	Giuseppe Roncalli was appointed Patriarch of Venice before being elected **Pope John XXIII** and instigating the second Vatican Council.
1953-1969	**Frank Lloyd Wright** (1869-1959) planned a student centre, the Masieri Memorial, to be built along the Grand Canal. In 1964 **Le Corbusier** (1887-1965) proposed designs for the Civil Hospital. **Kahn** (1901-74) undertook a project for a new Congress Hall. None of these undertakings ever saw the light of day.
1966	During the month of November the high tide rose to an alarming level. The waters flooded the *Murazzi* at Pellestrina and reached many of the city houses.
1969	Albino Luciani, Patriarch of Venice, is elected Pope in 1978, assuming the name **John Paul I** which he bore for little more than a month.

The lagoon lives on

If the glory of Venice belongs to a bygone era, its lagoon provides a continuous link with the past, preserving a quality and style of life unique to its shores, regardless of the threat of subsidence or flooding. In 1925 alone, the Piazza San Marco, the "salon of Venice", was flooded eight times: since then it has succumbed to inundation on a further 50 occasions.

Pollution, today's worst enemy – The 20C is the era of industrialisation. Marghera was created in the 1920s and, after the Second World War, the areas taken up by industrial activity expanded quite considerably. Oil was known to seep into the canal, threatening the ecological balance of the lagoon, whose precarious state was further endangered by the draining of land to build industrial areas and the Marco Polo airport.

Between 1950 and 1970, the wastage turned out by refineries and by chemical as well as metallurgical factories at **Porto Marghera** would often end up in the lagoon. During the 1980s a number of purification plants were set up nearby and they now recycle an estimated 80% of the area's industrial refuse. Pollution, caused by excessive amounts of nitrogen and phosphates, chemical fertilizers and insecticides, and organic substances generated by industrial complexes and urban communities, destroys part of the lagoon flora and fauna, encourages the proliferation of algae and stunts that of the phanerogamic species, whose roots are extremely useful since they prevent the onslaught of erosion.

1973	The Italian State declared that the preservation of Venice was of "pre-eminent national interest".
1988-1992	The Mo.S.E. prototype, a huge mobile sluice-gate devised to regulate the movement of the tides, was installed in the lagoon waters on an experimental basis.
1996	The opera house **La Fenice** burned down on 29 January.

More detailed information about the lagoon can be found in the section: The Venetian lagoon.

*The chapter on art and architecture in this guide
gives an outline of artistic creation in the region,
providing the context of the buildings
and works of art described in the Sights section.
This chapter may also provide ideas for touring.
It is advisable to read it at leisure before setting out.*

The arts

BUILDING IN VENICE

The history of architecture in Venice cannot be divorced from the physical and geographical constraints which, throughout the ages, the Venetians have had to overcome with mastery and ingenuity.

Houses on piles – The city is not built on water, but in the water. It was built either on sandbanks above the water level, which gave rise to real islands, or on small sandy mounds which had remained at the water's surface.

In either case, great larch or oak wood **pali** are driven deep through the sand, mud or silt, forming an unstable lagoon floor, to the bedrock of hard clay. These 2-4m/6ft 6in-13ft piles are organised in concentric circles or spirals starting from the outer perimeter of the building to be constructed, at intervals of 60-80cm/24-32in. In this way the piles provide a base onto which a raft-like platform *(zattera)* of horizontal beams *(zatterone)* may be secured. To reinforce this wooden floor, it is lined with boulders of **Istrian stone** that provide a solid course for the brick and mortar on which it is possible to build.

The number of piles used can sometimes be considerable: 1 106 657 for the Church of Santa Maria della Salute, and 10 000 for the Rialto Bridge!

Building materials – Unfortunately, since the lagoon offers very little in terms of building materials, it is necessary to import these from other areas.

Most of the **timber** is brought from the Cadore forests and the Balkans. It is used not only for the foundation piles, but also for the frames and ceilings of the houses. Occasionally it is incorporated into masonry walls not so much as reinforcement but rather as "shock absorbers": this lends greater flexibility to the structure, which resolves some of the problems raised by the instability of the subsoil. **Marble**, used to front façades, is principally sourced from the Euganei Hills *(south of Padua)* or from Greece. **Istria limestone**, hard, white and marble-like, has the added advantage of being resistant to salt-erosion; it is therefore frequently used in Venice for bridge copings and to face *palazzi*, churches, bell-towers etc. Only **brick**, which in Gothic times lent its charming pink hues to I Frari and many other quaint buildings in Venice, is made on site from local clay.

Originality of Venetian architecture – All the houses, palaces and churches that have been erected by the Serenissima through the ages survive on these reinforced, drained, dried and consolidated areas reclaimed from the lagoon. It is almost as if the early Venetians made a pact with the lagoon that they would live with it rather than view it as a problem to be reckoned with. And so from the water rise mists and fogs that swirl and fade again to confer a thousand different moods on the urban landscape: one moment the millpond mirrors a perfect reflection and in another the choppy, churlish surface dissolves the shimmering profile according to whim. The lagoon intensifies the ethereal sunlight to sparkle and glitter and lend a festive air to the place, but it may also invade the landscape with the spirit of melancholy. Water consorts with the changing light and density of the air, to exaggerate or deform the delicate stone lacework, the crenellated roof ornaments, the many recesses, loggias and arcades. But poetic descriptions of atmosphere are an insubstantial preoccupation in comparison to the physical problems posed by the lagoon: it is rather the remoteness of mainland resources and the instability of the subsoil that preoccupy the Venetian authorities. Initially, it was the cost and transport of building materials that dictated a patron's choice and influenced an architect's design of a private palace or church. Up to the 16C, local brick had been the most obvious raw material available. However, when more sophisticated and reliable forms of transport were discovered, the economic factor became considerably less important. A second major element in the equation was the risk of subsidence. To reduce this threat, houses were erected to no more than two or three storeys high, except in the Ghetto where squat buildings had low ceilings so that the total weight was proportionally less. A constant reminder of instability was the angle at which certain palaces (Palazzo Dario) and bell-towers (Santo Stefano, San Barnaba) inclined, and the regularity with which the quays (Riva degli Schiavoni) and St Mark's Square flooded. Through determination, patience and perseverance in an unpredictable environment, strengthened by a spirit of enterprise and ambitious business acumen, the Venetians learnt to construct and embellish their magnificent city. Yet despite everything that has been accomplished and all the expertise acquired, the unpropitious site for this wonderful city means that it will forever be at the mercy of natural forces: the corrosive action of salt and water, and the instability of the lagoon floor.

The campo – A square provides a point at which all roads, streets and alleys converge: it is at the very heart of community life where housewives chat and hang out their washing, where children play in the open. It is not to be confused with the **corte**, a closed public courtyard with a single entrance or with the **cortile**, a private courtyard hidden within a patrician town house.

The *campo*, sometimes dotted with a few trees, is encircled by fine patrician houses, Gothic or Renaissance in style and blessed with its own church. At its centre, a well might occupy a choice spot. Given that the town was built on salty water and therefore had no natural drinking-water supply, rain water had to be collected, purified and stored in cisterns that were excavated to a depth of 5-6m/16-20ft. The brick-lined tank collected water through several apertures in the *campo* floor, filtering it through fine river sand. Often the well-head or **vera da pozzo**, would have been paid for by a patron and would therefore have been sculpted as a veritable work of art.

When Venice ran short of drinking water, supplies taken from the rivers Brenta and Sile would be sent to the city in containers stocked on barges. These operations were carried out by the guild of water vendors, which was founded in 1386.

Domestic architecture – Throughout Venice, with the exception of the Grand Canal, palaces rub shoulders with modest houses. Simply built in pink brick or stone, most are low in height; a few retain their openwork external staircase, double façade and "double" front entrances: one on the street and one onto the canal with its "water porch". The inner courtyard is modelled on the Roman atrium – shaded in summer and protected from the wind in winter. On the first floor or **piano nobile**, a **portego** runs perpendicular to the main front, from the street, across the internal *cortile*, through the entire width therefore of the house to open out onto a loggia on the canal side.

The **altana** is a veranda built on a tiled roof where typical Venetian high funnel-shaped chimneys known as *fumaioli* can be seen projecting; these distinctive features were immortalised by Carpaccio in his paintings. Forever short of space, the Venetians have made clever use of their rooftops by installing these charming terraces in order to increase their living area. The façades are enhanced with flower-decked balconies, small carved disks, ornamental reliefs and sculpted cornices... Down the side walls, houses with *barbacani* have corbelled projections to support the timber beams of upper floors (Calle del Paradiso).

Like at roof level, the lack of space at ground level means that there are very few gardens in Venice, and those that do exist are small, sometimes consisting of a single tree or a few flower tubs, often jealously guarded from the public eye behind high walls.

ARCHITECTURE AND SCULPTURE: AN APPRECIATION OF CRAFTSMANSHIP

The city of Venice still bears the stamp of the former Byzantine empire but over the years the streets have also succumbed to the influence of Renaissance, Classical and Baroque architecture. Artists too have played a role in forging the atmosphere of the town, while remaining faithful to the Venetian spirit.

Veneto-Byzantine

The oldest monuments preserved by the Venetian lagoon are to be found on the Island of Torcello: the **Cattedrale di Santa Maria Assunta** and the complex of **Santa Fosca** bear witness to the close ties which once allied Venice with Ravenna, the Western heir to a Byzantine legacy.

For several centuries, Venice, through its conquests and trade links with the East, maintained a close relationship with Greece and Constantinople: the Basilica of St Mark, rebuilt in the 11C, was modelled on the 6C prototype of Byzantium churches, the Church of the Holy Apostles in Constantinople that was destroyed in the 13C (the immense and sumptuous Higha Sophia was built subsequently by the same architect along the same lines). St Mark's therefore directly transposes an expression of the Eastern Church in terms of form, structure, volume and style into the West.

This Oriental Christianity was a major force in the fusion· of an original "Veneto-Byzantine" style from the late Middle Ages onwards. The artistic iconography, strongly influenced by Byzantium, incorporates Islamic elements (decorative motifs, horseshoe arches), Palaeo-Christian features (*transennae*, capitals) and Roman details from sculpted fragments (marble blocks, column shafts, flat bricks) salvaged from villas along the Adriatic coast that had been destroyed during the Barbarian invasions of the 5C and 6C.

Churches – The Byzantine-style churches like Santa Fosca, Torcello Cathedral, Santa Maria e Donato on Murano and St Mark's Basilica, best demonstrate the Eastern influence. This is clearly visible in the centrally-planned Greek cross church or longitudinal hall church (nave and two aisles) prefixed by a narthex (covered porch which evolved into an arched portico) but independent of a free-standing baptistry (like at Torcello). Structurally, Byzantium provided the expertise to erect domes over open spaces unincumbered by piers; it inspired the use of precious marble column shafts crowned with variously shaped capitals (basket-shaped, inverted pyramid) and carved ornament (organic decoration like foliage, symmetrically arranged animals). The practice in Ravenna (12C-13C) of applying decoration in the form of shallow relief, open fretwork, or *niello* (deeply cut engraving) and mosaic with flat gold backgrounds to both internal and external walls, was quick to be emulated by Venetian mosaicists who copied subjects from the Old and New Testaments. Other features to be accommodated include Palaeo-Christian *transennae* (open-work window screens), *plutei* (marble tablets) and *paterae* encircled within a twisted rope moulding, acanthus leaves and vine leaf tendrils, Palaeo-Christian figurative motifs (gryphons, eagles, peacocks and lions often quoted from embroideries or manuscript illuminations), marble *ambos* (pulpits before the chancel), and *iconostases* (screens in Greek churches separating the sanctuary from the nave).

The **Romanesque style**, which seems to appear in Venice during the 11C and 12C is also in its own way modelled upon Byzantine art. The main forces at play were revived by the Lombard invasion from the northwest and from Ravenna in the south through which the Crusader armies would have passed.

Typical of the Venetian Romanesque style is the external appearance of high, solid, austere walls, pierced with tiny windows, relieved only by simple decoration afforded by blind arcading. The interior featured a raised nave, a vestige of Palaeo-Christian civilisation, and two aisles. Churches were planned as basilicas with a tall nave flanked by side aisles. In more simple terms it is a compromise of "Western" Romanesque and "Eastern" Byzantine styles, and it is precisely from this period that Venice's oldest churches survive: San Giacomo (Rialto), San Nicolò dei Mendicoli, San Zan Degolà, San Giacomo dall'Orio and Sant'Eufemia (Giudecca). Although these churches were heavily rebuilt in the following centuries, many have retained their original massive, square, brick *campanile* or bell-tower, articulated with pilasters and blind arcading, capped with a loggia that screens the bells (San Barnaba). Only the roof, added later, differs from the original by being hexagonal, pyramidal or conical in shape. In some cases, the original church has long gone, but the Romanesque tower remains as at San Zaccaria *(illustration: see SAN ZACCARIA)* and San Samuele. All that survives of the famous 12C Sant'Apollonia monastery, is its superb cloister, a rare vestige of Romanesque architecture.

Domestic buildings – The **Veneto-Byzantine palazzo** is no doubt the most original product of 11C to 13C Venetian architecture. Known as the *casa-fondaco* (from the Arabic *funduk* meaning depository or warehouse), this "storehouse" effectively combines the purpose of storage, commercial office and family home into one compact unit. The best preserved are the Fondaco dei Turchi, Ca' Farsetti, Palazzo Loredan and Ca' Da Mosto (*Ca'* being an abbreviation of *casa* meaning house).

These houses further testify to the prodigiously rapid growth of the city's merchant aristocracy, empowered and enriched by maritime trade which in turn, nurtured an interest and appreciation for Eastern Byzantine and Muslim craftsmanship.

As the need for defensive fortifications receded – on a scale seen at the first Doges' Palace – patrician town houses erected in the 11C began to conform to a set type that allowed for an easy and comfortable lifestyle. The structure would remain unchanged for several centuries to come, whereas its applied decoration would evolve according to contemporary taste. Split into three horizontal tiers, the main entrance into the storage or commercial area would have been on the canal side, through the **"porta d'acqua"**. On the first floor, the *piano nobile*, a continuous gallery or *loggia* would run the length of the façade between two solid walled towers, whereas at the top, a series of decorative crenellations would conceal the roofline. Only later would additional storeys sometimes be added.

Veneto-Byzantine arches have several forms: stilted round-headed arches (narrow arches with their springing line raised), horseshoe arches, Moorish ogee arches and high-pitched pointed "lancet" arches. These are often supported by highly-prized marble shafts with decorated capitals, bearing Byzantine stylised and/or symmetrical foliage or animals. Further decoration might include Byzantine *paterae* (small carved discs) illustrating real or mythical animals (peacocks, griffins etc) or medallions of different coloured marble, crosses or historical emblems.

Venetian Gothic

The term "Gothic", a label attributed in the 17C to the style developed by the barbarian Goths, assumes a distinctive meaning when applied to Venetian building design from the 1400s. For it is this delicate, ornamental, elegant style that has given the city its most distinctive characteristics and its architectural unity. It graces nearly all the *campi* and houses giving onto the banks of canals, styling a pointed arch or a loggia's filigree stonework. Unlike the structural changes that facilitated a new form of civil engineering in France, England and Germany, Venice merely used the Gothic style to ornament, flatter and decorate her buildings until the late 16C.

The Foreign Merchants of Venice

Venetian trade also benefited from the different cultures brought over by foreign visitors to the city. In those days, a great many nationalities were living side by side, all engaged in commercial activities - Albanians, Armenians, Dalmatians, Jews, Greeks, Persians, Germans and Turks. In this context the storehouse *(fondaco)* played an essential role as it was used for stocking goods and was seen as the heart of the business community. In Venice, the warehouses belonging to Persian, Turkish and German merchants were particularly active.

Churches – Politically, Venice was reinforcing her strength and autonomy. This prosperity allowed institutions to flourish both in the secular and religious domains, as demonstrated by the large-scale building projects undertaken by the principal monastic communities (I Frari, San Zanipòlo). With time, these were endowed by aristocratic patrons who wished to celebrate and publicise their wealth and standing (Madonna dell'Orto, Santo Stefano) entrusting to the churches their refined funerary monuments. These were days in which the plague was rapidly spreading and they were characterised by a strong sense of urgency: poverty and charity were preached by the Mendicant Orders, and measures were taken to build monasteries and *scuole*, the characteristic Venetian institutions that sustained their confraternities in exchange for charity. Thus around 1245, with the benediction of **Doge Giacomo Tiepolo**, the Dominicans and Franciscans began erecting the city's most beautiful churches.

Exterior – As from the 14C, designers of religious buildings began combining curved and rectilinear features in drafting their façades (San Giovanni in Bragora, I Frari, Scuola Vecchia della Misericordia). While the structures remained austerely simple, **porches** and **windows** suddenly became encrusted with Gothic features. The severe flat-brick west front was divided into three parts: the central, nave section soaring high above the flanking aisles. Plain surfaces were relieved with decorative elements in white Istrian stone: portals were framed with engaged columns and pediments, hood mouldings articulated the gables, a cornice was supported by a frieze of niches that curved around the lateral walls. Only porches made in marble or white Istrian stone carry ornamentation: crowned by recessed arches with acanthus leaf motifs as well as elegant relief decoration such as cable fluting, knot-work and foliage, they are often flanked by statuettes or engaged columns. At the east end, apses proliferated and extruded to form chevets (I Frari, San Zanipòlo), whereas the tall square pink-brick *campanile* point skyward with a white marble open loggia (St Mark's, I Frari, Madonna dell'Orto).

Interior – The Gothic church, based on the T-shaped Latin cross to accommodate the long processions required by the liturgy down the nave, was abutted by aisles; at the east end, a wide transept could accommodate a chancel and numerous transept chapels endowed by private patrons (I Frari, San Zanipòlo). Sometimes the internal space was enclosed by a fine open timbered roof built by local shipwrights in the form of an inverted hull (Santo Stefano, San Giacomo dall'Orio) and articulated by arches painted with string-courses of acanthus leaves, or by carved wooden tie-beams.

Domestic buildings – Gothic fronted *palazzi* enclose every *campi* and line the secondary canals; but the most magnificent examples are to be found along the Grand Canal which began to resemble a wonderful "triumphal waterway".

Fanciful creativity – The Venetian-Gothic **palazzo** was derived from the Byzantine model, retaining its three main characteristics: portico, loggia and decorative merlons. However, it now assumed a more noble, confident and sophisticated canon of ornamentation that continued to be implemented until the fall of the Republic. As the patrician families stabilised their social status, they affected changes to their houses, most notably on the *piano nobile*. The simplicity of the earlier Veneto-Byzantine façades (portico and continuous loggia) was replaced by a centralised, more important arcaded loggia with cusped arches and quatrefoil motifs. In the corner section, single isolated windows interrupt the solid wall area now enhanced by the use of brick and stucco in two-tone colour combinations.

Interior layout – The *palazzo* is traditionally U-shaped in plan: a central block with perpendicular wings extended around a courtyard *(cortile)* with a well-head. Access to the *piano nobile* would have been via an open external stairway supported on Gothic arches up to a colonnaded portico with wooden architrave (Palazzo Centani). On the first floor, a broad passageway or, if enclosed, a reception hall *(portego)* ran the entire width of the house to open out onto the loggia on the canal-side.

Extrovert beauty – Unlike the Florentine *palazzo*, austere, plain and impersonal, the Venetian façade may be seen as an extrovert, openly flaunting its charms to those who walk by. The windows are therefore natural vehicles for additional decoration.

Venice is still laden with oriental references both Christian and Muslim, and the characteristic loggias are strongly reminiscent of Palaeo-Christian stone fretwork; windows borrow from their Moorish counterparts a profile that echoes a cusped lancet and still the temptation of inserting sculpted Byzantine *paterae* is too great to resist.

By looking at the windows and their arched profiles, the various phases of Venetian Gothic may be discerned. 14C curvilinear arches of Moorish influence sometimes rest on colonnettes (Corte del Million); early-15C three-cusped, four-light centred arches are often topped with a finial (Palazzo Duodo); late-15C Gothic or High Gothic arches, the most original and varied phase which might be compared with the French Flamboyant, grace the Doges' Palace. Here, one or more rows of quatrefoil oculi surmount the three-cusped arches of the loggias. The Ca' d'Oro, where **Marco d'Amadio**, a member of the **Bon** family, worked from 1421 to 1461, is also expressive of this joyful, endearing exuberance.

Gothic sculpture – As with building, the first notable works of sculpture by known craftsmen date from this period. With **Pier Paolo** and **Jacobello delle Masegne** (d 1403 and d 1409 respectively) a style, explored by the School of Pisa, was evolved out of the static Byzantine tradition towards greater movement and expression, and combined with a taste for Gothic ornaments. Their work combines the use of delicate and complicated architectural elements with figurative statuary (iconostatis at St Mark's).

T. Zane

A traditional Venetian *altana* where girls used to sit and sunbleach their hair.

An upstairs loggia and famous *fumaiolo* chimney

E. Zane

A *sottoportego*

C. Boisvieux

A carved well-head

SIMACOURBE/RAPHO

S. Gerometta/HOAQUI

The *porta d'acqua* or waterside entrance

The Venetian School of Sculpture seemed unable to truly inspire the artistic community. The Serenissima was forced therefore to continue soliciting foreign artists or awarding commissions to unsuspecting craftsmen passing through the city.

Following in the footsteps of Pisa, Venice succumbed to the influence of Florentine art, to that of **Niccolò Lamberti** and to Sienese artists such as **Jacopo della Quercia**. Marco Cozzi, a remarkable wood carver from Vicenza, created the splendid wooden chancel in the Church of the Frari, the only example of such work to survive in Venice.

Funerary monuments – The earliest 14C tombs consist of a simple sarcophagus with the recumbent figure of the deceased in front and the figures of the Madonna and Child and saints incorporated at the four corners; above, set into a recessed arch is a lunette, painted or sometimes sculpted. Later a Gothic baldaquin of stone drapery was added, seemingly suspended in the middle from the ceiling, its drapes drawn aside by figures (angels or warriors). It is in this vein that the Delle Masegne brothers worked from the 14C to the 15C.

Portals – Almost all the 15C portals that adorn the Venetian churches are attributed to the architect **Bartolomeo Bon** (Santo Stefano, San Zanipòlo, Madonna dell'Orto, I Frari). Each is made of stone or marble to contrast dramatically with the main fabric of the brick building, and each is decorated with a series of hood mouldings and courses of twisted rope with cusps of foliage around the pointed ogee archway; elements are further embellished with acanthus leaves, the gable is surmounted with a free-standing statue, and inside the portal shelter small niches or aedicules. Bartolomeo's unquestionable masterpiece is the elegant Porta della Carta, the main entrance to the Doges' Palace, executed in Flamboyant Gothic.

Venetian Renaissance

The success and popularity of the International Gothic canon was such that it delayed the adoption of Renaissance principles in Venice. However, once introduced, the style quickly took hold and soon graced the traditional structures with a new refined magnificence. During the 1400s, under the patronage of **Doge Francesco Foscari**, the Serenissima's civilisation changed direction: artistic links with Tuscany and Lombardy were strengthened and after the fall of Constantinople in 1453, ties with the Eastern Empire were severed. Humanism flourished: it drew its inspiration from Hellenistic culture and was enriched by the sagacity of Greek scholars who had fled from Constantinople.

In 1495 the printer Aldo Manuzio began publishing the Ancient Greek classics as the city witnessed the divide between **Scuole Grandi** and **Scuole Minori** (see I Carmini). By the second half of the 15C, Florentine supremacy had dwindled. The new style, which originated from Tuscany, spread throughout Italy thanks to the wandering lifestyle of her artists, and gradually began to display regional characteristics - elements which Venice, in her inimitable fashion absorbed and interpreted in her own way...

In the beginning – The earliest traces of the **Early Renaissance** are to be found in archways.

The entrance to the Arsenale (1460) survives as the first full expression complete with its Classical lions, mythological figures and Greek marble columns. Three other examples betraying the same characteristics include the portal of San Giobbe, one at the Gesuiti in the Zattere quarter, and the Foscari doorway at the Doges' Palace.

In terms of sculpture, the Florentine masters Donatello and Verrocchio endowed the Serenissima with only two works, both of major importance: an evocative wooden polychrome figure of John the Baptist (1438) at I Frari, and an impressive equestrian monument in bronze of the Condottiere Bartolomeo Colleoni from Bergamo (1458) that now stands in the *campo* before San Zanipòlo.

Lombardo dynasty – At the turn of the 15C, the spirit of innovation that was to animate contemporary sculpture and architecture was largely due to the genius and expertise of the **Lombardo family** – from Lombardy as their name clearly implies – and in particular to **Pietro** (1435-1515) and his two sons **Antonio** and **Tullio**. Seeking to promote a complete re-evaluation of contemporary design and the widespread implementation of the new canon, the Lombardo family fashioned the highly public façade of the Scuola San Marco dominating its prime site, the Church of Santa Maria dei Miracoli and the unusual yet noble Ca' Dario giving onto the Grand Canal: in each case structural and decorative elements (porphyry medallions, marble rosettes) interact to form a perfectly-balanced ensemble governed by a harmonious system of proportions.

Stone and marble replace the brick used earlier by Gothic builders. Façades may be asymmetrical, articulated with cornices, sculpted busts, figurative statues, pilasters – fluted or with cartouches of delicate graffiti (Classical reliefs featuring masks, the attributes of the Liberal Arts and the Gods of War), friezes of vines or festoons of foliage, animals and putti...

In the field of sculpture, Pietro undertook for San Zanipòlo a series of important and distinguished funerary monuments to commemorate doges in Istrian stone (those of Pietro Mocenigo, Pasquale Malipiero and Nicolò Marcello). Tullio, meanwhile, who worked extensively with his father, is responsible for the fine reliefs set into the front of the Scuola San Marco, and for the monuments to Giovanni Mocenigo and Andrea Vendramin in San Zanipòlo.

Cushion capital
Torcello (9-10C.)

Pluteus with peacocks
Torcello Cathedral (11C)

Composite capital
Torcello

Campanile di San Barnaba

Fretwork stone screen
San Alipio door, St Mark's

Patera with Pascal lamb

The Lombard tradition is reflected in the formal design of such memorials: triumphal arch on several levels with superimposed niches housing allegorical statues of the Virtues, acting as a cornice over the sarcophagus. On the other hand, the fine workmanship of the figurines, along with the poise and elegance of their stance, undeniably testify to Tuscan influence.

Mauro Codussi (1440-1504) – This architect from Bergamo, a contemporary of the Lombardo brothers, seemed happier to celebrate the decorative rather than the structural function of architecture and to this end returned to the Tuscan vernacular for inspiration. Despite adhering to the guidelines pronounced by the Humanist Alberti in his treatises on architecture for a Canon of Beauty formulated according to mathematical proportion and harmony of component parts (spatial organisation, symmetrical elevations, correct application of the Classical orders – Doric, Ionic and Corinthian, entablature – architrave, cornice and frieze, rustication and niches), Codussi's designs appeared to lack homogeneity. Instead, he forged a personal style distinguished by semicircular pediments for the fronts of churches and the Scuola San Marco which he completed, rustication on the ground floor of his *palazzi*, engaged columns and cornices to differentiate superior storeys, circular oculi inserted between the coupled arches of an arcade supported on coupled columns.

His early projects, which included the Clocktower, the Church of San Giovanni Grisostomo, all showed trace elements of Byzantine styling (portico decoration, Greek cross floorplan), whereas his more mature works, the sumptuous *palazzi* Corner Spinelli and Vendramin Calergi on the Grand Canal, conformed to his distinctive style. This developed into an even bolder statement at San Zaccaria and San Michele, his masterpiece, where marble or white Istrian stone were applied across all three carefully articulated sections of the elevation – both on the horizontal and vertical axes; the nave towers over the aisles linked with semicircular pediments, whereas friezes, shell niches and porphyry roundels provided ornamentation. Two additional designs by Codussi included Santa Maria Formosa and the beautiful Istrian stone campanile of San Pietro di Castello.

Antonio Rizzo – Antonio Rizzo (d 1499) was responsible for the internal (courtyard) facade of the Doges' Palace and the monumental Giant's staircase faced in marble. Examples of his sculpture included the poised figures of Adam and Eve that once flanked the Foscari arch. He also varied the design of the archetypal funerary monument initiated at I Frari for Doge Niccolò Tron in 1473 by articulating it with five orders up to a semicircular pediment, and ornamenting it with several niches filled with free-standing figures.

Venetian High Renaissance – A heightened Classicism affirms itself only in the 16C, marking a distinctive, second phase of Renaissance design.

Rome, which had displaced Florence, the capital of the Arts at the beginning of the previous century, as the seed-bed for new ideas, was badly damaged by Charles V's Imperial army which sacked the Holy City in 1527. From 1530, Venice established herself as the model city of Italy. For a short period, she basked in the limelight, implementing a new Classicism that soon, alas, degenerated into Mannerism.

Arcaded porticoes proliferated at ground level with ever bigger openings, supporting ordered storeys above. Imposing *palazzi* with carefully articulated lines are rusticated the entire length of the ground floor; punctuated by large centrally-planned openings and ornamented with masks: for the *piano nobile*, rectangular windows, framed with fluted or coupled columns, are pedimented with circular or triangular tympana in symmetrical formation; projecting balustraded balconies add to the sculptural effect. Whereas below the entablature, the rhythm is maintained by a series of small oval apertures.

Sansovino, master of the Classical style – The Florentine-born Jacopo Tatti, known as Sansovino (1468-1570), an accomplished sculptor and architect, was responsible for introducing to Venice a Classical canon of design formulated from the Antique. Seeking refuge in Venice after the Sack of Rome (1527) where he had been apprenticed to Bramante and Raphael, Sansovino succeeded Bartolomeo Bon as *"proto"* or Chief Architect to St Mark's. He was thus entrusted with the Serenissima's ambitious plans for reconstruction and embellishment, beginning with the reorganisation of the Piazza San Marco. He drafted designs for the new Library, its portico based on an archaic model, the Fabbriche Nuove in the Rialto, Palazzo Corner della Ca' Granda on the Grand Canal, the elegant loggia at the foot of St Mark's campanile – for which he also produced the bronze statues and low-relief panels, the heavily rusticated, Tuscan-inspired Palazzo della Zecca, the imposing but incomplete Scuola Nuova della Misericordia and the Golden Staircase. Robust, but not overly austere, his initial projects (including Ca' Granda) show Sansovino completely at ease with the traditional Venetian vernacular style (buildings around the Piazza San Marco and the Piazzetta), enriching his Classical forms with original and majestic ornament; decorative detailing encrust the portico arches and enhance the flat surfaces, whereas statuary, low-relief panels and festoons add a touch of fantasy and convey a vivid sense of movement.

To affirm Sansovino's brilliance as a sculptor, one need but cite the figures of Mars and Neptune that grace the Giant's Staircase and the highly expressive John the Baptist in I Frari – they speak for themselves.

Grandiose domestic buildings – At this time, the Grand Canal assumed its claim to be a true "triumphal way" fronted by ever more elegant and ennobled patrician houses.

San Giovanni in Bràgora

Four-light window of Palazzo Sagredo

Three-light window
with quatrefoil tracery

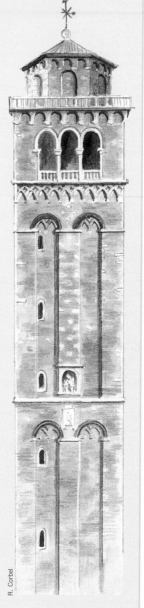

I Frari belltower

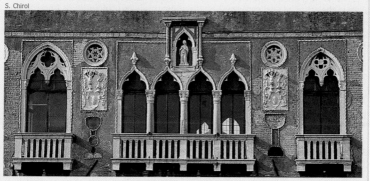

Four-light window on Murano

Veronese Sanmicheli (1484-1559) having served his apprenticeship under Sansovino, earned recognition for his military projects (Fortress of Sant'Andrea on the Lido) and for his design of the Palazzo Corner Mocenigo in the San Paolo *sestiere* and the Palazzo Grimani on the Grand Canal.

Meanwhile, a pupil of Palladio, **Vincenzo Scamozzi** (1552-1616), born in Vicenza, inherited Sansovino's projects for the redevelopment of the Piazza San Marco and erected the Procuratie Nuove (1586) modelled on the Classical example proffered by the former Library nearby. What is new, however, is the interplay of decorative elements that pre-empt the advent of the Baroque. Also by Scamozzi, is the Palazzo Contarini degli Scrigni on the Grand Canal.

Lo Scarpagnino completed the Fondacco dei Turchi and the Scuola di San Rocco initiated by Bartolomeo Bon. His style echoes that of Cordussi (openings on the ground floor) although now there is a greater sense of movement and dramatic contrast, achieved in part by the use of free-standing columns that project from the façade. He was also involved in the rebuilding of the Palazzo dei Dieci Savi and the Fabbriche Vecchie in the Rialto district.

Spavento began the Classical façade onto the small Senators' courtyard of the Doges' Palace, while Guglielmo dei Grigi, better known by his epithet **il Bergamasco**, was working on the Palazzo Papadopoli and the Palazzo Camerlenghi on the Grand Canal.

Andrea Palladio (1508-80) – Late in the 16C, the architect Andrea Palladio, a Paduan by birth, moved to Venice. He had established his reputation by designing villas in the Brenta Valley. His distinctive style, which is characterised by a balanced sense of proportion and formulated from a profound appreciation of Classical architecture, was applied to buildings that were designed to suit their purpose, their site and, most importantly, were practical to inhabit. Encouraged by the Humanist Trissino, Palladio visited Rome on several occasions to study Classical architecture in the context of theories outlined by Vitruvius (1C BC); in 1570, he published his theories based on observation in a treatise entitled *I Quattro Libri di Architettura* *(The Four Books on Architecture)*. This grand opus was to have far-reaching consequences in the spreading of Classicism to the rest of Europe. The essential principle of this "modern" Classicism is structural simplicity, achieved with the use of basic geometric volumes of space (cube, sphere and pyramid) and symmetry. Designs for building elevations conform to the same rules, with a façade having a central portico (San Giorgio Maggiore). Palladio received commissions, in particular, from the Serenissima's important and wealthy patrician families with estates in the hinterland (La Malcontenta on the Brenta). These variations on the villa design provide a new canon for informal domestic buildings that reflects both their function as country retreats and their location: besides boasting pure Classical form and a sound knowledge of decoration as well as gardening, these houses blend in perfectly with the surrounding landscape. The scenery therefore may be enjoyed from the house and the house may be admired as a point of interest punctuating and enhancing the scenery. This consideration was later explored and developed in garden design by the 18C English exponents of Palladianism (Campbell, Burlington, Kent, Adam, Capability Brown and the like). Palladio based many of his villas on Antique pagan temples; only the domestic buildings have forsaken monumentality for utilitarian considerations.

In Venice itself, Palladio's sense of austerity and perfect harmony is reflected in his magnificent churches: San Giorgio Maggiore, Il Redentore, le Zitelle, San Francesco della Vigna. Recurring features in his architecture are long, slender engaged columns, Corinthian capitals, triangular pedimented porticos borrowed from Roman temples, huge domes thrown into contrast by symmetrically arranged geometric forms; whereas inside, the enclosed space is airy and light.

After Palladio's death, Vincenzo Scamozzi saw a number of his master's projects to completion, ensuring the final effect was true to Palladio's vision, and thereby perpetuating his reputation even further.

High Renaissance Sculpture – Together with Palladio and Sansovino, the third important figure to import the artistic spirit of Michelangelo to Venice was **Alessandro Vittoria** (1525-1608). Famous for his austere and dignified portraits, Vittoria sculpted two lively representations of St Jerome now at San Zanipòlo and I Frari. He demonstrated further skills in the art of applied decoration by executing the stucco ceiling of the Libreria Vecchia and the fine gilded coffered vault of the Golden Staircase of the Doges' Palace.

Other artists of note working during the 1500s include **Lorenzo Bregno**, to whom are attributed several funerary monuments (namely that of Benedetto Pesaro) and the high altar at I Frari; **Girolamo Campagna** (bronze figures – I Frari and Correr Museum); **Tiziano Aspetti** (bronzes in Correr Museum, statues of Hercules and Atlantes flanking the Golden Staircase) and **Andrea Riccio** (bronzes in Correr Museum).

Venetian Baroque – sober and solemn dignity

Throughout the 17C the predilection for the Classical style was underpinned by the continued popularity of Palladian design: as a result, Venetian Baroque is more tempered than it ever was in Rome or elsewhere.

Baldassare Longhena (1598-1682) – This architect and sculptor is both the instigator and leading representative of Baroque art in the City of Doges. His lasting legacy was to inspire a taste for stone and a solemn architectural language, which, some say, verges on the whimsical. It is essentially Classical in inspiration but with charged ornamentation, frequently copied from the Antique.

Scuola di San Marco, front design
by the Lombardo family and Codussi

The funerary monument
to Doge Pietro Mocenigo
by Pietro Lombardo at San Zanipòlo

San Zaccaria façade
by Codussi

The Marciana Library by Sansovino

R. G. Everts/RAPHO

SCALA

SCALA

SCALA

His undoubted masterpiece is the Church of the Salute. It is also the most eloquent embodiment of this peculiarly Venetian strain of Baroque: it exudes confidence and an air of triumph with its vast proportions, towering dome, sense of movement conveyed by modillions featuring curved scrolls, and crowds of angels and prophets.

Charged with designing the finest Baroque *palazzi* along the Grand Canal, Longhena turned to Sansovino for inspiration. He endowed both Ca' Rezzonico and Ca' Pesaro with grand entrances, heavily rusticated ground floors, superimposed orders of tall windows deeply recessed into archways, separated by large columns and richly ornamented with masks; particular emphasis is given to the *piano nobile* with sharply defined architectural elements like cornices, balustraded balconies, and dramatically sculpted putti or coats of arms. A similar boldness marks his high altars and commemorative monuments of which perhaps the most exuberant is the sepulchre of Doge Giovanni Pesaro at I Frari.

After Longhena – Following the death of Longhena, the completion of his main projects was supervised by **Antonio Gaspari** (Ca'Pesaro) and **Giorgio Massari** (Ca' Rezzonico). The remarkably exuberant ornamentation (deeply cut garlands of fruit, niches, entablatures, pediments, fluted columns, crowning statuary) is evidenced in the Church dell'Ospedalletto with its great and ponderous atlantes. The three churches designed by **Sardi**, a collaborator of Longhena, are Santa Maria del Giglio which houses depictions of naval battles and is planned like a military fortress, the Church of the Scalzi and of San Salvador. Two other Baroque churches are San Moisé by Tremignon (1668) and finally, San Stae. Among the bell-towers, there are those of Santa Maria Formosa and All Saints.

The architect responsible for the great Church of the Gesuati (18C) is **Domenico Rossi**: who also designed its splendid white and green marble decoration imitating huge draperies falling into heavy folds. In contrast, the interior ceilings painted by **Giambattista Tiepolo** attain an unchallenged brilliance and lightness more often associated with Rococo. In sculpture, however, perhaps the main representative of the Venetian Baroque is the Fleming artist **Juste Le Court** whose works include altar fronts, allegorical figures and panels of low relief (Santa Maria del Giglio).

Neo-Classicism

During the 18C, Venice improved her image by erecting new buildings and remodelling a number of existing ones. In counter-reaction to the Baroque, the city reverted to a pure form of Classicism that was to be labelled neo-Classicism – well before any revival had taken hold anywhere else in Europe. The emergence of rational thinking during the Age of Enlightenment had affected all disciplines, including architecture, and given birth to a novel trend dubbed neo-Classicism. One of the advocates of this new style was a Venetian Franciscan, **Carlo Lodoli** who claimed *"only that which has a definite function or is born out of absolute necessity is worthy of existing in architecture"*; and so artists turned to Antiquity for inspiration. Simple arcading, domes and *pronai* (projecting vestibules fronted with columns and pediments) grace monumental *palazzi* and churches. The linearity of each structural element is clearly defined and elaborate schemes for interior decoration are replaced by plain, simple arrangements based on the Palladian or the Baroque model. The buildings that best illustrate this trend are the Palazzo Grassi by Massari and the Napoleon Wing enclosing the Piazza San Marco.

The architects **Andrea Tirali** (1660-1737), **Scalfarotto**, **Visentini**, and **Temanza** all implemented a neo-Classical style founded on simple form and basic geometry derived from Palladio (including the use of the *pronao*); a sense of grandeur was imparted from **Giovanni Battista Piranese** (1720-78), the Venetian-born architect and engraver who studied Roman civilisation and published the famous *Carceri d'Invenzione* (c 1745).

Perhaps the figure who dominates the artistic output of the period, however, is **Giorgio Massari** (1686-1766) from whom we have inherited such grandiose statements as the Gesuati Church on the Zattere with its Palladian façade, the Church of the Pietà, and the main door of the Accademia (1760). Tirali employed neo-Classical principles in designing the façade of the Church of the Tolentini, endowing it with a large *pronao* and Corinthian columns: a design that was to be inspirational later for other buildings. Other neo-Classical monuments of note include the Church of San Simeone Piccolo, erected in 1720 by Scalfarotto on a circular plan, with a gigantic porch copied from that of the Tolentini, reached up a massive staircase, unfortunately somewhat overwhelmed by the gigantic green dome; **Temanza**'s Church of the Maddalena also built on a circular plan that is crowned by a great dome, but with a foreshortened *pronao*.

Antonio Canova (1757-1822) – The last great personality in the Serenissima's illustrious history of art is Canova, who in many ways embodies the very essence of neo-Classicism in sculpture. Highly esteemed by his patrons at home and by Napoleon, Canova left the Republic to work both in Rome and Paris, where the spirit of the style was distilled into painting by J L David, another imperial protégé.

His work exudes great purity and sensitivity. The velvety polish imparted to the white marble – his favourite material – together with the fluid compositions and elegant forms, in which line rather than texture is emphasized, combine to suggest fragile sensuality. Venice still retains a series of low reliefs in the style of the Antique and the famous group of *Daedalus and Icarus* (Correr Museum). His grandiose memorial can be visited in I Frari: it was executed by pupils and lies opposite the monument he designed for Titian.

La Malcontenta by Palladio

The façade of San Moisé designed by Tremignon

From eclectic to modern times

The second half of the 19C was dominated by an eclectic assortment of revivalist styles in architecture: neo-Byzantine (Hotel Excelsior on the Lido, 1898-1908), neo-Romanesque, and most especially neo-Gothic (Pescheria by Rupolo, 1907, Palazzo Cavalli-Franchetti by Camillo Boito, 1895); the curious Mulino Stucky on the Guidecca (1883), remodelled in the International Gothic canon has high walls punctuated by a spired corner tower.

Since then, no particular trend has dominated Venice: only a few isolated personalities have had interesting projects built, now well integrated into the urban landscape: these include the residential districts around Sant' Elena from the 1920s, the railway station (1954) and the Savings Bank designed by Pier Luigi Nervi and Angelo Scattolin on Campo Manin (1968). Certain developments drafted by important personalities never got beyond the drawing board: a student hostel by the American Frank Lloyd Wright intended to stand on the Grand Canal (1953) and a public hospital by Le Corbusier (1964).

In conclusion, the area that accommodates the Biennale provides space for various contemporary experimental projects. Even if the gardens where the pavilions are built are dismissed from being part of the urban environment, it is worth acknowledging the more original and obsolete: Hoffman's Austrian Pavilion (1933), the Venezuelan designed by Carlo Scarpa (1954) and the Finnish by Alvar Aalto (1956).

Daedalus and Icarus by Canova
(Museo Correr)

The most famous 20C Venetian sculptor is **Arturo Martini** (1889-1947).

VENETIAN PAINTING – A SYMPHONY OF COLOUR AND LIGHT

Venice's pictorial tradition has one constant – its profound sensuality achieved by a predilection for colour and for light, which lends a strong poetic touch to the landscape. It is an art that mirrors the personality of the lagoon city as a watery world where everything is suffused with light: the blur of the skyline, the shimmering volumes, the haze rising above the canals that adds a bluish tinge to the scene. It is this distinctive greyish light, opaque and iridescent at the same time, that inspired the artists of the 18C.

Mosaics – The art of mosaic, inherited from the Romans, came to the lagoon long before the art of painting. In the 12C and 13C, Venice, inspired by the art of Ravenna, proceeded to arrange the mosaic murals from Torcello *(Last Judgement)*, Murano and St Mark's Basilica. After the fall of Constantinople in 1204, Greek decorators and mosaic artists came to Venice to work on the great Golden Altarpiece and the mosaics in St Mark's. Consequently, the biblical iconography of the Eastern Church became markedly oriental, with Christ featuring as the central character (central apse), opening and closing a story which unfolded along walls, arches and cupolas, thus observing established biblical chronology *(see PIAZZA SAN MARCO)*.

The use of mosaic was continued throughout the city's history. The very last ones to grace San Marco were executed over a rather long period running from the 16C to the 19C. The assumption that early mosaics were more impressive can be explained by the simple fact that artisans were unable to arrange the small pieces of glass in a regular fashion: the myriad uneven surfaces lent "flexibility" to the mural. This effect was enhanced by the light, which caught irregularities, acting as a kaleidoscope of twirling colours and reflections. If they were all aligned on a perfect flat plain, the effect would be dull and lifeless.

Quattrocento Primitives

A few artists began to paint in fresco in the 13C, a process that involves applying pigment to small sections of wet lime-plaster. Paintings from this period however, if they have survived, are all badly damaged. As regards the style of these first Venetian frescoes, they soon conformed both in design and subject-matter to Byzantine iconography, drawn for the most part from portable devotional icons typical of the Eastern Church, where the Madonna and Child usually occupy pride of place.

St Michael
by Michele Giambono
(Accademia)

St Augustine
by Bartolomeo Vivarini
(San Zanipòlo)

St Sebastian
by Mantegna
(Ca' D'Oro)

The Madonna of the Orange-Tree by Cima da Conegliano (Accademia)

The Barbarigo Altarpiece by Giovanni Bellini (San Pietro Martire, Murano)

SCALA

Paolo Veneziano – This artist, also known as Paolo da Venezia (active 1333-1358), emerged as the first distinctive personality in Venetian painting, his name appearing together with that of his son Giovanni on a *Coronation of the Virgin* (now in the Frick Collection in New York). Working in the Byzantine tradition, his painting showed him moving away from archaic stylisation (gold backgrounds, flat and confrontational compositions, hieratical attitudes) towards greater decorative refinement and distinctive use of line. This freedom of expression and sensitive treatment of Western subject-matter forestalled the evolution of the International Gothic style characterised by graceful movement and elegant form. The work of **Lorenzo Veneziano**, traced to the years 1356-72, is characterised by expressive faces, vigorous bodies and a subtle use of strong, bold colours. (Note: these painters were not actually related, the epithet *Veneziano* simply means Venetian.)

Venetian International Gothic – At the beginning of the 15C, the work of **Gentile da Fabriano** and **Pisanello** and that of the Paduan **Guariento**, who were engaged in painting a cycle of frescoes in the Doges' Palace (destroyed by fire in the 16C), marks the city's endorsement of the "International Gothic" – a refined, bejewelled style that combined Tuscan elements already assimilated in Padua (derived from sculpted Antique decoration on the one hand and by Giotto's cycle of frescoes in the Scrovegni Chapel on the other) with a more courtly style practised in Ferrara (notably portraiture).
The stimulus provided by these two influences blended with the local, Venetian predilection for naturalism, elegant linearity, fluid movement and strong decorative appeal (even the gold-embroidered and brocade clothing is celebrated) led to a distinctive regional style akin to the International Gothic that flourished in Siena, Prague and Avignon.
Other painters worthy of note include **Nicolò di Pietro** (recorded 1394-1430), **Jacobello del Fiore** (recorded 1394-1439), a pupil of Gentile da Fabriano who practised a detailed and intricate style, and, most especially, **Michele Giambono** (recorded 1420-62) who produced highly refined works in which Eastern Oriental influence can be felt (*St Crisogono* – San Trovaso, *St Michael* – Accademia).

A new pictorial tradition – By the mid-15C, attempts at perspective are reflected in the portrayal of floors and ceilings, whereas depth of field is suggested in the background by landscape scenes or buildings.
The first hint of the Renaissance is to be found in the works of the **Vivarini** family from Murano. The shift in emphasis comes with the break of the generations: the earlier pictures have the same quality as Gothic goldsmithery and are markedly influenced by Byzantine iconography – these pictures are by **Antonio** (active 1441-50) – the father and collaborator of his brother-in-law, **Giovanni d'Alemagna** (*Triptych with Madonna and Child with Saints* – Accademia, polyptychs – San Zaccaria); and the brother **Bartolomeo** (*Triptych of St Mark* – I Frari). If these are compared with works by the son **Alvise** however, his awareness of the Renaissance becomes evident (*St Anthony of Padua* – Correr Museum, *Triumph of St Ambrose* – I Frari, *Christ carrying the Cross* – San Zanipòlo). Strangely, in the following generation, **Marco Basaiti** (1470-1530) a pupil of Alvise Vivarini, is decidedly backward-looking in his delicate treatment of landscape and use of colour (*Vocation of the Sons of Zebedee* – Accademia).

Serenity in Early Renaissance Painting

Long after the flowering of the Renaissance in Florence in the early 1400s, Venice's artists turned their attention to defining three-dimensional space and volume, and to an improved articulation of landscape and topographical views during the latter half of the century. They also gave up the abstract use of gold background and the Gothic taste for overty decorated and complicated pictures.

Bellini family – First Jacopo, the father (d 1470), followed by his two sons, Gentile and Giovanni managed to emancipate Venetian painting from Byzantine and Gothic influences. The actual founder of the Venetian School is probably **Giovanni Bellini** (1430-1516) also known as Giambellino, who admired Florentine painting for its pure, idealised forms, and Flemish painting for its clarity in terms of light and observed realism. He was markedly influenced by his master and brother-in-law, the Paduan-born **Andrea Mantegna** (1431-1506) who settled and worked in Venice. Mantegna was fascinated by Roman Antiquities which were commonly traded in Padua at the time – an interest acquired from his adoptive father, the painter-archaeologist Squarcione: from his study of relief carving, he forged a bold style that is completely uncompromising to the point of coldness, where perspective is almost obsessively defined, and details are drawn with scientific precision (*St Sebastian* – Accademia).
This powerful source of inspiration is in some ways tempered by the example of **Antonello da Messina** who worked in Venice c 1475-76 (*Pietà* – Correr Museum) after learning to use oil paints in Flanders. Giovanni adopted this medium and developed his own deeply sensitive style that is characterised by a playful suggestion of light, a delicate and harmonious use of colour, elegant rendering of form and a strong sense of realism derived from Mantegna. Landscape assumes a dominant role and is used to convey the atmosphere of the picture: it provides a context in which the figures appear as pawns, set below an expanse of sky relieved by drifting clouds. These expressions

Sacra Conversazione by Palma Giovane (Accademia)

*Madonna
di Ca' Pesaro,*
by Titian
(Santa Maria Gloriosa dei Frari)

*The Stealing of the Body
of St Mark*
by Tintoretto
(Accademia)

SCALA

65

of mood are worked over and over again in countless Madonnas looking tenderly down at a sleeping cherub or a Christ Child in benediction (*Madonna degli Alberetti* – Accademia), in portrayals of the Dead Christ and many *Sacre Conversazioni* (*St Vincent Ferrer Polyptych* – San Zanipòlo).

His brother **Gentile** (1429-1507) was the first artist to be nominated Venice's official painter, a position which underpinned a brilliant career. He emerged as a talented portrait painter (Doge Giovanni Mocenigo) and applied his observational skills to portraying views of Venice, known as *vedute*, which became an influential genre in itself in the 18C. The overall objective was for painting to be true to life: *The Procession of the Relics of the True Cross in Piazza San Marco* (Accademia), for example, is a factual or documentary representation of 15C Venice, even if the painter, conscientious in every detail, was careful to align the façades and order the attendant crowds.

The advent of High Renaissance – **Vittore Carpaccio** (1455-1526), following in the wake of Bellini and Antonello, suffuses a lesson learnt from Flemish painting with his own personal creativity to execute the cycles of paintings commissioned by the "Scuole" *(see I CARMINI – The Venetian Scuole): Miracle of the Relic of the True Cross at Rialto* for Scuola di San Giovanni Evangelista; *Legend of St Ursula* (Accademia) in which Brittany is represented as a Venetian Renaissance city, *Legends of St George and St Jerome* for Scuola di San Giorgio degli Schiavoni, which depicts an exotic Orient. Carpaccio surpassed Bellini in sensitivity and in his inimitable talent for story-telling. His pictures are imaginatively populated with well-observed and delightful details: he even manages to reconcile his penchant for miniaturist precision with a love of broad views. In his landscapes, a key element in his paintings, are representations of a luxuriant, flowery vegetation, peopled with a host of animals (dogs, birds, rabbits, peacocks, parrots and deer). Renaissance buildings stand out, embellished with marble inlays that might have been designed by the Lombardo family, surrounded by numerous Oriental motifs (palm trees, Moorish turbans). All of Carpaccio's works display the same distinctive features: boldness of line, luminosity, vivid colours, perfect sense of proportion, attention to detail and crowd scenes.

Giambattista Cima (1459-1518), known as Cima da Conegliano, drew on Giovanni Bellini for his strong, radiant light and on Carpaccio for his love of detail. His are the glorious portrayals of dignified figures, pictured in beautiful landscapes under broad open skies (*Madonna of the Orange Tree* – Accademia, *Adoration of the Shepherds* – I Carmini). By the close of the 15C, Venetian painting had reached the height of its artistic expression.

Reform – His name was Giorgio di Castelfranco but he went by the name of **Giorgione** (1475-1510). It was he who revolutionised the course of painting in the early 16C despite his short-lived existence. Giorgione is considered in the history of painting as the first "modern" artist. A Renaissance man in every sense, he drew inspiration for his work from Humanist ideology, making it intellectual and sometimes shrouded in mystery, as well as open to controversial interpretation. Few works have been attributed to him with any certainty, and these are poetic in feel, almost dream-like, but always charged with allusions to literature, music and philosophy: ephemerality and vulnerability are the subject of *The Tempest*, while in *La Vecchia* it is the passage of time (both in the Accademia). His style appears more sensual than Classical. The landscape now plays an essential role in the painting; man is no longer the main subject, it is Nature itself that becomes the true protagonist – human drama is reduced to being just one element in the force of Nature (such as in *The Tempest*).

Palma il Vecchio (1480-1528) followed in the same vein, although in later life he betrays the influence of Titian's handling of light, his juxtaposition of contrasting colour and the asymmetry of his altarpiece compositions. Palma il Vecchio specialised in *Sacre Conversazioni (see SAN ZACCARIA)* and painted the portrait of Paola Priuli (Querini-Stampaglia Collection). His art does not match that of the most talented masters but its appeal is one of spontaneity and exuberant colour.

The Bergamo-born **Lorenzo Lotto** (1480-1556) is another major early 16C painter with a distinctively personal style. His pictures are disconcerting and strange, they betray the influence of Dürer's scientific treatment of detail (Dürer visited Venice in c 1495) and the painter's liking for bold contrasts (*Portrait of a Young Gentleman in his Study* – Accademia). He avoided the sensual, colourful appeal of Giorgione and Titian, preferring to employ a rather frigid, angular style modelled on the precise, slightly archaic style of Alvise Vivarini.

16C Masters and their pupils

In the 16C, Venetian painting affirmed its supremacy; this was the era of the great European masters and highly-skilled painters who, thanks to their respective talents, succeeded in establishing a distinctive style which was to become the hallmark of Venice and which soon earned her European recognition.

Titian – Tiziano Vecellio, known as Titian (c 1485-1576), is unquestionably the most famous artist of his time. Born in Pieve di Cadore, he remained highly active until his death, aged 90. He served his apprenticeship under Giovanni Bellini and was subsequently influenced by Giorgione (some of whose works he completed) and then

Christ in the House of Levi by Veronese (Accademia)

The Fortune Teller by Giambattista Piazzetta
(Accademia)

Pulcinella by Giandomenico Tiepolo
(Ca' Rezzonico)

View over the Rio dei Mendicanti by Canaletto (Ca' Rezzonico)

Raphael. The author of large altarpieces undertaken for churches (I Frari) and Scuole (La Carità) alike, he favoured colour over form and breathed life into his canvases with a dynamic handling of paint and bold composition (*The Assumption* – I Frari, *Martyrdom of St Lawrence* – Gesuiti). His reputation far outreached the realms of the lagoon city, and led to him being commissioned to paint portraits of all the leading lights of his time at the courts of Ferrara, Mantua, Florence and Urbino; he worked for the Pope, François I and Charles V who knighted him in 1553.

During the early part of his career, Titian's painting was fundamentally Classical in inspiration. However, between 1535 and 1545, he was seduced by Mannerism before reverting to a more dignified and serene style. At the end of his life, the melodramatic tension inherent in some compositions (*The Pietà* – Accademia) betrays the artist's mysticism at the imminence of death.

In conclusion, Titian was largely responsible for reviving interest in the large altarpiece. He succeeded in taking painting to unimagined heights of monumentality by abandoning symmetry of composition (*Pesaro Altarpiece* – I Frari), opting for large contrasting blocks of colour, displaying a sure stroke and a perfect sense of harmony.

Il Tintoretto – Contemporary with Titian, Venice harboured the genius of Jacopo Robusti, known as *il Tintoretto* (1518-94), the most original and most prolific of the Venetian masters. He was born the son of a dyer (whence his name) and never left Venice (save once, maybe, to visit Rome), but he never really enjoyed success in his lifetime. Tireless and passionate about his work, an ardent admirer of Michelangelo, he preferred Biblical subjects to those of Classical Antiquity (Scuola di San Rocco) and chose to portray common people instead of focusing on the excesses of the nobility. He developed a restless style: despite the interaction of rapid precise brush strokes and gentle soft touches, his work is always lyrical – a quality that apparently is projected from his dynamic handling of paint and from the arrangement of figures in groups or alone, brought together by strong lines of composition (*Crucifixion* – Scuola di San Rocco). The use of *chiaroscuro* (strong contrasts of light and shade), juxtaposed complementary colours, elongated figures, daring foreshortening and a filtering light that blurs the contours of figures and architectural settings, all contribute to reinforcing the charged atmosphere of his Mannerist work.

His best pictures include the *Miracles of St Mark* painted for the Scuola di San Marco (Accademia), the *Marriage of Cana* (Santa Maria della Salute), *Paradise* (Doges' Palace, Grand Council Chamber), *The Triumph of Venice* (Doges' Palace), *The Presentation of the Virgin in the Temple* (Madonna dell'Orto) not forgetting the 50 paintings, the largest cycle of its kind in Venice, executed for the Scuola di San Rocco on which he worked for 23 years in collaboration with his son **Domenico Tintoretto**.

Veronese – In direct contrast with Tintoretto, **Paolo Caliari** (1528-88), born in Verona, hence his nickname *Veronese*, specialised in portraying the wealthy, opulent and carefree aristocracy of the Renaissance, in luminous colour (including the famous "Veronese green") that set off the most sumptuous fabrics used for their clothing to theatrical effect. His works in the main are endowed with optimism, fantasy and spontaneity, they seem permeated with spring light: towards the end of his life, however, Veronese's paintings change to more sombre and melancholic mood, muddied by the influence of Tintoretto's *chiaroscuro* and Bassano's style. Mythological scenes proliferate on the walls and ceilings of the Doges' Palace *(Apotheosis of Venice)*. The subject of *The Last Supper* was reworked by Veronese several times for the refectories of Venetian monasteries, including the famous, huge canvas *Christ in the House of Levi* (Accademia), commissioned for the Dominican monastery of San Zanipòlo contrived as a depiction of an entirely profane meal while providing an excellent pretext for a work of grandiose proportions. The magnificent decoration of San Sebastiano is another masterpiece, appropriate perhaps given that it was his chosen ultimate resting place.

Mannerism in Venice – While Tintoretto forged his style from Titian and Michelangelo, and Veronese was heir to Bellini, Giorgione and Raphael, their legacy, like that of Titian, was both powerful and influential beyond the confines of Venice, for several generations. It also naturally led to Venetian Mannerism.

Titian had many followers: **Palma il Vecchio** (1480-1528); **Pordenone** (c 1483-1539) who worked successfully in Venice from 1535 to 1538; **Paris Bordone** (1500-71) who delighted in Venetian Renaissance architecture (*Handing the Ring to the Doge* – Accademia, *Martyrdom of St Theodore* – San Salvador) and charged his canvases with vivid colours; the prolific **Palma il Giovane** (1544-1628), the grandson of Palma il Vecchio, with an eclectic style, who provided nearly all the city's churches with large-scale paintings.

An exponent of the sensuality and silky colours explored by Giorgione and Titian, **Andrea Schiavone** (c 1510-63) moved away from realism in favour of elongated form and restless movement typical of Mannerism, in the style of Parmigianino.

Impressed by Tintoretto's painting, **Jacopo Bassano** (Jacopo da Ponte, 1512-92) paints in a provincial style marked by an exaggerated preoccupation with naturalism (*St Jerome Meditating* – Accademia), while using light effects to suggest the intensity of the scene (*Nativity* – San Giorgio Maggiore). His sons Leandro and Francesco shared this tradition of *maniera* painting in which the pastoral and rustic element becomes the prime subject rather than the religious or profane content.

18C revival

Venetian painting, in decline during the 17C and overshadowed by the great person-alities of the previous century and the Roman Baroque, enjoyed a new creative and glorious burst of energy during the era of lavish receptions and shimmering lights.

Decorative painting – Long after the taste for grandiose interior decoration had flourished in Rome and Florence during the 16C-17C, Venice revived her interest in the decorative art of Veronese found on the walls and ceilings of her churches and *palazzi* and in the Palladian villas along the Brenta.

Sebastiano Ricci (1659-1734), the Baroque painter of rather sentimental religious pictures, reinforced his strong compositions with bright colour (*Madonna with Saints* – San Giorgio Maggiore). It was with **Giambattista Piazzetta** (1682-1754), who excelled in religious paint-ing, that huge ceiling compositions became popular, and that figures began to be shown from below, aspiring to dizzy heights among the clouds, drawn awkwardly towards a mystical light (*Glorification of St Dominic* – San Zanipòlo). Influenced by Caravaggio, Piaz-zetta also painted genre pictures (featuring people from common, everyday life in mun-dane surroundings) with strong *chiaroscuro* (*The Fortune Teller* – Accademia).

Piazzetta influenced the greatest artist of the century: **Giambattista Tiepolo** (1696-1770), the pre-eminent genius of Venetian Baroque decoration and creator of huge compositions of great virtuosity full of delicate colour, golden light and infinite space. He painted vast altarpieces and covered entire ceilings with frescoes (Palazzo Labia, Scuola dei Carmini, Church of the Gesuati, Ca' Rezzonico), turning his hand as easily to religious subjects (*Our Lady of Mount Carmel* – I Carmini) as to mythological ones, including huge Virtues set before grandiose architectural backdrops.

Portraiture and Genre – Long-established patrician families and those of an aspiring middle class bourgeoisie, altered their household arrangements to reflect changes in lifestyle. In keeping with fashions elsewhere, it became acceptable to have informal, intimate and private rooms, separate from grandiose function or occasion rooms, in which to conduct everyday business, and this trend was reflected in contemporary art. Painters were asked to provide portraits that were both flattering and informal, a genre favoured by **Rosalba Carriera** (1675-1758) who produced delicate, vibrant pastels that earned her international fame (Ca' Rezzonico, Accademia) and by **Alessandro Longhi**. Around the same time, Venetians appeared to appreciate the small-scale interior scenes painted by **Pietro Longhi** (1702-85): masquerades, dances and duck hunting scenes (Hemingway's future pastime in Torcello), all revealing his acute powers of observation (Ca' Rezzonico, Querini-Stampalla Collection).

Topographical painters – Besides the *maniera* and genre scenes devoid of religious, allegorical or mythological meaning, landscape for its own sake began to provide artists with a worthy subject for easel pictures. In Venice, studies of the environment focused on the city herself, and it is for these views, or *vedute* in Italian, that Antonio Canal (1697-1768), known as **Canaletto**, became so famous. In his pictures, he delin-eates in minute detail his on-the-spot observations of the city. Although his vision is almost photographic, he exaggerates perspective and paints huge, monumental build-ings. He was also known to portray festivals and regattas. Alas, few works have remained in Venice as they are to be found in museums of many foreign countries. Canaletto inspired a great many artists, namely **Bernardo Bellotto** (1720-80), one of his pupils who was also a relative.

Quite distinct from Canaletto, **Francesco Guardi** (1712-93) was bewitched by the atmo-sphere of the lagoon city; his vision is no longer photographic, instead his bold use of paint succeeds in freezing the ripples of the water and the reverberation of flickering light – a preoccupation that was to fascinate the English Romantic painter Turner and the French Impressionists a century later. Besides views of the lagoon, he also painted scenes of everyday life in the manner of Pietro Longhi: *Nuns' Parlour*, *Interval Time in the Foyer* (Ca' Rezzonico), as did his brother **Giovianni Antonio**.

Freed from the influence of his father, after painting the Stations of the Cross in San Polo, **Giovanni Domenico (Giandomenico) Tiepolo** (1727-1804) painted 18C Venetian society on the Brenta Riviera with humour and irony, depicting the holiday-makers as buf-foons (Ca' Rezzonico: Villa Zianigo frescoes).

Modern and contemporary age

Between the 19C and the 20C Venetian painting continued on academic lines, ever faithful to the traditions set in the 18C with landscapes or urban scenes by Caffi and Ciardi, and the fine portraits by Alessandro Milesi.

Motivated by mainstream developments in Europe during the early 20C, several painters produced interesting work (International Museum of Modern Art in Ca' Pesaro): **Federico Zandomeneghi** (1841-1917) who was born in Venice, worked with the Macchiaioli group before moving to Paris where he befriended Degas; **Umberto Boccioni** (1882-1916) was a founding member of the Futurist movement and painted in a style reminiscent of Signal (*The Grand Canal*); **Fragiacomo** was an Impressionist much inspired by Turner (*St Mark's Square*); **Casorati** was a Symbolist painter and portraitist.

Members of the **Burano School** (Scuola di Burano), Moggioli, Gino Rossi, Sibellato, Semeghini painted the islands of the lagoon, experimenting with techniques inspired by Van Gogh, Gauguin and Cézanne, and of the Post-Impressionists Bonnard and Vuillard.

Composers in Venice

Prelude to Vivaldi

Renaissance – While in Rome a brilliant revival in music flourished under the auspices of **Giovanni Pierluigi da Palestrina** (1525-1594), who headed a polyphonic school dedicated to sacred music *(see THE GREEN GUIDE ROME)*, patronage in Venice was limited to more secular applications. Perhaps the turning point is marked by the Flemish **Willaert** (c 1490-1562), the choirmaster at St Mark's who set a trend that was to be continued by his pupil Andrea Gabrieli.

Andrea Gabrieli (c 1510-86) – Organist at St Mark's, Gabrieli emerged as an important composer and influential teacher of organ and choral music in the Venetian tradition. His innovative use of the *concertato* (a small group of instruments or voices) contrasted with the *ripieno* (a larger body of musicians) forestalled the implementation of the *concerto* form developed and exploited later by Corelli. This allowed Gabrieli to experiment with harmony and dissonance by combining various "parts" for choir, or the human voice with instruments. His most lasting contribution is a large body of choral works setting both sacred (motets for four to twelve voices, masses for six voices, the *Psalms of David* for six voices) and secular texts (madrigals for three to twelve voices).

Giovanni Gabrieli (c 1557-1612) – Andrea's nephew Giovanni inherited the position of organist at St Mark's and further propagated the fame of the Venetian School abroad (the Dutch master Sweelinck, Hans Leo Hassler, Heinrich Schutz, Bach's precursor and founder of German church music, were already pupils). Among his compositions, which comprised sacred, secular and instrumental pieces, the most notable are his motets, the **Sacred Symphonies**. His more *avant-garde* works include **sonatas** for violin which he used to explore antiphonal effects: for at the time the violin was the instrument that best sustained the popular taste for monophonic music (following a single line of notes). By adding a **basso continuo** or figured bass line, with long drawn notes, he was able to develop harmonies with the accompaniment, thereby providing sustained and textured melody. This Gabrieli applied not only to choral arrangements but to instrumental pieces for two violins and clavichord or cello.

Baroque – With the 17C began another rich and fruitful period for Venetian music. Melodrama became a formal genre; formulated from accounts of contemporary historical events or legends, exaggerated stories were re-enacted to audiences in elaborately contrived stage settings. Francesco Cavalli (1602-76) choirmaster at St Mark's, Marc'Antonio Cesti, (1623-69) and Giovanni Legrenzi (1626-90) choirmaster at St Mark's, all collaborated at an operatic school in Venice which in 1637 opened the first commercial opera house, San Cassiano. Here Monteverdi's operas were later performed.

During the 17C, thanks to Claudio Monteverdi, who conducted the choir at San Marco, Venice became known as the world's leading centre for operatic art, placing herself ahead of Florence and Mantua. In those days, the lagoon city boasted altogether 17 theatres.

18C – By the mid-1700s, Venice was renowned for the more typically Neapolitan kind of comic operas by **Baldassarre Galuppi** *(see BURANO)*, who, together with Giovanni Platti (1700-63) contributed to the development of the sonata (literally meaning "sounded" implying music that is instrumental rather than sung) for strings and keyboard. In response to works by the Bach dynasty in Germany, they composed pieces for one (harpsichord) or two instruments (harpsichord and violin) in homophonic (several lines of notes moving in chords) and polyphonic (several lines of notes each with its own distinctive pattern) arrangements in several movements (usually three).

The harpsichord enjoyed particular favour, despite the advent of the piano, built by Bartolomeo Cristofori (1655-1732) by substituting hammers for quills. Among the most famous players of the harpsichord besides Galuppi and Platti, there were the two **Marcello** brothers, **Benedetto** (1686-1739) who also composed sacred music and concertos for five instruments, and **Alessandro** (1684-1750) who wrote sonatas for violin and basso continuo and concertos for oboe and strings that hitherto have been attributed to Benedetto. Also active in Venice in this period was **Tomaso Albinoni** (1671-1750) who more closely followed in the German Baroque tradition and foreshadows Vivaldi in his instrumental compositions.

Antonio Vivaldi (1678-1741)

It is undoubtedly Vivaldi who best epitomises Venetian music: even J S Bach (1685-1750) drew openly on the compositions of the *"Prete Rosso" (see SAN GIORGIO degli SCHIAVONI)* who was literally rediscovered in the mid 20C, after years of oblivion.

Vivaldi was a prolific composer, using a three-movement form of the concerto, *allegro-adagio-allegro*, and freeing-up the *Sonata da Camera* as a series of contrasting descriptive passages as in the Four Seasons, the Goldfinch and Night *concerti*. Altogether, Vivaldi composed over 500 concertos for violin, viola d'amore, cello, mandolin, flute, oboe, bassoon, trumpet, cornet and string orchestra.

His parents – Giovanni Battista Vivaldi, father of Antonio, was both a professional barber and musician: this would be surprising today, but many Venetians of the time combined both professions. Giovanni Battista, nicknamed *il Rosso* after the colour of his auburn hair, obviously a family trait, was a violin virtuoso in 17C Venice, more specifically in the area around **San Martino** where most of the city's musicians congregated at the Scuola, the *Sovvegno di Santa Cecilia*, whose patron naturally was St Cecilia.

Camilla Calicchio, mother of Antonio, came from the area around **San Giovanni in Bràgora** *(see ARSENALE)*, where Antonio was baptised a second time, having been subjected to the formalities of a blessing at home on 4 March 1678, shortly after his birth when it appeared that he might not survive.

Vivaldi – the "Prete Rosso"

Il Prete Rosso – Antonio was ordained at **San Giovanni Novo** even though he dedicated himself rather to the cause of music than to the priesthood, content to remain a secular priest or abbot. He took up residence in Fondamenta del Dose, near the Ponte del Paradiso, before abandoning the Castello *sestiere* in favour of St Mark's where he lived on the Riva del Carbon. When he left these lodgings in 1740 it was to leave Venice completely, dying in poverty in Vienna the following year.

The Musician – Vivaldi's main musical activity is associated first and foremost with the Pietà and the Theatre of San Angelo.

The Pietà was one of the **great foundling hospitals** which, between the 17C and 18C, doubled as one of the musical conservatories of Venice, each having its own church where concerts were held. These "hospitals" functioned as charitable institutions and orphanages for girls *(ospitaliere)*, who received an education and, if gifted, musical instruction to enable them to take part in the choirs and orchestras of which the establishment was so proud.

Associated as it is to the fame of Vivaldi, the Pietà became the best known of the hospital-cum-churches. Standing on the Riva degli Schiavoni it cannot be mistaken or missed, although it is as well to acknowledge that the present church is not the original one where Vivaldi had been music teacher and composer, for the former church stood where the Metropole Hotel now stands, slightly to the right of the present church.

The San Angelo Theatre alas no longer exists. It was there that the violin virtuoso acted as musical director, impresario, composer and performed more secular works.

After Vivaldi

The musical splendour of Venice, which regaled contemporary ears for three centuries and continues to survive today in churches and concert halls, faded with the passing of its most illustrious representative. In more recent times, one interesting composer emerges from

> **Famous Organ-Builders**
>
> **Gaetano Callido** (1727-1813) built about 400 organs throughout the Veneto, Dalmatia and even the Holy Land: all three organs at St Mark's were restored by him in 1766. Four years later, he was appointed the official, permanent organ-maker to the city. His sons Agostino and Antonio continued their father's activity until 1821.

the Venetian and German traditions and that is **Ermanno Wolf-Ferrari** (1876-1948) who was particularly impressed by Mozart's operatic works and inspired by the theatre of Goldoni: both influences are evident in his own life's opus *Gioielli della Madonna, Le Donne Curiose, I Quattro rusteghi, Il Campiello*....

Yet more recently still, the city has resumed its role as a lively and innovative artistic centre by playing host to such experimental musicians as **Bruno Maderna** (1920-73) and **Luigi Nono** (1924-90).

Venice was also the birthplace of the conductor Giuseppe Sinopoli, who was to become an authority on Mahler's work.

Venetian by adoption

Tribute should also be paid to visiting composers who died in Venice.
Claudio Monteverdi (1567-1643) was one genius who breathed personality and characterisation into opera: he lies buried at I Frari *(see I FRARI)*. **Domenico Cimarosa**, (1749-1801) often regarded as the Italian Mozart, died in Campo Sant' Angelo *(see La FENICE)*, whereas the apparently aloof and detached **Igor Stravinsky** (1882-1971) is buried in the cemetery of San Michele.
It was **Richard Wagner** (1813-83), "the most controversial composer in musical history", however, who most desired to be adopted by his beloved Venice. The *maestro* died on 13 February in the Palazzo Vendramin Calergi *(see Il CANAL GRANDE)* in the company of his wife, Cosima and the gondolier Gigio Trevisan, nicknamed Ganassete.
During Wagner's peaceful stay in Venice, he would go to St Mark's Square daily where, seated at Quadri's or Florian's, he was sometimes recognised by the leader of the municipal band who would ask him to conduct: Wagner would agree, happy to direct his own compositions for the Venetians. It was here that Wagner composed the second act of *Tristan* (the English horn part having been inspired by the evening song of the gondoliers), that he wrote part of *Parsifal* and initiated work on the *Maestri cantori* inspired by Titian's *Assumption* that he so admired at I Frari.

Literature in Venice

1200 to 1500 – This history of Venetian literature begins in distant times, in 1271 when "Master **Marco Polo**, a wise and noble citizen of Venice" embarked on a journey to the Orient. Despite his tender age, the 16-year-old decided to accompany his father Niccolò and uncle Matteo, both Levantine merchants, on a very long expedition to the court of "Kublai, the Great Khan of the Mongols". Never before had such an ambitious journey to those parts been undertaken by Westerners. Unfortunately the return journey was to prove Marco's undoing for during one of the many naval battles between the Venetians and the Genoese, the explorer was taken prisoner by the enemy. As he languished in prison, he came to know a writer from Pisa, Rustichello, who undertook to set down on paper an account of the Venetian's experiences: and so **The Book of the Wonders of the World** was born which achieved success under the title *Il Milione*, an epithet given to Marco Polo when he described the quantities of gold he claimed to have seen. In the years that followed the death of the traveller, Venice appeared to dedicate itself less to literature than to commerce. Indeed Venetian literary circles seem to have been affected by Humanism.

It would appear that the title of Marco Polo's book was in fact inspired by the word "Emilione", which was the nickname given to the family of the great navigator.

It was not until **Aldo Manuzio**, the *"ante litteram"* publisher arrived in Venice that the situation changed. In 1499 he published the *Hypnerotomachia Poliphili*, an amusing, anonymous work written in an explosive style, vernacular language bastardised from Venetian and Latin. Its success was modest but it seems to have heralded one of the most successful literary spells in Venice.

Bembo to Goldoni: a period of great splendour – A more conventional writer to be published by Aldo Manuzio was **Pietro Bembo**. Born into a very aristocratic family in Venice in 1470, Bembo was the touchstone for literary developments for almost a century. His importance is largely due to *The Prose of Vulgar Language* which came out in 1528, and which contributed to the age-old debate regarding the use of vernacular language in literature: in it Bembo argued himself to be violently opposed to the

Marco Polo (Museo Correr Library)

language adopted by Dante, and offered a convincing alternative, that in part has influenced the evolution of Italian into the language of today.
The Paduan-born **Angelo Beolco** (1496), meanwhile, was moving in a different direction. His nickname *il Ruzzante* (The Playful One) was derived from the peasant protagonist of his plays, whom the author often impersonated and so the character and his creator became synonymous. The most famous play, *Il Parlamento del Ruzzante*, is a merciless portrait of peasant conditions at the time of a long and bloody war between the French and the Venetians.

In the Foyer during the Interval, genre by Pietro Longhi (Ca' Rezzonico)

Ca' Rezzonico, Venezia/SCALA

Contemporary with Ruzzante was the unknown author of the **Veniexiana**, an entertaining comedy in dialect which depicted the vices and virtues (mainly the former, to be truthful) of the inhabitants of the lagoon city. Its significance, however, lies not so much in the amusing story it tells, full of melodramatic action, but in its marking a turning point in the cultural milieu of Venice. For between 1530 and 1540, the popular trend suddenly passed from foreign imported theatrical productions to the blossoming "original" domestic plays.

This radical change was no doubt precipitated by the presence of **Pietro Aretino** who, as his surname suggests, was born in Arezzo. After a stay in Rome, Aretino reached Venice in 1527 just in time to publish *Il Marescalco* and *La Cortegiana*, two of the most popular and well-crafted comedies of the 16C. Their success was immediate and very well exploited by Aretino, who was astute enough to engage the new resources proffered by the printing press to increase his fame. This collaboration was in fact to make both the Tuscan and his publisher Marcotini a fortune. Aretino, furthermore, showed himself capable of using popular, vernacular language for literature to nothing short of tumultuous effect. His plays mocked and lampooned the authorities, attracting audiences from all walks of life, but most notably from among those in power who were anxious to know what was indeed being said. It was no surprise therefore, that he soon earned the epithet "the scourge of the princes".

Thus during the 17C, the Republic's somewhat liberal attitude must have excused the considerable freedom of thought and action enjoyed in Venice: one cannot otherwise explain the success of Aretino, nor indeed of other such lax publications that would have been prohibited elsewhere. Venice became an important publishing centre drawing types of all kinds who wished to take particular care over typographical layouts and to oversee the output of their own book, or even those who used it as an excuse to make a short trip to the shadow of the bell-tower of St Mark's. Soon hundreds of printers mushroomed to service hundreds of authors, dependent one upon the other.

Comedy – The theatre became a passion for citizens of all social classes. Plays proliferated, almost all written and produced on the spot. Comedies enacted in dialect enjoyed the greatest popularity; these were often based around sets of particular Carnival characters identified by their traditional mask and costume, such as **Harlequin**. The needs of a growing number of theatre devotees coupled with those of an important and thriving port founded the beginnings of a modern news-spreading media.

Journalism – The advent of journalism in Italy could only have been feasible in a milieu like Venice. In 1760 Gasparo Gozzi launched the magazine *La Gazzetta Veneta* which appeared twice a week for about a year. Conceived along the lines of an English periodical, features included articles on orders of the day and useful practical information on life in the city (financial announcements, public notices, advertisement listings, stock exchange reports and such like). It was in *La Gazzetta* that Goldoni published his first reviews on Rusteghi.

Carlo Goldoni (1707-93) – Goldoni's father was a doctor who wished his son to follow in his footsteps but when aged 13, the boy absconded from school to join a ship in Rimini that was carrying a troupe of actors to Chioggia, from where he went on to join his mother in Venice. Goldoni resumed his studies and qualified as a lawyer, but lacking the will to succeed, he soon turned his hand at challenging the tradition of the Commedia dell'Arte to improvise dialogue along the lines of a given plot.

Carlo Goldoni

In 1743 Goldoni wrote the script for *La donna di Garbo*. In 1750 the provocative comedy playwright impudently waged a bet with his rival Pietro Chiari that in less than a year he could write 16 new comedies: in actual fact he wrote 17, including the splendid *La Bottega del Caffè (The Coffee Shop)* set in Venice and satirising the bourgeoisie. The ingredients were simple: he used colloquial language for immediacy and formulated rounded characters based on observation of real life. He avoided political incorrectness by importing his gentrified personalities from afar, able therefore to exaggerate airs and graces. *Arlecchino, Servitore di due Padroni (Servant of Two Masters)*, *La Locandiera (The Inn Keeper)* are all constructed according to the same format. Goldoni died in France.

An account of Goldoni's stay in Venice can be found in the author's memoirs *(Memorie)*.

How the 18C and the 19C saw Venice – Venice as depicted by Goldoni, full of humour and moral integrity, was a vital place that attracted the talented, the eccentric and the curious. These included **Lorenzo da Ponte**, Mozart's celebrated librettist and author of the *Marriage of Figaro*, who lingered there for "a couple of years of adventurous libertinage", and that specialist master of licentiousness **Giacomo Casanova** (1725-98) who, between one amorous assignation and another, found time to write his interesting *Memoirs*.

Another reprobate of the same school, if the term is appropriate, the poet **Ugo Foscolo**, landed on the Riva degli Schiavoni in 1793. He stopped in the city for four years during which time he demonstrated the true colour of his personality on numerous occasions. Abandoning his regular studies, he embarked on teaching himself the Greek and Latin classics so as to engineer his infiltration of the very refined salon of Isabella Teorochi Albrizzi, with whom he initiated a passionate affair, he aged 16 and she 32. In the meantime, he wrote the famous *Ode to the Liberator Bonaparte*; only the "liberator" in his political intrigue paid no heed to the revolutionary ideals of the young Foscolo, but rather ceded Venice to Austria to further his own hegemonic aims. The repercussions on the writer were enormous, forcing him to seek refuge in Milan where he devoted himself to drafting *The Last Letters of Jacopo Ortis*, a prose account of the delusion he had suffered. During his sojourn in Venice, however, Foscolo also became involved with **Melchiorre Cesarotti**, an important forerunner of the early Romantic movement.

Cesarotti was a tutor in an aristocratic household whose salon Foscolo frequently attended. In 1760 Cesarotti came across a collection of poems by Oisin, a legendary bard, published by a certain MacPherson: in six months, Cesarotti had translated them into Italian verse which he published in 1763. *Le Poesie di Ossian*, as they appeared in Italian, shot Cesarotti to fame, oblivious of the fact that these "Ossianic poems" were to be one of those most famous cases of literary fraud to be uncovered over the last 200 years. **James MacPherson** (1736-96) claimed them to be a translation of a series of surviving fragments of some ancient Gaelic mythical poetry when in fact they had been fabricated, for the most part, by the Scotsman himself. Poor Cesarotti was one of the many innocents to fall for the trick. By the end of the century, the foundations of Italian Romanticism had been laid. The Piedmontese **Silvio Pellico**, the fervent patriot and anti-Austrian agitator, was soon to write his famous and doleful *Piombi*. In *Le mie Prigioni*, Pellico narrates his whole experience from the day of his arrest (13 October 1820) to that of his release (September 1830) thereby securing a place in the heart of the Nation as a hero.

Throughout the Romantic period, Venice reigned supreme. This was not so much as a result of her literary output but rather because she continued to distract so many intellectuals, such as **Lord Byron**, on their travels through Italy happy to meet up under the shaded porticoes of the Procuratie, a custom that was to extend well into the next century.

"What a funny old city this Queen of the Adriatic is! Narrow streets, vast, gloomy marble palaces, black with the corroding damp of centuries and all partly submerged; no dry land visible anywhere, and no side-walks worth mentioning; if you want to go to church, to the theatre, or to a restaurant, you must call a gondola. It must be a paradise for cripples, for verily a man has no use for his legs here."

Mark Twain - The Innocents Abroad, 1869

In 1886 the Russian author **Anton Chekhov** published a collection of short stories. *Story of a Stranger* recounts his overwhelming passion for Venice, to such an extent that he feels "intoxicated with life".

20C – The modern history of the lagoon city rests almost exclusively in the hands of foreigners, many of whom sought refuge there from persecution at home and soon enjoyed a protected social scene. Not only were there no Venetian-born writers of note to emerge, few Italians were attracted to the decadent beauty of the Serenissima. **Gabriele D'Annunzio** was a notable exception.

Marcel Proust arrived in 1900, inevitably accompanied by his mother, with whom he began translating the English writer **John Ruskin**, author of the famous *Stones of Venice*, while refining his own literary style. Proust's sojourn was a particularly happy one, reflecting in *A la Recherche du temps perdu*, he writes "*However did the images of Venice give e such joy and confidence as to render me indifferent to death*".

The reflections of **Thomas Mann** by contrast are of a very different order: in *Death in Venice*, the city is portrayed in a state of decay. The protagonist of the novel is Gustav von Aschenbach, a German writer who after a lifetime of rigorous discipline feels attracted by a city described as crumbling and overrun with cholera.

In 1918 the Viennese author **Arthur Schnitzler** wrote *Casanova in Spa*, a book set in Venice which was loosely based on his amorous adventures.

Among the most recent illustrious visitors to the city was **Ernest Hemingway** who set down his suitcases in the Hotel Gritti in 1948. He loved to be called "Papa" and while away the time with glasses of Montgomery, a strong Martini, at Harry's Bar. Far removed from the more rugged places one associates with the writer, Hemingway once confessed to his translator Ferdinanda Pivano: *"Sitting by the Grand Canal and writing near where Mr Byron, Mr Browning and Mr D'Annunzio wrote makes Mr Papa feel he has arrived at where he is meant to be"*.

The same year saw the publication of *Cantos* by the American poet **Ezra Pound**, who died in Venice *(see his cemetery in San Michele in Isola under SAN ZANIPÒLO)* and who wrote about the city in Canto LXXVI.

"Papa" Hemingway and his wife Mary Welch, before the Salute

Hemingway Collection/John F. Kennedy Library, Boston

In the early sixties, the Italian author **Giorgio Bassani** used the Ghetto district as a backdrop to his novel *Il Giardino des Finzi Contini*, which was made into a famous film by **Vittorio de Sica**.

The Russian writer **Josif Brodskij**, who received the Nobel Prize for Literature in 1987, was fascinated by Venetian water and canals, a passion he recounted in *Watermark*.

Another Slav author who evokes the lagoon city was Polish-born **Gustaw Herling** who, in *Portrait of Venice* (1994), evokes his "sentimental involvement with Venice".

A Venetian lexicon

The living breath of Venice is its dialect: besides the gossip exchanged in shops, along the *calli* or in the *campi*, place names and shop signs are often in Venetian. To hear the Venice of the Venetians it is worth recognising the most common terms used in conversation and in local cuisine. Accents have been used to facilitate pronunciation.

Colloquial terms

Barèna	low-lying sandbanks that emerge in the lagoon at low tide, often covered with scrub vegetation.
Baùta	a carnival mask comprising a black hood and a lace shawl.
Brìcola	a large wooden pole used for mooring boats, or if roped to others to delineate navigable channels.
Carèga	chair
Ciàcola	gossip or chatter
Fèlze	the gondola awning or cover set up in winter to protect the main seat.
Ocio!	Look out!
Ostreghèta!	Good heavens!
Pantegàna	the least salubrious inhabitant of the city, a large rat.
Putèo	a child
Tòco / tochetìn	a piece / little piece

Eating and drinking

Armelìn	apricot
Bacalà mantecà	boiled salt-cod, mixed with oil, garlic and parsley to a creamy consistency.
Bàcaro	a Venetian bistro, "the" meeting place *par excellence*, for a bite to eat and a glass of wine – usually crowded from early morning.
Bagìgi	peanuts
Baìcoli	typical dry, flat, cutlet-shaped sweet biscuits sold in nearly all bakeries and pastry shops.
Bìgoi	wholemeal spaghetti, generally served in *salsa* with a lightly fried mixture of anchovies and onions.
Bìsi	peas
Bussolài buranèi	an S or ring-shaped biscuit from Burano.
Càpe sànte	scallops
Cichèto	famous Venetian tit-bit that accompanies a glass of wine. It might be a bite of salt-cod, marinated sardine or a meat-ball.
Dìndio	turkey
Frìtole	carnival pancakes made with raisins and pinenuts.
Lugànega	a long thin sausage.
Narànsa	orange
Ombra, ombrèta	the traditional and much respected glass of wine taken standing at a bar.
Parsùto	ham
Peòci	mussels
Pòmi	apple
Rìsi e bìsi	rice and peas traditionally eaten during the Feast of St Mark.
Sàrde in saòr	fried sardines, served with a sweet-and-sour sauce made with onions, vinegar, pinenuts and raisins.
Sgropìn	a lemon sorbet made with vodka and *prosecco* – dry sparkling wine. Most refreshing after fish.
Sprìz	the famous Venetian aperitif: white wine with a dash of bitters and soda water.
Stracaganàse	dried chestnuts, literally translated as "jaw-acher".
Soprèssa	fresh salami
Tiramisù	the now world-famous dessert made of biscuits soaked in coffee, layered with full-fat *mascarpone* cream cheese blended with egg and sugar, powdered with bitter cocoa. Exquisite whatever the calorie count: its name literally means "pull-me-up".

Place names

These are as distinctive as Venice's system of house numbers which can reach remarkable heights (up to almost 7000) as these refer to individually numbered addresses within the whole *sestiere* rather than to a particular street or square: so do not try to apply common sense or logic in finding even numbers on one side of the street and odd ones on the other!

A somewhat confusing numbering system

Streets, squares and picturesque corners bearing dialect names have ancient and unusual derivations. Some of the most characteristic are listed here, whereas others are explained in context within the main Sights Section of the guide.

Altàna	a wooden roof-terrace or veranda, where Venetian girls used to sunbathe and bleach their hair. The distinctive crownless straw hat allowing the top of the head exposure to the sun is known as a *solana*.
Assassini	a canal or street name that might allude to where some murderer might have sought refuge.
Beccarìe	butchers that have lent their name to streets, squares, bridges or in-filled canals.
Calli	derived from the Latin *callis*, almost all the streets in Venice bear this name. Variations are *calli larghe*, *callette* and *calleselle*.
Campiello	a little *campo* or square.
Campo	Venetian for a square. There is only one *piazza* in Venice and that is the Piazza San Marco.
Cannaregio	one of the six *sestieri* of Venice from the Latin *cannarecium* or *canaleclum*, a marshy area where cane grows.
Castello	one of the six *sestieri* of the city alluding, perhaps, to the Roman fortification at Olivolo.
Dorsoduro	another *sestiere* of the city named after the type of hill on which it developed.
Fiubèra	buckle sellers that have lent their name to streets or vaulted arcades where they once set up shop.
Fondamenta	a road which runs parallel with a *rio* or canal.
Fòntego	a warehouse building where foreign merchants lodged.
Fornèr	a common name that would have identified where the local bread ovens were.
Frezzerìa	the famous commercial zone around St Mark's that was once the site of an arrow factory.
Lista	the stretch of street in front of an Ambassador's residence. Diplomatic immunity is indicated by its white stone.
Luganeghèr	commonly found in place names indicating a grocery store.
Megio	millet. This name alludes to grain (millet or wheat) warehouses storing supplies for times of hardship or might be given to a bridge and street in its vicinity.
Milion	the nickname of Marco Polo's family who lived over the Million courtyard behind San Giovanni Grisostomo. It is also the title of the adventurer's travel experiences.
Paradiso	this name given to a street or bridge, refers to the lamps that were used on Good Friday to light the area of Santa Maria Formosa.
Parrocchia	literally meaning "parish", this locality around a church serves as a subdivision of a *sestiere* and plays havoc with the numbering system!
Pescarìa	a fish market.
Piazzetta	there are only two *piazzette* or little squares in Venice: Piazzetta Leoncini and Piazzetta San Marco.
Piovàn	common in Venetian topography relating to a priest.
Piscina	place where there used to be a pool or sheet of water.
Pistòr	the baker who kneaded dough when making the bread.

Ponte	there are about 400 bridges in Venice, and all are marked by name.
Ramo	a side street.
Rialto	from the Latin *Rivoaltus*, a word which indicates the islands from which the city originated.
Rio terà	a street formed by a land-filled canal.
Ruga	from the French *rue*, is a synonym for street, usually one devoted to a commercial activity.
Salizzarda	from the word *salizo* or paving stone, denotes a paved street.
San Stae	the Venetian contraction of San Eustachio – St Eustace.
San Stin	another Venetian contraction of San Stefanino.
San Zan Degolà	refers to San Giovanni Decollato – the beheaded John the Baptist.
Scaletèr	a doughnut seller, from the word *scaleta*, a doughnut with marks like a flight of steps.
Sestieri	the six sub-divisions of Venice: San Marco, Castello, Cannaregio, Santa Croce, San Polo and Dorsoduro (which includes the Giudecca).
Sottopòrtego	a vaulted passageway running perpendicular to the building's façade on the ground floor, at one time lined with shops.
Squèro	a shipyard where gondolas are built and repaired.
Tette	the name of a bridge or street where bare-breasted women of easy virtue used to lean out of windows.
Zattere	the name given to the long *fondamenta* which extends to the Giudecca Canal, recalling the *zattere* or wood-laden rafts which used to stop there.

Pasta

Cannelloni – stuffed tubes, topped with tomato and bechamel sauce, baked in the oven

Farfalle – butterfly or bows

Fettuccine – freshly made egg pasta, thin tagliatelle served with a creamy sauce

Fusilli – twists of pasta designed by aerodynamics engineers to hold sauces of particular consistencies

Gnocchi – made with potato and flour – an acquired taste

Lasagne – sheets of pasta layered with meat or fish, tomato and bechamel sauce and baked in the oven

Maccheroni – small tubes

Paglia e fieno – thin threads of freshly made egg and spinach pasta (literally meaning straw and hay)

Pappardelle – broad flat ribbons of freshly made pasta, very often served in a rich sauce (wild boar – *cinghiale*; hare – *lepre*; *porcini* mushrooms...)

Polenta – a starchy semolina mixture served baked or with tomato sauce

Ravioli – cushions of freshly made egg-pasta stuffed with meat, fish or spinach and cheese *(spinaci e ricotta)*; delicious with butter and sage *(burro e salvia)* or meat sauce *(al ragù)*

Spaghetti – long threads of pasta served with shellfish *(frutta di mare)* or clams *(vongole)*

Tagliatelle – freshly made egg-pasta in long ribbons

Tortellini – little packets of freshly made egg-pasta stuffed with meat or cheese, served either in a sauce or in clear broth *(in brodo)*

Venice in the movies

Venice is a natural film set, but come September, she herself goes to the movies during the International Film Festival.

Cut! – The first rather primitive moving images of Venice are shot by Albert Promio in 1896, just one year after the birth of cinema. Since then, Venice has become one of the oldest, ageless, most sought-after *divas* ever!

1935 – Mark Sandrich films *Top Hat* with Ginger Rogers and Fred Astaire.

1955 – David Lean chooses Venice as the backdrop to the meeting between Rossano Brazzi and Katharine Hepburn in *Summertime*.

1963 – In the second James Bond film, *From Russia with Love*, Sean Connery goes to Murano in search of a particular glassmaker... Special effects include an amphibian gondola scattering pigeons in St Mark's Square.

1971 – Based on the novella *Death in Venice* by Thomas Mann, Luchino Visconti directs *Morte a Venezia* with Dirk Bogarde in the lead role; panoramic shots sweep across the sultry waters of the lagoon – a classic!

1976 – Fellini films *Casanova*, based on the life story of the notorious Venetian.

1979 – *Don Giovanni* is a beautiful film adaptation of Mozart's opera, populated by masked figures stepping out of swirling mists from boats in the Brenta Valley.

1982 – Giuliano Montaldo recreates Malamocco in the 1200s for his film *Marco Polo*, starring Ken Marshall.

1988 – Steven Spielberg gets archeologist Harrison Ford to jump out of the library into Campo San Barnaba in *Indiana Jones*.

1995 – In *Carrington*, Christopher Hampton directs Emma Thompson (Dora Carrington) and Jonathan Pryce (Lytton Strachey) on a visit to Venice.

1996 – Woody Allen directs and stars in a delightful musical called *Everyone Says I Love You*, set in three famous cities – New York, Venice and Paris. Those familiar with the lagoon city will recognise many quaint, secluded spots of the city, as well as the glorious Scuola di San Rocco.

Filming *Carrington*

Venice Carnival

During the 18C, the Venice Carnival opened at the beginning of October and ended on the Tuesday preceding Lent, with only one short interruption for Christmas festivities. In those days, masks were worn throughout the carnival but they were also used in other circumstances: during the Fiera della Sensa lasting for two weeks, on the occasion of doges' elections and their sons' weddings, and when famous personalities would arrive in town.

Legend has it... – Masks were introduced to Venice in 1204 when Doge Enrico Dandolo brought veiled Muslim women back to Venice after his conquest of Constantinople.

"Buongiorno, siora mascara" – As in Mozart's opera *Don Giovanni* (Act 2), this was how masked people greeted each other during the 17C. To go about one's business dressed in the *baùta* – a mask complete with its hooded black shawl – was so normal that a formal request was lodged by the clergy for Venetians to remove their "disguise" at least in church.

Return of the Carnival – The greater the decline of Venice, the sharper her sense of fun. Come 1797 when the French assumed power, thereby concluding the glory of the Venetian Republic for all time, the city continued her revelries, thriving on her taste for jokes and riddles, laughter and carnival which eventually was revived late in the 19C.

Even when this modern carnival was reinstated, with an open invitation to all to congregate in Piazza San Marco – the only time the space is truly filled by the crowds – it was a masked attendance. Whether it be with the *baùta*, the full-length cloak *(tabarro)*, the three-horned hat *(tricorno)* or the long-nosed mask *(maschera a becco)* that doctors used to use during the plague epidemics, the rule of the game is always the same: never investigate the identity of he who wears the mask.

The need to don a mask seems to come as second nature to a Venetian. Maybe because, in the words of Silvio Ceccat: *"The streets are narrow, the population is small. You meet someone at every corner. Everyone knows everyone else's business. Today there are no cars to protect anonymity as yesterday there were no coaches in which to hide... People used to and presently feel naked in Venice. So naked, indeed that clothes are not enough and so the need for the mask..."*.

Carnival attire

Eating out

Venice has traded with the Orient since the dawn of time; she has therefore throughout her history, been cosmopolitan in every sense of the word. A thousand different ethnic types have crowded the streets and squares as they have populated the pictures of Titian and Veronese: they have added colour to the Venetian scene, idiom and dialect to the vernacular language and, above all, exotic spice to the indigenous cultural and culinary traditions. The perfumes and fragrances exchanged in Venice have been blended and refined through time with more homely scents and flavours. Nothing has been lost. Only now the multicoloured multitude of merchants has been replaced with crowds of tourists, and so the alchemy continues.

Social history has also played its part: besides the gastronomic refinement inherited from an aristocratic past, solid peasant cooking still underpins many local dishes even if the poorest have long since been enhanced by every sort of ingredient the mainland can provide before returning as a regional speciality.

Tourism has nurtured a demand for restaurants that alternate between luxurious and anonymous "tourist" catering, but the age-old rhythm of the city and the convivial habits of its citizens still survive and flourish: **un ombra di vin** (measure of wine) and a **cichèto**, (a bite of squid, salt-cod or such like) consumed in a **bàcaro** are luxuries that the Venetians would be loath to renounce.

Pasta all'inchiostro di seppia – a dish prepared with squid ink

Out of the sea and into the frying pan! – Venetians are especially proud of their seafood. A traditional plate of *antipasto (hors d'œuvre)* offers a chance to relish a wonderful selection of local shellfish including **peòci, caparòsoi, bòvoli** and **canòce**, as well as **crab, granseole** and **gransipori**.

As a *primo* or starter, **bigoi in salsa** (thick, coarse spaghetti served with lightly-fried onions and anchovies) is one of the most popular first courses but there are also many types of risotto made with meat and/or vegetables grown locally in market gardens, or more especially with fish or **'in tecia'** – with cuttlefish.

Fish from the Adriatic is often served grilled with, in spring, **castraùre** (young fried artichokes); eels – **bisàto** in dialect, on the other hand are either broiled or poached.

One common ingredient is vinegar used in all kinds of ways but notably for pickling and preparing **saòr**, a kind of carp. For a truly typical dish, try a bite of **baccalà mantecato**, salt-cod beaten to a smooth cream with oil, garlic and parsley and served with polenta.

Meat dishes – Among the most traditional *secondo* or main course, there is **fegato alla veneziana**, (calf's liver and onions), a combination created in Venice but now popular everywhere. The defining factor for Venetians however, is how thinly the meat is cut, and the long gentle cooking it undergoes.

During the Feast of the Madonna della Salute, **castrato** is eaten. This is succulent, sweet meat from a castrated lamb, slightly fatter than the norm but more delicate in flavour. At this time it is traditionally served with Savoy cabbage.

For flavoursome country cooking, taste **panàda venexiana** a wholesome soup made with bread, garlic, oil, bayleaf and Parmesan cheese or the **pastissàda**, an ingenious concoction of green vegetables, cheese, sausage, pasta or polenta bound together traditionally to use up left-overs!

"Of all the spectacular food markets in Italy, the one near the Rialto in Venice must be the most remarkable... The gentle swaying of the laden gondolas, the movements of the market men as they unload, swinging the boxes and baskets ashore, the robust life and rattling noise contrasted with the fragile taffeta colours and the opal sky of Venice – the whole scene is out of some marvellous unheard-of ballet..."

Elizabeth David in Italian Food

Dolci – For dessert, try the famous **baìcoli** biscuits, which according to local custom are dunked in drinking chocolate or dessert wine; the **bussolài**, biscuits moulded into ring or "s" shapes – called essi buranèi; or the **Veneziana**, a kind of *brioche* covered with chopped almonds and sugar. For Carnival, other seasonal goodies replace our Shrove Tuesday pancakes: **frìtole** are made from a dough flavoured with raisins and pine nuts. At Epiphany come the **pìnsa**, a biscuit flavoured with fennel seeds, raisins, dried figs and candied peel.

For a toast – The most commonly found wines are the **Suave** (white) and the **Cabernet del Friuli** (red). For dessert, there is the Verduzzo di Ramandolo DOC, Torcolato di Breganza or the Recioto. As an *apéritif*, there is the famous **Bellini**, one-quarter

Polenta features regularly on Venetian menus

measure of peach juice to three of *prosecco* – a dry Italian sparkling white wine; the **Tiziano**, made with a special strawberry-flavoured grape juice; the **Mimosa**, a blend of tangerine and orange juices; the **Rossini**, with strawberry juice added. **Ernest Hemingway** was a frequent visitor to Harry's Bar, where he would order his own special cocktail, the **Montgomery**, named after the famous general: it was made with one measure of vermouth to 15 measures of gin and is only served by that particular establishment...

Tourists who enjoy browsing round the shops to discover new culinary specialities should make a point of visiting the stores that offer various kinds of coloured pasta, each with a different flavour: brown for chocolate, black for squid ink...

Italian coffee

Espresso – very short, sharp, black and very strong

Caffè lungo/caffè americano – a short, strong espresso with added hot water

Caffè corretto – an espresso with added brandy or *grappa* (eau-de-vie)

Caffè macchiato – an espresso with a dash of cold milk

Cappuccino or **cappuccio** – an espresso topped with hot fluffy milk and powdered chocolate

Caffè latte – a glass of hot milk flavoured with an espresso coffee

Ice cream flavours

Gelato is best bought from a *gelateria*

Stracciatella – plain with chocolate chips. **Gianduia** – smooth chocolate and hazelnut. **Bacio** – milk chocolate. **Fior di latte** or **panna** – plain milk or cream. **Crema** – vanilla enriched with egg. **Cioccolato** – chocolate. **Nocciola** – hazelnut. **Frutta di bosco** – fruit from the forest (blueberries, blackberries). **Limone** – lemon sorbet. **Fragola** – strawberry. **Pistacchio** – bright green pistachio nut. **Pesca** – peach. **Albicocca** – apricot. **Lampone** – raspberry.

Sights

This area is permanently thronged by people on the move: locals on business of their own, tourists and visitors drawn to the Gallerie and students milling outside the nearby University lend a very artistic feel to the area. It is always worth stopping, however, for a short break at one of the bars or trattorie. Seeing the Squero di San Trovaso from this unusual angle and the view of the Giudecca from the Zattere add the finishing touches to this very short but pleasant itinerary.

The suggested route and tours take about half a day.

A good pizza or a simple meal. Fish perhaps?

Try the **San Trovaso** taverna, on Rio di San Trovaso, at 1016 Dorsoduro. Another good local is the cantinone **Già Schiavi** at 992 Dorsoduro.
If the idea of a trattoria is more appealing, consider going to **da Montin** at 1147 Dorsoduro, fondamenta Borgo.

Ponte dell'Accademia (**7**, DX) – The **Accademia Bridge** is one of only three bridges to cross the Grand Canal. This wooden bridge replaces an old iron construction built by the Austrians in 1854 to allow their "peace-keeping" forces free access to both sides of the city. As then, it links the elegant and spacious Campo di Santo Stefano with the Accademia, eventually leading right up to the Zattere.

★★★**Gallerie dell'Accademia** ⊙ (**7**, DX) – The **Academy of Fine Art** exhibits a most important collection of art works encapsulating the development of Venetian painting from the 14C to the 18C, in a complex of buildings converted in the 19C: these include the Monastery of Lateran Canons, designed by Andrea Palladio (1508-80), the Church of La Carità, an atmospheric building which was redesigned

The Tempest by Giorgione (Accademia)

A Reflection on the Altarpiece of San Giobbe

Anyone who is familiar with the Brera Altarpiece by Piero della Francesca will recognise the compositional format of the Sacra conversazione: this consists of an arrangement of figures, often the Virgin and Child with Saints, within a defined architectural space.

This altarpiece bears the name of one of the Patriarchs present in the group (the figure standing closest to the Madonna, on the right), to whom the church for which it was destined is dedicated: the persepective and architectural detailing of the picture is matched exactly to the position it was intended to occupy above the second altar on the right *(see GHETTO: San Giobbe)*.

Bellini was certainly influenced by the San Cassiano altarpiece by Antonello da Messina, although he imbues his figures with a more solemn dignity, culminating in the most important of the group, the Madonna, and the bright light which is refracted across the mosaic floor.

by Bartolomeo Bon (recorded 1441-64) and the Scuola Santa Maria della Carità, the first Scuola Grande *(see I CARMINI – The Venetian Scuole which was erected in 1260)*. The tour starts in the large Sala Capitolare at the top of the 18C staircase.

Room I – The Sala Capitolare is where from the 15C, the Scuola Grande of the Santa Maria della Carità used to meet. This large room has a gilded panelled ceiling by Marco Cozzi (1484), divided into sections with a cherub in each. The figure of God in the central tondo, attributed to Alvise Vivarini (1445-1505), replaces that of the Madonna della Misericordia, the patron who would have occupied the section originally. The room is devoted to Venetian Gothic masters from the 14C and the first half of the 15C including Paolo Veneziano (*Coronation of the Virgin* at the top of the stairs straight ahead) and Lorenzo Veneziano. The huge painting, the *Coronation of the Virgin in Paradise* at the end of the room is by Jacobello del Fiore *(right)*. Note Michele Giambono's polyptych also on display here; flourishing between 1420 and 1462, Giambono is the most important artist to work in the International Gothic style in Venice.

Room II – This room displays eight important 15C altarpieces. On the entrance wall: the *Crucifixion and Apotheosis of the Ten Thousand Martyrs of Mount Ararat*, by Vittore Carpaccio (c 1465-1526), depicts the legendary massacre of the Roman soldiers betrayed by their own captains after beating the Armenian rebels *(right)*. On the wall to the right hang the famous **Virgin and Child with Saints**, also known as the Pala di san Globbe, by Giovanni Bellini (c 1470-1516) (1) taken from the Church of San Giobbe; the *Agony in the Garden* by Marco Basaiti (c 1470-1530) *(right)* and the *Presentation of Christ in the Temple* by Vittorio Carpaccio *(left)*.

On the end wall: the *Madonna of the Orange Tree*, by Cima da Conegliano (1459-1517) *(right)* hangs alongside his *Incredulity of St Thomas and the Great Bishop* in which the three figures are silhouetted against the sky with a village in the distance *(left)*. The **Calling of the Sons of Zebedee** (2), by Marco Basaiti, is a particularly beautiful and engaging treatment of the subject of Christ recruiting his Apostles, the variety of scenery with the focus on the water and the magical quality of the colour *(centre)*.

On the wall to the left: the *Mourning of the Dead Christ*, by Giovanni Bellini and assistants *(right)* and the *Madonna with Child Enthroned*, by Cima da Conegliano *(left)*.

Room III – This contains works by Sebastiano del Piombo, Cima da Conegliano and Giovanni Bellini. *Cross to the far end for access to the small adjoining Rooms IV and V, among the most important rooms in the gallery.*

Room IV – **St George** (3) by Andrea Mantegna (1431-1506) hangs on the wall to the left, one of only two paintings by the master who so influenced Bellini and consequently the evolution of Venetian painting. The painting has a Tuscan feel about it: the knight, a synthesis of Humanism is reminiscent of Donatello.

On the wall to the right, Giovanni Bellini's **Madonna with Child between St Catherine and Mary Magdalene** (4) depicts four figures thrown into relief by a strong transverse light that lifts them out of the darkness; note, however, the suggestion of serene beauty and tender spirituality so typical of Bellini. In contrast, on the right, is the *Portrait of a Young Man* by the Dutch artist Hans Memling (c 1435-94) with its sharp delineation of features and characterisation; lost in tranquil meditation the young man's face is imbued with inner calm.

Room V – **The Tempest** (5) by Giorgione (c 1467-1510) is the crystallisation of a state of mind rather than representation of a specific moment in time, an attempt at capturing the essence of a poetic narrative taken from literature. The protagonists of this "fantasy picture" are the three figures, the ruins, the water and the village dramatically caught in an irridescent green light by a flash of lightning.

Another famous work by Giorgione hangs on the left. **The Old Woman** (6) is a compelling portrait, appealing yet uncompromising. Self-explanatory, it has been described as a "hymn to fleeing youth" touched with the inevitable sadness of realised awareness, highlighted by the inscription in the cartouche *"col tempo"* –

Portrait of a Young Gentleman in his Study
by Lotto (Accademia)

with time. The picture is especially charged with meaning if one considers how Giorgione's untimely death in 1510 from the plague cut short a life full of promise. To the right of the door are the *Allegories* by Giovanni Bellini, particularly exquisite small paintings intended as decorative panels to be set into a piece of furniture or mirror.

On the wall in front of the exit hang the *Madonna and the Seraphim* and the *Madonna under the Trees* by Giovanni Bellini. The title of the latter refers to the trees which serve as foreground to the landscape, channelling perspective across the countryside to distant snow-capped peaks.

Room VI – This long room houses the *Assumption of the Virgin* by Tintoretto (1518-94) and the frieze from San Giacomo della Giudecca by Veronese (1528-88) and pupils.

Room VII – This little room is home to the famous 1524 ***Portait of a Young Gentleman in his Study*** (7) by **Lorenzo Lotto** (c 1480-1577), in which the sitter's concentration seems to have been interrupted by a thought or a memory; distracted from his reading, his long delicate fingers idly flick through the pages as he muses perhaps upon the passing of time, staring into the distance, his pale, chiselled face contrasted by his black coat.

After **Room VIII** which houses works by Vasari, Palma il Vecchio and Titian, follows **Room IX** *(bookshop). Access to Room X is through Room VI.*

Room X – The *Madonna with Child Enthroned* by Veronese *(left of the entrance)* recalls the Pesaro altarpiece in the Frari *(see I FRARI)*. The *Pietà* (8) by Titian (1490-1576) *(right of the entrance, in the middle)*, was intended by the artist for his own tomb at the Frari but remained unfinished on his death. Note down on the right, at the Sibyl's feet, the hand raised in supplication.

On the wall with the doorway into the next room there is Veronese's ***Betrothal of St Catherine*** *(left)*.

Opposite the entrance hang Tintoretto's canvases depicting the life of St Mark. From left to right *St Mark's Dream* (in fact the dream of St Mark's son, Dominic), *St Mark Saves a Saracen, St Mark Liberates a Slave* – the oblique lighting effects heighten the drama of the scene with St Mark falling headfirst; the *Theft of the Body of St Mark* (the final panel in the series, the *Finding of the Body of St Mark* is now in the Brera Collection in Milan). Note how the figures in the foreground of the painting appear thrown into relief by the use of *chiaroscuro*, where forms, picked out by strong light are contrasted against another recessed into shadow; here phantom-like figures fade into the darkness, sloping off in search of safety in the palace.

The whole of the right wall is taken by Veronese's controversial ***Christ in the House of Levi***, conceived as a *Last Supper* (1573) for the refectory of SS Giovanni e Paolo *(see SAN ZANIPÒLO)*. Shortly after the painting was unveiled, Veronese was summoned before a tribunal of the Inquisition on a charge of heresy for not adhering to the description of the event as related in the Gospels *("And does it seem fitting to represent the Last Supper with buffoons, drunkards, German soldiers, dwarfs, and similar scurrilities?")*: Veronese defended himself on the grounds of artistic licence. He promptly changed the painting's title to suit a more secular subject that might also justify the painter's predilection for such opulent textures as brocade, glass, gold... *("I paint my pictures with such judgement as I have and as seems fitting.")*

Room XI – This room accommodates works by Giambattista Tiepolo (1696-1770) including the frieze that depicts the *Castigation of the Serpents*, the fresco pendentives from the Scalzi Church (destroyed in 1915) and a series of canvases with a mythological theme. *Dinner in the House of Simon* by **Bernardo Strozzi** (1581-1644) is particularly vibrant, notably animated by the expressive face of the figure filling the chalice. The *Crucifixion of St Peter* composed around its strong diagonal axes by Luca Giordano (1643-1705) is also here.

On the left wall hangs the masterpiece by **Bonifacio de' Pitati** (c 1487-1553). The *Rich Man Epulone* (9) projects a tranquil scene, rich with incidental detail and contrasting personality, populated with musicians, a beggar, huntsmen and lovers converging in a wood, as a fire rages on the right.

GALLERIE DELL'ACCADEMIA

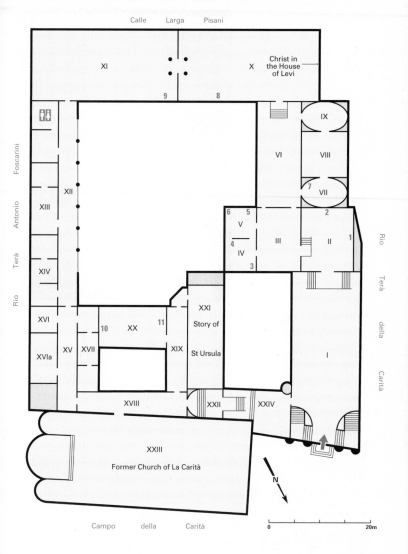

Room XII is dedicated to landscape painting straddling the 17C and 18C; these include Marco Ricci, Giuseppe Zais and Francesco Zuccarelli. Access to the two side rooms, **Rooms XIII** (in which hang several works by Tintoretto, including his portrait of the Procurator Jacopo Soranzo) and **XIV** which show works from the 16C and 17C is through Room XII. The corridor then becomes **Room XV** which leads to side rooms on the left (**Room XVII**) full of the most typical Venetian paintings: Canaletto (1697-1768) – although a prolific Venetian painter, all save a handful of his works hang in collections abroad having been sold to foreign gentlemen on the Grand Tour or requisitioned by Napoleon; Bernardo Bellotto (1721-80); **Francesco Guardi** (1712-93); **Giambattista Piazzetta** (1683-1754); **Rosalba Carriera** (1675-1758) whose series of informal pastel portraits are provocative studies of personality; **Pietro Longhi** (1702-85) (the famous *Dancing Lesson*).

Room XVIa accommodates works from the 18C including the *Fortune-teller* by Piazzetta.

Room XVIII serves as a passageway into **Room XXIII**, the old Church of La Carità, which now contains works from the 15C Venetian School.

The *Annunciation* by **Antonello da Saliba** (active 1497-1535) displayed in **Room XIX**, is in fact a copy of a work bearing the same title in the Galleria Nazionale di Palermo in Sicily, executed by Antonello da Messina, Da Saliba's uncle. *Access to Room XX is through Room XIX.*

Room XX – This room contains the famous collection of paintings illustrating the story of the ***Miracles of the Relic of the True Cross***, executed by various artists between the 15C and 16C, for the Scuola di San Giovanni Evangelista.

The *Procession in St Mark's Square* (10) by Gentile Bellini (1429-1507) covers the wall facing the entrance. The work is an important representation of the square in the mid-15C *(see PIAZZA SAN MARCO)*. Other paintings by Gentile Bellini on the right wall include *(from left to right)* the *Healing of Pietro de'Ludovici* and the *Miracle of the Cross on the Ponte di San Lorenzo* in which Andrea Vendramin is shown retrieving the Reliquary of the True Cross from the canal. Note that Caterina Cornaro *(see RIALTO — Ca'Corer della Regina)* is just visible on the left-hand side of the latter work. On the same wall hangs a work by Giovanni Mansueti (active in Venice from 1485 to c 1526): the *Healing of*

Portrait of a Lady by Rosalba Carriera (Accademia)

Benvegnudo's Daughter of San Polo which sets the scene in a beautiful Renaissance interior *(right)*. Carpaccio's **Miracle of the Relic of the True Cross at Rialto** (11) can be seen on the entrance wall. Interestingly, the subject of the painting — the miraculous healing of a madman taking place on the first floor loggia on the left — seems secondary to the profusion of topographical detail showing Venice at the end of the 15C: the wooden Rialto Bridge *(see RIALTO)*, the Fondaco dei Tedeschi on the right as it was before the events of 1505 *(see La FENICE)*, the Ca' da Mosto *(see Il CANAL GRANDE)* and the bell-towers of San Giovanni Grisostomo and the Church of Allsaints *(see RIALTO)*.

Miracle of the Relic of the Holy Cross by Carpaccio (Accademia)

Room XXI – This room contains the colourful and magical series of canvases by **Carpaccio** that retell the *Story of St Ursula* (1491-98). *Start with the wall facing the entrance (left) and proceed clockwise.*

The first panel, *Arrival of the English Ambassadors,* shows the ambassadors arriving at the (Catholic) court in Brittany bearing a proposal of marriage from their English (pagan) prince, Hereus. Ursula *(to the right)* is shown dictating her conditions of marriage (including his baptism and promise to undertake a pilgrimage accompanied by Ursula and a large number of virgins), in the presence of her wet nurse seated on the steps.

The English Ambassadors taking their Leave (detail)
by Carpaccio (Accademia)

Accademia, Venezia/SCALA

The next scene shows The *English Ambassadors taking their Leave* where the King hands over the reply: it may well be that it is being written up by the scribe who is concentrating on his task.

In the *Return of the Ambassadors* the cortège bringing the reply to the King is followed by a crowd to the edge of the lagoon – the towers suggestive of the Arsenale. Certain details of the painting are particularly noteworthy: the central scene is almost theatrical, the eye is caught by the handsome youth turning away as if in afront; the figure sitting on the bank is the "Steward" whose duty it is to herald the arrival of the ambassadors, invited by the doge, with music, while a monkey on the right watches a guinea-fowl.

The *Meeting of Ursula and Hereus and the Departure of the Pilgrims* is a composite scene, divided by the pennant, showing the prince taking his leave; Hereus and Ursula bid farewell to the rulers of Brittany before departing for Rome. Note the sharp contrast in the harsh, darkened representation of the English capital on the left and the colourful Breton town on the right represented according to Humanist ideals.

In *Ursula's Dream* the scene is more compact, set in Ursula's room where the light reveals more domestic details: reminiscent of *St Augustine in his Studio (see SAN GIORGIO degli SCHIAVONI)* the angel reaches out for the palm of martyrdom. The *Meeting of the Pilgrims with Pope Cyriac under the Walls of Rome* takes place against the background of the Castel Sant'Angelo, between two groups of virgin pilgrims (Ursula's companions) to the left and the prelates to the right. In the centre, the betrothed are waiting to be crowned. Note Carpaccio's delight in using strong and contrasting colours, notably red and white. The *Arrival in Cologne* depicts how, on their arrival in the city, Ursula and her father, who has joined the pilgrims, learn that the city is in the hands of the Huns. Ursula's eventful life on earth concludes with the *Martyrdom of the Pilgrims and Ursula's Funeral,* in which the two scenes are separated by the column. In the centre the warrior is removing blood from his sword. The final panel in the cycle, however, showing the *Apotheosis of St Ursula and her Companions* is perhaps the saddest.

Room XXIV, on the way out, is the former Sala dell'Albergo. It houses one of the collection's highlights: Titian's **Presentation of the Virgin to the Temple** (1530s).

The way to San Trovaso, parallel with the Grand Canal on the right of the Accademia, passes through an area bustling with people on the move where tourists mingle with the Venetians.

San Trovaso (**7**, **DX**) – *The entrance is on the canal side.* Like the Churches of San Marcuola and San Zanipòlo, this church is dedicated to two saints (Gervasius and Protasius – the protomartyrs of Milan) whose names have been contracted to "Trovaso". The original church was built in the 9C, but underwent much subsequent reconstruction culminating in its total remodelling by architects of the Palladian School between the 16C and 17C. It boasts two lateral façades serving two clans of rival factions, the Castellani and the Nicolotti *(see I CARMINI – Ponte dei Pugni);* both are similar with two huge windows in an arched semicircle, a relatively common feature in Venice.

Latin cross in plan, it has a single nave with side chapels. In the presbytery, a chapel off to the right, hangs *Christ Crucified between the Two Marys,* by Tintoretto's son Domenico (c 1560-1635) and the resplendent Gothic *St Chrysogonus on Horseback,* by Michele Giambono (active 1420-62). Two further wall paintings are by Domenico Tintoretto: the *Adoration of the Magi (right)* and the *Expulsion of St Joachim from the Temple.*

Squero di San Trovaso

The chapel to the left of the presbytery contains the *Temptation of St Anthony* by the more famous father (1518-94): note the devil dressed as a woman.

Also by Jacopo Tintoretto is a realistic depiction of the *Last Supper* – even the straw stuffing of the large chair is visible – on the right wall of the last chapel of the left transept *(directly opposite the entrance)*. By contrast, in the next chapel to the left is the *Pietà* by Palma il Giovane (1548-1628), whose three other works here include the *Birth of the Virgin* above the first altar in the nave, the *Madonna with Child in the Glory and Saints* over the next altar and the *Annunciation* in the left arm of the transept. *The Marriage at Cana*, above the entrance, is by Andrea Vicentino (late 15C-early 16C). The organ (1765) against the internal wall of the façade overlooking the square, was made by Gaetano Callido.

Further along the Rio di San Trovaso between the church and the Zattere is a quaint boat-yard.

Squero di San Trovaso (🔟, DX) – This is one of the few *squeri* still in operation in Venice and is certainly the most famous, possibly on account of its unusual character. In this city of elegantly refined Byzantine *palazzi*, this building seems idiosyncratic, built of wood, with its geraniums tumbling from the balcony in summertime it looks more like an alpine chalet. Elsewhere this little yard would be merely picturesque, here it continues to function as a gondola dockyard.

To reach the Church of the Gesuati proceed along the Zattere towards the Dogana.

Gesuati (🔟, DY) – The Church of Santa Maria del Rosario ai Gesuati is dedicated to the Madonna of the Rosary, honoured by an ancient (14C) order of laymen, the Clerici apostolici S Hieronymi – not to be confused with the Jesuits. Shortly after the order was dissolved by Pope Clement IX in 1668, the incumbent order of Dominicans commissioned the architect Giorgio Massari (c 1686-1766) to remodel the building. For the new façade he borrowed elements from the Church of San Giorgio Maggiore and chose spirited statues to represent Prudence, Justice, Strength and Temperance.

The luminous interior comprises one nave lined with three chapels on either side. The elaborate sculptural decoration is almost entirely attributable to Giovanni Maria Morlaiter (1699-1781). Typical in style of the 18C, the church has only one element which does not belong to this century, even if it was restored in the 18C by Piazzetta: the *Crucifixion* by Tintoretto (1518-94) above the third altar on the left.

The first altar on the left is adorned with the *Three Saints* by Sebastiano Ricci (1659-1734). The *Three Saints* by Piazzetta (1683-1754), opposite Tintoretto's *Crucifixion*, overlooks the third altar. This is one of Piazzetta's masterpieces and depicts San Vincenzo Ferrari, San Giacinto and San Ludovico Bertrando, all Dominican saints. The next bay on this side is dedicated to St Dominic. In the following bay sits a *Madonna between the Three Saints Honoured by the Dominicans, Catherine of Siena, Rose and Agnes*, by **Giambattista Tiepolo** (1696-1770).

The ceiling (1737-39) is divided into three sections which contain scenes from the life of St Dominic and the *Devotion of the Rosary*, by Tiepolo.

Chiesa della Visitazione (🔟, DXY) – Nearby, the Church of the Visitation was built in its present form between the 15C and the beginning of the 16C.

For those wishing to continue into neighbouring districts, turn to the sections on La SALUTE and I CARMINI.

ARSENALE ★

(**10**, HX)
Vaporetto: Arsenale or Riva degli Schiavoni

This offshoot of the Castello *sestiere*, renown for its shipyards, famous towers and the earthenware lions at the gate – easily spotted from the *vaporetto* on the Rio dell'Arsenale – is a more secluded part of Venice. But more than anything else, it is the tantalising glimpses of the churches that evoke the area's artistic heritage.

The suggested itinerary given here takes about three hours.

Enclosed within medieval walls punctuated with towers, the Arsenal has two main entrances along the Rio dell'Arsenale – one for land-based craft and one for the water-borne.

The **land entrance**, a grand Renaissance triumphal arch, constitutes the most important gateway dating back to c 1460, presided over by the lions from Ancient Greece (Athens and Piraeus), brought over by Francesco Morosini after his victory over Morea in 1687.

The **water entrance** (**10**, HX), through which the *vaporetto* passes, is marked by two towers which were rebuilt in 1686.

History – The first recorded dockyard in Venice, the **Arsenale Vecchio**, dates back to about 1104 when the demands of the crusades stimulated shipbuilding activity. The chosen zone, between the towers and the Galeazzi Canal, was protected and linked to the Bacino di San Marco by a canal that was only wide enough to accommodate one boat at a time. At one time, there were 24 active boat-yards. Along the slipways, the hulls were aligned in two rows.

By vaporetto

Even if the quickest way of getting around Venice is on foot and the most important sights can be reached this way, it is worth taking *vaporetto* no 52 along the Riva degli Schiavoni or the Fondamenta Nuove. This becomes almost obligatory if Venice's long and glorious maritime past is to be appreciated to the full as it was along this very canal that the galleys used to pass.

A quick snack?

Some way off the tourist trail, the area has some typically Venetian *osterie* (eating places) such as **Da Dante**, in Corte Nova *(2877 Castello)*.

In the 14C, the Arsenal was extended towards the southeast **(Arsenale Nuovo)**. Altogether 16 000 *marangoni* were employed, men apprenticed as joiners and trained as shipwrights. The boat-building techniques were highly advanced for their time, as the Venetians were already implementing on production lines.

During the second half of the 15C, the **Arsenale Nuovissimo** was extended to the north of the area – on the Galeazzi Canal (1564).

Having been destroyed during the French occupation (1797), the Arsenal was then rebuilt by the Austrians between 1814 and 1830.

After the Venetians attacked it in 1848 the area was abandoned during the third Austrian occupation (1849-66). Reconstruction work was initiated during the second half of the 19C, and continued up to 1914.

Buildings – In addition to being the naval base, a depository for arms and equipment and a workshop where maintenance work was carried out, the Arsenal also served as the main shipyard – popularly thought of as the very heart of the Venetian State. The toponymy serves as a reminder of the various trades and activities of each street: Calle della Pegola (fish), dei Bombardieri (cannon-ball founders), del Piombo (lead), delle Ancore (anchors). Mills continuously churned out hemp rope, then there were the sail lofts, the artillery warehouses and the slipways.

Beyond the towers, along the canal, is the **Scalo del Bucintoro** *(second on the right after the towers)*, designed by **Sanmicheli** (1484-1559). This dock is home to the famous ship that was built by the *arsenalotti*, a group of specialist artisans who worked in teams to build the vessels. The *arsenalotti* were also known for their prompt intervention in the event of a fire.

On entering the Galeazzi Canal the first building on the right is the **Complesso degli Squadratori**. This group of buildings which dates back to the 18C is where the skeletons of the ships were squared.

On the right, before the Galeazzi Canal reaches the lagoon, the final buildings are the shelters which housed the *galeazzi*, the oar-propelled galleys, as they were being built.

Alongside the Tana Canal to the south runs the **Tana**, a warehouse used to store hemp before being made into hawsers, which originated in the 14C but which was rebuilt between 1578 and 1583 by the architect Antonio da Ponte. Its name is borrowed from *Tanai*, the city formerly known as Don from where the hemp was imported.

The Maritime Archeological Museum is situated in Campo San Biagio.

Entrance to the Arsenale

★**Museo Storico Navale** ⊘ (**10**, HX) – This vast naval museum will delight any boat enthusiast and prove a veritable treasure trove to anyone intrigued by Venice's ship-building industry, for it was thanks to her ships more than anything else that Venice flourished as a maritime power.

The museum comprises four floors and houses a large collection of artefacts: a torpedo, taffrail lights, mortars, cannons, scale models of the city and her fortresses, firearms and sabres.

On the **first floor** are examples of wooden sculptures which decorated the galleys, coats of arms, naval weaponry, nautical instruments including compasses and octants, parchment *portolani* (pilots' charts and navigation material specifying details of coastal areas, harbours, anchorages and dangerous waters), engravings, models of ships, fine examples of galleys' broadsides, the supposed remains of Lazzaro Mocenigo's flagship which disappeared in the Dardanelles in 1657 and a model of the State barge, the *Bucintoro* (*see PIAZZA SAN MARCO – Museo Correr*). The **second floor** is dedicated to naval history during the 19C and 20C and includes scale models and naval uniforms.

The **third floor** displays an extensive collection of ex-votos (offerings given to a church in thanks or commemoration of an event), a luxury vessel from the 18C, gondolas and a model of a working boat-yard, the Squero di San Trovaso (*see ACCADEMIA*).

On the **fourth floor** there is a section dedicated to the Swedish navy and its relationship with Venice. The rescue expedition involving the airship Italia is remembered here.

On leaving the main building, follow the Rio dell'Arsenale to the second section of the museum on the right.

Even though the vessels are not displayed in their full glory in this setting, the pavilions house some interesting craft: a 1932 hydrofoil used for racing, a torpedo-launch (1942), an 1890 diving vessel and the remains of the steam ship *Elettra.*

Further along the Fondamenta di Fronte is the bridge which leads into Campo dell'Arsenale, under the watchful eyes of the famous lions. Here the visitor enters an almost "traffic–free zone", where silence is conducive to pondering life's trials and tribulations. A short, peaceful walk through the *calli* and squares will eventually lead to the Church of San Francesco della Vigna (**10**, HU 67).

Through calli and campi where silence speaks of art

Proceed along the Fondamenta di Fronte into Campo San Martino. Cross the bridge at the Fondamenta Penini and turn left into Calle delle Muneghette. In Campiello Due Pozzi, take Calle del Mandolin on the left. Turn right into Calle degli Scudi which leads directly to Campo di San Francesco della Vigna.

Coming from the south is particularly interesting as the route passes between the columns of an unusual 19C portico, of a delicate pinkish brown colour, which links the Naval headquarters with the Renaissance Palazzo Gritti, otherwise known as *La Nunziatura* (the Nunciature). Originally owned by **Doge Andrea Gritti** (1523-38), it was ceded by the Republic to Pope Pius IV (1559-65), who allowed it to be used by Apostolic delegates.

★**San Francesco della Vigna** (**10**, HU) – There really were vineyards here when the Franciscans first erected a church on land donated to them by Marco Ziani, son of Doge Pietro Ziani. Construction of the current building commenced in 1534, according to plans by Sansovino (1486-1570). The main façade with its crowning pediment was designed by **Palladio** (1508-80). Being one of the highest in Venice, the campanile serves as a point of reference from the most distant corners of the city. According to the records, it echoes the bell-tower of St Mark's.

Fashioned as a Latin cross, the church has one long nave which opens out onto five side chapels.

Begin along the left side of the nave.

Note the *Four Evangelists* on the ceiling in the third chapel, an early work by **Giovanni Battista Tiepolo** (1696-1770). The fifth chapel houses a *Virgin with Child* by **Veronese** (1528-88). The north transept links up with the chapel which contains a *Madonna with Child and Saints* by **Giovanni Bellini** (1432-1516).

In the chapel to the left of the presbytery (the Giustiniani Chapel dedicated to Saint Jerome) stands a marble altar (1495-1510) carved with a *Last Judgement* by Pietro Lombardo and his pupils, as are the *Virgin and Child with Two Angels and Putti* and the *St Jerome*. On the walls are painted the New Testament Evangelists and Old Testament Prophets, whereas above is a frieze of scenes from the life of Christ.

The construction of the presbytery was commissioned by Doge Andrea Gritti (1523-38) who is buried here. At the sides stand the two majestic Gritti monuments: the composite columns are by Sansovino. Serving as a pantheon for illustrious Venetians, the church also accommodates the tomb of **Doge Marc'Antonio Trevisan** (1553-54), in front of the presbytery.

The church's most famous masterpiece is to be found in the south transept: a *Madonna and Child Enthroned*★ painted in 1450 by the monk **Antonio da Negroponte**. This archetypal late-Gothic piece recalls works by Vivarini as regards structural format, figure types and decorative detail.

Veronese's *Resurrection of Christ* is housed in the chapel of the Resurrection on the right side of the nave.

From Campo San Francesco della Vigna take Calle San Francesco and then, to the left, Calle de Te Deum. Continue south, crossing the canal for the first time to reach the Fondamenta San Giorgio degli Schiavoni. Take the next bridge and proceed towards the Scuola di San Giorgio degli Schiavoni (see SAN GIORGIO degli SCHIAVONI).

By following the Fondamenta dei Furlani southwards one reaches the **Church of San Antonin**, which was founded in the 7C and rebuilt by Baldassare Longhena (1598-1682). Salizzada San Antonin leads into **Campo Bandiera e Moro** (**9**, HX). Although the square opens up on to the back of Riva degli Schiavoni, it is a peaceful area with few tourists. The heroes of the Risorgimento, Attilio and Emilio Bandiera, were born here and remembered in the name of the square together with Domenico Moro, another patriot who was shot down with them.

★**San Giovanni in Bràgora** (**9**, HX) – The name of this church has several possible derivations: from the Greek *agorà* which means piazza, or from the dialect *bragolà* (market square) or *bragolare* (to fish). Vivaldi was baptised here in 1678.

The current building, with its obvious brick façade, was erected in the late 15C.

The interior comprises a nave with a trussed ceiling and two aisles. In the left aisle, near the font, a copy of a deed confirming the baptism of Antonio Vivaldi is displayed. Further along, note the four panel paintings on wood from the workshop of Jacobello del Fiore (first decade of the 15C). The *Madonna and Child* by Alvise Vivarini (c 1445-1505) can be found further up the same aisle.

Hanging in the chapel in the left apse is a large wooden 15C *Crucifix* whereas the central bay is dominated by the *Baptism of Christ*★★ by Cima da Conegliano (c 1459-1517), between the *Washing of the Feet* by Palma il Giovane (1544-1628) *(left wall, lower panel)* and a *Last Supper* by Paris Bordone (1500-71) *(right wall, lower panel)*.

The Resurrection★ by Alvise Vivarini (c 1445-1505) is to be found in the right aisle; to the right of the door to the sacristy by Cima da Conegliano is *St Helen and Emperor Constantine at the Side of the Cross*. A stylised, truly Gothic *Madonna and Child with St John and St Andrew*★ (1478) by Alvise's uncle, Bartolomeo Vivarini (1432-c 1491) and *St Andrew with St Martin and St Jerome*, the work of Francesco Bissolo (c 1470-1554) are further up the right aisle.

For those wishing to continue into neighbouring churches, turn to the sections on SAN GIORGIO degli SCHIAVONI, SANT'ELENA E SAN PIETRO, and SAN ZACCARIA.

CA' D'ORO ★★★

Exploring the Cannaregio district offers a variety of pleasures: it is the tranquil and poetic *sestiere* of *calli*, squares and the Ghetto quarter so typically Venetian and amazingly unfrequented by tourists. It is also the *sestiere* that boasts the station and the lively Strada Nuova.

This is where each and everyone can formulate their own impression of Venice: another Thomas Mann could be inspired to write a novel depicting the city's fading decadence, a modern playwright with the panache of Goldoni might discover a limitless source of material for a lively performance in dialect. For anybody who does not harbour literary aspirations, however, the area offers a wealth of boutiques and shops of every type and trade.

The suggested route through the area takes about half a day.

A quick drink

If the idea of an Irish pub appeals why not try the **Fiddler's Elbow** *(3847 Corte dei Pali)*, half way between the churches of Santa Sofia and San Felice, for a beer or an Irish coffee.

There are various little alleyways leading off the Strada Nuova or Nova which are home to some very old and very busy *bacari* (Venetian bars). Try the **Vedova** *(3912-3952 Ramo Ca' d'Oro)*, a stone's throw from the Fiddler's Elbow, the **Promessi Sposi** *(4367 Calle dell'Oca, near Campo SS Apostoli)* or the **Bomba** *(4297 Calle dell'Oca)*.

An unusual *osteria*, where food is served accompanied with music and poetry, is **Al Paradiso Perduto** at 2540 Fondamenta Misericordia.

★★★**Ca' d'Oro (4, ET)** – As the expression of the ultimate in Venetian Gothic domestic architecture the current appearance of this *palazzo* does not justify its name "House of Gold" which is a vestige of its history. When Marino Contarini commissioned the construction of his *domus magna* at the beginning of the 15C, the French artist Jean Charlier, known as Zuane de Franza di Sant'Aponal, painted the façade in blue, black, white and gold, hence the name given to the palazzo.

Several Lombard masters, followers of Matteo Raverti (active 1385-1436), were involved in the construction of the Ca' d'Oro and under the leadership of Giovanni (c 1360-1442) and Bartolomeo Bon (active 1441-64) the Venetian masters took over. The well-head at the centre of the courtyard is attributable to Bartolomeo Bon, the son of Giovanni. The figures represent the three theological virtues of Fortitude, Justice and Charity.

Nowadays it is the façade and its reflection in the Grand Canal which most captivates the visitor. After a long period of restoration the subdued colours have regained their magical intensity and the delicate marble tracery and crenellation are complete. Although it is harmonious in its asymmetry, there might originally have been plans for a left wing.

The original structure commissioned by the Contarini was subject to various alterations requested by numerous owners who lived there over the course of the centuries. Restoration work started in the 19C when Prince Troubetskoy bought the Ca' d'Oro as a present for the ballerina Maria Taglioni. The restoration, however, was not faithful to the original construction. At the end of the 19C more accurate restoration work was undertaken by **Baron Giorgio Franchetti** who was responsible for the implementation of the Gallery which now houses a very varied collection of painting, Renaissance bronze sculpture and medals dating from a long and fertile period spanning seven centuries from the 11C to the 18C.

Galleria Franchetti ⊙ – The first floor, where the tour starts, is dedicated to Veneto-Byzantine Art from the 11C to the 13C. Particularly notable for its luminosity and poignancy, is the central panel of the polyptych dedicated to the *Passion* by Antonio Vivarini (c 1420-84) of the Crucifixion. Another significant work is the English, 15C *Scenes from the Passion of St Catherine*.

The undoubted highlight of the Galleria Franchetti is, however, Andrea Mantegna's uncompleted **Saint Sebastian★★**, in a niche at the end of the corridor on the right. Two similar treatments of the same subject by Mantegna exist, one in the Kunsthistorisches Museum in Vienna and one in the Louvre in Paris, but this is the most dramatically tragic version. Note the *memento mori* attached to the candle stating *Nihil nisi divinum stabile est – Coetera fumus (Nothing but the divine is eternal – all the rest is smoke)* and that the candle has just been blown out by the wind which ruffles St Sebastian's hair. The surge in popularity of St Sebastian during the early

Ca' d'Oro

Renaissance is often thought to be associated with his martyrdom by multiple arrow wounds, a fate involving the similar searing pain endured by those afflicted with the plague: the other being an opportunity for a painter to depict the nude torso of the young man modelled upon Classical sculpture. The other saint invoked by the plague-stricken is the pilgrim San Rocco (or Roch – *see SAN ROCCO*) who was believed to have protected Venice from the epidemic. The saint seems to indicate where the bubonic swellings have appeared by the position of his arms.

Among the bronzes, the work of one man particularly stands out: **Pier Giacomo Bonaccolsi** (c 1460-1528), the official sculptor at the Gonzaga court at Mantua, better known for his emulation of sculptures after the Antique and thereby nicknamed l'*Antico*, embodies all the Classical ideals of Humanism (note the *Apollo* on display in one of the small showcases).

Note also the *Annunciation* which appears to be set in Venice itself and the *Death of the Virgin*, painted by **Vittorio Carpaccio** (c 1465-1526) and studio for the Scuola degli Albanesi.

The *Flagellation* by Luca Signorelli (c 1445-1523) is to be found on the same floor along with the vibrant sequence from the *Life of Lucrecia* in two paintings by Biagio d'Antonio (active to 1508). The latter depicts the departure of Sesto Tarquinio from the Roman camp at Ardea, the rape of Lucrecia, her suicide and funeral. The *Virgin with Child and St John*, a tondo by Jacopo del Sellaio (1442-93) is also on display here.

Exhibits on the floor above include the *Portrait of the Procurator Nicolò Priuli* by **Tintoretto** (1518-94); Flemish tapestries from the second half of the 16C; *Venus with a Mirror* by **Titian** (1490-1576) which is incomplete on the right-hand side; *Portrait of a Gentleman* by **Sir Anthony van Dyck** (1599-1641) and *Venus Asleep with her Lover* executed by **Paris Bordone** (1500-71). Two more specifically Venetian scenes are by **Francesco Guardi** (1712-93): *St Mark's Square* with the view of the Church of San Giorgio that was very dear to the artist and the *View of the Wharf towards the Basilica of Santa Maria della Salute*.

Of great importance despite being very damaged are the frescoes by Giorgione (1476/77-1510) and Titian for the façades of the **Fondaco dei Tedeschi**. All that remains of Giorgione's work is the *Nude*. Titian's work is still discernible in the frieze with the *Justice* and the great coat of arms.

Other interesting works include paintings by Flemish artists, notable for their exquisite depiction of domestic interiors and landscapes. The *Crucifixion* by a follower of Van Eyck (executed during the early 15C) is remarkable for its clarity and minute, topographical detail particularly with regard to the fortified city that emerges from the background. The impact of Northern painting on the Venetians was considerable. Oils, a more meticulous medium than fresco, allowed the painter to revel in richer textures, greater colour contrast and finer detailing. Space was rendered from acute observation of light and shadow rather than by calculated perspective.

The Franchetti collection of ceramics is displayed in the adjoining Palazzo Duodo.

On leaving the Galleria Franchetti one is immediately sucked into the constant coming and going of the Strada Nuova, part of the throbbing artery which starts at the Santa Lucia station and snakes through the Cannaregio sestiere. It runs almost parallel to the Grand Canal and eventually leads to the Rialto.

Coming out onto Calle di Ca' d'Oro, follow the Strada Nuova round to the left taking the Fondamenta San Felice off the campo *of the same name.*

IN SEARCH OF VENICE'S MAGNETIC MELANCHOLY

Once past the Church of San Felice which houses *St Demetrius with his Follower* by Tintoretto (1518-94), the canal follows the *fondamenta* and emerges in a corner of the city that is rarely frequented by tourists. It is so peaceful, almost sleepy here: the temporal dimension seems to gradually disappear as the hubbub of the Strada Nuova recedes. Having reached the corner where the street veers naturally to the left the **Ponte Chiodo** appears, the only bridge in Venice that has no parapet, and which is vividly portrayed in many paintings (depictions of the fist fights in the Correr Museum and the Galleria Querini Stampalia). The way eventually leads to Campo della Misericordia, dominated by the **Scuola Nuova della Misericordia**, a building designed by Sansovino in 1534 as the "new" seat of the Order and built in brick, but never completed. Further along the Fondamenta della Misericordia there is a delightful square imbued with a dreamy atmosphere of melancholy and abandon.

Campo dell'Abbazia (◪, FT) – The centre of this square, paved in brick in a herring-bone pattern, is marked by a fine well-head. Bordering on the Rio della Sensa and the Misericordia Canal, the campo is hemmed in by the **Church of Santa Maria della Misericordia** (◪, FT), otherwise known as Santa Maria Valverde after the island on which it was built in the 10C, and by the **Scuola Vecchia della Misericordia** (◪, FT). The Baroque façade of the church, the work of Clemente Moli (1651-59), contrasts sharply with the Gothic brick façade of the Scuola of 1451.

The Church of Madonna dell'Orto, via the Peloponnese – The sense of struggle that is perpetrated through Venetian art will be reinforced if this evocative corner of the Cannaregio district is further explored. Continue under the porticoes of the old abbey to the bridge over the Rio dei Muri from where one of the few active *squeri* is visible. Retracing one's steps, the Corte Vecchia which heads off to the left leads to a corner of Venice that reveals the city's most genuine nature, one that is sometimes masked by an ephemeral or unreal, contrived beauty. Here is the perfect balcony overlooking the **Sacca della Misericordia** (◪, FST), the cove that is normally so buffeted by the wind, from where the view stretches into the distance, punctuated only by the Island of San Michele, the tranquil cemetery on the water.

Alongside the Rio della Madonna dell'Orto stands a palazzo that will undoubtedly intrigue anyone exploring the Fondamenta Gasparo Contarini. The building will probably impress as much for its general harmonious impact as for its Gothic detailing, the corner column and the low-relief featuring a man pulling a camel. This is the **Palazzo Mastelli del Cammello** (◪, ES) which belonged to a family of merchants from Morea in the Peloponnese who settled in Venice in 1112. The name Mastelli was coined after the thousands of *mastelli* (buckets) of gold *zecchini* or Venetian sequins that they were meant to own.

★**Madonna dell'Orto: the Tintoretto Church** (◪, ES) – The parish church of the Tintoretto family enjoys a magnificent position overlooking a quiet square paved in brick herring-bone pattern. The richly ornamented façade, also in brick, betrays the various stages of construction and refurbishment from its foundation in the 14C, through early-Gothic and Renaissance periods. Aisle windows were inserted later, in the 1550s; among the statues in niches stand figures of the Apostles, and over the central ogee of the main door, a St Christopher by Bartolomeo Bon (known 1441-64) to whom the church was originally dedicated. Patronage was entrusted to the miracle-working Madonna dell'Orto (Our Lady of the Vegetable Patch!) almost as soon as a statue of the Madonna and Child was found in a sculptor's garden. The bell-tower culminates in a conical brick dome.

Madonna dell'Orto

The spacious hall-church interior (single nave with aisles) is full of warm light and accommodates several important works of art: along the right aisle, in the first bay is a masterpiece by Cima da Conegliano (1459-1517), **John the Baptist;** the second has an altarpiece showing *St Vincent* by Jacopo Palma il Vecchio (c 1480-1528); in the last hangs the *Martyrdom of St Lawrence* by Daniel van den Dyck (1614-63). Over the entrance to the Mauro Chapel is the *Presentation of the Virgin in the Temple* (1551) by **Tintoretto** (1518-94) whose burial place is marked by a slab in a chapel on the right. Two other large works by the master dominate the presbytery, the **Last Judgement** and the **Adoration of the Golden Calf**. The main altarpiece depicting the *Annunciation* is by Palma il Giovane (1548-1628), whereas behind in the apse vault, the figure of *Faith* by an unknown 17C artist, is flanked by Tintoretto's *Virtues* and below, two panels represent the *Beheading of St Christopher* and the *Vision of the Cross to St Peter.* Palma il Giovane's *Crucifixion* is in the chapel off the left apse.

Down the left aisle, in the Contarini Chapel, is Tintoretto's *St Agnes Raising the Roman Prefect's Son* and in the Morosini Chapel the *Nativity* by the master's son, Domenico Tintoretto (c 1560-1635). The beautiful Madonna and Child by **Giovanni Bellini** (c 1426-1516) that once stood in the Valier Chapel was tragically stolen in 1993: all that remains is a life-size photograph.

Next to the church is the **Scuola dei Mercanti (4, ES)**, the seat of the Guild of Merchants since 1570 when it transferred itself there from the Frari. Palladio participated in its renovation (1571-72) and is responsible for the portal which overlooks the fondamenta. Alas, nothing remains of the works of Tintoretto, Veronese (1528-88) and Aliense (1556-1629) since Napoleon passed through.

Campo dei Mori (4, ES) – This peaceful corner of the Cannaregio *sestiere* seems even more motionless under the watchful eyes of its curious 13C statues that seem to lean against the houses watching what goes on in the square as the centuries pass by. The square's name alludes to the Moorish or Levantine Mastelli brothers *(see above).*

The figure on the corner of the building is Sior Antonio Rioba, the Paquino of Venice, whose nose is used as an object of satire when lampooning local politicians and visiting dignitaries. Further along the Fondamenta dei Mori is a fourth statue, near which stands the house where Tintoretto died in 1594, at no 3399.

Continue along the Fondamenta della Sensa and turn right into Calle del Capitello to reach the Church of San Alvise.

Ch. Boisvieux

One of the "Moors"

★**San Alvise** (**3**, **DS**) – Like the Church of Madonna dell'Orto, the Church of St Alvis is situated in a secluded, albeit busier, square. The simple brick façade is pierced merely by a rose window and a portal under a delicate prothyrum. The statue in the lunette is of St Louis of Anjou who lived towards the end of the 13C and named Alvise by the Venetians. Antonia Venier, a Venetian noblewoman, dedicated the new church to the saint after he appeared to her in a dream in 1383.

Originally Gothic in style it was greatly modified during the 16C, when the single nave was given its rich internal decoration. The almost opulent ornamentation in stark contrast with the simple linearity of the exterior comes as a pleasant surprise.

The 17C frescoes by Antonio Torri and Pietro Ricci lend an evocative threedimensional effect to the flat ceiling. The entrance area is overlooked by the *barco*, the pensile choir stalls used by the nuns, supported by columns with 15C capitals and Gothic buttresses. Above the columns stand 15C statues of *Christ the Redeemer* and *John the Baptist.* The *barco* connects directly with the Convent of the Canossiane. The wrought-iron grills date back to the 18C. On entering note the 15C **tempera panel paintings** on the left, which were executed by a pupil of Lazzaro Bastiani (active 1449-1512). These depict the *Giant with Feet of Clay, Solomon and the Queen of Sheba, Tobias and the Angel, Rachel at the Well, The Adoration of the Golden Calf, The Revelation of Joseph, Joshua and the Fall of Jericho* and *The Poverty of Job.*

On the right wall of the church are Tiepolo's *Flagellation* and *Crown of Thorns* (1740), whereas his *Christ's Way to Calvary* (1749) is in the presbytery. The 16C wooden polychrome statue of Sant'Alvise shows the saint dressed in a Franciscan habit with a splendid crown.

TOWARDS THE STRADA NUOVA

Turn back in the direction of Campo dei Mori and head towards the Grand Canal along the Calle Larga and the Fondamenta della Misericordia; this will lead to the bridge, on the other side of which is the **Chiesa di San Marziale** (Church of St Marziale) (**4**, **ET**). The austere exterior contrasts sharply with its rich Baroque interior. The ceiling decoration is the work of Sebastiano Ricci (1659-1734).

Continue as far as Campo Santa Fosca dominated by the church of the same name and a monument to **Paolo Sarpi** (1552-1623), a Venetian monk who defended the Republic while the Senate claimed the right of autonomy in the religious courts when pontifical claims were made. In addition to his excommunication, his opposition to the Church of Rome resulted in an attempt on his life which he survived *(see Introduction – Over a thousand years of glory: Another interdict).*

Strada Nuova (**4**, **EFT**) – As if waking from a dream, the charm of the lesser-known Venice gradually fades as the visitor gets caught up in the thick of the one sort of traffic in this city. Even if the traffic is only of the pedestrian kind it varies so in pace and intensity as Venetians speed along very purposefully and tourists are necessarily and willingly distracted.

The Strada Nuova, which opened in 1871, is vibrant with the uninterrupted flow of people as visitors shuttle to and from the station and the Rialto, and locals do their shopping. The street is lined with all sorts of shops, particularly along the stretch of Rio Terrà S Leonardo near the station and around the lively market. Fish stalls run the length of the Fondamenta della Pescaria, alongside the Cannaregio Canal.

For those wishing to continue into neighbouring districts, turn to the sections on GHETTO and SAN ZANIPÒLO.

"Venice is like eating an entire box of chocolate liqueurs at one go."
Truman Capote – "Sayings of the Week", The Observer, *26 November 1961*

Il CANAL GRANDE ★★★

"Arriving in Venice by train is like entering a palazzo by the tradesman's entrance" was the considered opinion of Gustav Aschenbach, the protagonist of Death in Venice.
The Grand Canal, the main artery and the backbone of Venice, enters the city by the tradesman's entrance. Once past the headland of the Dogano da Mar, the magnificence of the Bacino di San Marco opens up with the sumptuous polychrome of the Doges' Palace and the square while beyond San Giorgio Maggiore, the brackish waters and the gulls circling above herald the open seas. All this is encompassed in the final stretch of the canal leading into the mouth of the basin which, way back in time, was most certainly a river."

Alvise Zorzi

THE MOST BEAUTIFUL STREET IN VENICE

Given the nature and the origins of Venice as it rises up out of the water and seemingly floating on an island, the Grand Canal is, in every respect, the city's high street.

The Grand Canal (3km/2mi long, 30-70km/18-44mi wide and, on average 5.5m/18ft deep) takes the form of an inverted S, with the bend marked by the Ca' Foscari. It is not the only way through the city and it is often quicker to go on foot but, with the best views of the *palazzi* and churches that overlook the Canal, it is an experience not to be missed.

From river to canal – the river-buses have been around since the year 1000 – The origins of the Grand Canal are lost in the mists of time that have drifted over the marshes through the centuries. The *traghetti* (gondolas which cross the river) have, however, provided a ferry service between the banks of the canal since the year 1000: some of the existing landing-stages have been in situ since the 13C, many either serving mills that were operated by the tides or *squeri* where the gondolas were built; then there were the workshops for the guild of wool Weavers and Clothmakers which employed the poor to card, finish, dye and press the textiles.

The finest walk takes one along the canal where the beauty of the city unfolds: façades of vibrant colours, resplendent with gilding, exude the festive spirit and optimism of the Venetians who have never known the threat of oppression, not even in the Middle Ages, when the rest of the world had to build fortresses and sombre palaces to defend themselves. The *palazzi* that flank the Grand Canal are the Venetian nobility's expression of pride and self-satisfaction: they were the only people who could vouchsafe a piece of this water garden *(see GHETTO – Palazzo Labia)*. While commercial, banking and State enterprises have been in operation along the canal since the Renaissance, churches and fine *palazzi* were being erected right up until the Republic breathed its last.

Bird's-eye view of the Grand Canal

Left Bank

Stazione di Santa Lucia (◨, CT) – The station has marked the entrance to the city since 1860 when the first station was built. The present building was erected in 1954.

Gli Scalzi (◨, CT) – This Baroque church was designed by Longhena (1598-1682), its most distinctive features being the niches in the façade holding statues, framed with paired columns *(see GHETTO)*.

Ponte degli Scalzi (◨, CT) – The original construction (1858) was undertaken by the civil engineer, Neville, who was also responsible for the first Accademia Bridge. It was rebuilt in 1934.

San Geremia (◨, CDT) – From the water all that can be seen of the Church of St Jerome is the Chapel of St Lucy which houses the remains of the Sicilian martyr.

★★**Palazzo Labia** (◨, CDT) – This elegant 18C residence on the corner of the Cannaregio Canal is slightly set back from the Grand Canal. The ground floor is rusticated, with Ionic and Corinthian pilasters on the two floors above: the large windows open out onto balconies. The eagles which protrude from under the roof refer to the heraldry of the Labia family *(see GHETTO)*.

San Marcuola (◨, DT) – This church is quite distinctive from others overlooking the Grand Canal: the roughly-bricked façade remains incomplete. Interestingly, this façade is actually the side of the church. Although its present appearance is Baroque in style, the church is altogether much older *(see GHETTO)*.

★**Palazzo Vendramin Calergi** (◪, ET) – This Renaissance palace was commissioned by the noble family of Loredan al Cordussi who worked in the city between 1502 and 1504. With composite three-arched windows, it is a magnificent synthesis of Byzantine and Gothic architectural features. From 1844, it was home to the Duchesse de Berry, the daughter-in-law of Charles X of France, who held extravagant "salons" for other exiled aristocrats. Here too, Richard Wagner lived and worked, composing the second act of *Tristan and Isolde* between 1858 and 1859. Despite dying in the Palazzo Vendramin where he had worked on *Parsifal*, his memory is enshrined in the **Sala Richard Wagner** ⊙. The building currently serves as the winter headquarters of the municipal casino, although plans are afoot to use it for a different purpose.

★★★**Ca' d'Oro** (◪, ET) – Much restoration work has recaptured the *palazzo*'s former glory; its façade, a subtle creation in the ornate Gothic style, presents a colonnade lapped by the water's edge – proof of its use as both a warehouse and a residence – and, on the upper floors, two enclosed loggias with arched windows interlaced with intersecting tracery and quatrefoils. Curiously, this decorative feature is not centred in the façade. The right section consists of a blank wall between single-arched windows. The corners are accentuated by cordons of marble *(see CA' D'ORO)*.

Fondaco dei Tedeschi (◪, FU) – This 13C *palazzo* served as the headquarters of German traders and as a warehouse for their goods. Devastated by fire (1505-08) it was rebuilt by Giorgio Spavento (active in Venice between the 15C and 16C) and by Scarpagnino (active in Venice between 1505 and 1549). The façade that overlooks the Grand Canal and, at one time, frescoed by Giorgione (1476/7-1510) and Titian (1490-1576) has a portico on the ground floor, as befitted a *fondaco* (warehouse). Nowadays the building houses the main post office *(see La FENICE)*.

★★**Ponte di Rialto** (◪, FU) – The **Rialto Bridge** is the most important crossing point between the two banks of the Grand Canal. While today's bridge is the sixth version – the original was built in 1175 – this is the first stone-built construction: the work of Antonio da Ponte, it was opened in 1591. The shops which are housed in the symmetrical arcades were originally used by moneychangers, bankers and moneylenders, in close proximity of the first Zecca (Mint – *see RIALTO*).

Palazzo Loredan (◪, EFV) – Also a *fondaco* (warehouse), this Veneto-Byzantine *palazzo* retains some original features: part of the portico and windows opening out onto the loggia, interlaced with pateras, run the length of the *piano nobile (first floor)*. Palazzo Loredan and the nearby Palazzo Farsetti now accommodate municipal offices.

Palazzo Lando Corner Spinelli (◪, EV) – This Renaissance palazzo erected in 1490 was most likely designed by Mauro Codussi. The façade in Istrian stone is heavily rusticated. The upper storeys are punctuated with typical two-light windows, and a Renaissance frieze of festoons runs below the attic windows. In many ways it resembles the Palazzo Vendramin Calergi.

Right Bank

San Simeon Piccolo (**8**, CT) – This is the first eye-catching landmark on leaving the station. Its distinctive features include a Corinthian *pronao* (front portico) up a flight of steps and a green dome. The church was designed by Scalfarotto (c 1700-64) in the tradition set by Palladio (1508-80) and Longhena (1598-1682).

Ponte degli Scalzi (**8**, CT) – Originally built in 1858, the bridge, named after the discalced (meaning unshod and pertaining to religious orders, such as the Carmelites and Franciscans, whose members wear sandals), was designed by the same civil engineer, Neville, as the first Accademia Bridge. It was rebuilt in 1934.

Fondaco dei Turchi (**8**, DT) – This Veneto-Byzantine *fondaco* dates back to the 13C, built as a private house and turned into commercial premises in 1621, although its current appearance is largely due to its extensive restoration during the second half of the 19C. With the side towers framing the façade, the portico and the floor above are laced with arches. Between 1621 and 1838 the warehouse was used by Turks, hence its name. Nowadays the building houses the Natural History Museum *(see I FRARI).*

Fondaco del Megio (**8**, DT) – The very distinctive building with its walls of roughly-hewn brick and tiny windows, dates back to the 15C. Note the lion that stands out below the ornate crenellation. The Fondaco del Megio was used as a general grain store, notably for millet *(miglio = megio* – hence the name).

San Stae (**4**, ET) – Dedicated to St Eustace, this church was completely renovated during the 17C. The elaborate Baroque façade (1709) dominated by a pedimented bay set between two roughcast wings, is attributed to Domenico Rossi (1678-1742). Its broken tympanum, crowned with statues over the entrance, is original. Inside a single nave are works by Piazzetta (1683-1754), Ricci (1659-1734) and Tiepolo (1696-1770) that forestall a shift in style towards the Rococo.

★**Ca' Pesaro** (**4**, ET) – At the death of Baldassare Longhena (1598-1682), completion of the building was assigned to Antonio Gaspari (c 1670-1730). Unusual is its diamond-pointed rustication of the ground floor and row of lion's heads. On the second and third floors, great arched windows with single columns give onto an open loggia. Today, the building is home to the Museum of Oriental Art and the International Gallery of Modern Art *(see RIALTO).*

Ca' Corner della Regina (**4**, ET) – Designed by Domenico Rossi (1678-1742), the heavily rusticated ground floor gives way to plainer upper storeys punctuated by balconies and windows framed with columns. Currently the home of the National Archives of Contemporary Art *(see RIALTO).*

Pescheria (**4**, ET) – The portico of this neo-Gothic building which dates back to the beginning of the 20C now accommodates the fish market, hence the name *(see RIALTO).*

Fabbriche Nuove (**4**, FU) – This rather plain building on the bend of the Grand Canal, was designed by **Sansovino** (1486-1570). Its rusticated ground floor at one time would have consisted of *magazzini* (small shops) and warehousing. The first floor was occupied by magistrates' courts ruling on commercial matters.

Fabbriche Vecchie (**4**, FU) – Destroyed by fire, the warehouses were rebuilt by Scarpagnino (active in Venice between 1505 and 1549). Even the "old workshops" boast their own columned portico *(see RIALTO).*

Palazzo dei Camerlenghi (**4**, FU) – This Renaissance palace situated in the lee of the bridge was designed by Guglielmo dei Grigi, known as Bergamasco (active in Venice between c 1515 and 1530 to the Camerlenghi who were government officials responsible for the State's financial affairs. The pentagonal building has large windows aligned below a frieze of festoons.

★★**Ponte di Rialto** (**4**, FU) – The **Rialto Bridge** is the most important crossing point between the two banks of the Grand Canal. While today's bridge is the sixth version – the original was built in 1175 – this is the first stone-built construction: the work of Antonio da Ponte, it was opened in 1591. The shops which are housed in the symmetrical arcades were originally used by moneychangers, bankers and moneylenders in close proximity of the first Zecca (Mint – *see RIALTO).*

Palazzo Bernardo (**4**, EV) – Gothic in style (1442), the building boasts splendid five-arched windows pointed on the first floor and quatrefoils on the second floor.

Palazzo Pisani Moretta (**7**, DV) – Also late Gothic, the Palazzo Pisani Moretta dates from the second half of the 15C. Like Palazzo Bernardo, the windows have five lights and intersecting tracery that enclose quatrefoils on the upper floors.

Palazzo Balbi (**7**, DX) – The façade of this *palazzo* which is attributed to Alessandro Vittoria (1525-c 1600) is divided into three sections. Above a rusticated ground floor, the central bay is pierced by an arrangement of three arched windows. Note the two distinctive large coats of arms and the obelisks on the roof.

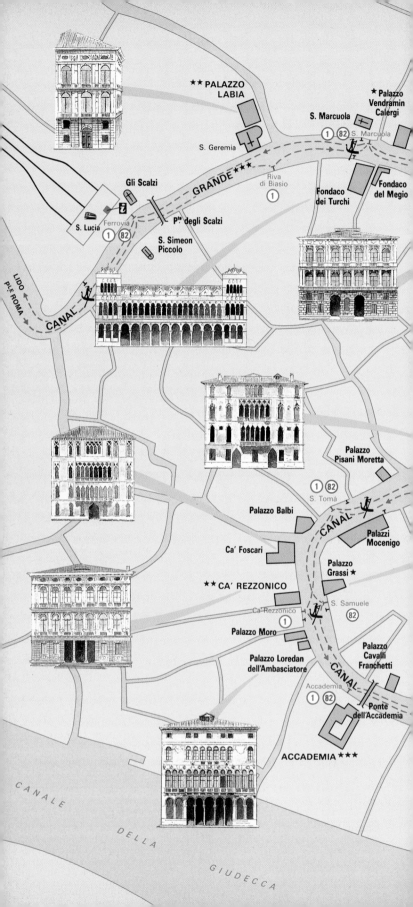

★★ **PALAZZO LABIA**

S. Geremia

S. Marcuola

★ **Palazzo Vendramin Calergi**

① ⑧② S. Marcuola

Gli Scalzi

GRANDE ★★★

Riva di Biasio

①

Fondaco dei Turchi

Fondaco del Megio

S. Lucia

Ferrovia

① ⑧②

P¹⁰ degli Scalzi

S. Simeon Piccolo

LIDO P.LE ROMA

CANAL

Palazzo Pisani Moretta

① ⑧② S. Tomà

Palazzo Balbi

CANAL

Palazzi Mocenigo

Ca' Foscari

Palazzo Grassi ★

★★ **CA' REZZONICO**

Ca' Rezzonico

①

S. Samuele

⑧②

Palazzo Moro

Palazzo Loredan dell'Ambasciatore

CANAL

Palazzo Cavalli Franchetti

Accademia

① ⑧②

Ponte dell'Accademia

ACCADEMIA ★★★

C A N A L E

D E L L A

G I U D E C C A

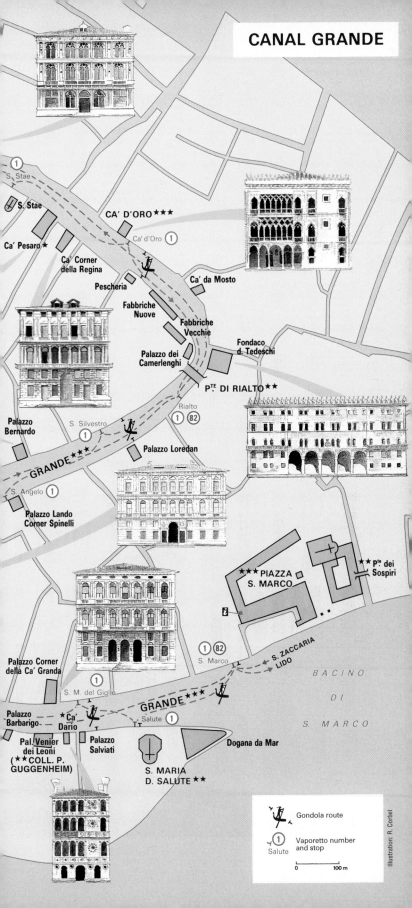

CANAL GRANDE

① S. Stae

S. Stae

Ca' Pesaro ★

Ca' Corner della Regina

Pescheria

CA' D'ORO ★★★

Ca' d'Oro ①

Ca' da Mosto

Fabbriche Nuove

Fabbriche Vecchie

Palazzo dei Camerlenghi

Fondaco d. Tedeschi

Pᵀᴱ DI RIALTO ★★

Palazzo Bernardo

S. Silvestro ①

Rialto ① ⑧²

GRANDE ★★★

S. Angelo ①

Palazzo Lando Corner Spinelli

Palazzo Loredan

★★★ PIAZZA S. MARCO

★★ Pᵀᴱ dei Sospiri

① ⑧²

S. Marco

S. ZACCARIA LIDO

Palazzo Corner della Ca' Granda

S. M. del Giglio ①

GRANDE ★★★

Salute ①

BACINO

DI

S. MARCO

Palazzo Barbarigo

★ Ca' Dario

Pal. Venier dei Leoni (★★ COLL. P. GUGGENHEIM)

Palazzo Salviati

S. MARIA D. SALUTE ★★

Dogana da Mar

Gondola route

① Salute — Vaporetto number and stop

0   100 m

Illustration: R. Corbel

Left Bank

Palazzo Mocenigo (**7**, **DX**) – This building comprises four adjacent *palazzi*. The first dates back to 1579 when it was rebuilt according to the designs of Alessandro Vittoria. The second and third buildings, which are identical, are from the end of the 16C, whereas the last, the so-called "Casa Vecchia", a Gothic construction, was remodelled by Francesco Contin during the first half of the 17C.

Previous inhabitants of this group of *palazzi* include Giordano Bruno (1548-1600) and the Romantic poet **Lord Byron** (1788-1824) who started work on his *Don Juan* here. The English "Don Giovanni" often swam home from a day at San Lazzaro *(see SAN LAZZARO degli ARMENI)*, or an evening at the Lido: a habit that instituted a swimming race that was held until 1949 and rewarded by the Byron Cup.

★**Palazzo Grassi** (**7**, **DX**) – Erected in 1749 by **Giorgio Massari** (1687-1766), possibly Venice's greatest architect in the first half of the 18C, this last Venetian palace to be built before the fall of the Republic is designed with all the majesty of neo-Classical domestic architecture at its best. Inside, the courtyard has a fine colonnade and a grand staircase frescoed by Alessandro Longhi (1733-1813) and populated with masked figures. Other rooms are frescoed by Jacopo Guarana (1720-1808) and Fabio Canal (1703-67). Today the building is used for prestigious temporary exhibitions.

Ponte dell'Accademia (**7**, **DX**) – Venice had to wait until 1854 for its second and third means of crossing the Grand Canal after the Rialto Bridge. The original iron construction, restricted in height, hindered the passage of the *vaporetti*. It was therefore replaced in 1932, this time built of wood due to lack of funds. The present bridge is a copy of its wooden predecessor *(see ACCADEMIA)*.

Palazzo Cavalli Franchetti (**7**, **DX**) – The splendid façade of this late-15C *palazzo*, complete with delicate tracery work, five-arched windows with intersecting tracery and quatrefoil motifs, casts its intricate reflection across the Grand Canal. It was rebuilt towards the end of the 19C by Camillo Boito, the brother of the musician.

Palazzo Corner della Ca'Granda (**8**, **EX**) – Nowadays this Renaissance palace is used as the police headquarters *(Prefettura)*. It was built for the nephew of Caterina Cornaro by Sansovino (1486-1570). The rusticated ground floor has a three-arch portico whereas elegantly aligned arched windows on the upper floors alternate with paired columns.

Next door, the little red house was used by Canova as his studio (1770s) and during the First World War by the novelist Gabriele d'Annunzio.

View of the left bank from Ponte dell'Accademia.
On the left, Palazzo Cavalli Franchetti.

Right Bank

Ca' Foscari (**7**, **DX**) – The glorious façade of this *palazzo* rises above the Grand Canal at the junction with the Rio Foscari. Perfect symmetry aligns the three orders of arched windows, arranged in groups that alternate with simple, single light openings and stonework. The original 14C building was rebuilt closer to the water's edge after 1550, resulting in an overall Gothic design with early Renaissance features (marble low relief above the ornate arcade of windows on the second floor). Nowadays it forms part of the University *(see I CARMINI)*.

★★Ca' Rezzonico (**7**, **DX**) – This house, commissioned by a wealthy Genoese banker, was to be the last palace to be designed by Baldassare Longhena (1598-1682) who only lived to see the completion of the first floor, before Giorgio Massari (c 1686-1766) took over. It presently contains the Museum of 18C Venice *(see I CARMINI)* and collections of Venetian finery that convey all the excitement of Carnival.
The similar architectural features articulate all three levels: engaged columns punctuate the bays of the rusticated ground level as well as the arched openings on the first and attic storeys. Note the extensive embellishment of the *piano nobile* and the fine configuration of balconies.

Palazzo Moro (**7**, **DX**) – Situated just beyond the Ca' Rezzonico vaporetto stop, beyond the gracious Palazzo Stern and its gardens overlooking the Grand Canal, this 16C *palazzo* is austere in its simplicity. It was here that the Moro family resided, one of whom suffered the tragic marriage that was to inspire Shakespeare (1564-1616) to write *Othello*, and portray the famous "Moor of Venice" as black.

Palazzo Loredan dell'Ambasciatore (**7**, **DX**) – The late-Gothic Palazzo Loredan – otherwise known as "The Ambassador's House" – has splendid arched windows with a quatrefoil design. Between the single-arched windows at the sides are two shield-bearing pages.

★★★Accademia (**7**, **DX**) – The Academy of Fine Arts has been housed in this group of buildings since the beginning of the 19C. While the former Scuola Grande della Carità is Gothic in style, its 18C façade is by Giorgio Massari and Bernardo Maccurzzi. The adjoining church, rebuilt between 1441 and 1452, most probably under the guidance of Bartolomeo Bon has been subject to considerable restoration through the ages: one such instance involved Palladio (1508-80) *(see ACCADEMIA)*.

Ponte dell'Accademia (**7**, **DX**) – Venice had to wait until 1854 for its two additional means of crossing the Grand Canal after the Rialto Bridge. The original iron construction, restricted in height, hindered the passage of the vaporetti. It was therefore replaced in 1932, this time built of wood due to lack of funds. The present bridge is a copy of its wooden predecessor *(see ACCADEMIA)*.

Palazzo Barbarigo (**8**, **EX**) – The mosaics which decorate the façade depict Charles V in Titian's studio and Henry III of France on Murano. These were installed by the glass-blower and mosaic-maker, the Compagnia Venezia e Murano, responsible for the reconstruction of the 16C palace towards the end of the 19C. It was this building that provided Henry James with inspiration for his novel about a love triangle and accompanying intrigue, *The Wings of the Dove*.

Palazzo Venier dei Leoni (**8**, **EX**) – It requires a great deal of imagination to conjure up a picture of how the palace was intended to look by its designer Lorenzo Boschetti in 1749, despite the scale model of the building in the Correr Museum. The Venier family were constrained to stop work on the building by financial problems, so what survives today is its rusticated ground floor.
The allusion to lions might stem from a story that the Venier family managed to tame a lion in the garden, or otherwise, more simply, to the lion masks along the base.
The building currently houses the Peggy Guggenheim Collection *(see La SALUTE)*.

★Ca' Dario (**8**, **EX**) – This small, late-15C *palazzo* is most distinctively embellished with polychrome marble decoration. It was built by the Lombardo family for Giovanni Dario, the Secretary to the Senate of the Republic at the Sultan's court. In recent times it has gained a sinister reputation as a result of mysterious circumstances surrounding the death of several of the buildings' owners.

Palazzo Salviati (**8**, **EX**) – Like Palazzo Barbarigo, the 19C Palazzo Salviati was owned by glassmakers who provided its fine mosaics.

★★Santa Maria della Salute (**8**, **FX**) – The massive white structure with its distinctive spiral volutes (the so-called *orecchioni* = big ears) is visible from afar. Designed by Longhena (1598-1682), it was erected upon the express wishes of the doge as a gesture of supplication to end the plague of 1630: a story recounted in the finest Italian novel by Alessandro Manzoni, *I Promessi Sposi (see La SALUTE)*.

Dogana da Mar (**8**, **FX**) – It was here on this extension of the Dorsoduro that goods used to be unloaded and duty on them levied. The present construction – dominated by a tower on which two Atlantes support the weight of the World and the figure of Fortune – dates back to the second half of the 17C *(see La SALUTE)*.

I CARMINI

This stretch of the Dorsoduro district is a lively mixture of the university life of Ca'Foscari and the daily markets which take place in the vast Campo Santa Margherita and along the Rio di San Barnaba: water-borne greengrocers sell the freshest vegetable produce – including the most delicate artichoke hearts – whatever the season. It is not difficult to find a café catering to the tastes of students and foreign tourists, or indeed a quintessentially Italian bar. There are plenty of opportunities to shop here, although the majority of outlets cater for everyday necessities, as one might expect. There is, however, the odd authentic *bottega*, particularly between San Barnaba and Campo Santa Margherita selling wood carvings and masks.

The suggested route and visits take about half a day.

Campo Santa Margherita

(7, CX) – The distinctive features of this large square are the Scuola dei Varoteri or Confraternity of Tanners, situated in the "centre" (the *campo*'s oblong layout hardly justifies the description) and the stunted campanile of the former Church of Santa Margherita. The cafés, shops and market stalls also add to the animation. Its truly populist appeal derives largely from its position alongside the Rio della Scoazzera (meaning sewage channel), now running underground, which dissuaded the nobility from building patrician *palazzi* in its vicinity.

★**Scuola Grande dei Carmini** ⊙ (7, CX) – The narrowest end of the great Campo di Santa Margherita becomes the Scuola dei Carmini (Guild of Dyers), beyond which is the square of the same name, dominated by the façade of their church.

The two façades of the Scuola have been widely

Something to take home from Dorsoduro

attributed to Longhena (1598-1682): that which overlooks the Campo di Santa Margherita comprises two tiers of paired Corinthian columns.

The guild associated with this Scuola were devotees of the Virgin of Carmelo, as borne out by the central picture on the ceiling of the Salone, *The Virgin in Glory Appearing to the Blessed Simon Stock, Consigning to him the Scapular* (a simple arrangement of two squares of white cloth tied together with strings over the shoulder – a standard part of the Order's costume).

This panel together with another eight were executed by **Giambattista Tiepolo** (1696-1770) between 1739 and 1744 – at the height of his career. Other works include those on the entrance wall by Gregorio Lazzarini (1655-1730) and opposite, by Antonio Zanchi (1621-1722).

The **Sala dell'Archivio** is decorated with 18C wall hangings. On the wall next to the entrance to the Sala dell'Albergo is Piazetta's (1683-1754) *Judith and Holofernes.* The central panel of the ceiling in the **Sala dell'Albergo**, which accommodated pilgrims and the poor, is by Padovanino (1588-1649).

Chiesa dei Carmini (⛫. CX) — Both the simple Renaissance façade of this church and its fine 14C porch, decorated with Veneto-Byzantine pateras, framing the portal on the left side are in stark contrast to the rich decoration of the interior. At first sight, the red columns dividing the three aisles, the dark colours of 17C and 18C paintings and the heavy black and gold of the statues lend a lugubrious atmosphere; however, the radiant luminosity of the

St Simon Stock (c 1165-1262)
Simon Stock was among the first Englishmen to join the Carmelite Order as it expanded into England. Born in Cambridge, he is meant to have had a vision of Our Lady bestowing the Carmelite Order with its badge. He acceeded to the Generalship in his old age (1247), during which time the Order was realigned to the values and practices of the Mendicant Friars. The name "Stock" alludes to the story that as a young hermit, Simon lived in the trunk of a tree.

internal space, the woodwork decoration typical of such 14C churches and its many paintings soften the initial impression.

The church, which is dedicated to Santa Maria del Carmelo, contains some interesting works of art:

– in the left aisle *(near the entrance)*, Padovanino's *San Liberale Saves Two Men Condemned to Death* and *St Nicholas between John the Baptist and Saint Lucy with Angels* by Lorenzo Lotto (c 1480-1556);

– the decoration of the choirstalls at the entrance to the presbytery is the work of Andrea Schiavone (c 1518-63) whereas inside, on the right wall, the *Feeding of the Five Thousand* is by Palma il Giovane (1544-1628);

– the *Presentation of Christ in the Temple* by Tintoretto (1518-94) hangs above the fourth altar along the right aisle, described by Ruskin as *"glorious... I do not know an aged head either more beautiful or more picturesque than that of the high priest";*

The Venetian Scuole
Instituted during the Middle Ages, the Venetian Scuole (literally meaning "school") were lay confraternities or guilds drawn from the merchant classes, which were active in all aspects of everyday life, be it devotional, charitable, spiritual, economic or professional, until the fall of the Republic. Patricians subscribed to the most prestigious Scuole, from which were excluded the poor, any person engaged in morally dubious activities, and women, unless they were part of a member's family. Each Scuola had its own patron saint and **Mariegola**, a rule book and constitution of the guild.
Various types of Scuole existed, such as the Scuola di San Giorgio degli Schiavoni and the Scuola degli Albanesi which were dedicated to foreign workers: it was their role to assist in the search for employment and provide financial and spiritual assistance at times of crisis. Others collected together artisans sharing a common trade, while those of a specifically religious nature were known originally as the **Scuole di Battuti** reflecting their devotional and penitential practices.
From the 15C, the Scuole were divided into *Scuole Grandi* and *Scuole Minori* as resolved by the Council of Ten. In order to qualify as a *Scuola Grande*, the guild had to be a *Scuola di Battuti*. Included among the *Scuole Grandi* were those of San Rocco, Santa Maria della Carità, San Marco, San Teodoro, San Giovanni Evangelista and the Misericordia. At the time, there were around 400 Scuole in existence: not all had permanent headquarters, but the buildings which housed the most important guilds were magnificent palaces, with their interiors decorated by famous artists.
It is precisely because of this rich artistic heritage that the Venetian Scuole are so celebrated to this day, despite the damage done to the many which were not fortunate enough to survive the sacking of the guilds and subsequent dispersal of their artistic treasures during the second French occupation (1806).
A selection of products manufactured by the various trade guilds is exhibited in the Correr Museum *(see PIAZZA SAN MARCO).*

– in the adjoining sacristy, a fine wooden ceiling complements the 14C terracotta arch and Palma il Giovane's *Annunciation;*
– the frescoes of the cupola over the third altar are by Sebastiano Ricci (1659-1734), the altarpiece in the second bay is by Cima da Conegliano (c 1459-1517) and depicts the *Adoration of the Shepherds with St Helen and St Catherine, the Young Tobias and the Angel.*
Many of these paintings were restored by funds from the American Committee to Rescue Italian Art *(see Introduction - Venice in Peril).*

Having crossed the bridge and turned immediately left, proceed to the end of the fondamenta which runs alongside the canal. The Church of San Nicolò dei Mendicoli is on the right.

San Nicolò dei Mendicoli (◖, BX) – The dedication of the church to the *Mendicoli* alludes to the beggars and down-at-heel who used to live in the area, notably the *pinzochere* (impoverished religious women) who sheltered in the portico.
The indications are that the church was founded in the 7C although this building dates for the most part from the 12C, as does the massive bell-tower. The central bay of the façade and its portico echo those of the Church of San Giacomo di Rialto *(see RIALTO).* The plain side wall is interrupted by a small 18C section faced with Istrian stone.

Interior – A single nave flanked by aisles terminates in its original 12C apse. The wooden statuary dates back to the second half of the 16C, when the iconostasis was given its present appearance. The paintings by followers of Veronese (1528-88) depict *Episodes from the Life of Christ.*
Go back along the fondamenta and cross the canal by the second bridge.

Beyond the **Church of Angelo Raffaele** (◖, BX), which contains the scintillating *Stories of Tobias and the Angel* disputedly by Gian'Antonio Guardi (1699-1760) on the parapet of the organ, Calle Nave branches off to the left towards the Church of St Sebastian.

★★San Sebastiano ◷ (◨, CX) – The white façade of the church betrays the complexity of the internal structure: columns in the lower section outline the form of the side chapels, whereas those in the upper part echo the choir stalls.
The "entrance" area is defined by the monks' choir stalls which extend across the aisles and side chapels.
The true beauty of the church, however, lies in the fabric of its rich interior decoration – Vasari described Veronese's paintings as "joyous, beautiful and well-conceived". It is well worth scanning the principle individual masterpieces before allowing time to absorb the overall effect.

Proceeding along the right side in the first side chapel hangs *St Nicholas* by Titian (c 1490-1576); in the third, is a *Crucifixion* by Veronese (1528-88); the *Tomb of Livio Podacattaro*, Bishop of Candia (Cyprus), is by Sansovino (1486-1570); opposite, next to the organ stands the bust of **Veronese** (1528-88) that marks the burial site of the master painter who so gloried in the beauty of the world and celebrated it with depictions of luxurious brocades of silk and velvet, buxom women in flesh and stone, surrounded by gold, glass and silver. On the left side, away from the main altar, is the Grimani Chapel that shelters the bust of Marc-Antonio Grimani carved by Alessandro Vittoria (1525-1608). The altarpiece in the last chapel, *Christ at Emmaus,* is by Andrea Schiavone (c 1518-63).

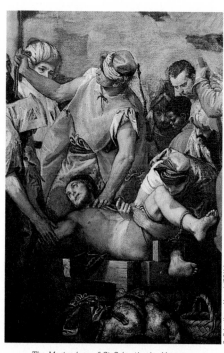

The Martyrdom of St Sebastian by Veronese
(San Sebastiano)

S. Sebastiano, Venezia/SCALA

A. Zane/MICHELIN

The water-borne vegetable stalls or *verduriere*

It is the opulent quality of Veronese's art that renders the Church of St Sebastian unique; it was with this cycle of frescoes that the painter was particularly preoccupied for the most significant part of his life. His friend and colleague, a monk with whom he shared the commission, left Veronese complete freedom of composition and expression: a free reign that was to result in a "misunderstanding" with the Inquisition *(see ACCADEMIA – Gallerie dell'Accademia: Room X)*. Veronese started with a *Coronation of the Virgin* on the ceiling in the sacristy, to include *Four Evangelists (side panels)*. Colour – notably red and blue – is used to associate the figure of Mary with the Christ-child, whereas God the Father, robed in greeny blue, remains a detached presence.

The ceiling is painted with *trompe-l'œil* architectural elements that complement the structural members and exaggerate the internal space to accommodate *Esther Crowned by Ahasuerus (centre)*, the *Triumph of Mordecai* and the *Rejection of the Vasti (in the ovals at the sides)*.

Looking down towards the altar, note the *Annunciation* on the sides of the main arch. Painted figures of *Sibyls* and *Prophets* nestle in niches between spiral columns as pendants to "real" sculptures by Girolamo Campagna (c 1550-1626). The depiction of the Sibyls, which extends down the side walls, is particularly significant as an allegory of the prophetic endorsement by Salvation of work completed by pagans. Prophets appear on the counter-façade among eight Apostles in the side chapels.

St Sebastian (San Sebastiano) recurs as the subject of many of the frescoes in this church: above Podacattaro's tomb and behind the statue *(right)* St Sebastian is shown pierced by arrows from archers on the wall opposite (frescoes may be seen from the *barco* ("nun's choir") ⊙ a depiction of *St Sebastian before Diocletian*, the saint wounded by an arrow, is watched by two people on the balcony as he reproaches the persecutor of the Christians. Opposite, the *Martyrdom of St Sebastian* seems to be theatrically enacted between four columns.

Other works include the *Presentation of Christ at the Temple* on the doors of the organ *(visible when the doors are closed)* – note the *trompe-l'œil* figure of a woman appearing from between two columns – one real and one mock. When the doors are open they depict the *Probatico Piscina* or *Pool of Bethesda*.

The principal altarpiece features the *Madonna in Glory* accompanied by Saints Rocco, Sebastian, Peter, Francis, Catherine and Elizabeth. In the presbytery are two more works by Veronese: the *Martyrdom of St Sebastian (right wall)* and *Saints Mark and Marcellian* (3C Roman martyrs whose lives are recounted in the 5C Acts of St Sebastian: twin brothers, they were charged during the persecutions of Diocletian and given 30 days' stay of execution. Ignoring the entreaties of friends and family, they were encouraged to uphold their faith by Sebastian, then an army officer. *Left wall*).

The long *calle* which links the churches dedicated to San Sebastiano and San Barnaba boasts few monuments or important sights but remains a particularly genuine part of Venice, lined with friendly eating places, paint shops displaying vast arrays of vibrantly coloured pigments, a delightful model-maker's shop selling intricate miniatures...

Campo San Barnaba (**7**, **CX**) – The buzz of this square is maintained by a flow of tourists and determined Venetians alike. It is confined by the simple white façade of the titular church, small shops, a bar and, above all, the food stalls along the Rio di San Barnaba near the Ponte dei Pugni.

Cross the canal, either by the Ponte dei Pugni or another bridge immediately to the left of the façade of the church, and continue towards the Grand Canal; the Ca' Rezzonico is on the way.

The Ponte dei Pugni

Since Renaissance times, the Venetians have been passionate about gamesmanship; participants of such sport, however, competed with such intense earnest, even violence, that the authorities were obliged to suspend such tournaments, constituting as they did for the most part, of a "war" to be settled on "battlefields". Confrontations of rival factions were held on bridges, as combatants fought with sticks or fists – hence the name Ponte dei "Pugni" (punches) or "della Guerra" (battle).

As the imprints on the bridge reveal, this bridge, around the corner from Campo San Barnaba, was one such battleground between the hostile *contrade* (clans), the Nicolotti and the Castellani.

★★**Ca' Rezzonico** (**7**, **DX**) –

The last *palazzo* to be designed by **Baldassare Longhena** (1598-1682), was in fact completed by **Giorgio Massari** (c 1686-1766). It is markedly the product of two very distinctive masters, who, despite their differences of opinion, worked towards the same ends. Whereas Henry James (1843-1916) considered the Ca' Rezzonico to be such a majestic piece of architecture as to be almost mythological, Ruskin (1819-1900), who detested the Baroque style, likened the pilasters to *"piles of cheeses"*. Originally commissioned for the Bon family, ownership was transferred incomplete, to a family from Lake Como; one progeny of which was to become Pope Clement XIII (1758).

Ca' Rezzonico was once owned by **Robert Browning** (1812-89) and his wife, the poet Elizabeth Barrett (1806-61) before passing to their son Pen (1849-1913), whose real name was Robert: the nickname Pen was coined as an abbreviation of *penini* which in Venetian dialect means small feet. Robert Browning junior was forced to sell the *palazzo* in 1906 when his divorce obliged him to return a large dowry.

Ca' Rezzonico now houses the Museum of 18C Venice.

Museo del Settecento Veneziano ⊘ – *(Presently undergoing restoration and reorganisation: details given here refer to arrangements before the museum was closed for works).* The tour of the museum starts at the top of an enormous staircase – designed as with the other state rooms on the *piano nobile* to impress guests and play host to elaborate carnival fancy-dress parties – in the **Salone da Ballo** (ballroom), dominated by the great coat of arms of the Rezzonico family and frescoed by the master of *trompe l'œil*, **Giambattista Crosato** (c 1685-1758). On the ceiling, *Apollo's Chariot* is flanked by the *Four Parts of the World*. Early-18C Venetian pieces include the ebony figurines and the delicate chairs that once belonged to the Venier family and which have painstakingly been recovered over the years.

The ceiling of the **Sala dell'Allegoria Nuziale** was frescoed by Tiepolo in 1757 for the society wedding of Ludovico, one of the members of the Rezzonico family, to Faustina Savorgan, the daughter of one of the oldest Venetian families.

Housed in the **Sala dei Pastelli** (Pastel Room) are portraits by Rosalba Carriera (1675-1757) – *Faustina Bordoni, Suor Maria Caterina, Gentleman in red*, and that of *Cecilia Guardi Tiepolo*, the wife of Giambattista and mother of the artist Lorenzo Tiepolo (1736-76). The furniture is Rococo, delicate, ornamentally fanciful and over-decorative.

The **Sala degli Arazzi** (Tapestry Room) is hung with three Flemish tapestries from the end of the 17C that tell the story of Solomon and the Queen of Sheba. The furniture here is also Rococo. The frescoed ceiling from c 1756 is by Jacopo Guarana (1720-1808): it depicts the *Triumph of the Virtues*. Note the yellow lacquer door with Chinoiserie decoration – which was very fashionable at the time.

The **Sala del Trono** (Throne Room) derives its name from the majestic golden throne adorned with nymphs, sea horses and *putti* that was used by Pope Pius VI on his visit to Venice in 1782. It is worth noticing Bernardino Castelli's particularly impressive portrait of *Pietro Barbarigo* (c 1780) set in its grandiose frame decorated with allegorical figures. The ceiling panel depicting *Merit* (crowned with laurel and attended by Nobility and Virtue) *Ascending to the Temple of Glory* was painted by Tiepolo (1696-1770).

Continue into the **portego**, the corridor that runs perpendicular to the façade of the *palazzo*, where a golden sedan chair covered in red silk is kept. The marble busts are from the 18C. The doorway onto the stairs, surmounted by the Rezzonico coat of arms, is ornamented with two sculptures by Alessandro Vittoria (1525-1608).

In the **Sala del Tiepolo** (Tiepolo Room) the ceiling depicts *Virtue and Nobility Bringing Down Perfidy*. The four *Heads* on either side of the chimney are attributed to Giandomenico (1727-1804) and Lorenzo Tiepolo. Other notable works hung here include the *Portrait of the Architect Bartolomeo Ferracina* by Alessandro Longhi (1733-1813) *(opposite wall)*. The *bureau-trumeau* in walnut is from the 18C; the games' table with carved legs dates back to the end of the 17C or early 18C; the 17C cabinet was used as a strongbox in the 18C.

Return to the portego for access to the second floor.

Upstairs in the *portego* are two topographical works by **Canaletto** (1697-1768) - *View of the Canal* and *View of the Grand Canal from Ca' Balbi to the Rialto Bridge;* the *Portrait of Marshal von Schulenburg* is by Gian' Antonio Guardi (1699-1760); *Alexander with the Dying Darius* is by Giambattista Piazzetta (1638-1754) and *Muzio Scevola with Porsenna* by Gian Antonio Pellegrini (1675-1741). Other works include the *Meeting of the Diplomats* by Francesco Guardi (1712-93) and the *Portrait of the Patriarch of Venice – Federico Corner* by Bernardo Strozzi (1581-1644).

Giandomenico's frescoes from the Tiepolo Villa at Zianigo, near Mirano, are now housed in a room at the end of the *portego*, on the right. It is worth pausing in the **Sala del Mondo Novo** (New World Room) where frescoes depict a crowd of peasants who, with their shoulders turned, are intent on watching the low house on which images of distant towns that they will never see are projected – the effect would have been achieved by means of a cosmorama (an effect used to enlarge or enhance panoramic images) or a diorama (a scene produced by the rearrangement of lighting effects in large paintings whereby the spectator appears to find himself within the picture plane). In the **Stanza di Pulcinella** (Pulcinella Room) the Neapolitan mask represents the reality of Venice's social position at the twilight of the Republic. The **Stanze dei Centauri e dei Satiri** (Centaur and Satyr Rooms) contain frescoes illustrating historical and mythological subjects.

Beyond the reconstructed villa is the **Sala del Clavicembalo** accommodating the early 18C instrument which gives the room its name. Works on display in the small corridor include *Pope Clement XIII Rezzonico Enthroned* by Pietro Longhi (1702-85), *View of Castel Cogolo* by Francesco Guardi (1712-39) – in poor condition, *a Pastoral Scene* by Francesco Zuccarelli (1702-88), *Teaching the Art of the Coroneri* (the *coroneri* being makers of crowns, rosaries and buttons) by Francesco Guardi and the *Tooth Drawer* by Pietro Longhi.

The **Sala del Parlatorio** (Parlour Room) contains paintings by Pietro Longhi and two well-known pieces by Francesco Guardi: the *Parlour of the Nuns of San Zaccaria* and a miniature of *Palazzo Dandolo to San Moisé.*

Access to the Sala del Longhi (Longhi Room) is back through the portego.

Twenty-nine paintings by **Pietro Longhi** (1702-85) from different periods of his life illustrate changes in the artist's style: note particularly his *Portrait of Francesco Guardi*. Longhi has been compared with the English-born William Hogarth as a social commentator of his own times, although the depictions of quiet Venetian patrician domesticity are more benign, lacking the wit and satirical bite of paintings by his English counterpart.

The son of this prolific artist Alessandro Longhi (1733-1813) was a successful Society portraitist. He published a book on contemporary Venetian painters (1762) which provides useful biographical details and comment.

The ceiling panel of *Zephyr and Flora* is by Tiepolo.

Chinoiserie predominates the **Sala delle Lacche Verdi** (Green Lacquer Room).

The *Triumph of Diana* on the ceiling is by Gian Antonio Guardi.

Note the evocative painting *Frozen Lagoon* (1788) by a follower of Francesco Battaglia.

Morning Hot Chocolate by Pietro Longhi (Ca' Rezzonico)

Ca' Rezzonico, Venezia/SCALA

The three frescoes in the **Sala del Guardi** (Guardi Room) are by **Giovanni Antonio**: *Venus and Love*, *Apollo* and *Minerva*. Little biographical detail exists about the Guardi brothers, Francesco (1712-93) and Giovanni Antonio (1699-1760), other than the fact that they relied on the tourist market for most of their trade. Francesco, the *veduta* painter uses paint freely to capture sparkling light in his topographical landscapes (a quality to be later admired by the Impressionists), whereas the elder brother animated his scenes with figures in a way that was to affect 18C British watercolour painting (Sandby, Girtin, Turner, Prout, Varley).

The **Alcova** (Alcove) is a reconstruction of a bedroom and boudoir; the pastel *Madonna* is by Rosalba Carriera. The 17C silver toilette service is the work of Augsburg silversmiths. Giandomenico Tiepolo is responsible for the ceiling of the wardrobe while the stucco decoration and the frescoes in the boudoir are by Jacopo Guarana.

Access to the third floor is via the portego.

The **Sala dei Dipinti** (Paintings Room) has two ovals by Tiepolo: *St Martin* and *San Biagio*. Other notable works include *Rebecca at the Well* by Gregorio Lazzarini (1655-1730), the *Portrait of Giambattista Piazzetta* by Alessandro Longhi and the *Architectural Caprice* which could be a signed copy of a painting by Canaletto from 1765.

The **Sala della "Sagra di Santa Maria"** (Festival Room) is dedicated to the Giudecca Canal Festival held on 29 July and the following Mondays in August, and includes a portrayal of the celebrations by **Gaspare Diziani** (1689-1767). Other paintings are by Pietro Longhi and his school: particularly famous is the *Dinner in the Nani Household*, a vibrant depiction of the banquet which was held on the Giudecca on 9 September 1755 in honour of the Elector Archbishop of Sassonia.

The tour of 18C Venice concludes with a reconstruction of the **"Ai Do San Marchi"** pharmacy, and a puppet theatre alongside Alessandro Longhi's *Portrait of Carlo Goldoni*.

Retrace the way back along the Fondamenta Rezzonico and turn right into Calle delle Botteghe. Take Calle della Malvasia on the right and then Calle del Cappeller on the left. Follow as far as Ca' Foscari.

Ca' Foscari (**7**, **DX**) – A famous example of the Gothic style, Ca' Foscari was built in 1452 for Doge Francesco Foscari. Today, it accommodates the headquarters of the University of Venice. The approach from Calle Foscari is not ideal as the view of the *palazzo* is restricted by the crenellated wall which surrounds the courtyard. Bustling with student activity, the Ca' Foscari is best seen from the Grand Canal, which in turn may be glimpsed from the *salone* on the ground floor *(see Il CANAL GRANDE)*.

For those wishing to continue into neighbouring districts, turn to the sections on ACCADEMIA and SAN ROCCO.

The length of time given in this guide
– for touring allows time to enjoy the views and the scenery;
– for sightseeing is the average time required for a visit.

La FENICE★

(**8** EX)
Vaporetto: S Marco, S Maria del Giglio, S Samuele, S Angelo or Rialto.

On 29 January 1996 La Fenice burnt down, succumbing to the same fate that befell it in 1836. Nonetheless, this chapter is dedicated to the theatre, which it is hoped will live up to her name as she did in the 18C (*Fenice* is the Italian for phoenix). Walking through the area in the loop of the Grand Canal takes in a very lively part of Venice. This area is known as the "seven *campi* between the bridges": a reference to the Campi di San Bartolomeo, San Salvador, San Luca, Manin, Sant'Angelo, Santo Stefano e San Vidal situated between the Rialto and Accademia Bridges. There are also plenty of shops in this district: bookshops in the Campo San Luca, bookbinders and mask shops between Campo Manin and Campo Sant'Angelo. The route between St Mark's and Campo Santo Stefano boasts many elegant shops and hotels around the Church of San Moisè which gradually give way to art, glass and bookbinding workshops.

The suggested route and tour takes about 2hr.

La Fenice interior – as it was

★**Gran Teatro La Fenice** (🎫, EX) – The opera-house and music-theatre, situated in a secluded and picturesque little square, was inaugurated in 1792 after its predecessor (1673) burnt down in 1774. Construction was initiated by **Giannantonio Selva** (1751-1819), a friend of Canova, who was awarded the commission by winning a competition. Almost completely destroyed by fire in 1836, it was rebuilt and renamed La Fenice (The Phoenix) in honour of its emergence from the ashes. Neo-Classical in style, La Fenice had two façades and two entrances, including one overlooking the canal. It is not difficult to imagine the difficulties posed by the spatial requirements of the auditorium which was much bigger than the apparently narrow façade, a problem overcome by means of an ingenious series of stairways. This "jewel box of a theatre" (Isaac Sterne) burnt down on 29 January 1996 when closed for restoration. Damage was exacerbated by the fact that fire services were unable to reach the scene along normal routes as several neighbouring canals had been drained for cleaning. Special funds were set up by the Venice in Peril Fund and the American Save Venice Committee *(see Introduction)*.

Campo San Fantin (🎫, EX) – Also situated in Campo San Fantin are the **Chiesa** and **Scuola di San Fantin** (🎫, EX).
The Renaissance church was begun by Scarpagnino (active in Venice between 1505 and 1549) and completed by Sansovino (1486-70). Inside, there are two works by Palma il Giovane (1544-1628): the *Doge Alvise Mocenigo Thanks the Virgin for the Lepanto Victory (left wall of the presbytery)* and the *Christ's Entombment (right aisle)*.

If you need to make a telephone call...

There are several telephones on the corner of Campo San Luca and in Campo San Bartolomeo *(see RIALTO)*.

Snatching a glass of wine

At a stone's throw from Campo Manin is the *enoteca* (wine shop) **Al Volto** *(4081 Calle Cavalli)* which serves a fine selection of wines.

Traditional stationery

The famous marbled paper can be bought in **Alberto Valese's** *(3135 salizada San Samuele, 3471 Santo Stefano, 1920 Calle della Fenice)*, as can ranges of wrapping and writing paper, elegant old-fashioned glass pens that come with a variety of pen-nibs, coloured inks and sealing wax. In fact, there is everything a graphomaniac could want in the shops in Calle della Mandola, between Campo Manin and Campo Sant'Angelo, and Calle del Piovan, between Campo San Maurizio and Campo Santo Stefano. Meanwhile, the **Legatoria Piazzesi** in Campiello della Feltrina, between Santa Maria del Giglio and San Maurizio, stocks beautiful cards printed using old-fashioned Venetian methods.

The Scuola belonged to the Guild of San Girolamo for *picai* (hangmen) whose rather sinister function was to escort those condemned to the gallows to the site of their execution and to oversee their subsequent burial. The front (c 1580) was designed by Alessandro Vittoria. Today, the building accommodates the **Ateneo Veneto** ⊘ (**❽**, **EX**). The Aula Magna on the ground floor has a fine wooden panelled ceiling decorated by Palma il Giovane; the Aula Tommaseo houses works by Antonio Zanchi (1631-1722) *(ceiling and, on entering, the right wall)* and by Francesco Fontebasso (1709-69) *(opposite)*. The Sala di Lettura (Reading Room) is decorated by Veronese (1528-88). From Campo San Fantin it is an easy walk to the Napoleon Wing of the Procuratie building in St Mark's Square, an area rendered all the more *chic* by the presence of prestigious hotels and boutiques.

Follow Calle delle Veste off Campo San Fantin to Calle Larga XXII Marzo which is closed off on the left by the sumptuous façade of the Church of San Moisé – in the other direction, Calle del Fruttarol leads to a bridge with a view of the *palazzo* on the canal where **Mozart** stayed during the Carnival in 1771, as marked by a commemorative wall-plaque.

San Moisé (**❽**, **FX**) – Undoubtedly, the most striking feature of the church is its façade: built by Longhena's pupil **Alessandro Tremignon** in the 17C with the help of the Flemish artist Meyring, a disciple of Bernini, it is the epitome of excess. Ruskin regarded the Church of San Moisé as *"Notable as one of the basest examples of the basest school of the Renaissance"* and coupled with Santa Maria Zobenigo as *"among the most remarkable in Venice for their manifestation of insolent atheism"*. The slating comments not only sum up Ruskin's disdain for Baroque architecture but also for the lack of religious iconography in the design of these churches used as vehicles to celebrate the vain-glory egos of the commissioning patrons.

Divided into three sections both horizontally and vertically, every sort of adornment has been lavished on the front. The lower tier is designed as a triumphal arch dominated by three memorials to members of the Fini family who died in 1660, 1685 and 1726.

The interior is also Baroque, its sense of dramatic gesture is conveyed in Tintoretto's *Christ Washing his Disciples' Feet* in the chapel to the left of the high altar.

At the other end of Calle Larga XXII Marzo is **Campo Santa Maria Zobenigo** situated in front of the church of the same name. The magnificent façade by Giuseppe Sardi (1621/30-99) is reminiscent of the façade of the Church of San Moisé in style and eulogy *(see above)*: in this case, the dedication is to a naval captain, Antonio Barbaro, who despite being dismissed by Francesco Morosini for ineptitude is here represented attended by Honour, Virtue, Fame and Wisdom. Its incompleted 18C bell-tower remains a sort of box covered with a small roof.

Inside hangs Tintoretto's *Four Evangelists (behind the high altar, under the organ)*.

Continue straight on for Campo San Maurizio and Campo Santo Stefano.

Campo San Maurizio (**❽**, **EX**) – The peace of this square is sometimes broken by a busy antiques market. To the right of the church is a view of the campanile of Santo Stefano. The former **Scuola degli Albanesi** *(see I CARMINI: The Venetian Scuole)* is on the left with its Renaissance reliefs. Previous residents of the *palazzo* opposite include the novelist Alessandro Manzoni (1785-1873) and Giorgio Baffo (1694-1768) who wrote salacious poetry in Venetian dialect.

Campo Santo Stefano (**❽**, **EX**) – This is perhaps one of the most elegant squares in the city. Dominated by a church in which concerts are regularly given, this lively meeting place is further animated by a news stand and *gelaterie* (ice-cream shops). Bustlingly busy during the day as people make their way between the Accademia Bridge and Calle dello Spezièr, it provides the perfect venue for an early evening stroll or *passeggiata* when it takes on a magical air, caught in silence, yet populated by the lights of the *palazzi* and a purplish hue from the streetlamps. Towering over the square is a monument (1882) to **Niccolò Tommaseo**.

The *palazzo* which in certain respects overshadows the square is the **Palazzo Loredan** (**❽**, **EV**), now home to the Venetian Institute of Science, Arts and Letters and its prestigious library. In 1536 the Loredan family commissioned Scarpagnino (active in Venice between 1505 and 1549) to rebuild the palace recently acquired from the Mocenigo family. Note its Palladian northern façade.

Straight ahead is the **Palazzo Pisani** (**❽**, **EX**), one of the largest private palaces in the city, on the square of the same name. Having been acquired by a noble family between the 17C and 18C, Girolamo Frigimelica (1653-1732) was commissioned to remodel the building. The *palazzo* is now the home of the **Benedetto Marcello Music Conservatory**.

Palazzo Morosini (**❽**, **EX**) which dates back to the 14C, was restored at the end of the 17C by Antonio Gaspari (c 1670-1730). Former residents include Francesco Morosini, Doge between 1688 and 1694. The *palazzo* is now the home of the New Consortium of Venice.

★Santo Stefano (**8**, EX) – Only one side of the Church of St Stephen faces on to the square of the same name, allowing its fine brick frontage to go almost unnoticed, giving as it does onto a constrictingly narrow alleyway. Clearly Gothic in style, the church comprises a central vaulted nave flanked by lower side

Niccolò Tommaseo (1802-74)

This man of letters, born in Sebenico, dedicated himself to studying language and linguistics – producing a dictionary of synonyms and a dictionary of the Italian language – before writing his masterpiece *Faith and Beauty*.

Involved in the Risorgimento movement in Venice, he left the city when the Austrians were reinstated.

bays. The 15C portal is by Bartolomeo Bon (known 1441-64); note the particularly attractive suggestion of movement in the acanthus leaves. The elegant sculptures are crowned by the figures of God blessing an angel. The pinnacles down the side, lancet windows and rose all contribute to the poise of the Gothic whole.

Construction of St Stephen's and the adjacent convent was initiated in the latter half of the 13C; the church, however, was modified and embellished in the 15C.

The campanile (60m/196ft 10in high) is one of the most famous in Venice. It is constructed in brick with a cornice in Istrian stone leading up to an octagonal spire. Like other bell-towers in the city, it boasts its own story: building on the 15C lower section was resumed in 1544; when it collapsed in 1585, it was the new masonry that crumbled, hit by lightning so violent that the bells melted. Further damage incurred by subsidence between the 17C and 18C has left the tower leaning at an angle like all the others.

OSVALDO BÖHM

The vaulted ceiling of Santo Stefano

The nave rises high above the aisles, vaulted by a fine wooden ceiling, shaped like an inverted ship's hull that was actually crafted by shipbuilders. Geometric designs relieve the red brick walls.

Like so many other churches in Venice, St Stephen's is a pantheon to the glory of the city: before the first altar of the left aisle is the tomb of **Giovanni Gabrieli** *(see Introduction: Composers in Venice)*, while the tomb of **Francesco Morosini**, the Peloponnesian, is in the central aisle. Baldassare Longhena's monument to the seafaring Captain Bartolomeo d'Alviano is at the far end of the left aisle, above the door.

In accordance with Gothic architectural planning, the wooden choir stalls would originally have been in front of the presbytery – as those surviving in the Frari Church *(see I FRARI)*; they were moved behind the main altar at the beginning of the 17C.

The high altar is by Gerolamo Campagna (c 1550-1626). In the sacristy *(at the end of the right aisle)* hang three works by Tintoretto (1518-94): the *Last Supper*, in which the dog and the cat allude to the dispute raging between the Catholic and Protestant Churches over belief in the mystery of the Eucharist and the two women on the left represent the Synagogue and the Church; *Christ washing his Disciples' feet*, *The Agony in the Garden* and *The Resurrection*. There are also some fragments from the polyptych by Bartolomeo Vivarini (c 1432-1491), a *Crucifixion* by Paolo Veneziano (active c 1320-62) along with a rendition of the *Holy Family* by Bonifacio de' Pitati (c 1487-1553).

Note in passing on the way to the Accademia the elegant **Palazzo Cavalli Franchetti** (■, **EX**), in Campo San Vidal *(see II CANAL GRANDE)*. The palace, originally Gothic in style, was restored during the second half of the 19C.

Campo Sant'Angelo (■, **EX**) – By day, one might pass through this rather austere square en route between St Mark's and the Accademia, without giving it a second glance: at night, however, the *palazzi* overlooking the canal turn the square into a veritable stage set.

The **Oratorio dell'Annunciata** (Oratory of the Annunziata) has replaced the church that gave the square its name, formerly associated to the Scuola dei Zoti, the guild for disabled sailors. Note the plaque on the wall of **Palazzo Duodo** commemorating the composer Domenico Cimarosa (1749-1801) who died there.

The Gothic portal on the bridge leads into the cloister of St Stephen (now the headquarters of the Regional Accountancy Board). Contemporary with the building of the church and the other cloister by the apse, this section was destroyed by fire and rebuilt during the Renaissance, possibly by Scarpagnino (active in Venice 1505-49) and frescoed by Pordenone (c 1484-1539).

Rio Terrà della Mandola branches left off Calle dello Spezièr and leads to the Palazzo Fortuny.

Palazzo Fortuny (■, **EV**) – Dating back to the 15C, the building's distinctive features include the two fine mullioned windows with five arches. The Palazzo Pesaro degli Orfei was acquired by the painter, photographer and textile designer, **Mariano Fortuny y Madrazo** (1871-1949) in 1899. The former music school is now a **museum** Ⓢ of the artist's work.

Campo Sant'Angelo

The Magician of Venice

Born in Granada, the ancient Moorish capital of Spain, into an illustrious family of Spanish artists, **Mariano Fortuny** lost his father to malaria at the age of three and grew up in Paris. Funnily enough it was Mariano's allergy to horses that prompted his mother to abandon Paris society in favour of Venice (1889). Here the young man immersed himself in studying art and experimented with photography. He visited Bayreuth and became captivated by the powerful music and imagery of Richard **Wagner**'s *Parsifal*. On his return to Venice, Fortuny explored the expressionist potential of the applied arts, experimenting with designs for theatre interiors, electric lighting, costumes and stage sets. He began manufacturing his own dyes, built his own printing-press, and created the **Delphos** dress.

In fashion design, his most lasting legacy, Fortuny combined the purest Classical forms of early Hellenist sculpture with the rich colours and textures of Carpaccio: this immediately appealed to the Symbolists, notably Klimt, but it is perhaps the poet **Gabriele d'Annunzio** who best transposes the magic into words: *"She was wrapped in one of those very long scarves of Oriental gauze that the alchemist dyer Mariano Fortuny steeps in the mysterious recesses of his vats, which are stirred with a wooden spear, now a sylph, now a hobgoblin and he draws them out coloured with strange, dreamlike shades, and then he prints on them with a thousand blows of his burnishing tool new generations of stars, plants and animals.* (From *Forse che si, Forse che no.*)

The *calle* that leads from Campo Sant'Angelo to Campo Manin is always busy with people coming and going, albeit willingly distracted by the many shops along the way. Particularly striking are the bookbinders' window displays.

The bridge over the Rio di San Luca leads into the modern Campo Manin.

Campo Manin (◧, EV) – Few features distinguish this square other than the monument to Daniele **Manin** (1875), the shops down along one side and the **Cassa di Risparmio di Venezia**, designed by Pierluigi Nervi and Angelo Scattolin which provides an idea of modern Venetian architecture.

Pierluigi Nervi (1891-1979) trained as a civil engineer, and collaborated on the construction of the UNESCO building in Paris, the "Pirellone" in Milan and the Olympic stadium in Rome. He was also responsible for the Exhibition Centre in Turin and the Sala Nervi where audiences are held in the Vatican Palace.

To reach the peaceful square that houses the Palazzo Contarini del Bovolo, take the calle to the left of the stationers and turn right after the bend.

The Renaissance Palazzo

Based upon Roman originals, the Italian *palazzo* was designed to fulfil commercial and residential demands. Arranged around a central courtyard, it most often comprises three storeys. The ground floor was used for storage or shops *(magazzini)* that opened out onto the street; to emphasise an impression of strength and permanence, this level tends to be heavily rusticated, its masonry worked to look rough-hewn. The first floor, or *piano nobile* was used by the occupying family as living quarters: externally lighter in texture, the interior had high ceilings and large windows providing ample light and ventilation. The top storey below the roof and much lower in proportion, served as quarters for servants and children.

★Scala del Bovolo ⊘ (◧, EFX) – The **Bovolo Staircase** is all the more impressive situated as it is off a tiny, peaceful courtyard overlooked by private houses. The delicate spiral staircase (*bovolo* in Venetian dialect) which seems to concord with a composite style drawn from both Gothic and Renaissance styles, is attributed to Giovanni Candi who died in 1506. Encased in a tower the staircase provides access to the *palazzo*'s loggias.

From the top extends a lovely, yet disorientating, **view★★** over the Venetian rooftops: churches may be identified by their bell-towers although the height and the distance may tax the most discerning topographer.

To get to Campo San Luca pass either to the left or to the right of the Cassa di Risparmio; to reach the church of the same name continue along the Salizzada.

Campo San Luca (8, FV) – This lively *campo* is one of the most popular meeting places in Venice. There is everything here: cafés, well-known stores, bookshops, telephones, travel agencies, fast food outlets and a host of shops in the immediate vicinity.

The **Church of St Luke** (San Luca) contains the *Virgin in Glory Appearing to St Luke While Writing the Gospel* by Veronese (1528-88).

When the floor was repaved at the beginning of the 20C the gravestones of those buried there, including the writer Aretino, were not relaid.

Further along Calle del Teatro is the **Goldoni Theatre** (8, FV). The reflection of the campanile of St Mark's in the canal can be seen from the bridge.

San Salvador (8, FV) – The 7C Church of San Salvador would have been consecrated by Pope Alexander III during his visit to Venice to meet with Barbarossa in 1177. Despite having been subjected to various phases of rebuilding, the 17C façade designed by Giuseppe Sardi (1621/30-99) survives with its cannon ball embedded in the masonry since 1849. The arch that opens on to the Mercerie is 16C. The main layout was designed by Spavento, a little-known architect, to be continued after his death in 1509 by

The Bovolo Staircase

G. Guittot/DIAF

Tullio Lombardo (1455-1532) and Sansovino (1486-70). Interestingly, Spavento combines an assured use of Classical structural elements with refined sculptural ornament, a style that foreshadows Mannerism and the bold Classicism of Palladio. Inside, three square bays are aligned to form a nave, each cubic space rising to a semicircular dome. A number of significant paintings include the main altarpiece, *The Transfiguration* by **Titian** (c 1490-1576) and, in the last bay on the right before the transept, his *Annunciation*. To the right of the main chapel hangs *The Martyrdom of St Theodoric* by Paris Bordone (1500-71); in the Santissimo Chapel on the left of the main altar is *The Disciples at Emmaus* by Giovanni **Bellini** (c 1432-1516) while the organ doors *(by the side door)* are painted by Titian's brother, Francesco Vecellio (1475-1560).

Campo San Bartolomeo (4, FU) is a busy crossroads between St Mark's, the Rialto, the Accademia and the Strada Nuova. Bars and tourist shops surround the square which is dominated by a fine spirited statue of Goldoni (1883).

Fondaco dei Tedeschi (4, FU) – What once served an association of German traders (13C onwards), now accommodates the main post office headquarters. Destroyed in a fire in 1505, the Fondaco was rebuilt by Giorgio Spavento (d 1509) and Scarpagnino (active in Venice 1505-49) who conceived the idea of a square courtyard. The frescos which adorn the façade facing the Grand Canal are the work of **Giorgione** (1476/7-1510) and the earliest known works by Titian (1490-1576) *(see also CA' D'ORO: Galleria Franchetti).*

To continue further to St Mark's Square and the Rialto see PIAZZA SAN MARCO and RIALTO.

I FRARI ★★★

(**3**, DV)

Vaporetto: S Tomà, Stazione, Riva di Biasio or S Stae

After visiting the Frari Church, it is well worth strolling in the vicinity of the nearby railway station. Being some distance – relatively speaking – from any major monument of great artistic merit or touristic interest there are few enticing colourful craftshop window displays to distract the eye. This is a residential quarter, even if the term seems inappropriate for Venice, that provides an insight into the sort of daily life that goes on in many other cities. That there are almost no canals along this route is particularly striking.

The suggested itinerary takes about half a day.

A couple of useful addresses

Ai Postali *(821 Santa Croce, Rio Marin)* near the Church of San Simeon Grande is a bar *osteria* that serves a tasty *bruschetta* (toasted bread rubbed with garlic) and crêpes. **Al Ponte** at 1666 Santa Croce, Ponte del Megio (so-called because of the proliferation of millet *(megio)* and grain stores that were so necessary when food was scarce) is the place to go for fish and seafood. **Alla Zucca**, next door at no 1762, is recommended for its varied and more exotic dishes. Special recommendations for the vegetable dishes.

★★★**I Frari** (**3**, DV) – This great church – whose name is derived from the abbreviation of Fra*(ti Mino)* ri – has often been compared with the Church of SS Giovanni e Paolo on account of its sheer scale and style.

Monumental in stature, flanked by the second tallest campanile (70m/229ft 6in) after St Mark's, this building is strikingly magnificent, massive yet articulated with fine architectural detail, conforming to Franciscan archetypes yet quite original. It impresses from every angle: the best view of the apses, the oldest part, is to be had from the Scuola di San Rocco; if contemplated from the bridge built by the monks in 1428, it appears just as breathtaking, its late-Gothic tripartite façade being a masterpiece of design. The doorway is surmounted by a *Risen Christ* by Alessandro Vittoria (1581), flanked slightly below by the *Virgin with Child* and *St Francis* by Bartolomeo Bon (active 1441-64) supported on two finely-crafted engaged columns. High above, inserted into the plain brickwork are four circular window openings edged in white Istrian stone.

Over the side door into the Corner or St Mark's Chapel *(at the end on the left)* the Madonna is shown restraining the Christ-child from struggling to break free.

Interior ☉ – On entering the church from the left side, the perspective through the interior space seems to combine with the structural architectural elements to inspire a sense of great awe that is almost disorientating.

Santa Maria Gloriosa dei Frari – the church's full title – is in the form of a Latin cross. The nave is divided from the aisles by 12 huge cylindrical piers which soar up to the crisscross of transverse and longitudinal timber beams that underpin the quadripartite vaults. The red and white floor tiles are from Verona.

Proceed down the left aisle and across the transept before returning down the right side.

The first noteworthy monument is neo-Classical and dedicated to **Canova** (1757-1822) (1). If it seems a little strange, this is because it was actually designed by the sculptor to commemorate Titian (1490-1576) but was never in fact completed. This piece would have been executed by the sculptor's workshop, and recalls a similar composition, the tomb of Maria Cristina of Austria, in the Augustinian church in Vienna. The allegorical figures before the pyramid represent Sorrow (portrait of Canova) with Venice *(left)*, in the company of Sculpture, heavily veiled, Painting and Architecture.

Beyond the Baroque monument to Doge Giovanni Pesaro (1658-59) is the famous **Madonna di Ca'Pesaro Chapel** dominated by Titian's altarpiece. In this Sacra Conversazione the Virgin sits to the right of the apex of the composition triangle with at her feet St Peter dressed in his yellow mantle, gesturing towards Jacopo Pesaro *(kneeling)* the Captain of the Papal fleet who defeated the Turks at Santa Maura in 1503. The coat of arms on the flag is that of the Borgias (the family of Pope Alexander VI); like the two slaves, the laurel symbolises victory. On the right, the two Saints Francis and Anthony also recommend the Pesaro family to the Virgin. The monument to Bishop Jacopo executed by the Lombardo studio (1524) is on the top right.

121

I Frari

Serving as a sort of glorious harbinger to the Maggiore Chapel and Titian's *Assumption* are the 15C **choir** stalls, executed by Marco Cozzi da Vicenza and comprising 124 decorated stalls. The two organs on the right are signed Gaetano Callido (1794) and Giovanni Piaggia (1732) respectively. Beyond, early-17C paintings by Andrea Micheli, known as Vicentino, illustrate the Works of Corporeal Mercy *(left)* alongside his *Creation of the World*, the *Brazen Serpent*, a *Last Judgement* and the *Glory of Paradise (right)*.

In the left transept, the first chapel on the left is the St Mark's or Corner Chapel which houses the *Triptych of St Mark* by Bartolomeo Vivarini (c 1432-91): here the Evangelist is flanked by John the Baptist and St Jerome, St Nicholas and St Peter respectively. High up on the wall opposite is *Christ's Descent into Limbo* by Jacopo Palma il Giovane (1544-1628). The marble baptismal font with John the Baptist is by Sansovino (1486-1570).

Next comes the Milanese Chapel with its *Sant'Ambrogio* altarpiece by Alvise Vivarini (1445-1505) and Marco Basaiti (c 1470-1530). St Ambrose, the patron saint of Milan, is depicted under an arcade with a scourge *(right)* and a staff *(left)* among saints, at his feet two angels play the lute and the mandola – a token gesture to one of the brothers of the Milanese School, **Claudio Monteverdi** (1567-1643) who is buried here.

Beyond the Chapel of St Michael and the Franciscan Saints, follows the Maggiore Chapel, the focal point of the magnificent perspective of the Frari Church. All points converge on Titian's *Assumption of the Virgin* which was commissioned by the Franciscans in 1516. This major work – the first religious subject undertaken by the painter – caused the friars quite some consternation on account of its unorthodox iconography: Mary at that time was more usually represented in prayer with an expression of divine rapture. Instead of restful contemplation, the painting of a crowded table (6.68m x 3.44m/22ft x 11.28ft) shows the 11 Apostles disturbed by the mystery of this supernatural event; *putti* and winged angels singing and playing music, emphasise the upward movement of the composition, as the (nervous) Virgin looking ever upwards towards God the Father is received in the Kingdom of Heaven in a triumph of light and colour. The brilliance of heaven is exaggerated by the careful portrayal of light from the realms of shadow and darkness on earth, via the more shaded zone occupied by angels up to the explosion of bright light pushing the figure of the Virgin into bold perspective.

Against the presbytery walls are two additional important monuments, one commemorating **Doge Nicolò Tron** by Antonio Rizzo (c 1440-1499) – probably the most important Renaissance sculptural group in Venice *(left)* – and the other, from the 15C to **Doge Francesco Foscari** attributed to Nicolò di Giovanni Battista.

In the right arm of the transept, the jewel of the Chapel of John the Baptist is the only Venetian work by Donatello (1386-1466), his *John the Baptist* depicted with the index finger of his right hand (unfortunately the finger is missing) raised against Herod as a sign of admonition. Beyond the former Santissimo Chapel – now dedicated to Maximilian Kolbe – comes the Bernardo Chapel containing the *Polyptych* by **Bartolomeo Vivarini** (1482).

Before going into the sacristy look out for:

– the equestrian monument to **Paolo Savelli** (d 1405) (2) who fought for Venice against the Carraresi. Its author is uncertain, although the style of the horse and rider have attributed the work to the Sienese artist Jacopo della Quercia (1367-1438);

– on the door to the sacristy, the 16C monument to **Benedetto Pesaro** (3), the captain who died in 1503 is by Giovambattista Bregno. Between the columns that frame the doorway, note the Lion of St Mark's holding the closed Gospel: a common practice in Venice during periods of political conflict, when the city, unable to listen to the Biblical teachings of peace, would "close" the Gospel and leave it under the lion's paw;

– the terracotta monument to **Scipione Bon, the Blessed Peacemaker of the Frari** (4) with the 15C portrayal of the Baptism of Christ in the lunette;

– to the right of the transept, the monument to **Jacopo Marcello** (5), the captain of the Venetian fleet who died in 1488 during the conquest of the city of Gallipoli. The work is by Pietro Lombardo (1435-1515).

The Assumption of the Virgin by Titian

123

The **sacristy** houses the splendid **Triptych** (1488) by Giovanni Bellini (c 1426-1516) which exudes sweetness: the gentle expression of the Virgin as she turns to the angels who play the lute and flute and the serene air of the figures of Saints Nicholas, Peter, Mark and Benedict *(from left to right)*. Opposite is a lunette (1339) by Paolo Veneziano that was designed to be set above the Byzantine sarcophagus of **Doge Francesco Dandolo** (1329-39) in the adjacent Sala del Capitolo *(closed to the public)* – the Capitolo being the periodic assembly of the various groups belonging to a religious community. In this rather fine painting, a Madonna with Child is flanked by St Francis and Elizabeth of Hungary presenting the patron Doge Francesco Dandolo and his wife.

Further along the right aisle, the **Chapel of St Catherine of Alexandria** (6) is decorated with an altarpiece by Palma il Giovane, illustrating the saint's salvation from the torture of the wheel. In the next bay, is the unusual statue of *St Jerome* (1564) (7) by Alessandro Vittoria which recalls the style of Michelangelo. The **altar of Purification** (8) is ornamented with a painting by Salviati (1520/25-75).

Titian's Mausoleum (9), hewn in marble from Carrara, was executed during the decade 1842-1852. Titian, who died of the plague in 1576, was buried in the Frari in accordance with his wishes but by the end of the 16C all traces of his body had disappeared. The artist is depicted between the Nature of the Universe and the Genius of Knowledge.

Cross the canal in front of the church and turn left to Campo San Stin. Then take Calle del Tabacco and Calle dell'Olio as far as the Campiello della Scuola.

Scuola di San Giovanni Evangelista ⊙ (**3**, **DU**) – The courtyard outside the Scuola of St John the Evangelist has been described by Sir Hugh Honour as *"a little masterpiece of Venetian Renaissance architecture – an exquisite composition of grey and white marble, stone, brick and stucco..."* and by Ruskin as *"sweet in feeling"*.

The Scuola was the second of the Scuole Grandi *(see I CARMINI – The Venetian Scuole)* to be founded in 1201 and honoured by a confraternity of flagellants who attended religious processions stripped to the waist and whipping themselves with scourges so as to strew blood along the streets. They are represented in the relief carvings inscribed and dated 1349 at the front. The front otherwise dates in the main from 1454 when the large ogee windows were inserted. The elegant Renaissance iconostasis with its crisply carved decoration, overlooked by the eagle of St John crouching in a lunette, was designed by Lombardo (1481), whereas the main door itself, framed below kneeling figures, dates from 1512.

The elegant double stairway inside, lit with large arched windows, was built by Codussi (c 1440-1504). On the first floor, structural changes were made by Giorgio Massari (1727) who added the oval windows and raised the height of the **salone** which now seems to resemble an 18C stage set, particularly around the high altar. The statue of John the Evangelist is by Gianmaria Morlaiter (1699-1781).

Various craftsmen are responsible for the decoration on the ceiling and the walls including Jacopo Guarana (1720-1808), Gaspare Diziani (1689-1767), Jacopo Marieschi (1711-94), Giandomenico Tiepolo (1727-1804), Domenico Tintoretto (c 1560-1635) and Pietro Longhi (1702-85).

The salone adjoins the Oratory of the Cross built to house Carpaccio's cycle of the *Miracles of the Relic of the True Cross*, now on display in the Accademia *(see ACCADEMIA)*.

Continue straight on as far as the Grand Canal, to come out opposite the Santa Lucia railway station. Turn right along the water's edge.

San Simeon Piccolo – *See Il CANAL GRANDE.*

At Ponte degli Scalzi, turn right and then left into Calle Bergami.

San Simeon Grando (◘, CT) – So-called to distinguish it from the Church of San Simeon Piccolo, the church is also known as San Simeon Profeta. Although its origins go back as far as 967, the building has undergone considerable remodelling, particularly in the 18C. The neo-Classical white façade dates from 1861.

The internal space is divided into nave and aisles by a series of columns crowned with Byzantine capitals and shrouded in heavy red damask drapes, as is fairly common in Venice. Although the ornamentation is generally heavy there is an exquisite *Last Supper* by Tintoretto (1518-94) on the left of the entrance.

Calle Larga dei Barbi, behind the church, leads into Campo Nazario Sauro. From here continue on to Campo San Giacomo dall'Orio, an open, often lonely space and down Ruga Bella or the parallel Ruga Vecchia, which comes out directly in front of another church.

★**San Giacomo dall'Orio** (◘, DT) – The church was founded in 976 but most of its present fabric dates from 1225. Its position and structure recall those of the Church of Santa Maria Formosa.

The centre of the main façade features a Veneto-Byzantine patera with a statue in Istrian stone of the Apostle St James the Great standing above the portal. The bell-tower, erected in the 12C or 13C, is reminiscent of that on Torcello. The three apses date back to different periods: the left to the 16C, the central apse to the 13C and the right one to the 17C. The transept frontage dates from around the 14C.

Interior – It is perhaps the Gothic lacunar **ceiling** that is most striking, shaped as it is in the form of an inverted ship's hull.

The nave is divided from its aisles by five baseless columns down each side – the fourth marking the division of the transept.

Beside the entrance, David is depicted with excerpts from Psalm 150. The unusual stoup for the holy water is made of cipolin (onion) marble from Anatolia. Of the paintings in the choir stalls attributed to Schiavone (1503-63), it is *The Apostles in the Boat* that is the most likely to be by him.

The organ was built by Gaetano Callido *(see Introduction – Composers in Venice)*.

In the transept off the right aisle, an exquisite 13C statue carved from Greek marble of the *Madonna in Prayer* nestles in its small niche. Above, hangs the ***Miracle of the Loaves and the Fishes*** by Palma il Giovane (1548-1628). Along with the works in the Santissimo Chapel this painting is based on the theme of the Eucharist – particularly significant given the differences between Catholic and Protestant factions at the time.

Over the altar dedicated to St Anthony, the *Madonna and Child in Glory with Saints* is by Giambattista Pittoni (1687-1767). It is most likely that the Ionic column of ancient green marble which was brought to Venice from Byzantium has been in the church since the 13C.

The Council of Trent

Established in 1545 and dissolved in 1563, the Council of Trent aimed to encapsulate Catholic ideals in dogma and to structure its ministry by disciplinary reform. Those opposed to the rationalisation of the Roman Church went on to precipitate the Counter-Reformation and found the Protestant faction.

This ecclesiastical body confirmed the Church's sole right to interpret the Bible and underlined the role of the clergy as sole intercessors between man and God. The value of the seven sacraments was reaffirmed, and the practices of Baptism and Confirmation were ratified. The acknowledged existence of Purgatory, the invocation of Saints, the veneration of relics, images and indulgences were also endorsed and rationalised, with the insistence of the doctrine of transubstantiation, whereby the consecrated bread and wine were actually transformed into the body and blood of Christ.

The Eucharist, however, was also interpreted as nourishment since that shared in the miracle of the loaves and fishes. Palma il Giovane's painting was therefore ad hoc at a time when Paolo Sarpi *(see Introduction – Over a thousand years of glory)* was interpreting the two opposing factions, one who believed in the transformation into the Body of Christ, and one in the symbol of the bread and wine.

In the **New Sacristy**, off this arm of the transept, are Palma il Giovane's *Crucifixion with the Virgin and St John* and a version of *The Marriage at Cana* also thought to be by him; by Francesco Bassano (1549-92) and his assistants are *The Preaching of John the Baptist* and *Madonna with John the Baptist and Nicolò da Bari*. The ceiling decorated with an allegory of *Faith and the Doctors of the Church* (St Gregory the Great, St Jerome, St Augustine and St Ambrose) is the work of the studio of Veronese (1528-88).

The right apsidal chapel, the **Santissimo Chapel**, is dedicated to faith in the Eucharist. Of note are the *Via Crucis* and the *Burial Tomb of Christ* by Palma il Giovane. In the arch of the vaulting, above the presbytery, is a wooden *Crucifix* attributed to Paolo Veneziano (c 1290-1362). The altarpiece, by Lorenzo Lotto (c 1480-1557), depicts the *Madonna and Saints*.

To the left of the presbytery is a beautiful 14C *Annunciation* in hard stone.

On the left wall of the left apsidal chapel are a pair of fine organ doors (1532) attributed to Schiavone.

The **Old Sacristy** *(apply to the custodian)* besides its fine wood panelling, is decorated with a cycle of paintings by Palma il Giovane dedicated to the subject of the Eucharist in accordance with edicts from the Council of Trent; scenes include the *Jewish Passover, Christ in the Tomb, the Parting of the Red Sea, the Brazen Serpent, Gathering Manna from Heaven, Elijah Being Fed by the Angel.*

Left of the entrance to the Old Sacristy, the figures of *St Sebastian, St Rocco* and *St Laurence* are by Giovanni Bonconsiglio, also known as **Marescalco** (c 1470-1535). In the left arm of the transept, the chapel dedicated to St Laurence is decorated with painted scenes from the life of the saint: Veronese's *St Laurence, St Jerome and St Prospero (centre);* whereas the *Distribution of Holy Wealth to the Poor* and the *Martyrdom of St Laurence* are by Palma il Giovane.

The pulpit shaped like a chalice is late-Renaissance.

Before leaving the church, note the 16C *Miracle of St James Raising the Gaul* and *Christ Borne by an Angel* by Palma il Giovane.

To get to Campo San Giovanni Decollato and the church of the same name (Zan Degolà in Venetian), take Calle Larga and branch left down Calle dello Spezier.

In this area, only a stone's throw from the hustle and bustle of the Grand Canal, the seasons blossom and fade as if suspended in time. Uniquely Venetian in its tranquillity, it is a place of sanctuary to rest the weary soul.

San Lorenzo

St Laurence (d 258) served as one of seven deacons under Sixtus II. He was martyred during the persecution of Valerian. According to the legend perpetuated by St Ambrose, when St Laurence was asked to turn in the Church's treasures to the Roman authorities, he gathered a huge crowd of poor, needy people and declared to the prefect: *"These are the treasures of the Church".* He is usually represented as being slowly roasted on a gridiron, although he is more likely to have been beheaded.

San Zan Degolà (**3**, DT) – Dedicated to the beheaded John the Baptist, this church's origins are ancient, there having been a parish church on the site by 1007. The terracotta façade is early 18C. A rose window is the main feature of the central section of the three-tier façade, framed by pilasters supporting a triangular tympanum. The relief on the right wall recounts the story of John's decapitation.

As with the façade, a harmonious simplicity pervades the interior: the three aisles are separated by four columns of Greek marble with 11C Byzantine capitals. The ceiling takes the form of an inverted ship's hull. The intense silence enhances the air of contemplation inspired by the frescoed chapels at the end of the side aisles. In the left one is an *Annunciation, St Helen and Saints* and, on the ceiling, the symbols of the *Evangelists*, conforming to the Veneto-Byzantine style. In the chapel to the right is a *St Michael the Archangel* dated from 1300 recently uncovered by restoration.

Follow the calle behind the church as far as the Grand Canal. At the end, right opposite the plain façade of the Church of San Marcuola, is the elegant palazzo that was the residence of the Turkish merchants (see II CANAL GRANDE).

Fondaco dei Turchi (**3**, DT) – This now accommodates the Natural History Museum (Museo di Storia Naturale).

Natural History Museum ⊘ (**3**, DT) – While most visitors to Venice, quite understandably, might be driven rather by an interest in art than in natural science, they should not exclude, if time allows, a quick tour around this rich collection. Displays are effectively arranged by theme using dioramas to complement the clear explanations given on the showcases: from cells to protozoa, porifers, worms, molluscs, arthropods, crustaceans and echinoderms. Fossils from Bolca, in the vicinity of Verona which is noted for its wealth of palaeontological finds, illustrate the evolution of vertebrates.

One room is dedicated to animal species from the lagoon, whereas another concentrates on an explanation of the insect world's defence facilities such as mimicry and camouflage.

The dinosaur room is worth visiting to see one particularly special exhibit, an enormous skeleton, brought to Italy from the Ligabue expedition to the Sahara in 1973.

> **When the *Vox Populi* is not the *Vox Dei***
>
> For the Venetians, the relief depicting the unfortunate John the Baptist would have represented a *Biagio luganegher* – every child's nightmare. Children who lived near the bridge where it was originally located were told about the strange culinary practices of this evil merchant who loved to "flavour" his food with human remains, particularly children. It was only in about 1968 that the parish removed the effigy of John to the church to which it actually belonged.

Molluscs and minerals follow on from the Bolca fossils, among which the most spectacular are those that show their progression and movement before succumbing to petrifaction.

For those wishing to continue into neighbouring districts, turn to the sections on SAN ROCCO and I CARMINI.

To find the description of a sight, a historical event, a monument ... consult the index at the end of the guide.

Il GHETTO ★★

(**3**, DT)

Vaporetto: Ferrovia, Ponte delle Guglie or San Marcuola

Around the corner from the station and its inevitable bustle, it is both enjoyable and stimulating to saunter through the squares and *calli* that are vibrant with the comings and goings of its market and numerous shops. What may be even more alluring, however, are the more peaceful squares and *calli* of this area, so close and yet cut off from the milling crowds that throng a neighbouring street.

For a quick bite...

Try **Alla Fortuna** at 1102 Fondamenta Cannaregio.

And given that this is the Jewish quarter...

Enjoy a kosher meal at **Casa di Riposo**, 2874 Cannaregio – it is advisable to book ☎ 041/71 60 02.

When hunting for Jewish bread and pastries, seek out **Volpe** (*1143 Ghetto*).

At 1122 Fondamenta Pescaria, at the entrance to the Old Ghetto stands **Gam-Gam**, a Jewish restaurant with a pleasant atmosphere.

In search of mystery – The Ghetto of Venice is a secret corner of the Cannaregio *sestiere* where the ambience is not dissimilar to the area of the Sacca della Misericordia (*see CA' D'ORO*). Despite their differences in customs, religion and even architecture, both areas have evolved a distinctive artistic celebration of their own history and faith.

Leaving behind the incessant hubbub of activity in the shops and market around Fondamenta della Pescaria and Rio Terrà San Leonardo, one is struck by the tranquillity of the squares and the *calli* – with their curious yellow signs and elegant Hebrew characters – that lead to the heart of the Ghetto.

The approach to Campo di Ghetto Nuovo from Calle Farnese might suggest that the area is fortified. From the bridge before the *sottoportego* the view is particularly evocative: unusually tall houses (for Venice at least) seem to tower out of the canal tenuously strung together by a crisscross of washing lines that seem permanently weighted with laundry. The *sottoportego* adds to the picture, appearing as it does like a raised drawbridge onto a mysterious world.

Story of a name and a place – The Ghetto of Venice is the ghetto *par excellence*, being the first Jewish quarter to be differentiated as such in Western Europe. The term which seems to testify rather to the barbarities and periods of persecution endured by the Jewish community, rather than a history enjoyed, was originally coined from the word *geto* in Venetian dialect that referred to a local bombard or mortar foundry – the "g", normally pronounced soft (as in George), was hardened by the first Jews who came from Germany.

The distinction of *Vecchio* (old) and *Nuovo* (new) should not be interpreted in any chronological sense: they are references to the old and new foundries. In fact, the Jews were first confined to the Ghetto Nuovo – then a fortified island – which was practically impenetrable. At the time, the houses were still rather squat and low-lying; the area was subjected to a form of curfew at nightfall after which time the drawbridge was raised and the area sealed off. It was only in 1866 that access to the Ghetto was freed up and that Jews were granted the same rights as other Venetian citizens. As long as the Jews were obliged to stay there, however, they were at least protected.

Indeed, it was precisely because their community was confined to this small area that their houses climbed ever taller. It seems odd, now, to acknowledge that Jews were prohibited from undertaking any kind of building work be it on their houses or any of the five synagogues, or *scuole*. Instead, they became *strazzaroli* (dealers in secondhand clothes and goods), doctors and bankers involved in moneylending activities: the colours of their stalls being red *(no 2912)*, green and black.

Above Eye Level

An 18C notice in the Old Ghetto warns Jews converted to Christianity not to frequent the Ghetto, and the houses of other Jews on pain of "hanging, prison, hard labour, flogging, pillory". The means by which the Serenissima authorities were to be informed is also advertised: by secret denunciation via the usual channels (the infamous holes-in-the-wall known as *bocche di leone*). These tablets also advertised the dues to be expected by the accuser, paid in recompense from the property of the accused.

This proclamation was sculpted in stone and publicised at all the busiest points in the Ghetto.

Museo ebraico ⊙ (**3**, **DT**) – The **Jewish Museum** collects together many precious artefacts relating to Judaism: decorative objects and ornaments or paraphernalia connected with their sacred scrolls *(rotoli della Legge)*.

Of all the Toràh covers in the collection, the one featuring the Jews encamped, the manna and the hand of Moses issuing forth water from the rock is particularly famous.

★★**Synagogues** ⊙ – Occupying the upper floors of various buildings, the five windows and the lanterns peeping out from under the roofs indicate the presence of a place of prayer. All five synagogues in Venice (Italiana, Levantina, Spagnola, Canton and the oldest Tedesca,) share the same bifocal layout in which the pulpit *(bimà)* and the cupboard which contains the scrolls *(aròn)* are placed, one in front of the other, along the smaller side of the room with the women's gallery above.

The Spagnola and Levantina Synagogues are situated in the Ghetto Vecchio which was assigned to the Jews in 1541. Their names indicate the different rites practised.

The **Spagnola Synagogue** (**3**, **DT**), the largest synagogue, was rebuilt by Longhena (1598-1682) in the 17C. Longhena and his followers were also probably responsible for the restoration of the Levantina Synagogue, which is used during the summer months. The Tedesca (Ashkenazi), Canton and Italiana synagogues are situated in Campo di Ghetto Nuovo.

The **Canton Synagogue** (**3**, **DT**), so-named either after the banker who commissioned its construction in the 16C or the Venetian term *canton* which refers to its corner position, is particularly renowned for its series of rare illustrations along the upper section of the walls. Concordant with the strict observation of the second commandment, which prohibits the representation of any creature in the sky, on land or in water, of God or of man; even a suggestion of landscape inside a synagogue could be considered as a distraction from prayer. However, the most important moments of Jewish history are recounted here. These include: the *Sending of Manna from Heaven*, the *Parting of the Red Sea* (interestingly, a hand can be seen protruding from the water, a detail that might indicate that the artist was Egyptian), *Moses Bringing Forth Water from the Rock*, the *Ark of the Covenant*, the *Symbol of the Jewish People who Crossed the River Jordan*.

Campo di Ghetto Nuovo

Campo di Ghetto Nuovo (**3**, **DS**) – A walk in this square will inevitably recall the most tragic moments in the history of the Jews in Venice: reminders include a relief (1979) by the Lithuanian artist Blatas and a monument to the deportees (1993) commemorates the Venetian Jews who died. At the same time, the square projects a picture of mundane tranquillity where ancient Jewish traditions live on: workshops manufacture objects related to the Jewish faith, glass ornaments and cards bearing images of rabbis for those who seek inspiration to devotion or who just want to buy a memento of a very special corner of Venice.

The Sacred Scrolls

For the Jews, the Law (*Toràh*, which literally means "teaching") comes in the form of the Pentateuch, the five Books of Moses comprising Genesis, Exodus, Leviticus, Numbers and Deuteronomy. Transcribed onto parchment, the scrolls are wound around two batons which are unfurled during readings.

The scrolls are stored in a rigid container or rolled up in a mantle, mounted with a crown and two pinnacled end-pieces (*rimonim*, the Hebrew for pomegranate).

The rolls are stored in the Holy Ark. Given their sacredness, they can be neither exposed nor touched so a silver holder is used during readings.

Campo di Ghetto Nuovo

Rousseaud/CAMPAGNE CAMPAGNE

STILL IN THE GHETTO

If approaching the Ghetto from Santa Lucia railway station, there are several distractions that might slow one's progress, such as window shopping in Rio Terrà Lista di Spagna (*lista* refers to the area around a foreign embassy that enjoyed diplomatic immunity – in this case the Embassy was Spanish); the delight of observing the fish stalls along the Fondamenta della Pescheria or the market in Rio Terrà San Leonardo; the temptation of exploring the Scalzi, San Geremia, and Palazzo Labia churches.

Among these, for anyone in the vicinity of the station, the most recommended would be a visit to Gli Scalzi.

Gli Scalzi (**3**, **CT**) – Literally the Church of "the Discalced", its name pertains to the Carmelite Order whose members, like the Franciscans, were obliged to go about their duties barefoot (today they wear sandals). Designed by Longhena (1598-1682), its Baroque façade is faced with Carrara marble.

The rather sombre interior shelters the tomb of the last doge, **Lodovico Manin** *(second chapel in the left aisle)*. Prior to its destruction during the First World War, the ceiling was decorated with a fresco by Tiepolo (1696-1770): the current painting dates from 1934. Fortunately, Tiepolo's frescoes in the vaults of the first chapel off the left aisle and second chapel off the right aisle survive *(see Il CANAL GRANDE)*.

Rio Terrà Lista di Spagna, lined with numerous workshops, eventually leads into Campo San Geremia.

San Geremia e Santa Lucia (**3**, **CDT**) – Bathed in light, the interior of this 18C church is similar in plan to the Church of la Salute. It is here that the body of St Lucy lies. Also of note is a painting by Palma il Giovane (1544-1628), *The Virgin Attending the Coronation in Venice*. The brick campanile, alongside, dates from the 13C *(see Il CANAL GRANDE)*.

San Geremia e Santa Lucia

St Jerome Emiliani (1481-1537) was born in Venice. Having served in the army, he was ordained in 1518 and dedicated the rest of his life to helping the poor and afflicted. He established orphanages, hospitals and refuges for fallen women. He was canonised in 1767 and made patron saint of abandoned children.

St Lucy died a virgin martyr in 304 in Syracuse, under the persecution of Diocletian. Her relics were pillaged by the Venetian Crusaders from Constantinople and brought to Venice in 1204.

According to her Acts, she would have been a Sicilian who refused marriage offers preferring to donate her property to the poor. Having slighted one suitor she was reported to the authorities and sentenced to "be violated in a brothel"; further sentences included attempts at burning her at the stake and having her eyes gouged out – at which point her sight was miraculously restored. She thus was adopted as the patron saint of the blind and is often represented holding her eyes in a saucer. Her feast day is celebrated in Sweden and Finland on the shortest day of the year (13 December).

★★Palazzo Labia ⊘ (**3**, **CDT**) – The construction of this *palazzo* – built of Istrian stone – was commissioned at the end of the 17C by a wealthy family of Spanish merchants, to whom the building owes its name. The three façades, adorned with eagles – the family emblem – overlook Campo San Geremia, the Cannaregio Canal and the Grand Canal – almost. "Almost" because one of the façades actually overlooks a small square rather than the actual Grand Canal. It was the exclusive prerogative of the Venetian nobility to have a residence in the most highly sought-after location overlooking the canal. The Labia family who had paid for the privilege of being listed in the Libro d'Oro *(see Introduction - Over a thousand years of glory: 1784)* had therefore to settle for a residence with a view of the Grand Canal without actually overlooking it.

The *palazzo* has a particularly strong connection with one member of the Labia dynasty, namely Maria Labia who lived in the 18C. It was in honour of her marriage that **Giambattista Tiepolo** (1696-1770) was commissioned to fresco the Salone delle Festa (Banqueting Hall) and it would appear that the depiction of Cleopatra was inspired by her beauty.

After the fall of the Republic, the family abandoned the *palazzo*, and when Napoleon handed it over to the Austrians, there began a long period of neglect that included nails being driven into walls to support washing lines.

In 1951 the palace was acquired by a wealthy Mexican oil magnate who organised a sumptuous ball in 18C costume to which all the international jet set were invited. Abandoned once again, restoration was postponed until the 1960s when, at last, it accommodated the Veneto arm of RAI, Italy's national television network. Today, it belongs to the Labia Services Company which holds seminars and conventions there.

The love of Anthony and Cleopatra – As mentioned above, Tiepolo was responsible for the frescoes in the Banqueting Hall. Cleopatra is depicted in 18C costume in two scenes, the *Encounter* and the *Banquet*, bold with blatant *trompe-l'œil* effects. In the *Banquet*, Cleopatra, dissatisfied with the presents she has received, asks for a glass of vinegar in which to dissolve the pearl that she is holding in her hand.

On the ceiling, *Genius Rides the Horse Pegasus; Time is Armed with a Halberd*, and *Venus Surrounded by Cupids before the Magic Pyramid*, a topographical detail denoting Egypt.

Other apartments, arranged around the *salone*, or main room, and the courtyard include the Stanza degli Specchi (Hall of Mirrors), its ceiling decorated in delicate hues and its *trompe-l'œil* walls; the Stanza degli Mappamondo (Map of the World)

The Ostentations of the Labia Family

Perhaps a little maliciously, legend has it that at the end of a banquet the Labia family would hurl their gold dinner plates and cutlery out of the window and into the canal to cries proclaiming their indifference to their wealth. The infamous family was more astute, however, than they might have appeared, for by placing fishing nets at the bottom of the canal, they were able later to retrieve their precious treasure for use another day.

The Encounter by Giambattista Tiepolo (Palazzo Labia)

and chapel adjacent; a corridor decorated with Cordoba leather; the Stanza degli Stucchi hung with portraits of the Labia family; the Tapestry Room accommodating a cycle of tapestries illustrating the *Adventures of Scipio the African* designed by Giulio Romano and woven in Brussels (1650); a room with a lively 18C representation of the *Signs of the Zodiac*, and one decorated with two hemispheres (1649) in which Greenland appears to be attached to the continent and Australia is referred to as *Terra Australis Incognita* (the Unknown Land of Australia).

Salizzada San Geremia leads to the Ponte delle Guglie.

Ponte delle Guglie (**3**, DT) – The Cannaregio Canal is crossed by two bridges *(ponti)*. Passing over the Ponte delle Guglie (1580) is practically obligatory given that it is the bridge linking the railway station to the Strada Nuova. It takes its name from the architectural features which adorn the balustrade. The second bridge, the Ponte dei Tre Archi is further along the Grand Canal.

To the left of Fondamenta Venier which runs alongside the Cannaregio Canal – level with Ponte dei Tre Archi – is the calle which leads to the Church of San Giobbe.

San Giobbe (**3**, CT) – Work on the church dedicated to Job, the figure in the Old Testament who rejected the view that suffering is the result of sin, was initiated by Antonio Gambello (recorded between 1458-81) in the second half of the 15C and completed by Pietro Lombardo. Its distinctive, plain façade is broken by a fine Renaissance portal above which preside the statues of San Bernardino, Sant'Alvise and St Anthony. St Francis and Job appear in the low relief enclosed in the lunette. The interior comprises a single nave, with side chapels to the left and altars to the right. The vault of the second chapel on the left is glazed in majolica tiles from the Florentine Della Robbia workshops active between 1400 and 1500.

Before the entrance into the presbytery is the coat of arms of **Doge Cristoforo Moro** (1462-71) who is buried alongside his wife Cristina Sanudo, in the presbytery: their tombstone is typically Lombard in style. Note the three mulberries, the fruit of the *moro*, included in the coat of arms, a synonym that was not wasted on **Shakespeare** (1564-1616) who wrote about a Moor in *Othello (see Il CANAL GRANDE – Palazzo Moro)*. Desdemona would have been based upon the first wife,

---

Bridge with Three Arches

Much appreciated by pedestrians who do not have to cope with a single steep ramp, the three-arched structure is less popular with the canal traffic which is forced to slow down and proceed with caution. It is therefore understandable that Palladio was unsuccessful with his plans for a three-arch Rialto Bridge *(see RIALTO)*. As if to confirm the impracticality of such a construction, all the three-arched bridges in Venice have disappeared with the exception of one, the **Ponte dei Tre Archi** on the Cannaregio Canal which was constructed at the end of the 17C by Andrea Tirali (c 1657-1737).

---

to whom interestingly, Othello gives a handkerchief embroidered with small berries. Important works of art that once graced the first bays on the right include the *Agony in the Garden* by Marco Basaiti (c 1470-post 1530), an *Enthroned Madonna* by Giovanni Bellini (c 1430-1516) where Job is portrayed among the Saints surrounding the Virgin and the *Presentation of Christ at the Temple* by Vittore Carpaccio (c 1465-1526). These are now displayed at the Gallerie dell' Accademia *(see ACCADEMIA)*.

Continue along Rio Terrà San Leonardo as far as Rio Terrà del Cristo on the right which leads to the Church of San Marcuola.

San Marcuola (**3**, DT) – Like Zanipòlo *(see ACCADEMIA – San Trovaso)*, this name is a contraction of the two saints' names – Ermagora and Fortunato.

The original construction dates back to around the 10C but the church was subsequently restructured during the course of the 18C, although the *campo*'s façade which overlooks the Grand Canal was never completed.

Inside, the altars are the work of Giovanni Morlaiter (1699-1781) who sculpted the high altar in the Church of La Salute. San Marcuola's most famous artwork, however, is the *Last Supper (left wall of the presbytery)* painted by Tintoretto *(see Il CANAL GRANDE)*.

For those wishing to continue into neighbouring districts, turn to the section on CA' D'ORO.

To best enjoy the major tourist attractions, which draw big crowds, try to avoid visiting at the peak periods of the day or year.

La GIUDECCA

(7, 8, 9, BGYZ)
Vaporetto: Zitelle, Redentore, Giudecca or S Eufemia

At one time dotted with the villas of wealthy Venetian nobles, the prestigious Cipriani Hotel is the only one left to perpetuate the luxurious past of this island. Nowadays it is a haven for visitors wishing to take in the island's relaxed and peaceful atmosphere, if only for an hour or so, and the contrasting views of Venice extending beyond the canal.

An extension of Harry's Bar...

This is to be found at **Harry's Dolci** on Fondamenta S Biagio *(773 Giudecca)*. Both restaurant and *pasticceria*, this is a little less expensive than its more famous sister establishment.

Fish, Jews and the Exiled in the history of a name – The eight islands which make up the Giudecca – laid out in the shape of a fish-bone – justifies its original name: **spinalonga** (long spine). The origins of the current name may be twofold: one, being a reference to the Jews *(giudei)* who lived there; the second being an allusion to the 11C *zudegà* (judgement) which guaranteed land to noble families who had been exiled from elsewhere.

Today the Giudecca offers the opportunity for a long meander along the various *fondamenta* following the canals that divide up the Giudecca, from the Church of San Giorgio Maggiore to Mulino Stucky.

Le Zitelle (🅱, FY) – The Church of Santa Maria della Presentazione was designed by Palladio (1508-80). The name *"Zitelle"* was coined from a reference to the girls accommodated in the adjoining hospice that forms part of the façade.

Characteristic features of the main front is the dominant triangular tympanum, flanked by bell-turrets, over a semicircular window.

★Il Redentore (🅱, EY) – Like the Church of La Salute, the Redentore was built as a result of a motion carried by the Senate: with Venice decimated by the plague which had been raging for more than a year, **Doge Alvise Mocenigo** proposed (1576) that a new church should be dedicated to the Redeemer, and every year thereafter, honoured by a solemn procession.

In designing the church, Palladio (1508-80) sought to make it fulfil its votive function over and above all else. Its longitudinal axis, which may only be fully appreciated inside, was necessary if the long procession of clergy and dignitaries was to be accommodated.

The flat, rigourously Classical façade is set up and back from a great flight of steps imaginatively inspired by Biblical descriptions of the Temple in Jerusalem. This idealised view of the Catholic Church accommodating a modern, classically ordered building was also to determine the setting for the *Presentation of Mary at the Temple* by Titian (1490-1576) at the Accademia, as well as the version by Tintoretto (1518-94) at the Church of the Madonna dell'Orto.

In the niches stand St Mark and St Francis, and above San Lorenzo Giustiniani, the city's first Patriarch, and St Anthony of Padua. The whole is overlooked by an allegory of Faith collecting in a chalice, the blood from the cross. Behind rises the dome of the Redeemer flanked by two integrated bell-towers.

Interior – Flooded with light, the unified internal space is contained in a single nave lined with side chapels: a plan charged with symbolic iconography that alludes to the theme of human suffering as endured by Jesus Christ through His incarnation and ultimate sacrifice *(altar)*, to be ultimately redeemed at the Resurrection. As with the architecture, so the paintings are arranged in such a way as to reveal their significance and unfurl the mystery of life as the procession progresses.

Starting therefore from the right.

Il Redentore

1st chapel: *The Nativity* by Francesco Bassano (1549-92).

2nd chapel: *The Baptism of Christ* by the School of Veronese.

3rd chapel: *The Flagellation* by the School of Tintoretto, followed by *The Road to Calvary* and *The Crucifixion* over the altar.

Follow down the left side, starting at the third altar.

3rd chapel: *The Deposition* by Palma il Giovane (1548-1628).

2nd chapel: *The Resurrection* by Francesco Bassano.

1st chapel: *Christ's Ascension to Heaven* by Tintoretto and assistants.

> ### The Feast of the Redeemer
>
> The Feast of the Redeemer is still held on the third Sunday in July perpetuating the tradition started by Doge Alvise Mocenigo. A bridge of boats across the Giudecca Canal used to be orchestrated to enable the procession to reach the island and allow free access to the faithful. In the evening of the preceding Saturday, a fireworks display would – as it still does today – illuminate the sky and the lagoon with sparkling lights, bewitching the vast and animated audience of Venetians and tourists gathered on the Riva degli Schiavoni.

In the **sacristy** *(off the third chapel on the right)* hang a *Baptism of Christ* by Veronese (1528-88) and a *Madonna with Child and Angels* by Alvise Vivarini (1445-1505).

Sant'Eufemia (**7**, CY) – This is the oldest church on the island, its origins dating back to the 9C. The late-16C portico on the left side, facing onto the Giudecca Canal, is from another church, now destroyed.

Still graced with the 11C Veneto-Byzantine capitals, the interior houses the colourful *San Rocco and the Angel* by Bartolomeo Vivarini (c 1432-91) *(first altar, right aisle)*, whereas the frescoed ceiling is by Giambattista Canal (1745-1825) and exalts the life of the Saint to which the church is dedicated.

Mulino Stucky (**7**, BY) – This prepossessing but rather awkward construction – which would perhaps be more at home in Dickens' London – is the work of late-19C German architects. It earns its name from the Swiss entrepreneur who commissioned it.

For those wishing to continue into neighbouring districts, turn to the section on San Giorgio Maggiore.

GRAND CANAL

see Il CANAL GRANDE

MICHELIN GREEN TOURIST GUIDES
Landscapes
Monuments
Scenic routes, touring programmes
Geography
History, Art
Places to stay
Town and site plans
Practical information
A collection of guides for your travels in France and around the world.

Every day, **St Mark's Square** is the meeting place and destination for thousands of visitors. In summer and on special occasions, such as the Carnival, there are so many people converging on the square that one might begin to doubt its attraction. It is advisable to avoid the "drawing room" of Venice at such times: the early hours of the morning and evening; the spring and autumn when the colours and the sounds are crisp and clear are infinitely preferable. Each person's impression of St Mark's is always unique, so much so that painters, photographers and writers have only ever managed to convey a snippet of the square's subtle, even sublime nature.

With the dawning of each day, St Mark's Square comes alive. Beyond the columns of St Mark and St Theodore, the gondolas and *vaporetti* come and go while noisy crowds gather around the hotly-contested souvenir stalls. Almost every language can be heard as the tourists follow their tour guide's raised umbrella into the basilica or loiter under the porticoes, bewitched by windows of *passementerie* and sparkling jewellery and glass. Small groups of musicians play to the *habitués* of the legendary cafés, while vendors of bird-feed continue to attract flocks of people and pigeons, by selling tokens of good luck.

The centuries do not appear to have left their indelible mark on the square; however, if one could journey back through time, it would be just as busy in the 14C. The passing of the hours, since time immemorial is still ceremoniously sounded by the Moors on the clock-tower and the mighty bells of the campanile.

For a thorough tour of the basilica, the Doges' Palace and the museums allow about half a day.

Hundreds of years ago...

– A canal once ran before the basilica. By covering it over in 1160, the length of the only piazza in Venice was tripled.

The new area, described by Napoleon as *"the finest drawing room in Europe"* already afforded a majestic view of the basilica: now a two-tiered colonnaded construction was planned on the north side to house offices for the Procurators.

The columns of St Mark and St Theodore *(see below)* were erected in the piazzetta, and the entire architectural complex, as adapted, became the setting before which Pope Alexander III met with Barbarossa (1177).

Glamorous cafés and bars

An absolute must are the **Caffè Florian** (Z), the **Quadri Caffé** (Y) and, very nearby, **Harry's Bar** (N) – see below under *The Procuratie*. It was here, as Ruskin observed, that *"the idle Venetians of the middle classes lounge, and read empty journals"* in *The Stones of Venice*.

For a less extravagant bite to eat, walk round to **Piero e Mauro**, at 881 Calle dei Fabbri, for a tramezzino, crostino or simply a good glass of beer! The decor is fun too!

Fortunately, it is possible to glean some idea of what the old Procuratie looked like from the minutely detailed background to *The Procession of the Cross in St Mark's Square*, painted by Gentile Bellini (1429-1507), and now in the Gallerie dell'Accademia.

At that time, contemporary with Bellini, the Procuratie Vecchie were not permitted to build houses and hospices: it was for Jacopo Sansovino (1486-1570), the Florentine sculptor and architect that had been active in Rome, to redesign the piazza, linking it to the piazzetta and removing the buildings that choked the campanile.

The illustrious architect is also responsible for the **Library**, whose lengthy construction was further protracted by 30 years when all work was suspended. Towards the close of the 16C, work was at last resumed and attention was turned to the redevelopment of the south side of the piazza, beginning with the removal of the existing old buildings considered to be so ugly, to make way for the Procuratie Nuove. A competition was organised to find an architect capable of undertaking the new project while overseeing the final completion of the Library. On his appointment, Vincenzo Scamozzi (1552-1616), the most important of Palladio's immediate followers, promptly decided to endow the square with the spatial reorganisation necessary to enhance the unusual points of reference – the basilica and the campanile.

The present trachyte paving was designed by Andrea Tirali (c 1657-1737) who also resurfaced the area known as the **Piazzetta dei Leoncini**, so-called after the two lions by Giovanni Bonazza (1654-1736). Tirali then conceived the idea of accenting lines of perspective in the piazza by in-laying four "fasciae" in Carrara marble in concentric geometric formation. Two such bands converge on the basilica whereas the other two running oblique to the first pair are aligned with the columns of St Mark and St Theodore: at their speculative point of intersection stands the square base of the campanile (best appreciated from above).

A bird's-eye view of the Piazza

Y. Arthus-Bertrand/ALTITUDE

Little changed, then, until the collapse of the campanile on 14 July 1902. Miraculously, the only damage incurred was to Sansovino's Loggetta and to a small part of the Biblioteca Marciana. By 1911, the new campanile, on the design of the old one, reinstated the square's traditional appearance.

And today... – The vast trapezoidal space (176m/577ft in length, 82m/269ft maximum width) is enclosed on the north side by the Procuratie Vecchie and by the later-16C Procuratie Nuove opposite. In between, the neo-Classical Napoleon Wing or **Ala nuovissima**, was built in accordance with the wishes of Emperor Bonaparte after the demolition in the early 1800s of the 16C Sansovino Church of San Geminiano.

★★★BASILICA DI SAN MARCO (8. FGX)

"Pax tibi, Marce, evangelista meus. Hic requiescet corpus tuum" (Peace unto you, Mark, my Evangelist. Here rests your body) is what the angel said to St Mark near the Rialto, as the Evangelist was journeying from Aquileia to Rome. Almost another 800 years were to elapse before the legendary prophecy was fulfilled, since when, and as far as the whole world was concerned, the symbol of St Mark has been synonymous with the Venetian flag.

According to legend – It is well known that the second Evangelist was in Rome with St Peter, and that following the Apostle's death St Mark (San Marco) became the Bishop of Alexandria in Egypt. In addition, therefore, to the famous visitation near the Rialto that foretold the association of the name of the saint with Venice for evermore, there is a story that tells of another portentious adventure in Egypt around the year 800.

Two merchants actually set out for Alexandria with the intention of stealing the saint's body as rumour had it that the relics would bestow upon Venice the prestige it needed to "compete" with Rome or, at least, to affirm its politico-religious independence from the capital.

Procession through Piazza San Marco by Gentile Bellini (Accademia)

This status was regularly reaffirmed by the Republic throughout its long history: even today, the city continues to enjoy the honorific title of Patriarchate. So the body was taken in a chest aboard a Venetian vessel. The theft was organised down to the last detail: in anticipation of any inspections, the cadaver was hidden under layers of pork to discourage any Muslim from examining the cargo too closely. The story is further endowed with a miracle, whereby the ship, venturing too close to some rocks, was saved when St Mark woke the captain in time. On arrival in Venice, the precious relic was placed in the chapel of a castle belonging to Doge Giustiniano Partecipazio, subsequently consecrated in 832 as the first church dedicated to St Mark.

History of the church – In this way the first patron saint of Venice, San Teodoro, *Todaro* in dialect, was demoted even if not forgotten.

The vicissitudes of St Mark's relic were not yet over. After the fire of 976 which seriously damaged the church, all trace of the body was lost. Only three people knew where it had been buried and they took their secret to the grave. Everyone was asked to fast and pray for its return: and then a miracle occurred: during the reign of Doge Vitale Falier (1084-96), on the occasion of the consecration of the third church to be erected on this site (25 June 1094), a part of a pilaster in the right transept crumbled to reveal a human arm. The sacred relic was removed to the crypt and later (19C) to below the high altar. The 11C basilica is modelled upon the Church of the Holy Apostles in Constantinople, and its building is thought to have been supervised by a Greek architect. Right from the start, it came to be the pride of the Venetians: **Doge Domenico Selvo** (1071-84) would ask merchants travelling to the East to bring back marble and other stone pieces (alabaster, jasper, porphyry, serpentine) for its embellishment, indeed it was thus that the mosaics in the domes and the vaults came about.

Exterior – A unique spectacle at any hour of the day, it appeared as a "vision" to Ruskin. Silhouetted against the sky are the Basilica's five 13C Byzantine domes which culminate in a cross over the lantern. The lateral façades face onto Piazzetta dei Leoncini and Piazzetta San Marco.

West front – The façade is articulated horizontally by a terrace and balustrade that extends down the lateral walls; vertically, the width is divided into five bays, pierced at both levels by arches, opening at ground level into porches.

The iconography of the 17C mosaics from the left arch is as follows:

1st arch: *Transportation of the Body of St Mark into the Church* (1260-70), the only complete mosaic to survive from the façade's original decoration;

2nd arch: *St Mark Venerated by Venetian Magistrates* (based on a cartoon by Sebastiano Ricci (1659-1734);

3rd arch: (main, central archway) the 19C replacement mosaics, *Christ in Glory* and *The Last Judgement,* are enclosed in an arch populated with figures amongst foliage; below the mosaics, the three archivolts (inner arches) are illustrated with Romanesque-Byzantine carvings representing the Three Kingdoms:

Accademia, Venezia/SCALA

Land, Ocean and Animal, the Labours of the Months and the Signs of the Zodiac, the Virtues and Beatitudes. Running along the intrados of the main arch (underside) are depictions of the typical Venetian trades: note the man on the left with the crutches, thought to allude to the architect of St Mark's, gnawing his hand, preoccupied by the imperfection of his work.

4th arch: *The Body of St Mark Welcomed by the Venetians;*
5th arch: *The Theft of the Relic of St Mark.*

Modern copies now replace the four bronze horses on the balcony, the originals are conserved in the museum. On the upper level, the arches terminate in Gothic cusps. The 17C mosaics *(see below)* depict (from left to right): *The Deposition, The Descent into Limbo, The Resurrection* and *The Ascension.*

Left side – It is worth walking down the left flank, overlooking Piazzetta dei Leoncini, to admire the Porta dei Fiori (4th arch, on the corner) with its Romanesque relief of *The Nativity.*

Right side – The south side abuts the Doges' Palace on the piazzetta. The first arch is framed by two columns surmounted with Romanesque griffins; the second arch contains the door to the Baptistry, framed with the **Acrean pillars** (1), possibly brought here by Lorenzo Tiepolo from the Church of St Saba in Acre in Israel as a trophy after the battle against the Genoese in 1258. Syrian in origin, two of the 6C columns have white marble shafts, whilst the one nearest the piazzetta is of porphyry. This porphyry column is also known as the **pietra del bando**, the proclamation stone from where laws would be announced. In 1902, when the campanile collapsed, this pedestal was damaged while protecting the corner of the Basilica.

The Tetrarchs

On the corner nearest the Palace stand the famous 4C **Tetrarchs ★** (2) or Moors – sometimes upheld to allude to the Emperors Diocletian, Maximilian, Valerian and Constantine. They are otherwise said to be Saracens who were turned to stone when trying to steal the treasure of St Mark, if, that is, the legend is to be believed! Entry into the basilica is through the large atrium that would have been reserved for the unbaptised and new converts. Decked with mosaics that relate stories from the Old Testament *(The History of the Fall of Man, The Lives of the Patriarchs up to the Receipt of the Law by Moses* and *The Fall of Manna from Heaven)*, these herald others inside the church that illustrate incidents from the New Testament. In effect, in the whole the mosaics transform the church into *"a great Book of Common Prayer; the mosaics were its illuminations, and the common people of the time were taught their Scripture history by means of them."*

Atrium ⊘ – At the end of the Fourth Crusade *(see Introduction – Over a thousand years of glory: 1201-1204)*, Venice entered a phase of self-esteem and celebration on the wave of victory after the conquest of Constantinople.

Romanesque and early Christian iconography in these early mosaics are borrowed from 5-6C illuminated manuscripts that appear to have reached Venice with the Fourth Crusade.

Start with the right dome, and follow towards the left.

The Creation according to Genesis (3) – These are the oldest mosaics in the atrium: in three concentric circles, in an anti-clockwise direction, they tell the story of Genesis, beginning with the dove, the smallest mosaic to the east. In synthesis with the tradition of the Eastern Church, based upon the Gospel of St John *(The word was God...)*, the figure of the Creator is that of Christ, beardless, to signify the period before the Incarnation. Each stage of the Creation is attended by the angels which gradually increase in numbers as the days go by.

Note, on the day of the creation of the animals, the lions before God that symbolise Venice's atmosphere of pride and self-congratulation; on the day on which the Creator blesses the seventh angel – the day of rest and the day that Adam and Eve were chased from the Garden of Paradise, how they are depicted dressed in clothes. On the eighth day, Christ is born heralding the beginning of a new Creation.

The **Arch of Noah** (4) depicts the story of Noah and the Flood: notice the ark's little window during the deluge.

Continuing with the iconographic theme initiated in the entrance, the mosaics of the **Arch of Paradise** (5), designed in part by Tintoretto (1518-94) and Aliense (1556-1629), exalt the mission of the Church as the Salvation of Man by means of the Cross, Paradise and Hell; represented as symbols that break with the narrative of the Old Testament stories illustrated previously. Before passing through the doorway, it is worth looking up at the vault, where St Mark in Ecstasy is based on a cartoon by Titian (1490-1576).

In the niches on either side of the doorway stand the Madonna, Apostles and Evangelists, the ornamentation is Byzantine.

The story of Noah continues in the next arch with a particularly beautiful depiction of the **Tower of Babel** (6) marking a prelude to the division of the human race.

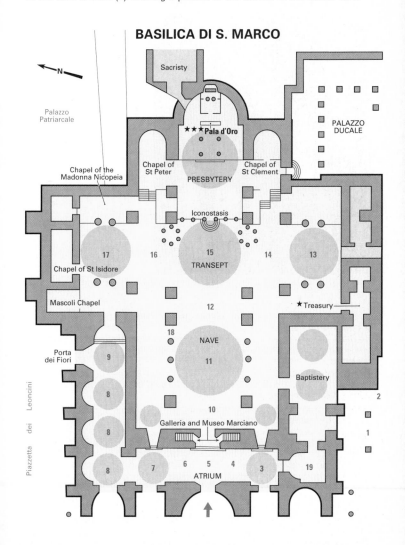

BASILICA DI S. MARCO

Story of Abraham (7) – The mosaics in the second dome comprise one cycle, dedicated to the life of Abraham. Between the various scenes are lunettes which illustrate God's promises to Abraham. In the next arch, Abraham is depicted with the confirmation in writing, as the prefiguration of Christ.

Story of Joseph (8) – The last dome on the left and the next two in the left arm illustrate the story of Joseph. In order to portray a person who is dreaming – in this case the Pharaoh – the mosaic artists resorted to a sort of bubble that unfurls. The second and third dome of this series post-date the first by about 20 years which explains why the images and landscapes appear richer and more vibrant.

Story of Moses (9) – In the last dome of the atrium, this part of the biblical cycle concludes with the life of Moses.

Above the door, the Madonna presents her Son, flanked by St John and St Mark. This concludes the Old Testament cycle and serves as a link to the New Testament by encouraging the visitor to carry on "reading" inside the Basilica.

A steep flight of stairs leads to the Galleria and the Museo Marciano.

Galleria and Museo Marciano ⊙ – Access to the Marciano Museum is via the Gallery, from where there is a marvellous view of the mosaics and an opportunity to look out over the piazza from the balcony. The museum houses tapestries, mosaics and some interesting documents relating to the history of the Basilica. The greatest draw of visitors must be the *Gilded Bronze Horses* ★★. They arrived in Venice as part of the booty from the Fourth Crusade but undoubtedly date back to a much earlier period, although opinion on their actual origin is divided between being 4-3C BC Greek works or 4C Roman works.

Given pride of place on the balcony, these wonderful equestrian statues were taken to Paris by Napoleon after his crushing Italian campaign, but returned in 1815. In 1974 they were removed from their original position for restoration and replaced with copies.

S. Grandadam/EXPLORER

The Bronze Horses

St Mark's interior – It is impossible to say what is most striking about St Mark's. It may well be the luminosity of this unique "tapestry" of mosaics which were first executed in 1071 by artists brought to Venice from Constantinople. It could be the eastern aura or the 12C pavement decorated with animal and geometric motifs; its uneven surface caused by subsidence only serves to heighten the sensation of having being inherited from a mysterious and sacred past.

In the form of a Greek cross, St Mark's has a raised presbytery separated from the central nave by an iconostasis.

★★★ **Mosaics** – It can be enormously bewildering to find oneself surrounded by such a plethora of images, their brilliance often accentuated by the two "eyes" of light in the right transept and above the portal.

As a general means of orientation, the lower part of the walls depict the saints, the middle section is reserved for the Apostles whilst the domes are dedicated to the Creator. The key to each story is held in the dome of the apse from where the story unfurls chronologically: Christ as Pantocrator towers over the four patrons of Venice: St Nicholas, St Peter, St Mark and St Ermagora, with the area above the atrium given over to the Last Judgement. These last mosaics are also the most recent dating as they do from the 16C.

The entrance door depicts the *Deesis*, the Saviour in benediction between the Virgin and St Mark.

The **Arch of the Apocalypse** (10) illustrates the visions described in the gospel of St John: the seven candelabra symbolising the seven churches.

St Mark's golden interior

The dome nearest the doorway is dedicated to the *Pentecost* (11). Between the windows, the populace listens to the preaching of St Peter in Jerusalem; to correspond with the angels, the Four Evangelists are illustrated in the pendentives. Approaching the central dome, the **West Arch** (12) presents a synthesis of the *Passion* and *Death of Christ*. Worthy of note are the cartouches in the hand of the Judeans, bearing Pilate and Christ.

In the right transept, illuminated by a Gothic rose window, the **Dome of St Leonard** (13) or the Saints of the Sacrament, is decorated with 13C mosaics representing Saints Nicholas, Clement, Blaise and Leonard. The **South Arch** (14) has Byzantine mosaics which depict the *Temptations of Christ* and *His Entry into Jerusalem*, the *Last Supper* and the *Washing of the Feet*.

In the centre is the **Dome of the Ascension** (15). This encapsulates the most important moments in the story of the Salvation. Witnesses to the *Ascension* include the Apostles, the Madonna and, between the windows, the Virtues and some of the Beatitudes. Christ in Benediction dominates the scene. Beneath the pendentives which depict the Four Evangelists are the Four Rivers of the Earth.

The **Presbytery Dome** is dedicated to the Season of Advent, dominated by Emmanuel in the company of Prophets, with the Virgin in the middle. The decoration of this dome dates back to the beginning of 1100. Symbols of the Evangelists adorn the pendentives.

The mosaics on the **North Arch** (16) designed by Tintoretto show *St Michael with Sword Drawn* with the *Last Supper* on the left and the *Marriage at Cana* on the right. In the centre, the *Healing of the Leper* is taken from a cartoon by Veronese

(1528-1588), the *Healing of the Bleeding Woman* and the *Resurrection of Naim's Widow's Son* are based on cartoons by Salviati (1520/25-75). The *Christ in Glory* is a 19C reconstruction.

The **Dome of St John the Evangelist** (17) is in the left arm of the transept. The 13C mosaics reproduce a Greek cross with biblical verses on the *Sermon on the Mount* and episodes from the Life of St John the Evangelist.

Continue along the left aisle.

In the north aisle is the **Capital of the Crucifixion** (18), a white and black marble structure with a pyramidal roof surmounted by an agate. The crucifix contained therein, coming from Constantinople, would have been the cause of much bloodshed.

The mosaic panels (c 1230) opposite the side aisles depict: *Christ Blessing the Prophets* – Hosea, Joel, Micah and Jeremiah *(in the left aisle)* and Ezekiel, Solomon, the Madonna in prayer, David and Isaiah *(in the right aisle)*.

★★★**Pala d'Oro** ⊘ – The Golden Altarpiece is preceded by a ciborium on **columns of alabaster**★★ inscribed with reliefs inspired by the Gospels and the Apocrypha. The exact date and provenance of these reliefs remain uncertain, however, but are usually classified as 5C-6C Greek (from Ravenna), Syrian, Egyptian or Coptic. Contained within the high altar rest the remains of St Mark, and beyond, towers the great altarpiece.

Commissioned and made in Constantinople in the 10C, the Golden Altarpiece is a masterpiece of the goldsmith's craft. Gleaming with precious stones set amongst enamelled panels, it continued to be embellished with new and valuable sections until the 14C.

The top section is dominated by the figure of the Archangel Michael in the centre, framed between scenes *(starting from the left)* of the *Entry into Jerusalem*, the *Resurrection*, the *Crucifixion*, the *Ascension*, the *Pentecost* and the *Death of the Virgin*. The focal point of the lower section is Christ Pantocrator (the Ruler of the Universe) flanked by the figures of the Evangelists. Below, the Virgin appears between the Empress Irene and the Emperor Giovanni Commeno, Prophets, Apostles and Angels. On either side, the iconographic cycle continues with episodes from the lives of Christ and St Mark.

In the apse, the doors to the tabernacle and to the sacristy are by Sansovino.

Chapels – Grouped around the presbytery it is worth stopping to look at the **iconostasis** (open-work screen) in polychrome marble. Eight columns support an architrave bearing figures of the **Apostles**, the **Madonna** and **John the Baptist** by Dalle Masegne (14C-15C). This great line is broken in the middle by a bronze and silver **Crucifix**. At either end, the iconostasis terminates with a pulpit, each reconstructed in the 14C. The **Double Pulpit** on the left comprises two sections from which lessons are read from the Gospels *(upper tier)* and the Epistles *(lower tier)*. To honour the Word of God, it is crowned with a fine golden cupola which is decidedly oriental in style.

The Golden Altarpiece (detail – San Marco)

The pulpit on the right, the **Pulpit of the Reliquary**, was where the relics would be displayed and where the newly elected doge would make his first appearance. Both chapels dedicated to **St Clement** *(right apse)* and **St Peter** *(left apse)* are screened off by their own iconostasis; the one for St Clement, complete with statues, is by Dalle Masegne. Outside each chapel, the wall is covered with mosaic (12C) illustrating episodes from the lives of St Mark and St Peter respectively, while in-side the domed vault of each are representations of the saints to whom each chapel is dedicated (St Peter is 13C).

The window on the right wall of the Chapel of St Clement enabled the doge to follow functions and services being held in church without leaving the comfortable confines of his palace appartments.

In the **Chapel of the Madonna Nicopeia** is a particularly venerated image of the Madonna and Child, called *Nicopeia* (meaning the Bringer of Victory or Leader), because she served as the standard of the Byzantine army. Coming from Constantinople, the figure may have been brought to Venice as booty from the Fourth Crusade.

The **Chapel of St Isidore** is off the transept, whose end wall bears *Mary's Genealogical Tree* which dates back to the end of the 12C.

The next chapel, the **Mascoli Chapel** is dedicated to the members of confraternity of male worshippers. The mosaics are the work of

Salome Dancing (San Marco)

Giambono (active 1420-62), Andrea del Castagno (c 1421-57), Jacopo Bellini (c 1396-1470) and Andrea Mantegna (1431-1506).

★**Tesoro** ⊙ – This treasury houses an extremely valuable collection of religious objects, reliquaries and ornaments which came into Venice's possession after the conquest of Constantinople in 1204 includes one notable exhibit, namely the *Artophoron*, an 11C container for the Bread of the Eucharist in the shape of a church, crowned with oriental-style domes.

Baptistery ⊙ – Divided into three interconnecting areas, the baptistery (battistero) boasts a series of 14C mosaics that recount episodes from the life of John the Baptist and the Infant Jesus. The most famous panel shows *Salome Dancing before Herod.* The baptismal font is by Sansovino (1486-1570), who is buried here, before the altar.

The mosaics in the **Cappella Zen** (19), the funeral chapel of Cardinal Zen who died in 1501, date from the 13C.

> *"Now the first broad characteristic of the building, and the root nearly of every other important peculiarity in it, is its confessed incrustation. It is the purest example in Italy of the great school of architecture in which the ruling principle is the incrustation of brick with more precious materials..."*
>
> *John Ruskin*

★★IL CAMPANILE ⊙ (**B**, FX)

Although the present bell-tower was erected at the beginning of the 20C *(see above)* it was rebuilt according to its predecessor's early 16C designs by Bartolomeo Bon, a native of Bergamo (recorded in Venice from c 1463 to 1529, and not to be confused with the Venetian of the same name active between 1441 and 1464).

Built in brick, the campanile stands 96m/315ft high, culminating in a golden angel weather-vein that turns in the wind. Contemporary written chronicles from the time of its inauguration, describe the occasion as being accompanied by musical fanfares and drunken revelry.

Solid in appearance, the square tower is articulated as if by a gigantic order of pilasters up to an arched white marble section pierced by a four-light loggia where the bells hang. Above a balustraded section, the four sides rise cleanly to a pyramid.

Once upon a time, the campanile... – The tower was also used by performing acrobats. According to tradition during the Carnival, on the Thursday before Lent, the doge attended the *svolo dell'Angelo* or *del Turco* (translated as the angel or

---

The Bells of San Marco

There are five deeply sonorous bells, each with its own name:
La Marangona, the largest of the clutch was salvaged when the tower fell. Its name derives from the fact that it tolled the working hours of the *marangoni* or carpenters. It also heralded times when the Major Council met; the second strike, known as *la Trottiera* acted as a signal for the nobles to "trot" quickly over to the palace. *La Nona* (the grandmother) rang at midday; *la Mezza Terza* (Middle Third) or Pregadi Bell *(see Palazzo Ducale – below)* was a sign that the Senate was in session, while the notorious knell of the *Renghiera* or Bad One marked an execution.

Turk's flight to earth). This was a spectacular performance involving an abseil down a rope that extended from the belfry to a boat or to the loggia of the Doges' Palace. A less amusing spectacle was the *supplizio della cheba* when priests accused of blasphemy were suspended from the top in a cage.

At the top, from where **Galileo Galilei** (1564-1642) once extended his telescope (1609), one has the "privilege" of enjoying a **view★★** that extends from the Giudecca Canal to the Grand Canal across a sea of roofs, chimneys and *altane* (wooden roof terraces) and beyond, to the islands in the lagoon. It is a privilege because at one time the campanile was almost inaccessible to outsiders: it was feared that spies would take advantage of the opportunity to seek out strategic hideaways and anchorages.

Loggetta Sansoviniana – At the base of the tower, and facing St Mark's, the richly decorated Sansovino Loggetta comprises three arches supported on columns reminiscent of a triumphal arch; columns also frame the niches that accommodate the figures of Minerva, Apollo, Mercury and Peace. The reliefs above depict *(from left to right)* the Island of Candia, Venice as an allegory of Justice, and the Island of Cyprus. The terrace at the front is enclosed by a balustrade, broken in the middle by a bronze gate designed by Antonio Gai (1686-1769).

At one time, wooden huts-cum-workshops would have been erected around the base of the campanile; these were banned in the 15C, when it was decided to rid the square of anything that might detract from the splendour and refinement of this corner of the city so symbolic of the nobility of the State and its religious spirit. And so the original Loggia or Ridotto dei Nobili was removed to a location nearby. The present *loggetta* was first built during the early part of the 16C by Sansovino (1486-1570) and rebuilt after the collapse of the campanile.

During sittings of the Grand Council it also provided shelter to the armed guard of *arsenalotti (see ARSENALE)*.

The day the campanile collapsed

★★★ PALAZZO DUCALE (DOGES' PALACE) (◘, GX)

The magnificent richness of the decoration and the uncommon attention to detail are such that every corner and every stone of the Doges' Palace – which is more like a part of the city than a *palazzo* – has a story to tell. Little by little, wherever one looks, its long history unfurls.

The old Palatium Ducis – The origins of this Byzantine, Gothic and Renaissance palace go back almost as far as those of Venice itself. It was **Doge Agnello Partecipazio** who decided, in 810, that the seat of his public offices should be located on the site of the present Doges' Palace. At the time, the buildings, which included the Church of St Mark, were more of a citadel than a government office.

The need for a fortified residence gradually ceded towards one with an institutional role with loggias and porticoes on the outside and a host of offices inside where various affairs of State could be conducted by the doge's staff.

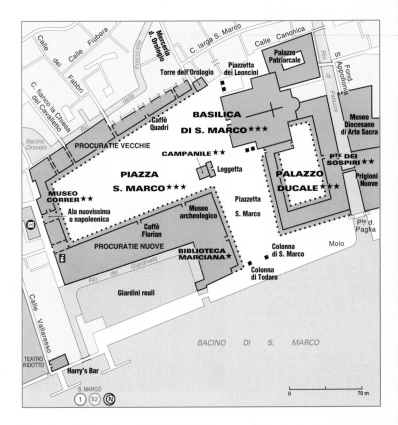

From the outside – Even at first sight, the harmony of the structural whole is striking: the "hollow" spaces of the portico and the loggia contrast with blocks of "solid" masonry in the upper section of the building. The effect is mitigated however by the rose-coloured tint of the upper floor and the darkness of the multi-arched lower floors. The narrative function of the mosaics inside the basilica is transposed here onto the sculptural iconography that adorns the capitals, the corners of the *palazzo* and its pillars. Decorating the palace are allegorical figures representing the Vices and Virtues, Labours of the Month, the Ages of Man and Signs of the Zodiac – all charged with moral example.

The façade onto the piazzetta, almost as long as that which overlooks St Mark's Basin, rises from an arcade of 18 pointed arches along the ground floor, supported on baseless columns. The first-floor loggia also runs continuously along the façade, the horizontal emphasis is accentuated by the balustrade and sequence of 34 roundels between the ogive, cusped arches, punctured with quatrefoil cut-outs. From between the two red marble columns, public announcements of capital sentences were made, later to be carried out between the columns of Saints Mark and Theodore in the square below *(see below)*.

The two upper storeys, which together are as tall as the two lower floors, seem lost in solid wall. From a distance, the building appears a distinctively soft shade of pinky-rose, with surface relief at closer proximity, provided by the interplay of terracotta and white bricks disposed in diamond patterns. Its massiveness is further offset by the delicate line of gables along the top.

On the first floor, the central balcony overlooking the piazzetta is from the 16C (artists unknown): the portrait above it is of Doge Andrea Gritti (1523-38). At each corner is a sculptural ensemble: that projecting into the square depicts the *Judgement of Solomon*, an allegory of Wisdom, thought to be by Bartolomeo Bon (active 1441-64) beyond which stands the Porta della Carta.

★★**Porta della Carta** – The "Paper Doorway" is the entrance to the palace *per se.* Flamboyant Gothic in style, it was constructed by Giovanni and Bartolomeo Bon between 1438 and 1442. Explanations for the name have been attributed to the many scribes that used the entrance which also served the archives *(cartarum)*. The super-imposed niches are occupied by the four Cardinal Virtues sculpted by Antonio Bregno (c 1418-c 1503). Above the doorway, kneeling before the winged lion is Doge Francesco Foscari who was in power when the portal was constructed. Above the window, in the roundel is St Mark, overlooked by Justice on the pinnacle.

To reach the canal quayside from the Piazzetta San Marco, walk round the full length of both sides of the palace.

The façade overlooking the Basin stretches between the corner sculpture groups of *(left) Adam, Eve and the Serpent* (late 14C) – an allegory of Sin – surmounted by the figures of Tobias and the Angel Rafael (late 14C) and *The Drunkenness of Noah* (14C-15C), showing the rare virtue of indulgence *(near the Paglia Bridge)*.

The second capital from the left, known as the Capital of the Sages *(dei Sapienti)*, is inscribed with the date 1344, the year in which this wing was constructed. The central balcony on the second floor was inserted in the early 15C, designed by Dalle Masegne.

The reason the last two, more decorative, windows appear out of alignment with the others is because of the internal room arrangement.

To the right, the Ponte della Paglia (literally translated as the Bridge of Straw) precedes that second and much more famous bridge across the canal.

The Drunkenness of Noah

J. Gabanou/DIAF

On the right side of the basilica, near the Porta della Carta, stand the vestiges of a tower decorated with low-relief sculptures; as they are not directly at eye level, they tend to elude the attention of visitors. However, if you crouch down a little, you will notice one in particular that is located under the Tetrarchs, just on the right. It represents two putti escaping from the jaws of two dragons. They are pictured framing an ancient inscription, believed to be one of the very first texts written in Venetian dialect.

★★**Ponte dei Sospiri** (🖪, GX) – Universally well known, the Bridge of Sighs owes its name to Romantic literary notions: overwhelmed by the enchanting view from the windows of this bridge, this was where the prisoners would suffer their final torment.

The bridge, constructed in Istrian stone, actually links the palace with the Prigioni Nuove (New Prisons). It was built during the dogeship of **Marino Grimani** (1595-1605) and bears his coat of arms. Inside, the bridge is divided into two passages through which visitors pass on their tour of the Doges' Palace. Given the number of rooms and the length of the tour, it is easy to lose one's bearings and to cross the bridge without realising it – so beware!

The entrance to the *palazzo* is to the right of the Porta della Carta (through which visitors pass on their way out). The courtyard is graced with a fine mid-16C well-head, the mid-15C **Porticato Foscari** leading through to the **Foscari Arch**, and the

Scala dei Giganti directly opposite. The Giants' Staircase, constructed at the end of the 15C, was designed by Antonio Rizzo (c 1440-99) and is dominated by two magnificent statues of Mars and Neptune (the gods of War and Sea) by Sansovino (1486-1570). It was at the top of these stairs that the doges used to be crowned.

The well-heads in the courtyard date back to the mid 16C, whereas the east end façade, designed by Rizzo, is early Renaissance in style.

Interior ⊙ – From the portico, take the **Scala d'Oro** or Golden Staircase up to the second floor. Sansovino initiated work on the staircase during the reign of **Doge Andrea Gritti** (1523-38) although work was not to be completed by Scarpagnino (recorded in Venice 1505-49) until after the appointment of Lorenzo Priuli (1556-59):

Ponte dei Sospiri

note the coats of arms of the two doges on the large arch. Its Baroque-sounding name comes from reference to the rich stucco decoration in white and gold around Giovan Battista Franco's (1498-1561) frescoes depicting *The Glorification of the Defence of Cyprus and Crete* and *The Virtues Necessary for Good Government*.

The portrait in the atrium of Doge Gerolamo Priuli was painted by Tintoretto (1518-94).

L'Appartamento Ducale – Before undertaking a tour of the *palazzo*, it is well worth following the signs through to the Ducal Apartment in which are displayed a *Pietà* by Giovanni Bellini and the famous *Lion* by Vittore Carpaccio.

Sala delle Quattro Porte – Referred to as the Chamber of the Four Doors, this first room is where the ambassadors would wait for their audience with the doge. The decoration post-dates 1574, following one of the many fires caused by the use of wood and candles. Propped up on the easel is *Venice Receiving the Homage of Neptune*, a famous canvas by Tiepolo (1696-1770). The frescoed ceiling is by Tintoretto, the four doorways are by Palladio (1508-80). The paintings on the walls depict allegorical scenes or historical subjects linked to Venice's glorious past. Among these, *Doge Antonio Grimani in Adoration before the Faith and St Mark in Glory* was started by Titian (1490-1576) and finished by his nephew. The painting commemorating a visit made by Henry III, King of France, in 1574, depicts the Triumphal Arch designed by Palladio that would have been made of *papier-mâché*, a material commonly used to create temporary stage sets for special occasions.

Sala dell'Anticollegio – Serving as an antechamber for diplomatic missions and delegations, the room houses the *Return of Jacob with Family* by Jacopo Bassano (c 1517-92) and the *Rape of Europa* by Veronese (1528-88) *(facing the windows)*. The paintings on either side of the doors are by Tintoretto and illustrate allegories of the Seasons: the inward harmony of the landscapes suggests the rewards of careful husbandry achieved under good government. The fresco on the ceiling is by Veronese.

Sala del Collegio – It was here in the College Chamber that the doge, his throne raised on the wooden platform, presided over meetings.

The "Full College" used to deal with legal matters that were subsequently presented to the Senate, and political relationships between Venice and foreign courts on diplomatic missions. The stalls date back to 1575. The principal theme of the paintings decorating the gilded wooden ceiling is the *Exaltation of Venice*; also by Veronese is the great panel above the throne depicting *Doge Sebastiano Venier Thanking the Redeemer after the Battle of Lepanto.*

The paintings on the wall with the clock set in black Belgian marble are by Tintoretto: to the left of the clock, *Alvise Mocenigo Thanking the Redeemer* commemorates the votive plea for an end to the plague of 1576 which, once granted, provoked the building of Il Redentore on the Giudecca *(see La GIUDECCA)*. Tintoretto's painting on the door continues in the same vein of celebration.

Sala del Senato – The Senate Chamber, or the "Pregadi Chamber", was where the members of the Senate were asked *(pregati)* to submit their written request to participate in the meetings. It was here that the assembly presided over all matters of State. The decor, refurbished after the fire of 1574, is peopled with the figures of doges and patron saints, in audience before the Redeemer or the Virgin. In the central panel of the ceiling Tintoretto depicted *The Triumph of Venice*. Behind the throne hangs *The Dead Christ Adored by Doges Pietro Lando and Marcantonio Trevisan. Doges Lorenzo and Girolamo Priuli Kneeling before the Redeemer* is the work of Palma il Giovane (1548-1628) as are the paintings on the wall opposite the windows. In the *Allegory of Victory over the League of Cambrai,* Venice appears as a young warrior

Palazzo Ducale

on the attack, preceded by the lion, while a laurel wreath is brought to Doge Loredan from Heaven *(on the door)*. The pulpit was used by those taking part in the debates.

Sala del Consiglio dei Dieci – The Chamber of the Council of Ten was where the powerful and notorious council, whose origins go back as far as 1310, used to meet. On the ceiling preside allegories of Good Government and the Power of the Republic: Veronese's *Juno Offering the Doge's Corno (cap) Amongst Jewels and Gold to Venice* is one of the most notable; the central painting of *Jove Descending from the Sky to Strike Down the Vices* is in fact a copy after Veronese – the original, "stolen" by Napoleon, is now in the Louvre. On the walls are depicted two important historical events: *The Peace of Bologna between Pope Clement VII and Emperor Charles V* by Marco Vecellio (1545-1611), a cousin of Titian *(left)* and *Pope Alexander III Blesses Doge Sebastiano Ziani after the Battle of Salvore* by Francesco da Ponte, also known as Bassano (1549-92), and his brother Leandro (1557-1622) *(right)*.

Sala della Bussola – The Ballot Chamber was also the waiting room for those who were to be interrogated by the heads *(capi)* of the Council of Ten. To the left of the ballot-box is a painting by Marco Vecellio, *Doge Leonardo Donà with St Mark in Adoration before the Virgin.* To the side of the main entrance is a small wooden hatch that allowed secret denunciations to be removed from the *bocca di leone* or lion's mouth outside *(see Introduction – Over a thousand years of glory: 1310)*. The ceiling is predominantly attributed to followers of Veronese, although the central painting, *St Mark in Glory Descending to Crown the Three Theological Virtues* is a copy – the original being in the Louvre.

Armeria – The various rooms which make up the Armoury house a variety of objects including: tournament armour, trophies and relics of war, the suit of armour of the infamous *condottiere* Gattamelata identified by the badge with a cat on the knee, a Turkish flag, the trophy of Lepanto, crossbows, maces, broadswords, a container for harquebus fuses, pistols and instruments of torture. The room dedicated to Francesco Morosini is marked with the sign CX, the Council of Ten's monogram.

Sala del Maggior Consiglio – The Grand Council Chamber is perhaps the highlight of the tour: especially if this enormous room (1300m²/14 000sq ft) is pictured as it might have been on most special occasions, rather than thronged with noisy

tourists. During sittings of the Grand Council, the legislative body which appointed almost all public offices, the doors of the Chamber would be closed and armed guards positioned outside the palace. Summons to meetings were sounded by the bell of St Mark's.

Here and in the nearby Sala dello Scrutinio, the constitutional election of the new doge was conducted according to set procedures as the number of nominees was gradually reduced. For the initial stage of the selection process, the *ballotte* (ballot papers), one for each voter present, were placed in the urn. Of these papers, only 30 bore the word *lector*; those whose *ballotta* was found to be blank were thereby dismissed and forced to abandon the field. The next stages involving the further

Sala del Maggior Consiglio

PALAZZO DUCALE

SECOND FLOOR

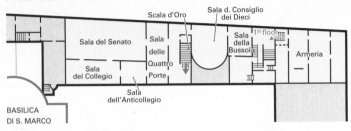

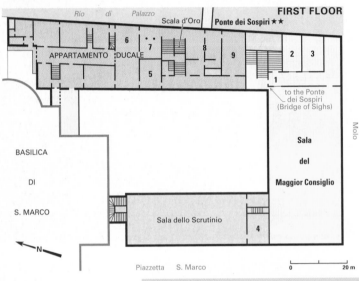

1	Corridoio o vestibolo	APPARTAMENTO DUCALE	
2	Sala della Quarantia Civil Vecchia	5 Sala degli Scarlatti	8 Sale Magistrato alle Leggi
3	Sala dell'Armamento	6 Sala dello Scudo	9 Sala della Quarantia
4	Sala della Quarantia Civil Nuova	7 Sala degli Scudieri	Criminal

elimination of 19 nominees were long-winded and complicated: the final objective, however, was to arrive at 11 men whose role was to appoint a body of 41 electors, who, in turn would elect the next doge, with a minimum majority of 25 votes.

The great fire of 1577 destroyed most of the paintings that originally decorated the room, the exception being the 14C Guariente fresco depicting the *Coronation of the Virgin*, now in the Sala del Armamento. The damaged panels were swiftly replaced, however, with ever more magnificent decoration. The subject of the long wall which overlooks the Basin is the Fourth Crusade. Other notable paintings include *Doge Enrico Dandolo and the Crusader Captains in the Basilica of St Mark Swearing Loyalty before Leaving for the Expedition* by Carlo Saraceni (1579-1620) and Jean Le Clerc (1585-1633), *Crusaders Besieging Constantinople* by Palma il Giovane, the *Conquest of Constantinople* by Domenico Tintoretto (c 1560-1635) and *Crusaders in Santa Sofia electing Baldovino of Flanders as Emperor of the East* by Andrea Micheli (1539-1614), also known as Vicentino. On the opposite long wall overlooking the courtyard, are the events that linked Doge Sebastiano Ziani, Alexander III and Barbarossa in opposition to the Pope. Of particular interest is the painting by Federico Zuccari (c 1542-1609), *The Emperor Kissing the Pontiff's Foot before the Basilica*. Despite the overall magnificence of this room, one cannot fail to be impressed by the vast and populated painting behind the throne depicting **Paradise**, executed by Tintoretto, his son and followers *(see Introduction – Over a thousand years of glory)*.

Below the ceiling runs a line of portraits representing the first of the 76 doges who governed Venice between 804 and 1554 with their coats of arms, almost all executed by Domenico Tintoretto, although the commission had been awarded to his more famous father. Marino Falier who, in the 14C, conspired against the State and was beheaded *(see Introduction – Over a thousand years of glory)* is remembered rather unfavourably: his likeness (on the wall facing *Paradise*) is obscured by a painted veil bearing the inscription: *"Hic est locus Marini Falethri decapitati pro criminibus"* (This is Marino Falier who was decapitated for his crime). Portraits of the last 39 doges spanning the years 1556 to 1797 are in the Scrutinio.

The trussed wooden ceiling is dominated by Veronese's **Apotheosis of Venice** (1582) in which Venice, attended by allegories of War (Mars crowned with the laurels of Victory), Peace (Irene before the olive branch), Wisdom (Minerva, patron of the Liberal Arts, with the caduceus and crown), Fertility (Ceres with the horn of plenty) and Justice (Themis with the dogal *corno*), appears as the matron on a cloud, being crowned by a winged figure. Below, her citizens (the nobility along the balcony of the *piano grande*) bear witness.

The other paintings on the ceiling celebrate Venice's victory in battle. The rectangular panel, *Doge Nicolò da Ponte Receiving a Laurel Crown from Venice* is by Tintoretto. It shows Venice, flanked by the winged lion, holding the palm of Peace and laurel crown of Victory, leaning down towards the new doge, thereby approving the process by which he has been appointed with the involvement of all the figures at each stage (represented up the stairs). The oval panel depicting *Venice Supreme, Crowned by Victory Welcoming her Subject Provinces* is by Palma il Giovane. The other 12 works to the sides are all based on the same theme: the valour with which Venice distinguishes herself at salient points in the Republic's history.

Sala dello Scrutinio – It was in this chamber that the *scrutinio* (counting) of the votes took place. The series of portraits of the Governors of Venice concludes with the last doge, **Lodovico Manin** (1789-97) who ceded to Napoleon and marked the subjugation of the Serenissima: obviously, only the first works are by Tintoretto and assistants, the following having been executed by various artists contemporary with the subsequent doges.

As with the Grand Council Chamber, the decoration of this room also celebrates grandiose events in Venice's history. The ceiling comprises five large paintings, interspersed with three oval and two rectangular panels – the most noteworthy of these being the end oval depicting *The Naval Victory of the Venetians over the Pisans at Rodi* by Vicentino (c 1539-1614/17) and its central counterpart showing *The Venetian Victory over the Genoese at Trapani* by Giovanni Bellini (c 1426-1516). The partition wall dividing this room from the **Sala della Quarantia Civil Nuova** bears Palma il Giovane's *Last Judgement* which replaced Tintoretto's painting destroyed during the fire of 1577.

The paintings on the side walls retell Venice's victorious sea battles including those waged against the Hungarians for the *Conquest of Zara* (by Tintoretto), and the *Battle of Lepanto* (1603) by Vicentino *(right wall)*. The end wall features *The Triumphal Arch* (1694) constructed in honour of the Peloponnesian, Francesco Morosini, after his victory against the Turks *(see Introduction – Over a thousand years of glory)*.

Just before the prisons, the Sala del Magistrato alle Leggi preserves *The Mocking of Christ* by the Flemish master Quentin Metsys (1466-1530) and the only works by Hieronymus Bosch (c 1450-1516) in Italy, namely the three of the four panels: the *Martyr of Santa Liberata, The Hermits, Paradise* in which the tunnel that leads towards the light is said to recreate pictorially the experience of someone awakening from a coma, and the *Fall of the Damned*. *Hell* which is rich with the same complex symbolism is the work of an imitator (initialled J S).

Prigioni Nuove – Steps lead up to the Bridge of Sighs *(see above)* and beyond to the New Prisons on the other side of the canal. These prisons also served as the seat of the magistrature of the **Signori di Notte al Criminal**, a sort of vice squad. Note the graffiti inscribed on the stone walls.

Cross the bridge to the palace.

Sala dei Censori – This chamber lined with wooden seats, known as the Censors' Chamber, accommodated a judiciary body. The paintings, mostly by Domenico Tintoretto, consist of formal portraits of magistrating censors in office.

Sala dell'Avogaria – The last room of the tour, the Avagoria Chamber, was the seat of another part of the former magistrature, whose members, the *avogadori* consisted of lawyers appointed by the State. Their duty was to ensure that the Law was obeyed. It is unusual for such portraits to have been presented in this way, a practise that hitherto was reserved for religious subjects.

The tour concludes with the **Sala dello Scrigno** and the **Sala della Millizia da Mar**.

A tour through the labyrinthine palace corridors ⊘ – The various magistratures that had seats in the palace operated in an environment that was anything but ostentatious. Many of the activities, most of which were secret, took place in very restricted surroundings just off the grand chambers. Linked by a maze of hidden stairs and passageways, these still exude an air of mystery. Although his office was small, the Grand Chancellor, the director of the Secret Chancellery (Venice's general archives), enjoyed such prestige that he was not obliged to remove his headdress in the presence of the doge. The **Cancelleria segreta** (Secret Chancellery) which resembles a ship's deck embellished with wooden fixtures, is ornamented with the Chancellor's coats of arms.

The impressive **Sala delle Torture** (Torture Room) betrays the more intolerant, if not more characteristic face of the Republic. After Florence, Venice was the second state in the world to abolish torture and the first to abolish slavery. Furthermore, the treatment of prisoners was guided rather more by diplomatic and political acumen than by mere human piety: in the instance of galley-slaves condemned to row the ships in battle, should their contribution lead to victory, they were rewarded with liberty; so with the "law of the repentent" *ante litteram* which applied to informers, whereby anyone with a relation accused of a minor crime could ensure their release from prison if they revealed valuable information that might lead to the capture and prosecution of an assassin.

In cases of murder, religious theft, crimes against children, criminal offences against the State, return from exile or causing pollution, however, the sentence resulted in capital punishment.

The prison cells located in the palace, meanwhile, were referred to as the **Pozzi e Piombi** (Wells and Leads): the *Pozzi* were the sinister, deep and damp dungeons for hardened criminals; the *Piombi*, so-called because they were roofed in lead, for prisoners "doing time" for a couple of months. Life in the cells was not necessarily that severe: prisoners were allowed to bring some furniture and a little money with them; lawyers were allowed to continue to perform certain professional duties. Punishment was intended to induce remorse by exerted psychological pressure rather than by inflicting physical suffering and harsh living conditions.

It was from the *Piombi* that **Giacomo Casanova** (1725-98) made his daring escape, emerging onto the roof above the Grand Council Chamber.

From here one can picture the view over Venice in former times when it was almost entirely built of wood.

After the fire of 1577, da Ponte (c 1512-97) was given a mere 16 months to complete the palace's reconstruction. He was therefore obliged to draw upon the skills of the formidable *arsenalotti (see ARSENALE)*, who, as demonstrated to Henry III of France on his visit to Venice in 1574, were capable of assembling a ship in one day. (This same day, pastrymakers were brought in to make the banquet into a particularly sumptuous occasion in honour of the sovereign. The table featured spectacular mythological and historical sculptures contrived by their skilled artistry – Henry III attempted to open out his napkin, which was fashioned out of sugar, so realistic it appeared before realising that it was a subtle joke.)

The **Sala dei Tre Capi del Consiglio dei Dieci** is the chamber where the three magistrates *(capi)*, who had been elected from the Council of Ten to preside over court cases, would meet. Of particular interest on the ceiling are *Virtue Driving Away Vice (centre)* by Zelotti (c 1526-78), and in the corner panels *Punishment of the Falsifier* and *Sin Overcome by Virtue* by Veronese. On the walls, the *Dead Christ Supported by Angels* is by Antonello da Saliba (active 1497-1535), after a painting by one of his uncles, Antonello da Messina.

In the **Sala dei Tre Inquisatori** (Inquisitors' Chamber) two members of the Council of Ten and one of the doge's councillors would pass judgement on crimes against the State. The ceiling features paintings by Tintoretto: *Return of the Prodigal Son* surrounded by *Justice, Faith, Fortitude* and *Charity*.

THE PROCURATIE (⟨8⟩, FX)

Procuratie Nuove – Replacing the Orseolo hospice, the second seat of the Procurators was planned by Scamozzi (1552-1616) and completed by Longhena (1598-1683) during the first half of the 17C. Under Napoleon, the Procuratie Nuove became the Palazzo Reale.

To get to the Museo Correr, go through the Ala Napoleonica.

★★**Museo Correr, the Museum of the City and Civilisation of Venice** ⊘ – The museum takes its name from **Teodoro Correr** (1750-1830), a Venetian gentleman who wanted to leave his rich collection of artefacts pertaining to the history and art of the Serenissima, to the city. The collection was first displayed in the Correr's family home before it was moved to the Fondaco dei Turchi and then to the Procuratie Nuove in 1922.

Up the magnificent 19C staircase, the tour proceeds through the neo-Classical **Sale Canoviane** (Canova Rooms) and on to the **History, Arts, Crafts and Games Departments** *(first floor)*.

Among its historical maps, the Museo Correr boasts one of the **De' Barbari maps** (c 1445-1515 – *see Biblioteca Marciana, below*) and the vivid, typically Venetian topographical works of the German artist Joseph Heintz the Younger (c 1600-1678), including *Bull Baiting in Campo S Polo*.

Among the sculptures by **Canova** (1757-1822) are his *Orpheus and Eurydice* and the celebrated *Daedalus and Icarus*, a harmonious piece which this artist from Possagno, at the age of 20, has managed to compose in a spiralling movement: the father, with his reassuring expression, is about to fix wings to the shoulders of young Icarus and attachments to Daedalus' ankles. Other works, by Francesco Hayez (1791-1882) betray Canova's influence.

Beyond the dining room, with its particularly neo-Classical decoration, one is thrown among displays of objects that testify to the nobility and rich symbolism of the city's history: exhibits include doges' *corni* (caps), staffs of command, *manine* (modelled hands used, along with the ballot urn, for counting votes in the lengthy procedure in electing a doge) *(see Sala del Maggior Consiglio, above)*.

A painting by Andrea Michiel, also known as Vicentino (c 1539-1614) records the *Arrival of the Doge's Wife, Morosina Morosini Grimani at the Doges' Palace* whereas one by Antonio Vassillachi, also known as Aliense (c 1556-1629) depicts the *Disembarkation of the Queen of Cyprus, Caterina Cornaro,* the unhappy Venetian whose story is allied to that of the Rialto. The portrait of *Doge Grimani Enthroned Receiving a Procurator Senator* is by Pietro Longhi (1702-85). The *Lion of St Mark's* attributed to Michele Giambono (active 1420-62) represents Venice in one of its most typical allegories.

The **Libreria dei Teatini**, complete with 17C furnishings, accommodates books from the Teatini Convent. The **Costume Rooms (sale dei costumi)**, meanwhile, contain official 17C and 18C garments worn by senators and procurators as reflected in their portraits on the walls.

The **Numismatic Collection (Collezione Numismatica)** comprises almost the entire series of coinage minted by the Republic, including the famous **zecchino** *(see Introduction – Over of thousand years of glory: 1284)* and the painting by Tintoretto of *Santa Giustina and the Treasurers.*

One room is dedicated in its entirety to the **Bucintoro**, the doge's ship aboard which the Marriage with the Sea took place *(see Introduction – Over a thousand years of glory: 1177)*. Being 35m/115ft long and 7m/23ft wide, the ship was a veritable show-piece. Propelled by 168 rowers, it could only sail in the calmest meteorological conditions, because, being as tall as it was, it would easily have tipped over.

A journey through the history of Venice would not be complete without reference to the Arsenal: in this case, relevant exhibits include a map, engravings and banners. Inevitably, one can linger to listen to the voice of the sea and tales that recount glorious victories like that of the Battle of Lepanto.

The section "Venice and the Sea" is followed by one dedicated to war which includes the weaponry and armour from the Correr and Morosini Armouries. This second collection also contains numerous objects once owned by the Peloponnesian, Francesco Morosini, including a triple galley light and the prayer book inside which a pistol is hidden.

From here, ascend to the second floor, and on to the **Quadreria** (Paintings Section) which presents a synthesis of the School of Venetian painting up to the early 16C.

Among the Veneto-Byzantine examples is perhaps the earliest Venetian painting on wood, the lid of a wooden chest depicting the *Blessed Giuliana with the Saints Biagio and Cataldo.*

The following rooms are dedicated to **Paolo Veneziano** (c 1290-1362) and **Lorenzo Veneziano** (1356-72), and their *Figures and Stories of the Saints and Christ Handing the Keys to St Peter* in which Christ's throne and mantle conform to the Gothic style.

More completely Gothic is the portrayal of *Doge Antonio Venier* by **Jacobello delle Masegne** (active 1383-1409) which besides presenting the noble bearing of the sitter reveals his deep and tormented personality. Among the other Gothic artists here represented is **Stefano Veneziano** (active 1369-81), who painted the *Madonna with Child Enthroned and St Christopher.*

International Gothic arrived in Venice at the beginning of the 15C. Examples include the paintings of Michele Giambono (active 1420-62) and Jacobello del Fiore (c 1370-1439).

The suggestive *Pietà*★ marked by brittle form and metallic colour, is the work of **Cosmè Tura** (c 1430-95) who came from Ferrara. His attention to detail, use of colour and sensitive modelling of the face of the Madonna may be influenced by Flemish painting which he would have come across at the court of the Estes.

The minute but bold *Portrait of a Young Man* is attributed to another 15C artist from Ferrara, Antonio da Crevalcore, characterised by strong contrasting colours.

The next room is dedicated to **Bartolomeo Vivarini** (c 1432-91) who came from Murano. His works betray the strong influence of Mantegna (1431-1506), notably in the exquisite rendering of detail and clear linearity of his style, and the pensive, hieratical expression of his subjects. His use of gold leaf background, however, is more archaic and Byzantine in style.

From the 15C Flemish School stands out an *Adoration of the Magi* by **Breugel the Younger** (1564-1638), a Holy scene set in a Northern landscape blanketed with snow. The influence of Northern oil paintings on Italian art is suggested in a *Pietà*★★, the only work here by **Antonello da Messina** (c 1430-79) who visited Venice in 1475/6. Unfortunately the ochre ground of the faces have permeated the delicate glazes that once modelled the features, damage which has been aggravated by earlier attempts at restoration. The landscape vignette of the Church of St Francis in Messina, however, is easily discernable.

The two other Flemish works in the room are the *Crucifixion* by Hugo van der Goes (c 1435/40-82) and the *Madonna Suckling the Christ Child* by Dieric Bouts (1415-75).

One painting from the later 15C and 16C **Flemish School** is the *Temptations of St Anthony* by a follower of Hieronymous Bosch; its complex symbolism adding a disquieting, nightmarish dimension to the subject.

The **Bellinis** are gathered together in one room: they include the *Crucifixion* by Jacopo (1400-c 1470), the *Portrait of Doge Giovanni Mocenigo* by Gentile (1429-1507) and four works by Giovanni (1430-1516) including the *Pietà*★ and the Crucifixion, in

Antonello da Messina

The work of this major Italian painter of the 15C betrays a large debt to the exquisite detail facilitated by oil-painting. He may have handled works by the Van Eycks in Italy as there is no reference to him having travelled to Flanders. His large altarpiece for San Cassiano was to significantly affect the development of Venetian painting, notably in the use of architecture to frame figurative subjects and in the treatment of portraiture. His influence was particularly assimilated by his contemporary Giovanni Bellini.

which the clarity of the landscape, painted in meticulous detail, betrays the influence of Mantegna.

Alvise Vivarini (c 1445-1505) and Venetian painters from the late 15C forestall the works of **Vittore Carpaccio** (c 1460-1526), one of Venice's most acclaimed artists. His enigmatic *Two Venetian Ladies* are apparently animated by a private joke, their slightly dismissive expressions giving rise to various explanations. According to some, the panel with the two courtesans is a fragment of a diptych, its companion piece (a valley hunting scene) being in the J P Getty Museum in Malibu. Together, the pictures might depict two bored ladies of noble birth, attested by the coat of arms on the vase, awaiting the return of their husbands or lovers from a hunting expedition.

The **Gentleman in the Red Cap**★★ is presently attributed to a painter from Ferrara-Bologna although in the past, it was thought to have been executed by Lotto (c1480-1556), Giovanni Bellini, Carpaccio. It is somewhat irksome and therefore disconcerting not to be able to meet the man's noble and inquiring look, as he turns his back on a landscape that is lapped by the water of a lake or a river.

The evolution of art through the **High Renaissance** continues with Lorenzo Lotto *(Madonna with the Christ Child at her Breast)* before being interrupted by displays of works by 16C and 17C Greek *Madonneri* (painters depicting the Madonna in the traditional manner), and 15C and 16C majolica extending to the room beyond the Manin Library.

Museo del Risorgimento – The Museum of the Risorgimento, housed on the same floor, documents the years which, in certain respects, do not belong to the story of Venice whose end came in 1797, when after 1000 years of glory, the Republic surrendered.

Themes explored therefore tend more towards social history touching upon free-masonry, the temporary Municipality (the Government which, on the arrival of the French, pursued the abdication of Lodovico Manin), the rule of Napoleon and the Austrians.

This period is divided into three eras. The first extends from the end of 1797 to 1805 when Venice became part of Napoleon's Italian Kingdom; the second lasts from the Vienna Congress (1815), through the Manin and Tommaseo period to 1848 *(see Introduction – Over a thousand years of glory: 1848);* and from 1849 to 1866, when Italy was unified.

Returning to the first floor of the Museo Correr, there is one room displaying Renaissance bronzes and an interesting section dedicated to the **Arts and Crafts (Arti e Mestieri)** of Venice where the insignia of the various guilds are displayed: the older ones, made of wood, feature an animated illustration of the work produced by that particular guild along with the name of the *gastaldo* (person in charge). St Mark's lion and the guild's patron saint are also represented.

Other exhibits include a collection of "end products", namely textiles made by the weavers' guild, shoes produced by the *calegheri* (cobblers) guild and examples of the workmanship of painters and *tagiapiera* (stone-masons).

The **Giochi** (Games) collection includes examples of the Strength of Hercules or human pyramids that were "built" on wooden platforms on Thursday before Lent and other particular feast days; fist fights *(Guerre dei Pugni – see I CARMINI)* that developed between the rival Castellani, who were mostly sailors, and Nicolotti, who were mostly fishermen; and bull-baiting *(Caccia ai Tori)* during which dogs that have been excited to a frenzy would be unleashed.

The exhibits also include various packs of cards, one of which might have been used as a teaching aid to Roman history.

Procuratie Vecchie (**8**, **FX**) – The original residence of the Procurators in the 12C, these ancient loggias were initially Veneto-Byzantine in style before being rebuilt up to the first floor probably by Scarpagnino (died in Venice 1549) or possibly by Mauro Codussi (c 1440-1504). Still incomplete, they were damaged by fire in 1512, after which, first Bartolomeo Bon (active c 1463-1529) then Guglielmo Grigi (active c 1515-30) added their mark, before Sansovino (1486-1570) completed the work in 1532.

Famous bars – In the arcaded portico of the Procuratie Vecchie, is located the **Caffè Quadri** (**8**, **FX Y**), which was founded by Giorgio Quadri in 1775 to serve Turkish coffee.

Opposite, on the other side of the piazza is the older **Caffè Florian** (**8 FX Z**), also named after its first proprietor Floriano Francesconi, which was opened in 1720. Its most renown previous *habitués* have included the playwright Goldoni (1707-93) and the neo-Classical sculptor Canova (1757-1822).

Yet without the basilica, the campanile and the Doges' Palace, St Mark's Square and the piazzetta which extends around the corner by the sea would not comprise the same harmonious symphony of architecture, colour and light that epitomises Venice, even in the mind's eye of those who have never set foot in the place.

LA PIAZZETTA
(**8**, **FGX**)

This extension of St Mark's Square – between the Doges' Palace and the Biblioteca Marciana –

Sipping a cappuccino at Caffè Florian

G. Guittot/DIAF

overlooks the sea through a magnificent portal framed by the two **Colonne di Marco e Todaro**. These two column shafts used as pedestals for Saints Mark and Theodore were brought back from the East in 1172, although their specific provenance remains uncertain. The second one is in fact a copy – the original being in the courtyard in the Doges' Palace. The lion, which the Venetians identify with their Evangelist-Saint, could be a chimera.

★**Biblioteca Marciana** ⊘ (**8**, **FX**) – **Sansovino** (1486-1570) worked on the library from 1537. This prestigious seat of Venetian culture is almost as glorious as its neighbour, the Doges' Palace, as was Sansovino's intention. On his death, the project was completed by Scamozzi (1552-1616).

Over the Doric portico runs the loggia, its windows framed by Ionic columns, true to the Classical architectural canon of orders.

As the first example of Classical architecture in Venice, the Biblioteca's sculptural decoration draws on Classical mythology: the keystones of the arches are marked by leonine protomes and mythological heads, while statues in various expressive poses overlook the piazzetta from the balustrade.

Inside, the Reading Room is located off the **Zecca** courtyard (the Mint).

Staircase – With its two flights, this staircase is reminiscent of the Scala d'Oro *(see Palazzo Ducale)*. The vaulted ceiling and cupola stucco decoration are by **Alessandro Vittoria** (1525-c 1600), the frescoes are by **Battista Franco** (c 1498-1561) *(first flight)* and **Battista del Moro** (c 1514-1575) *(second flight)*. The thematic iconography is defined by a neo-Platonic concept of Man, who, influenced by cosmic forces *(first flight)* and fashioned by the Virtues *(second flight)* finally achieves Universal Knowledge – symbolised by the book and the circle.

First floor – One important exhibit is the famous map of Venice by **Jacopo De' Barbari** (c 1445-1515) executed in 1500, the other version being in the Museo Correr *(see above)*. It would appear that to achieve such topographical detail, the city would have had to be observed from her many towers, viewpoints that have successively assisted in determining any changes to the city's distinctive profile.

Nearby is the *Mappamondo* (1457-59) by Fra Mauro, the Camaldolite monk from San Michele in Isola. The planisphere is painted, in colour and gold, on parchment stuck down on wood.

Vestibolo – Sansovino intended the Vestibule as a salon for Humanist lectures. Instead, it was turned into the Republic's Sculpture Museum when the Patriarch of Aquileia, Giovanni Grimani, donated his collection of sculpture and statuary to Venice; some pieces have overflowed into the Archaeological Museum *(see below)*.

On the ceiling, *Wisdom* – painted by Titian (1490-1576) – has been inserted into a trompe-l'œil perspective by Cristoforo and Stefano Rosa, executed around 1559.

Salone Sansoviniano – At the heart of the original library, the Sansovino Room houses the codices and manuscripts bequeathed to the Republic by **Cardinale Bessarione** (1403-72), the famous Greek humanist.

The grotesque ceiling decoration, the work of Battista Franco, is completed with 21 tondos illustrating mythological subjects, virtues and disciplines against a gold background.

The artists responsible for this ultimate "manifestation of Mannerism in Venice" are Giovanni De Mio (1510-70) author of the first trio *(best viewed walking backwards away from the entrance)*; Giuseppe Porta, known as Salviati (c 1520-75) (second trio); Battista Franco, (third trio); Giulio Licinio (1527-93), whose third tondo, in poor condition, was replaced with one by Bernardo Strozzi (1581-1644) depicting Sculpture; Giambattista Zelotti (1526-78) whose third painting was also replaced, this time by a panel representing the *Nile, Atlas, Geometry* and *Astrology* by Padovanino (1588-1648), Veronese (1528-88) and Andrea Schiavone (1510/15-63). Portraits of philosophers line the walls including two by Veronese *(door side)*; four by Tintoretto *(left)* then two by Schiavone, and another two by Tintoretto – although the attribution of the one on the right is uncertain *(end wall)*; one by Salviati, one by Franco and one by Lambert Sustris (1515/20-recorded up to the end of 1568) adorn the right wall.

Museo Archeologico ⊘ (**8**, **FX**) – The Archaeological Museum is housed in the Procuratie Nuove, two doors away from the Biblioteca Marciana. It houses Greek sculpture, Egyptian and Roman fragments and a collection of coins and medals.

One of the Moorish bellstrikers in action

The recommended route through the collection starts in the loggia containing the Greek inscriptions and passes through the coins and medal section before reaching displays of the most ancient Archaic pieces; the famous **Grimani** Greek statues (5C-4C BC); sculpture from the 5C-4C BC including the Classical and Hellenistic phases; small sculptures from the times of Alexander the Great to the 1C BC; the art of Pergamon – the capital of the Attalidi Kingdom in Asia Minor (3C-2C BC); Roman busts – from the end of the Republic to the 3C AD; Latin inscriptions; Assyrian-Babylonian and Egyptian antiquities; Cypriot and Mycenian vases; early Venetian ceramics and Etruscan *buccheri* (clay drinking vessels).

From the quayside, the view of the piazzetta is punctuated by the Clock tower.

Torre dell'Orologio ⊘ (**8**, FX) – Designed by Codussi (c 1440-1504), the Clock tower was erected between 1496 and 1499, and constitutes the main entrance to the Mercerie, Venice's principal shopping street *(see RIALTO)*.

The striking astronomical quadrant probably attracts less attention than the two Moors who sound the hour on a big bell at the top of the tower. Below it stands the lion passant of St Mark set against a starry background. Below this tier comes a Virgin and Child before whom, on Ascension Day, appear mechanical figurines of the Three Kings. To the left, the Roman numerals tell the hour, while the minutes are marked out at intervals of five to the right.

TUCKED AWAY IN THE CORNER

Piazzetta dei Leoncini (**8**, FX **126**) – This small area tucked away between the Basilica, the Palazzo Patriarcale and the side of the former Church of San Basso was designed by Longhena (1598-1682). Its name is derived from the red marble lions from Verona, sculpted by Giovanni Bonazza (1722).

Follow along Calle della Canonica and cross the canal: the Diocesan Museum of Religious Art is on Fondamenta S Apollina on the right.

Museo Diocesano di Arte Sacra ⊘ (**9**, GX) – The building was once part of the Benedictine Convent of Sant'Apollina (12C-13C), its cloister, meanwhile, so inspired D'Annunzio (1863-1938) that he described it in his work *Il Fuoco* (The Fire).

Romanesque in style, its arches have double-arched lintels, supported along the longer sides, by paired columns. The well-head in the centre is 13C.

Fragments of Roman, Byzantine and Veneto-Byzantine (9C-11C) stone-work line the walls.

Originally conceived by the Patriarch of Venice, **Albino Luciani** (1912-78), and Pope Giovanni Paolo whose reign lasted just one month, the museum houses paintings and sculptures, sacred objects and congregational banners from deconsecrated churches. Its collection boasts works by artists such as Antonio Zanchi (1631-1722), Palma il Giovane (1544-1628) and Jacopo Guarana (1720-1808).

For those wishing to continue into neighbouring districts, turn to the sections on SAN ZACCARIA, RIALTO and La FENICE.

The Michelin on-line route planning service is available on a pay-per-route basis, or you may opt for a subscription package.
This option affords you multiple route plans at considerable savings.
Plan your next trip in minutes with Michelin on Internet: www.michelin-travel.com.
Bon voyage!

RIALTO ★★

Situated in the heart of the commercial area, the Rialto Bridge across the Grand Canal, in some respects, continues the long line of shops that snakes its way from St Mark's Square, along the Mercerie, to terminate with the side stalls and market in the San Polo *sestiere*.

Given the overwhelming hustle and bustle of the small workshops and market stalls, it is easy to forget the significance and long history of the Rialto which was so fundamental to the development of Venice.

To follow the prescribed route allow about three hours.

Should you need to phone...

At the epicentre of the city, at the end of Campo San Bartolomeo – *Bartolomio* in dialect – is the **Posto Telefonico Pubblico** (Public Telephone Exchange). This has several card and cash pay-phones, as well as *"scatti"* phones – where calls may be made from metered telephones and paid for at a cash desk.

Stamps...

Stamps can be bought at a *Tabaccheria* (tobacconist) or stationer's but any queries regarding airmail, parcels and recorded letters should be dealt with at the Poste Centrali (Central Post Office) near the Public Telephone Exchange now at the Fondaco dei Tedeschi.

For a quick drink...

Try **Da Pinto** which is a very popular, typically Venetian bar near the market *(367 Campo delle Beccarie)*.

For a beer...

Try **Olandese Volante**, (The Flying Dutchman) at 5658 Campo San Lio between Campo Sta Maria Formosa and the Rialto, which offers a broad range of salads and snacks with a kindly smile.

Osterie and trattorie...

There is absolutely no reason to starve in this area: in Calle Bembo stands the trattoria **Antica Carbonera** *(4648 di San Marco)* with its distinctive interior shaped as a boat; the *osteria* **Antico Dolo** *(778 di San Polo)* has on its menu such colourful local delicacies as *trippa, crostini, polenta* and *bacalà* (salt cod); **All'Arco** *(436 di San Polo)* meanwhile serves a fine glass of wine and snippet of scrumptiousness; **A la Campana** *(4720 di San Marco, Calle dei Fabbri)* is a truly Venetian establishment; **Ai Do Ladroni** *(5362 di San Marco, Campo San Bartolomeo)* prepares appetising sandwiches and other local fare; the **Leon Bianco** *(4153 di San Marco, Salizzida San Luca)* is a good bet whether you are in a hurry or prefer eating your meals sitting down; **Ai Rusteghi** *(5529 di San Marco, Campo San Bartolomeo)* has a wonderful selection of panini and a good choice of wines; another typical venue is **Da Sergio** *(5870/a di Castello)*. More names include **Alle Testiere** *(5801 di Castello, Calle del Mondo Novo)*; **Il Vecio Fritoin** *(2262 Calle della Regina)* round the corner from Ca' Corner, offers a reliable selection of Venetian dishes; **Al Volto** *(4081 di San Marco, Calle Cavalli)* offers a delicious glass of wine.

Pasta all shapes, sizes and colours...

Seek out **Rizzo** in one of the little side streets leading to San Giovanni Grisostomo, a stone's throw from the church.

Whipped cream...

For a frothy delicacy of a different kind, assiduously beaten by hand, **Da Zorzi** in Calle dei Fuseri at 4359 di San Marco is recommended.

For special purchases: collectable books, cards, writing paper...

Luna in Campo San Cassiano has an extraordinary selection of goods on sale.

When Venice was the Rialto – Out of this very group of islands, referred to in Latin as the *Rivoaltus,* evolved Venice. This came to pass during the reign of Charlemagne, who after his coronation on Christmas Eve in the year 800, ruled the Eastern Empire. Meanwhile dissidents from both empires disrupted the lives of the Venetians.

When Charlemagne's son and King of Italy, Pepin failed in his attempt to capture the lagoon which the Venetians resisted with dogged force, **Agnello Partecipazio** (811-27), Venice's first doge, transferred the seat of government from Malamocco to the Rialto.

★★**Ponte di Rialto** (▨, FU) – The first bridge over the Grand Canal built in 1175 was to be a significant factor in the commercial development of the area. The wooden bridge had to be replaced several times following its deliberate destruction during the uprisings led by Baiamonte Tiepolo *(see Introduction: Over a thousand years of glory: 1310),* and two subsequent occasions when it collapsed. Its design proved to be ever complicated by the requirements of both the established shopkeepers and boatmen.

At one time Palladio (1508-80) proposed a cumbersome Roman-style design with three arches, but it was dismissed on the grounds that it might hinder canal traffic *(see GHETTO).* Eighty or so years later, one of these considerations became less of an issue as restrictions were imposed upon larger ships using the Grand Canal.

Ponte di Rialto

The new construction, designed by **Antonio da Ponte** (1512-97) was simplified to a single span thereby ensuring ease of use for boats and barges as well as safeguarding a flow of water that prevented stagnation and maintained the delicate equilibrium of the lagoon.

The present bridge consists of a single stone archway, 28m/92ft long and 7.5m/25ft high, that supports a central graduated alley lined with commercial units, flanked on either side by a narrower parallel passageway. Access from one aisle of shops to another is from either end of the bridge or via transverse arches in the middle. The whole complex is sheltered by a sloping roof.

The Rialto was to remain the only means of crossing from one bank of the Grand Canal to the other until the mid 19C when the Accademia and Scalzi bridges were built.

★**Mercerie** – The countless number of shops selling innumerable varieties of goods give rise to the name of this very historic commercial street in Venice. The *mercerie* (traditionally these were haberdashers selling cloth, ribbons, and other miscellaneous merchandise) provide access between St Mark's and the Rialto. In the past, this was the route chosen by nobles intending to make some triumphal entry into the Piazza San Marco.

The Mercerie which are as busy today as they were in the Middle Ages fall into three main sections, starting from the Clock tower: **Merceria dell'Orologio** (▨, FV 121), **Merceria di San Zulin** (▨, FV 124) and **Merceria di San Salvador** (▨, FV).

At 149 Merceria dell'Orologio there is a relief which records the event that set panic among the group of rebels led by Baiamonte Tiepolo *(see Introduction – Over a thousand years of glory: 1310)*, that disbanded when a stone mortar was dropped on a standard-bearer.

San Zulian (**4**, FV) – This is the first church encountered along Merceria di San Marco. The façade, cramped by adjacent build-

> **Not just pedestrian traffic ...**
>
> In the Middle Ages, the main way to travel in Venice was on horseback, to such an extent that on occasions, movement became impossible through the streets given the number of horses! In 1291, it was decreed that horsemen should dismount their charges in Campo San Salvador before continuing on foot, and that in any event, horses should not be allowed into the Piazza. Instead, they had to be left by the Clock tower, where – as hard as it might be to imagine – stood a copse of elder.

ings, is richly ornamented. Above the portal, Tommaso Rangone, the benefactor of the church, is portrayed by Sansovino (1486-1570). Note also the columns that frame the cartouches and the windows below pediments. Under the main tympanum is a typically Venetian feature, a "*serliana*" consisting of a window with three openings named after Sebastiano Serlio (1475-1554/55).

The church, founded in the 9C, was remodelled during the late Renaissance by Sansovino and Alessandro Vittoria (1525-c 1600). The square internal space extends to a presbytery with two side chapels.

The *Glory of St Julian* in the centre of the ceiling is by Palma il Giovane as are the *Assumption* in the second bay on the right, the *John the Baptist with Saints Joseph and Anthony* in the side chapel on the right and the *Resurrection* above the arch in the side chapel to the left.

The *Dead Christ Upheld by Angels and Saints* is painted by Veronese (1528-88).

San Salvador (**8**, FV) – *See La FENICE.*

AT THE JUNCTION

From Campo San Bartolomeo *(see La FENICE)* one can choose to go in one of three basic directions: towards the Accademia, the Strada Nuova or across the Rialto Bridge.

Towards Strada Nuova

This route makes its way past all kinds of shops; it is nonetheless attractive for being a busy urban area between the Accademia and the Mercerie.

Fondaco dei Tedeschi (**4**, FU) – *See La FENICE.*

E. Zane/MICHELIN

A day in 1310 when a mortar was dropped on a standard-bearer

San Giovanni Grisostomo (**4**, FU) – Shoe-horned between the houses into a rather narrow passageway is the simple yet remarkable reddish façade of the **Church of St John Chrysostom.** Founded in 1080 the church was given its current appearance by Mauro Codussi (1440-1504) and his son Domenico who completed the project at his father's death. The compact and well proportioned interior, dominated by a dome resting on four piers, is in the form of a Greek cross.

In the first chapel on the right is a painting on canvas representing *Saints Jerome, Christopher and Augustine* by Giovanni Bellini (1426-c 1516); the second chapel is dedicated to St Joseph with an altarpiece by Johann Karl Loth (1632-98). The presbytery meanwhile is literally plastered with 17C scenes from the life of the church's patron saint coupled with episodes from the life of Christ. The central section by Sebastiano del Piombo (c 1485-1546) is particularly impressive, and depicts Saints John Chrysostom, Paul, John the Baptist, Liberale, Mary Magdalene, Cecilia and Catherine.

In the left transept, the marble *Coronation of Virgin* is by Tullio Lombardo (c 1455-1532).

Continue straight on to the large but crowded Campo SS Apostoli.

Campo SS Apostoli (⚃, FT) – This square is in some ways the start of the Strada Nuova, and as such it serves as a busy thoroughfare with shops and bars in almost all the nearby *calli*.

Only one side of the **Church of All Saints** *(dei Santi Apostoli)*, rebuilt in the 16C and restored in the 18C, gives onto the square. The tall campanile, so visible from afar, is here detached from the church. It is a composite structure, comprising a stone pedestal at ground level that soars up to a belfry with three-arched openings.

> ### St John Chrysostom (c 347-407)
>
> This Doctor of the Church is remembered essentially for his honesty, asceticism and direct interpretation of the Scriptures (Chrysostom literally means "golden-mouthed") which he gained from his study of the law in Antioch and from living as a hermit. Appointed Patriarch of Constantinople (398) against his will, he fell from grace when he began criticising the corruption and excesses of the city's court, clergy and people.

Inside the rectangular church nestles the 15C **Corner Chapel**, attributed to Codussi (1440-1504) that contains the *Communion of St Lucy* by Tiepolo (1696-1770). On the left wall of the presbytery is a depiction of *Manna Sent from Heaven* drafted by Veronese (1528-88) and executed by "Heredes Pauli", whereas in the chapel on the right are a series of early 14C Byzantine-style frescoes.

On the far side of the canal stands the 13C **Palazzo Falier** (⚃, FTU) named after its most eminent resident, Doge Marino Falier *(see Introduction – Over a thousand years of glory)*. At ground level, the portico shelters a number of shops and restaurants, whereas the two superior levels are decorated with pateras and arcaded windows.

Beyond the Rialto Bridge

San Giacomo di Rialto (⚃, FU) – Partially hidden by the stalls and the market in Campo San Giacomo di Rialto. The best view of the church is to be had approaching the Rialto from the San Polo *sestiere*.

This church is traditionally considered to be the oldest in Venice: according to one document – although of dubious authenticity – the city was born on 25 March 421 when three consuls arrived from Padua to establish a commercial seat at the Rialto and this church, which is also referred to as San Giacometto and was built to celebrate the event. Its present appearance dates from the 11C when it was rebuilt to accommodate local residents drawn to the market in the square.

The façade boasts several striking features, namely the clock (despite being a 1938 reproduction), the campanile which houses the clock and the bells, and the 14C portico.

Inside, planned as a Greek cross, its original Greek marble columns survive complete with 11C Veneto-Byzantine capitals carved with organic decoration. On the left is an altar by Scamozzi (1553-1616) and bronzes by Gerolamo Campagna

---

The Hunchback of the Rialto

Some of the statues in Venice, such as the Moors in Campo dei Mori *(see CA' D'ORO)*, adopt rather curious poses and expressions. One such statue is the 16C **"gobbo di Rialto"**, a hunchback who is bent double beneath his burden, patiently supporting the stairs before the column from where the *comandador* would proclaim government decrees.

The gobbo di Rialto lending an ear to a cat

A. Zane/MICHELIN

(c 1550-1626) who was also responsible for the altar in the Church of San Giorgio Maggiore. On the right is an *Annunciation* by Marco Vecellio (1545-1611), a cousin of Titian's. The main altar is by Alessandro Vittoria (1524-1608).

Just off the square used to stand the **Banco Giro**, a public bank founded in 1619. The *"giro"* in those days, took the form of a written transfer from one account to another: this allowed clients, who at the time could not draw cheques, to go to the bank to register an order for payment in favour of a third party. No receipt was issued as everyone put their trust in the bank register which effected the official record. In this way, Venice could save on paper and, more importantly, the bank's clients could go about their business unencumbered by unwieldy bags of cash.

In addition to being home to banks and the magistrature, the Rialto has always been a commercial area as the names of the *fondamenta*, *campi* and *calli* testify to this day. These commemorate times of trade in such commodities as oil *(olio)*, fish *(pesce)*, wine *(vino)*, spices *(spezie)*, chickens *(polli)*, meat *(beccarie)*, sausages *(luganegher)*.

Further along the canal stretching down as far as the Pescaria are the Fabbriche Vecchie and Fabbriche Nuove, a group of buildings, simple and functional in structure, which once served as commercial offices.

Fabbriche Vecchie (◪, FU) – This building – set back from the Fabbriche Nuove – was designed by Scarpagnino (active in Venice 1505-49), as was much of the surrounding area destroyed by fire in 1514. The ground floor is rusticated, broken by an open colonnade, whereas the upper floors, punctuated by simple windows, seem light-weight and less imposing.

Fabbriche Nuove (◪, FU) – These premises directly overlooking the Grand Canal, on the bend, were designed by Sansovino (1486-1570). As the rusticated ground floor is interrupted by its portico, so the upper storeys are articulated by windows framed with pilasters and surmounted with pediments.

Campo della Pescaria (◪, EFU) – Under the porticoes of the impressive building overlooking the square is the famous fish market which takes place daily. Today, as in days gone by, the fish market provides a good opportunity to witness animated vignettes from everyday life.

The same vivacious atmosphere pervades **Campo delle Beccarie** (◪, EU), which at one time housed the public abattoir, now sheltering a traditional Venetian *bacaro* (wine bar) and various market stalls.

Follow the crowd of people streaming their way from the Rialto to Campo San Cassiano nearby – the route is almost unavoidable: left along Calli dei Botteri to the other side of the canal, then right into Calle Corpus Domini Christi.

San Cassiano (◪, EU) – While the origins of this church are rooted in the 9C, it has been subjected to various attempts at restoration: its present appearance is largely the result of 17C remodelling.

The overall impression of the interior can be over-bearing: the three aisles are separated by columns hung with red and grey damask drapes.

The right chapel off the apse houses three works by Leandro Bassano (1557-1622): a *Visitation*, *Annunciation to Zaccariah* and *Birth of John the Baptist*, and one by Palma il Giovane (1544-1628), *The Crucifixion*.

In the presbytery are three works by Tintoretto (1518-94): a *Resurrection with St Cassian and St Cecilia*, the *Descent into Limbo* and the *Crucifixion*.

Cross the canal to the side of the bookbinder's shop and follow Calle della Regina off to the right.

Daily business in the Rialto market

N. Bosques/MICHELIN

Caterina Cornaro (1454-1510)

At the age of 15, Caterina was betrothed in marriage to James II, King of Cyprus, on condition, signed and sealed, that in the event of the king dying without an heir, that the Kingdom of Cyprus be turned over to Venice. Within months of the marriage, James died suddenly leaving the queen pregnant with their son.

From then began the most tragic sequence of events: beginning with a bloody *coup d'état* on the death of her son, and ending with her abdication, enforced by the Republic of Venice. In compensation, she was given a *palazzo* which stood where Ca' Corner was subsequently erected, some land in Cyprus and the Asolo Seignory. Largely thanks to Pietro Bembo, a member of her court and man of letters *(see Introduction – Literature in Venice)*, artistic patronage flourished at Asolo until it too was lost as a consequence of the Battle of Cambrai.

Ca'Corner della Regina (🗺, **ET**) – It was here, in the house of her brother, that Caterina Cornaro, Queen *(Regina)* of Cyprus resided after her fall from grace. The *palazzo* was then fashioned in the Gothic style. The present building, dating from the 18C, is decorated with a series of frescoes in the style of Tiepolo that recount the unhappy events of her life *(see Il CANAL GRANDE)*.

Since 1976, Ca' Corner della Regina has housed the **Archivio Storico delle Arti Contemporanee** (Historical Archives of Contemporary Art) ⊙, a rich source of information on the Biennale and 20C arts, libraries of books, newspapers and periodicals, and an archive of photographs, film and famous recordings *(see SANT'ELENA E SAN PIETRO)*.

Return to Calle della Regina and turn right into Campo S Maria Materdomini.

Santa Maria Materdomini (🗺, **ET**) – Slightly set back from the square and the 14C-15C Palazzo Zane with its distinctive trilobate five-arched window, is the Church of Santa Maria Materdomini. Fundamentally influenced by the Tuscan style, it is an assured expression of Renaissance design: the simple Istrian stone façade, hemmed in between the houses, has been attributed to Sansovino (1486-1570), although the overall project may owe more to **Pietro Lombardo** (1435-1515) and **Codussi** (1440-1504).

The ordered, simple marble-faced interior comprises three aisles and a domed apse. The most striking paintings are the large scale dramatic renderings of *Finding of the True Cross* by **Tintoretto** (1518-94) in the left transept and a *Last Supper (opposite)* attributed to Bonifacio de' Pitati (c 1487-1553). The exquisite altarpiece in the second bay on the right is also worthy of note. Painted by the close associate of Giorgione and Bellini, **Vincenzo Catena** (c 1480-1531), the scene shows *St Christina of Bolsena* emerging from Lake Bolsena on the millstone that was meant to have drowned her. The panel is full of serene beauty and delicate colouring.

The fine terracotta *Madonna* by the main altar is 15C by Nicolò di Pietro Paradisi, whereas the more

Even the capitals in the Rialto are inspired by the sea

N. Bosques/MICHELIN

subtle early 16C marble altarpieces *(right of the entrance and left of the main altar)* are carved by Lorenzo Bregna. In the presbytery is a delicate relief by the Lombardo brothers.

Proceed towards the Grand Canal to get to Ca' Pesaro and the International Gallery of Modern Art.

★**Ca' Pesaro** (◨, **ET**) – This *palazzo* was commissioned by the Pesaro family. Initiated by Longhena (1598-1682), it was completed by Francesco Antonio Gaspari (c 1670-post 1730). It now houses an important collection of oriental art and a museum of modern art *(see Il CANAL GRANDE).*

Museo d'Arte Orientale ⊘ – The Museum of Oriental Art is housed on the upper floor (at the top of about 100 steps) and contains a collection of Japanese armour from the Edo period (1615-1868), swords, lacquer-work, puppets, musical instruments and Chinese porcelain.

Galleria Internazionale di Arte Moderna ⊘ – The gallery hosts important works of modern art from the end of the 19C onwards, notably from the Futurist movement. These include examples by Klinger (1857-1920), **Chagall** (1877-1985), **Klimt** (1862-1918), **Bonnard** (1867-1947), **Matisse** (1869-1954), **Kandinsky** (1866-1944), Klee (1879-1940), **Tanguy** (1900-55), **Henry Moore** (1898-1986), **Mirò** (1893-1983), **Ernst** (1891-1976), Boccioni (1882-1916), Rosso (1858-1928), De Pisis (1896-1956), **Morandi** (1890-1964), **De Chirico** (1888-1978), Casorati (1883-1963), **Carrà** (1881-1966), Sironi (1885-1961), Pizzinato (1910).

There is also a permanent exhibition of works by Guglielmo Ciardi (1842-1917) who perpetuated the Venetian landscape tradition, and from the latter half of the 19C, Venetian pieces by Luigi Nono (1850-1918), Alessandro Milesi (1856-1945) and Giacomo Favretto (1849-87).

Caterina Cornaro by Titian (Uffizi, Florence)

Uffizi, Firenze/SCALA

Museo di Palazzo Mocenigo ⊘ (◨, **ET**) – This museum provides an idea of Venetian life among the noble classes in the 17C and 18C. The Mocenigo dynasty provided the Serenissima with a total of seven doges, whose portraits hang in the entrance way.

Today the interiors are used to display fabrics and costumes belonging to the **Centro Studi di Storia del Tessuto e del Costume** (a foundation dedicated to the study and conservation of fabrics and costumes). On show are a range of woven materials and textiles from the rise of the Republic.

Ponte and Fondamenta delle Tette

Venetian toponymy is full of surprises. In this case, the focus is on an area located between Campo San Cassiano and Campo San Polo, where, in the 16C, Venetian women of dubious morality would hang out of the window, baring their *tette* – slang for breasts. This display was not only accepted but encouraged by the religious authorities, who saw the practice as a way of reducing the risk of homosexuality so prevalent among sailors.

For those wishing to continue into neighbouring districts, turn to the sections on PIAZZA SAN MARCO, La FENICE, SAN ZACCARIA and SAN ZANIPÒLO.

La SALUTE ★★

(⊠, FX)

Vaporetto: Salute, Accademia

Despite the hoards of tourists visiting La Salute or the Guggenheim Collection, this corner of the Dorsoduro *sestiere* is very peaceful. It is an area that is not really conducive to browsing in shops or lingering in cafés and wine bars, which are more common in the San Trovaso and San Barnaba districts. The artists' workshops and the nearby Anglican church, along with the numerous enthusiasts of modern art – often Peggy Guggenheim's fellow countrymen – give these streets an Anglo-American flavour: some of the directions are even given in English.

To follow the suggested route visiting the recommended sights, allow about 3hr.

The Basilica of Santa Maria della Salute is, surely, one of the most important and obvious points of reference on the skyline of Venice. It is also very dear to the Venetians: in 1630 when their city was racked by plague, they pledged a solemn vow to erect a church once the epidemic subsided. Their prayers were answered and in 1631 **Baldassare Longhena** (1598-1682), the preeminent Venetian Baroque architect, was granted leave to develop his project.

An evening in a piano bar?

Try **Linea d'Ombra** at 19 Dorsoduro, just round the corner from the Dogana.

★★**Santa Maria della Salute** (⊠, FX) – This impressive basilica is rendered all the more majestic by its magnificent flight of stairs up to the entrance. Dominated by the towering central dome, the great round volume emerges from an octagonal base: a geometric shape that radiates to eight façades presided over by a figure flanked by two angels over each pediment. Like Palladio before him, Longhena uses Classical architectural forms to build bold outlines and articulate every subsidiary part of his design: he employs figurative sculpture to punctuate profiles, to relieve flat planes and to reiterate the human dimension. The proliferation of statues at every level may be put down to the fact that Longhena was born into a family of stonecarvers. Akin in itself, to a free-standing sculpture, the church occupies a prominent position from every angle.

At the apex of the overall composition is a figure of the Madonna clutching the baton of the *Capitana de Mar* (Captain-Generalship of the Sea), poised above the balustraded lantern; so too is there a figure of the patron presiding over the main pediment of the façade.

On the lesser dome stands St Mark, flanked by the weather-vanes of the two *campanili* beyond, marking the far end of the church. At the drum level, great concentric volutes also known as *orecchioni* (big ears), link the lower level of the outer section with the dome: an integral part in the design fabric of this distinctive and universally famous church, their very boldness contrasts with the clean profile of the delicately ridged cupola, echoed on a smaller scale around the lantern of the lesser dome.

Interior – The interior space is dictated by the main cupola with the central area opening out into six chapels.

As if to concentrate the power of design, the polychrome marble floor converges on a central circle of five roses which, together with the other roses of the wider circle, suggest the idea of a rosary. The central inscription in Latin states that it is from here that the health *(salute)* and salvation accorded to Venice emanates: tradition has it that the city was born on the Feast of the Annunciation – 25 March 421 – to signify the protection accorded to Venice by the Virgin.

On the left side, the last bay before the high altar is ornamented with the *Descent of the Holy Spirit*, painted by **Titian** (1490-1576) in 1555.

At the high altar is a 12C icon, the *Madonna della Salute*, also referred to as *Mesopanditissa* because it came from a place of the same name in Candia (Crete). The sculptural group above (1670-74) represents Venice – liberated from the plague – at the Virgin's feet: it is the work of the Flemish artist Juste Le Court (1627-79). The Plague is depicted on the right, being chased away by an angel.

The sacristy boasts a wealth of treasures: the most eye-catching being the *Wedding at Cana* by **Tintoretto** (1518-94), in which the artist has included himself (the first Apostle on the left), his friends and their wives.

Titian's *St Mark Enthroned with Saints* (Sebastian, Roch, Cosmas and Damian: the first two to be invoked against the suffering of the affliction; the twin patrons of physicians for the healing thereof), on the left wall above the altar, reflects Giorgione's influence. On the right is the *Madonna of La Salute* by Padovanino (1588-1649). To the left of Tintoretto's panel is *Samson* by Palma il Giovane

(1544-1628) and a *Madonna and Child* by Palma il Vecchio (c 1480-1528): to the right is Palma il Giovane's *Jonah the Prophet*. *The Last Supper* on the wall opposite the organ doors is by Salviati (c 1520-75), as are the paintings of *Joshua*, *David's Triumph over Goliath*, *Melchisedek* opposite Tintoretto's works; the various depictions of the *Madonna in Prayer* are by **Sassoferrato** (1605-85).

La Salute and the Dogana

The paintings on the ceiling on the theme of *Sacrifice* are by Titian: they portray vivid depictions of David and Goliath, Abraham and Isaac, Cain and Abel, in which the drama of the moment reveals extraordinary, if not convincing, power.

On leaving the sacristy, in the corridor before the chapels *(right)* are three notable altarpieces by **Luca Giordano** (1634-1705): a *Nativity of the Virgin*, an *Assumption* and a *Presentation of Mary at the Temple*. The feast of the Presentation of Mary is the occasion of solemn celebrations on 21 November.

La Dogana (🖸, FX) — Further along the Fondamenta Dogana, with its very evocative view over St Mark's Basin, is the Dogana da Mar. Dating back to the 15C, it originally served as the customs point for goods arriving by sea — a Dogana di Terra on the Fondamenta del Vin in the Rialto district served as the equivalent for imports brought by land. The building's present appearance dates from the 17C. Fashioned to resemble a ship's hull, a statue of *Fortune* towers over a golden globe — representing the world — supported by two atlantes.

The Feast of the Madonna della Salute

Venice has been celebrating the end of the plague of 1630 for over 300 years. On 21 November, a bridge is made of boats stretching across the canal to La Salute to allow devotees and pilgrims to reach the basilica with ease. Celebrations for the Feast of the Madonna of La Salute — which have a certain parochial air about them — last all day. This particular day is remembered by Venetians with the lighting of a candle.

★**Le Zattere** (🗗, 8, CFXY) — A walk along these Fondamenta provides a thrilling view that might be expected from a long balcony with a perfect prospect over the Giudecca Canal, a rougher stretch of water than the Grand Canal, to the Island of the Giudecca itself on the other side. While the panorama here is less illustrious than the city it overlooks, the majestic buildings of the Giudecca have their own stories to tell: from the Mulino Stucky to the Redentore, combined with that of the Zitelle, these provide the most exuberant expressions of religious fervour in Venice. The name Zattere was coined from one function served by the Fondamenta in the 17C, and that was its transportation of wood on rafts or *zattere*.

Peggy Guggenheim (1898-1979)

This colourful personality, who did so much to popularise modern art, was born in New York and educated in France; she spent most of her working life in England and died at a respectable age in Venice. In 1939 she decided to open a museum for contemporary art in London, but during the period leading up to the Second World War, when she resolved to *"buy one picture a day"*, it became increasingly obvious that it was safer to return home. In October 1942, when she opened her gallery "Art of This Century" in New York with a collection of Cubist, Abstract and Surrealist art, she wrote *"I wore one of my Tanguy earrings and one made by Calder, in order to show my impartiality between Surrealist and Abstract art."* She was briefly married to the Dadaist and Surrealist Max Ernst.

Her autobiography *Out of This Century* was published in 1979.

The buildings evoke a past that involved hard work and profound religious faith. There is the former **Magazzini del Sale**, a 14C warehouse used to store salt *(sale)*, that primordial ingredient so abundantly produced in Venice. Next comes the former Convent and **Church of the Spirito Santo**, from where the bridge of boats stretched across the water for the Feast of the Redentore. Looking towards the Church of the Gesuati (belonging originally to the order of Poveri Gesuati that was replaced by the Dominicans in 1668) is the **Ospedale degli Incurabili** (Hospital for Incurables) which served in the 16C as a hospice for syphilis sufferers before being used as a home for abandoned children; later it accommodated a musical conservatory *(see Introduction – Composers in Venice)*.

The length of the route is dotted with bars which, in spring and summer, set tables outside on wooden platforms lapped by water.

Take Calle della Scuola and proceed straight on to the entrance of the very beautiful, if ill-famed, Palazzo Dario (see Il CANAL GRANDE). Turn left in the direction of Palazzo Venier dei Leoni.

★**Collezione Peggy Guggenheim** ⓥ (**8**, **EX**) – The Peggy Guggenheim Collection is housed in the incomplete Palazzo Venier dei Leoni (1749), which was designed by Lorenzo Boschetti, the architect of the Church of St Barnabas *(see Il CANAL GRANDE)*.

Maiastra (1912) by Constantin Brancusi

The entrance is through the peaceful sculpture garden, in the shade of whose surrounding wall are two stones that mark the final resting places of Peggy Guggenheim herself and her "beloved babies" – her dogs. The niece of the American industrialist Solomon R Guggenheim who instigated the museum of the same name in the famous spiral building by Frank Lloyd Wright (1869-1959) in New York, **Peggy Guggenheim** built up her Venice collection between 1938 and 1979. She acquired the *palazzo* after the Second World War and lived there until her death, whereupon, according to her express wishes, both the *palazzo* and the collection it housed were handed over to the Solomon Guggenheim Foundation. Like its counterpart in New York, the museum is arranged thematically, displaying parallel collections of Abstract and Surrealist works by the same artists *(see THE GREEN GUIDE NEW YORK)*.

The collection which is particularly strong in Surrealist art contains works by **Braque** (1882-1963); **Picasso** (1881-1973); Mondrian (1872-1944); Boccioni (1882-1916); **Brancusi** (1876-1957); **Kandinsky** (1866-1944); **Chagall** (1887-1985): *The Rain;* Balla (1871-1958): *Abstract Speed+Noise;* Severini (1883-1966): *Sea = Ballerina;* **Mirò** (1893-1983); De Chirico (1888-1978): *The Red Tower;* **Max Ernst** (1891-1976); Klee (1879-1940); Magritte (1898-1967) *Empire of Light;* Dali (1904-1989); **Pollock** (1912-1956); **Calder** (1898-1976): *Mobile;* Vasarely (1908-1990) and **Moore** (1898-1986).

Among the most notable individual compositions are the 23 sculptures designed by Picasso and executed by Egidio Costantini (1964) positioned in the window, so as to exploit to maximum effect their evocative transparency set against the intense blue of the Grand Canal beyond.

Outside, the erect sculpture that stands guard over the Grand Canal is *The Angel of the City* by Marino Marini (1901-80).

Since 1997, Palazzo Venier dei Leoni has temporarily accommodated the **Mattioli Collection** which includes works by the Futurist painters Carrà (1881-

An American in Venice: Peggy Guggenheim

1966) – *La Galleria di Milano;* Severini – *Ballerina in Blu;* Boccioni, Balla (1871-1958) and other important masters such as Morandi (1890-1964); Sironi (1885-1961); Modigliani (1884-1920) and Soffici (1879-1966).

For those wishing to continue into neighbouring districts, turn to the section on ACCADEMIA.

Surrealism

The *First Surrealist Manifesto* was published in Paris in 1924 by André Breton (1896-1966), promoting ideas drawn from the latest contemporary psycho-analytical theories on the unconscious and subconscious states of mind. The manifesto challenged the traditional views on art and life, it encouraged artistic expression inspired by natural dream activity, drug-induced hallucinations and other suspended states of mind. Breton defined the essence of Surrealism as *"pure psychic automatism, by which it is intended to express verbally, in writing, or in any other way, the true process of thought. It is the dictation of thought, free from the excise of reason, and every aesthetic or moral preoccupation".*

Pictorially, Surrealism emerged from various movements, drawing on particular aspects of that movement: Cubism (refracted form), Futurism (movement and automation) and Dada (humour and absurdity), pioneered among others by Picasso, Ernst, Klee, Dalí, Miró and Magritte.

SANT'ELENA E SAN PIETRO ★

(**1** , KLXY)
Vaporetto: S Elena, Giardini Biennale

The Sant'Elena and San Pietro districts of the Castello *sestiere* are peaceful and yet vibrant with life, as their green spaces attract crowds of people. The view from the public gardens and the Park of Remembrance (Parco delle Rimembranze) over the lagoon and St Mark's Basin is nothing short of magnificent. At this extremity of the Castello *sestiere*, the colours of washing hung between the houses interplay with the light refracted from the gleaming canals. Movement and activity pervades the area around the Rio di S Anna with its floating market, and extends to the bustling commercial activities of the only real street in Venice, via Garibaldi.

Places for a sandwich, a pizza or a particularly cheap *"menu a prezzo fisso"* (set price meal) proliferate.

The route suggested takes about three hours.

For anyone venturing to this outlying *sestiere*, the area offers an unusual prospect of Venice. Separated from the rest of the lagoon by the green space of the Park of Remembrance, it is a quiet neigh-

> ### A taste of Venice
>
> At 24 Calle Chinotto in the *sestiere* Sant'Elena nestles the trattoria **Dal Pampo**; at 738 di Castello, in Seco Marina, **Dai Tosi** is both a trattoria and a pizzeria.

bourhood; devoid of canals, the area is reminiscent of a small forgotten town in days gone by. On the far side of the Rio di Sta Elena rises the Church of Sant'Elena, flanked by a stadium and military base.

ISOLA DI SANT'ELENA (**11**, KLXY)

Up until the 11C, the island was known as *cavana* (refuge), providing sheltered anchorages to boatsmen and fishermen. Its present name is derived from the name of St Helen (c 257-336), mother of Emperor Constantine, whose relics are still housed in the church (first chapel on the right) brought to Venice in 1211, after the Fourth Crusade.

The small monastery, already established in 1060, was built by Benedictine monks from Monte Oliveto Maggiore (Tuscany) in 1407. Subsequent rebuilding was undertaken during the period between 1439 and 1515.

In 1684, the State authorities installed bakers' ovens here to supply its navy with bread and biscuits.

A colourful array of linen drying over the rooftops of Sant'Elena

As happened to other religious institutions during Napoleon's rule, the monastery was disbanded and its assets sold and dispersed; the church became used as a warehouse and troops were billeted in the convent buildings.

During the latter half of the 19C and beginning of the 20C, the area around the church and monastery was at last extended and urbanised by popular demand.

Today, the church and convent accommodate Servite monks.

Church (**11**, LY) – The Gothic façade is dominated by its portal (1467). The striking sculptural group above is by Antonio Rizzo (c 1440-99) and shows the Capitano da Mar (Sea Captain-General), **Vittore Cappello**, kneeling before St Helen.

Through the gate to the left of the façade, extends the beautiful cloister.

The campanile, however, erected in 1956, does not conform with the essentially Gothic structure of the church.

Inside the luminous interior, a single nave terminates in an apse pierced with tall windows, accommodating its wooden choir stalls. The chapels dedicated to St Helen and to the Crucifixion radiate off the apse on the right.

It is particularly enjoyable to gently stroll through the park and along the Viale dei Giardini Pubblici, as if through a gently shaded terrace, with the lagoon beyond, to the end from where an all-encompassing panorama of Venice extends. In the Castello Gardens stand the Biennale pavilions.

The Biennale (**11**, KY) – The 100-year history of this international exhibition of modern art is long and controversial. From its earliest beginnings, in 1895, it caused an outcry by exhibiting a painting called *Il Supremo Convegno* by **Giacomo Grosso** (1860-1938), which was deemed to be in poor taste. The Impressionists were only "invited" to exhibit their work much later as the organisers, up until 1912 at least, preferred to orientate themselves towards art from Middle Europe rather than Paris.

The exhibition has always been held in the Castello Gardens where the pavilions of the various countries have been erected. One particularly spectacular inauguration was that of the Russian pavilion in 1914, which was celebrated with an Orthodox mass in the presence of the Grand Duchess.

Since the 1930s, other artistic venues have proliferated: there is now the Festival of Music, the Poetry Conventions, the Exhibition of the Cinema held on the Lido since 1937 and the Theatre Festival.

In 1995, the centenary of this important, if controversial, institution was celebrated: for the occasion, Venice was mobilised and further embellished with various works which were put on display in locations other than the traditional venues. Anyone arriving by water would have been surprised and perhaps confused by the strange appearance of the normally immutable Riva degli Schiavoni, curiously bedecked with metal sculptures, the symbolism of which was so complex as, for some, to remain virtually unintelligible. Besides all the controversy, the usual organisational problems, the philosophical and political diatribes, the Biennale has stood its ground: *"The Biennale is one hundred years old and in certain ways, it is showing its age"*, said the Mayor of Venice. It may well be, however, that its uncomfortable position in the "eye of the storm" ensures a restlessness that guarantees its very vitality.

Campo San Giuseppe (**10**, JX) – Beyond Viale Trento lies this little square stretching before the 16C Church of San Giuseppe which houses in the first bay on the right, *St Michael and Lucifer Fighting over the Soul of Michele Bon* by Jacopo (1518-94) and Domenico (c 1560-1635) Tintoretto.

Cross over the bridge that lies just left of the square and follow Calle Correra to Fondamenta Sant' Anna. Turn right, cross the bridge on the left, and continue straight on up Calle Larga San Pietro to the Church of San Pietro di Castello.

Throughout the entire district, glimpses of the cheerful hustle and bustle of everyday life may be snatched: these scenes reflect a genuine picture of a Venice unspoilt by the tourist trade.

ISOLA DI SAN PIETRO DI CASTELLO (**11**, KX)

This island was inhabited before the city of Venice was even founded.

Originally known as **Olivolo** – perhaps after its olive groves – the "modern" name of the *sestiere* commemorates a castle that was either built or found there by the earliest Venetians. Since time immemorial, it has been the religious symbol of the city. Not only the seat of Bishop Castellano, and a dependent of the Patriarch of Grado, it still shelters the body of the first Patriarch of Venice, Lorenzo Giustiniani, who resided there in the 15C.

The basilica stands in an open, grassy area, the venue for lively celebrations on the occasion of the Feast of San Pietro di Castello.

★San Pietro di Castello (**11**, KX) – Despite the fact that its fame has always been usurped by St Mark's, the Church of St Peter at Castello was regarded as the official cathedral of Venice up until 1807, during which time St Mark's was merely considered the doge's chapel.

It was erected in the 8C on the foundations of a church that dates back to 650. Reminiscent of the Redentore, the façade conforms to Palladian design. On the right is the former late-16C Patriarchal Palace. The nearby campanile which leans to one side was rebuilt by Mauro Codussi (c 1440-1504).

The 17C interior reflects the influence of Palladio (1508-80): comprising a Latin cross with three aisles, a large dome covers the central crossing. Above the main portal are represented *The Feast of the Jewish Passover* by Malombra and Vassillachi (16C-17C) *(right)* and *The Feast in the House of Simon* by Jacopo Beltrame (16C) *(left)*.

In the left aisle note the painting on canvas of *St John the Evangelist, St Peter and St Paul* by **Veronese** (1528-88) and beyond, in the left transept in the Gothic **Lando Chapel**, the mosaic altarpiece based on a cartoon attributed to Tintoretto (1518-94). The antependium or altar front comprises a 9C, Veneto-Byzantine marble transenna (open-work screen) inlaid at the base with 2C mosaics. The portrait bust is of San Lorenzo Giustiniani.

The **Vendramin Chapel** alongside is by Longhena (1598-1682): the *Madonna and Child with the Damned* is by Luca Giordano (1634-1705).

The very elaborate high altar is based on designs by Longhena.

Returning down the right side, the *See of St Peter with Four Saints* is by Marco Basaiti (c 1470-1530); the marble seat known as **St Peter's Cathedra** is from Antioch: note the unusual back adapted from

an Arab-Muslim funerary stele, decorated with inscriptions from the Koran in Cufic script.

Return to the Fondamenta Sant'Anna to peruse its quite amazing water-borne market. At the mouth of the canal begins the long and busy **Via Garibaldi** (**11**, JX), the only street in Venice to be called a *"via"*. From here, there is a fine view of the Church of La Salute, and plenty of shops alternating with all kinds of bars and *pizzerie*.

For those wishing to continue into neighbouring districts, turn to the section on ARSENALE.

SAN GIORGIO MAGGIORE★★

(**9**, GHXY)
Vaporetto: S Giorgio

The island fulfils almost any preconception one might have of Venice, as well as providing a first-rate view over the whole city, a particularly evocative panorama that is punctuated with churches that might be identified by their *campanili*, and which feature in the background of many a painting.

San Giorgio does not tend to be haunted by tourists – there are no bars or restaurants. For this reason alone, it is a "must" for anyone searching for a unique view of Venice and for those attracted to the serenity of monastic life, even as an escape for an hour or so. It is also a "must" for Palladio fans.

History of the Benedictines, artists and soldiers – The name of the island pertains to the dedication of a church which was erected there in 790, the term *maggiore* is used to distinguish it from another island, San Giorgio in Alga. Since 982, the year in which **Giovanni Morosini** founded a Benedictine monastery there, the island's history has been associated with this monastic order.

It became especially favoured by doges, who on 26 December would come and attend mass in celebration of the Feast of St Stephen, sung by the Benedictine choir and that of St Mark's. The tradition for this occasion became so entrenched that it had to be taken into consideration when Palladio was commissioned to redesign the church.

Over the centuries, the island has gradually been endowed with fine artistic and monumental buildings. The first monastic church, at the centre of the island, would have been built in the Gothic style: but unlike what we have now, it would have conformed with other contemporary island monastic churches, by being inward looking and enclosed within a cloister rather than facing outwards over St Mark's Basin or, indeed any other stretch of water. When the complex was rebuilt in the Renaissance style between 1400 and 1500, it was given a Florentine cloister adapted from designs brought to Venice by the exiled Cosimo de'Medici, who came to San Giorgio in 1433 accompanied by Michelozzo (1396-1472), a Florentine architect and collaborator of Donatello.

The island only came to enjoy its true moment of glory however, 100 years later with the arrival of **Andrea Palladio** (1508-80).

Its eventual downfall, coinciding with that of the Republic of Venice, was protracted into the 1850s. After both Napoleon and the Austrians had defiled the exquisite artistic and spiritual beauty of the island, its finest buildings continued to be devastated by various armies passing through – this includes the Italian army using the *manica lunga* as military stores during the First World War *(see below)*.

The island's present serenity – The restoration of the island to its former beauty is largely due to the Cini Foundation and the Benedictines, who, for more than 1 000 years have faithfully preserved the original liturgical tradition and Gregorian chants of San Giorgio, assisted by the Salesians who are active in all fields of education and guidance.

No-one lives on the Island of San Giorgio besides these dedicated souls. It is a place of retreat, of profound learning and deepest religious faith. There is nowhere to stay, nowhere to eat or drink, for such places would distract the spirit and attract an influx of indiscriminate visitors.

The proposed tour takes about two hours.

Isola di San Giorgio

★**San Giorgio Maggiore** (🄘, GY) – The rebuilding of the church to designs by Palladio was initiated at the beginning of 1566, and dedicated to St George and St Stephen, who occupy the niches in the marble façade between the busts of doges Tribuno Memmo (979-91), who ceded the island to the Benedictine monk Giovanni Morosini, and Sebastiano Ziani (1172-78). The front is dominated by a great triangular pediment supported by four columns: a feature borrowed from a Classical temple and applied here as an ordered entrance to the new church.

The bright interior compliments the clarity of design, enhancing the ample Latin cross space enclosed within its vaulted ceiling and apsed transepts.

Proceeding from the entrance up the right aisle, in the first chapel is a dark *Adoration of the Shepherds* by Jacopo Bassano (1517/19-94); in the third chapel, *The Martyrdom of Saints Cosmas and Damian* is by **Jacopo Tintoretto** (1518-94) who also painted the two large paintings in the presbytery of *The Last Supper (right wall)* and *The Gathering of Manna from Heaven*.

The main altar is ornamented with late-16C sculptures by Gerolamo and Giuseppe Campagna. Behind the balustrade, bearing the exquisite figures of St George and St Stephen (1593), extend the wooden choir stalls sculpted with scenes from the *Life of St Benedict* – the work of a Flemish artist, Albert van der Brulle (1594-98). The door to the right leads into the chapel *(open for Sunday services)* decorated with Tintoretto's last work, his **Deposition from the Cross**. The doorway in the left wall, meanwhile, provides access to the campanile.

The paintings depicting *The Risen Christ with St Andrew the Apostle* and *St Stephen, the Protomartyr* by Jacopo and Domenico (c 1560-1635) Tintoretto are in the left transept where the relics of St Stephen, the first martyr stoned to death (Acts 7, v6) lie. According to legend, these remains were transferred from Constantinople in 475.

Campanile ⊙ – The bell-tower was given its present form by Scalfarotto in 1726. It offers the best possible **view★★★** over Venice.

Fondazione Giorgio Cini ⊙ (**🔢**, **GY**) – The Giorgio Cini Foundation, a private institution, is responsible for the programme of restoration work undertaken on many of Venice's monuments, for various cultural initiatives connected with Venetian civilisation and, supported by various other institutions, for administrating new problems. Research carried out by the Foundation may be sourced through a broad range of media available in its libraries and microfiche facilities that are always installed in some unique, sumptuous room full of artistic splendour. The Cini Foundation also addresses a broad spectrum of other issues; it has organised important conventions, for example, on the development of international relations. The Giorgio Cini Foundation was in fact founded by **Vittorio Cini** (1885-1977), a man who showed great courage and philanthropy during his life as a financer and government minister who dared to speak out against the war, impervious both to Mussolini and Göring. He was also an enlightened patron, wealthy and modest in equal measure, who strove to help every kind of humanity. The institution of this benevolent foundation commemorates his son Giorgio who died in a plane crash, and is devoted to supporting and endowing cultural and humanist initiatives.

★**Biblioteca** ⊙ – *The entrance to the library is off the first cloister and up the main staircase on the right.* Like the staircase, the library (1641-53) was designed by Longhena (1598-1682). It is decked with shelving and ornamented with carved wooden figures: the ceiling was decorated in the 17C Mannerist style.

Chiostri ⊙ – This ancient monastery has two cloisters. The first, the **Chiostro dei Cipressi** (with the cypresses) after the island's original name, was designed by Palladio (1579-1618) and is elegantly articulated with paired columns and windows opening below curved and triangular pediments. This leads into the **Teatro Verde**, an open-air theatre with marble seats for use during the summer. The second cloister, which is older, was originally known as the **Chiostro degli Allori** (with laurels). Giving onto the cloister is the **Refectory** *(Refettorio)* on which Palladio worked with Veronese (1528-88). For the end wall, Veronese painted a *Wedding at Cana*, a panel Napoleon had sent back to Paris, and now hangs in the Louvre. Its replacement representing *The Marriage of the Virgin*, is from the School of Tintoretto.

Dormitorio (la manica lunga) – The dormitory building is impressive for its sheer size and lightness, and for the fine view it enjoys over the Riva degli Schiavoni. Known as the *manica lunga*, meaning the long sleeve, it was conceived by Giovanni Buora at the end of the 15C: 128m/420ft long, it opens up onto 50 rooms.
On the outside, there is a 16C relief depicting *St George and the Dragon*.

Conclave Meeting in Venice

The Conclave Room is now used by the Benedictine monks as a choir room. It was in here that the conclave met in difficult circumstances to elect Pope Pius VII in December 1799-March 1800 while Rome remained occupied by French troops. Each stall is still inscribed with the name of the 35 cardinals who took part in the conclave. When finally the appointment was made, and it was revealed that Napoleon's favourite had not been elected, the cardinals were prohibited from holding the pontifical mass in the Basilica of St Mark's, and so it was celebrated at San Giorgio.
At the altar is a canvas by **Carpaccio** (c 1465-1526) depicting *St George Slaying the Dragon*, a later version of the masterpiece in the Scuola di San Giorgio degli Schiavoni (a copy of which is contained in the Chapel of the Deposition). Outside the room itself is the chimney where the used ballot-papers were burnt.

For those wishing to continue into neighbouring districts, turn to the section on La GIUDECCA.

---

*Constantly revised **Michelin Maps**, at a scale of 1:200 000, provide much useful information:*
– latest motorway developments and changes;
– vital data (width, alignment, camber, surface) on motorways or tracks;
– the location of emergency telephones.
Keep current Michelin Maps in the car at all times.

SAN GIORGIO degli SCHIAVONI ★★★

(🝚, HV)
Vaporetto: S Zaccaria or Riva degli Schiavoni

Tucked away behind Riva degli Schiavoni, a small section of the Castello *sestiere* is spirited by an energy level that falls midway between the frenetic, milling activity around St Mark's Basilica and the absolute peace surrounding the Church of San Francesco della Vigna. Borrowing a little of the atmosphere from both, this area of Venice forges its own charm and personality.

The suggested route takes about two and a half hours.

A drink and a bite even at some unsociable hour

Tucked away in Campo Santi Filippo e Giacomo, at 4357 di Castello, there is an enterprising establishment offering a whole range of wines and a broad choice of things to eat – and that is **All'Aciughetta**. The **Birreria Forst**, like all self-respecting brasseries, promotes beer-drinking with black-bread German sausage sandwiches. Alternatively, seek out **Devil's Forest**, another brasserie in Calle degli Stagneri at 5185 di San Marco, where darts are played. By Ponte San Provolo, at 4625 di Castello, stands the trattoria **Rivetta** where a drink and a bite can be snatched at the bar.

★★★**Scuola di San Giorgio degli Schiavoni** ☉ (🝚, HV) – The original 15C buildings were remodelled by Giovanni de Zan in 1551, but the original layout of the interior was retained. By this time, Carpaccio had already started working on his cycle of paintings in 1502, intended for the upper hall.

The *scuola* was founded by the Confraternity of the Schiavoni, or Slavs from Schiavonia (equivalent today to Dalmatia) who for the most part, traded with the Levant. Their patron saints were the three protectors of their homeland, St George, St Tryphon and St Jerome.

The *Cycle of St George*★★★ by **Vittore Carpaccio** (c 1465-1526) took the artist five years to complete (1502-07). It was moved downstairs in the 16C, to the intimate ground-floor, well-lit, gallery, with its fine wooden ceiling providing an ideal location to best show off the paintings' warm colours.

Iconographically, it is best to read the panels from the left wall even if this does not follow the chronological order of execution; Carpaccio having started with the episodes from the Life of St Jerome.

St George and the Dragon catches the very moment when the knight attacks the dragon: the event is

The Legend of Saint George

Little is known about this early martyr's life whose cult became particularly important in the 6C. The legend of him slaying the dragon seems to have emerged late in the 12C when popularised in the **Golden Legend**: a story possibly founded on the myth of Perseus killing the sea monster at Arsuf or Joppa. What is certain, however, is that the traditional veneration of the saint as a soldier, which originated from Palestine and was embraced by the crusaders, is shared by both the Eastern Orthodox and Western churches.

The symbolism inherent in the valiant saint slaying the dragon and saving the virtuous princess was exploited by the church as a parable about the church being saved from the devil.

narrated pictorially with all the romance of heroic chivalry, a veritable *chanson de geste* on canvas. The noble bearing of the saint and his steed, the dignified composure of the emotional princess and the architectural precision of the composition are true to the idealised legend but contrast sharply with the macabre portrayal of skulls and hideously mutilated bodies.

The Triumph of St George dramatically depicts the saint on the point of killing the wounded dragon: the exotic figures are set against a background of Renaissance architecture, although the centrally-planned temple is not positioned in the actual centre as this would have disturbed the harmony of the composition.

The group of musicians is also present in the next scene, *St George Baptising the Heathen King and Queen*, as witnesses to the solemnity of the occasion: this is tempered only by the timorous pose of the saint who is shown full of hesitation. The rich details also seem charged with expression: note the animals and the turban lying on the steps. The pre-eminent significance given to the chivalry of St George may be due to the financial support given to the *scuola* by the Knights of Rhodes who considered the saint to embody all the ideals of the perfect knight.

St Tryphon Exorcising the Daughter of the Emperor Gordianus is a rare representation of the saint. Although thought to have been painted by Carpaccio and his assistants, a master's touch is recognisable in the architectural details and the distinctive personalities of the figures. The two small paintings, the *Agony in the Garden* and the *Vocation of St Matthew*, exceptions to the cycles dedicated to the lives of the *scuola's* three patron saints, serve as a prelude to episodes in the life of St Jerome.

In the first canvas, *St Jerome Leading his Lion into a Monastery*, the depiction of the monks is nothing short of humorous as they flee from the lion that is more concerned with obediently following St Jerome. Panic is carefully conveyed in the dashing movement of the monks towards the left,

St Jerome (c 342-420)

Eusebius Hieronymus was a biblical scholar and a great traveller. Born in Dalmatia, he studied rhetoric in Rome before journeying through Gaul, Palestine and Syria where he spent four to five years as a hermit, before visiting Antioch, Constantinople and Egypt. He settled with monastic life in Bethlehem and devoted his mature years to study. His most significant work was the translation of the Gospels and Old Testament into vulgar Latin, which aroused opposition from Rome.

In art he is often depicted as having a red cardinal's hat and in the company of the lion from whose paw he is said to have removed a thorn. His portrayal as a scribe surrounded with books was especially popularised by the Renaissance Humanist patrons, while representations of the aesthete in the desert may be used as a penant to his natural successor John the Baptist in the New Testament. He sometimes holds a stone that alludes to his aesthetic life as a hermit.

right and up the stairs. The building in the background is the Scuola di San Rocco. By contrast there is no such animation or humour in the *Funeral of St Jerome*, only solemn tragedy. Set in the peaceful, ordered precinct of a monastery, the composition centres around the saint laid out on the floor, attended by monks. A basic, yet serene, sense of inevitability pervades the scene, as suggested by the animals in the courtyard that represent the continual natural rhythm of life and death.

St Augustine in his Study also alludes to the legend of St Jerome: the Venetian version of the story tells of St Augustine wishing to address a letter on a matter of theology to St Jerome, who had already died: his divine presence appeared in St Augustine's study admonishing him for his presumption (a Venetian edition of the letter was published in 1485). The study is flooded with natural light that highlights every detail including the dog's bemusement, the scrolls and the little knobs. The quality of rendering and exquisite attention to the furnishings, especially the open door into a second room, are reminiscent of Flemish domestic interior painting. The facial traits of St Augustine are in fact those of **Cardinal Bessarione** (1402-72), a scholar of Greek Humanism.

Crossing this part of the Castello sestiere to reach the Scuola di San Giorgio degli Schiavoni from Riva degli Schiavoni, one is confronted by the Pietà.

St Augustine in his Study by Carpaccio (Scuola di San Giorgio degli Schiavoni)

La Pietà (🖪, GX) – The white façade with its broad pediment supported on columns, finally added in 1906, is the distinguishing feature from afar of Santa Maria della Visitazione, better known as "La Pietà" (the merciful one) after its hospice, dedicated in the 14C to abandoned children.

Initially the church would have been integrated within the institutional complex, but in the 18C, when it was all to be remodelled by Giorgio Massari (c 1686-1766), it was decided that the church should be designed as a concert hall given that the orphans' education was orientated towards music – at one time under the inspired leadership of **Antonio Vivaldi** *(see Introduction – Composers in Venice)*.

The internal structure is vaulted to optimise the acoustics: oval in shape, its atrium successfully muffles sounds from Riva degli Schiavoni. The orchestra and the choir are positioned along the side walls.

Music is also the theme of the superb frescoes on the ceiling. *Fortitude and Peace, The Triumph of Faith* and the *Cardinal Virtues* are by **Giambattista Tiepolo** (1696-1770).

A contemporary description of music at La Pietà relates: *"They sing like angels, play the violin, flute, organ, oboe, cello, bassoon – in short no instrument is large enough to frighten them... I swear nothing is so charming as to see a young and pretty nun, dressed in white, a sprig of pomegranate blossom behind one ear, leading the orchestra, and beating time with all the grace and precision imaginable"*.

Continue down the right side of the church along Calle della Pietà and Calle Bosello. Turn left into Salizzada dei Greci and then left again at the canal.

San Giorgio dei Greci ⊙ (🖪, GV) – The closed complex designed by Longhena (1598-1682) and distin-

> **Outside, along the right wall**
> An inscription from Paul III's Papal Bull, dated 12 November 1548, denounces the families who abandoned their children to the Pietà.

guished from afar by its gently leaning tower, comprises a 16C church and college buildings reserved for its Greek Orthodox community, and the Icon Museum.

Founded originally by a colony of Greeks, a confraternity evolved to form the **Scuola di San Niccolò**; after the fall of Constantinople in 1453, its numbers increased remarkably. Since 1539, first Sante Lombardo (1504-60) and then Giannantonio Chiona (active in Venice 1548-54) were charged with the church's expansion.

The long and narrow façade with its prominent pediment owes much to the influence of Sansovino. The cupola was added in 1571.

Inside, the great rectangular space is completely sealed by a magnificent **iconostasis★** embellished with holy figures against a gold background that screens off the apsed area beyond, reserved for the clergy. The walls are lined with wooden stalls for use by the congregation partaking of the long Orthodox rituals.

Museo di Icone Bizantine-postbizantine ⊙ – This museum houses a rich collection of Byzantine and post-Byzantine icons and paintings portraying various religious subjects that range from episodes from the Life of Christ (*Christ with John the Baptist*, the great 17C icon), the Saints, the Virgin, the Tree of Jesse, to exquisite illuminated manuscripts and religious artefacts.

Return along Salizzada dei Greci past **San Antonin** (🖪, HV) – a church which dates back to the 7C but which was rebuilt by Longhena (1598-1682). The mid-17C campanile rises to an Eastern-style cupola.

Before turning back towards Riva degli Schiavoni, one comes to Campo Bandiera e Moro with its church **San Giovanni in Bràgora★** (🖪, HX) *(see ARSENALE)*, where Vivaldi was baptised. And so ends this itinerary fringed with musical associations: having started with Vivaldi at the

> **Byzantine Icons**
> Icons are votive or devotional images used in Orthodox branches of the Eastern Church. The style of such pictures in small-scale diptychs appears intimate whereas their large-scale counterparts – often in mosaic – seem somehow inanimate. Iconographically, the figures tend to be stylised according to set rules and traditional symbolism, and pictured against a flat gold background like a decorative cameo jewel – a far call from the more realistic narrative painting that evolved in Western churches during the Renaissance.

Pietà it concludes with the *"Prete Rosso"*, a nickname pertaining either to Vivaldi's red hair or to his red uniform *(see Introduction – Composers in Venice)*.

For those wishing to continue into neighbouring districts, turn to the sections on ARSENALE and SAN ZACCARIA.

SAN ROCCO ★★★

Vaporetto: S Tomà

A walk around the area of San Rocco is ideal for the tourist: not only does it accommodate important sights, it also boasts its own local colour. What's more, quiet bars and cafés are situated near the main points of interest so one can always find a place for a coffee or a pizza, and break off from the cultural "tour".

To follow the suggested route and visit the places listed requires at least two and a half hours.

San Rocco (c 1295-1327) – Little is known of St Roch, protector of the sick and plague-stricken, other than that he was born in Montpellier in southwest France. According to his Venetian biographer, Francesco Diedo, Roch travelled to Italy where he miraculously cured plague victims with the sign of the cross (Aquapendente, Cesena, Mantua, Modena, Parma...) until he too succumbed to the disease in Piacenza and recovered enough to return home. He is most often represented with a pestilential sore on his leg, with a shell hanging from his belt or staff, and accompanied by the dog who brought him food and licked his wounds clean. On his return to Montpellier, he was taken to be a spy in Angers and incarcerated. He died there in prison.

While San Rocco was particularly venerated in Venice, the eponymous port also helped to spread the epidemic. Spared from Napoleon's edicts, the Confraternity of St Roch is still active today. Annually, on 16 August, Venice celebrates the saint with the most traditional pomp and circumstance *(see Traditional events)*.

The prestige of the *scuola* was further enhanced in 1485 when the saint's relics were transferred to its care. The "shrine" therefore was initiated in 1516 by Bartolomeo Bon, who was dismissed in 1524 after a major disagreement with the leaders of the *scuola*, when the project was entrusted to Scarpagnino (active in Venice 1505-49) who worked on the building until his death.

Putting this setback aside, the magnificence of the *scuola* resides in its interior decoration which has an interesting history of its own.

Bars and restaurants

The trattoria **Dona Onesta** operates from 3922 di Dorsoduro. **Ai Nomboli**, at 2717 Calle Goldoni, also in the *sestiere* di San Polo, is a bar specialising in tramezzini sandwiches. **Alla Palatina** *(2741 di San Polo, Calle Saoneri)* has banks of vegetable antipasti on offer (including, of course, roast potatoes) as well as a standard table service. **Da Vivaldi** in Calle del la Madoneta *(no 1457)* stands a short distance from Campo San Polo; it boasts a colourful menu of local dishes.

Tintoretto's shrewd move – In 1564, a competition was launched for the decoration of the Salla dell'Albergo *(a small room on the first floor where the Chapter met)*. While several illustrious artists including Paolo Veronese (1528-88), Andrea Schiavone (1503-63), Giuseppe Salviati (1520/25-75) and Federico Zuccari (1540-1609) submitted their drawings, **Tintoretto** (1518-94) quickly completed a painted panel for the ceiling depicting *St Roch in Glory* and promptly donated his work as a gesture of his devotion.

In such circumstances, the work, irrespective of what admiration it solicited, could not be refused – and so Tintoretto went on to furnish the entire *scuola* with his paintings.

Scuola Grande di San Rocco ⊘ (⬛, CDV) – Despite displaying a certain homogeneity, the façade draws together a variety of styles, most notably evident in the windows: those on the ground floor are early Venetian Renaissance whereas those above are Mannerist in design. The rear façade, facing onto the canal, is simpler in format with a portico and finely carved details (note the heads on the pilasters on the first floor).

★★★**Interior** – It is best to start from upstairs: so take either of the two flights that then feed into the single, grand staircase. Above, Scarpagnino's barrel-vaulted ceiling is painted with *St Roch Presenting the Sick to Charity, who Bears the Torch of Religion* by Giannantonio Pellegrini (1675-1741), whereas the walls show *Venice with Saints Mark, Roch and Sebastian in Supplication for an End to the Plague* by Pietro Negri (1673) *(on the left)* – note the inclusion of the Church of La Salute which was erected as a votive gesture at the end of the plague in 1630; and *(on the right) The Virgin Appearing to the Plague-Stricken* (1666) by Antonio Zanchi (1631-1722).

Sala dell'Albergo – On entering the Albergo Room one is struck by the impact of the huge and dramatic *Crucifixion* straight ahead.

A disconcerting, diagonal shaft of light suggests an unnerving presence of the supernatural, while a luminous ray of light behind the cross heralds the Resurrection. The picture's two compositional axes extend from the outside the picture and converge on the horizon, behind the Crucified Christ from whom emanates a supernatural luminosity.

In the left section of the entrance wall, *Christ Appearing before Pilate*: the intensity of the scene is concentrated by light focusing exclusively on the figure of Christ, thereby exaggerating the brilliance of his white garment and intensifying his spirituality. In the middle section is depicted *Ecce Homo*, and to its left, *Christ Bearing the Cross*, a realistic rendering of the tragic journey which Tintoretto populates with a weary cortège of figures moving in the opposite direction.

Scuola Grande di S. Rocco, Venezia/SCALA

The Crucifixion by Tintoretto

The *Three Apples* on the bench, reminiscent of something by Cézanne, is a fragment from the ceiling that was discovered above the door after four centuries behind one of the capitals.

Despite some controversy, the easel picture of *Christ bearing the Cross* has been attributed to Giorgione (1476/77-1510) and that of *Christ in Pietà* to his followers.

Sala Capitolare – The large chapter-house interplays subjects from the Old *(ceiling)* and New *(walls)* Testaments (1575-81). The principal themes treated are those that underpin the charitable aims of the scuola: providing drink for the thirsty, food for the hungry and care for the afflicted.

The central panel on the ceiling depicts *The Brazen Serpent* in which Aaron brandishes his rod (the rod that budded with leaf in endorsement of his authority as a priestly intercessor), foreshadowing another cross that presages the delivery from sin. This is framed by two square panels depicting *Moses Striking the Rock*, swirling with movement like a vortex around the central biblical

> **The Brazen Serpent**
>
> Number 21 *(v4-9)* describes how fiery serpents were sent among the Israelites as they grumbled about journeying through the desert, cursing Moses and God. On realising their wrong-doing, they sought forgiveness, so *"the Lord said unto Moses, Make thee a fiery serpent and set it upon a pole: and it shall come to pass, that every one that is bitten, when he looketh upon it, shall live."*

character, and *Manna Sent from Heaven*. The two large oval panels illustrate *Ezekiel's Vision* and the *Fall of Man*. The other eight panels painted in green chiaroscuro conclude the cycle of the Old Testament.

On the side of the corridor leading from the Albergo Room, is depicted *The Ascension (nearest the door)* followed by *The Pool of Bethesda* (described by Ruskin as *"All the great Italian painters appear insensible to the feeling of disgust at disease; but this study of the population of a hospital is without any points of contrast,* and I wish Tintoretto had not condescended to paint it"). The Temptation of Christ boasts a splendid Lucifer that echoes images of Eve tempting Adam with the apple.

On the wall opposite, the Adoration of the Shepherds is followed by The Baptism in which the protagonist is the Divine light that throws the faces of Jesus and John the Baptist into shadow; in the central section opposite The Ascension, The Resurrection of Christ shows Christ seemingly bursting from the tomb as the two Marys walk in the morning light beyond; whereas in The Agony in the Garden, the hour of the day imbues the scene with a faint reddish light. The focal point of perspective in The Last Supper is the bright halo hovering over the little figure of the Saviour. Unfortunately, little remains of the full glory that might have graced The Miracle of the Loaves and Fishes which succumbed to damage over the years from the light of the windows. Of The Resurrection of Lazarus Ruskin commented "... the upper part of it is quite worthy of the master, especially its noble fig tree and laurel, which he has painted, in one of his unusual fits of caprice, as carefully as that in the Resurrection of Christ opposite... The grass and weeds are, throughout, carefully painted, but the lower figures are of little interest, and the face of Christ a grievous failure".

The room also accommodates a large altarpiece, depicting the Vision of St Roch painted largely by Tintoretto, assisted by his son and Studio; a Self-Portrait showing Tintoretto in a religious pose and one of his versions of The Visitation. The Annunciation, however, is by Titian (1490-1576) and the two other easel canvases by Tiepolo (1696-1770), Hagar and Ishmael comforted by the Angel and Abraham visited by the Angels.

Sala Terrena – On the Ground Floor hang Tintoretto's last canvases, dedicated to Mary. Along the wall opposite the entrance are The Annunciation – a more "popular" version if compared to the aristocratic rendering by Titian precedes The Adoration of the Magi, The Flight into Egypt, The Massacre of the Innocent (imbued some might say by a sharp sense of realism and desperate tragedy by a Tintoretto overwhelmed with grief at the death of his son), and a Mary Magdalene. In the other paintings, St Mary of Egypt, The Presentation at the Temple and The Assumption, Tintoretto succeeds in creating a tension between the vertical and horizontal axes of the composition by suggesting an upward movement out of the broad horizontal picture plain.

All Tintoretto's canvases conform to the aesthetic principles outlined by the Council of Trent scorning all artifice and loftily intellectual iconography in favour of a more direct appeal to the common people. This art is contrived to be popular and emotionally charged with legible messages pertaining to the Salvation of Christ.

San Rocco (**3**, **CDV**) – The present façade of the church, built in the mid-1720s was substantially remodelled by Bernardino Maccaruzzi (d 1789) in the latter half of the 18C. The statues of the Saints (including the very fine Rococo figures of David and St Cecilia inside) and the Blessed are by Marchiori (1696-1778) and the Austrian-born Gianmaria Morlaiter (1699-1781) who also carved the relief of St Roch Tending the Sick. A few of the original Renaissance features designed by the Bon from Bergamo (1489) survive on the side overlooking the scuola: these include the portal and rose window.

A tour of the church perfectly concludes the full survey of the scuola's artistic heritage. Above the entrance door, the **old organ door panels** painted by Tintoretto depict The Annunciation – "a most disagreeable and dead picture" according to Ruskin – and The Presentation of St Roch to the Pope.

In the first side chapel of the left aisle, the altarpiece depicts St Helen and the Recovery of the True Cross by Sebastiano Ricci (1659-1734); the two tall panels by Pordenone (1484-1539) show St Martin and St Christopher, whereas the panel below, Christ Chasing the Moneychangers from the Temple, is by Fumiani (1650-1710) who also painted the Charity of St Roch on the ceiling. Over the second altar is an Annunciation and Angels by Solimena (1657-1747).

Four further canvases by Tintoretto meanwhile are to be found in the presbytery: (on the left) St Roch Administers to the Plague-Stricken and, St Roch in the Desert; (on the right) St Roch Heals the Animals and St Roch in Prison Comforted by the Angel. In this last work, Tintoretto shows the saint being arrested on his return from France on suspicion of being a spy.

Heading down the other side of the church, towards the way out, the first altarpiece on the left is dedicated to The Miracle of St Anthony by Trevisani (1656-1746). In the middle, between the two altars hang two more canvases by **Tintoretto**, St Roch Captured at the Battle of Montpellier and below The Pool of Bethesda; the latter, Ruskin criticises for its "corrupt Renaissance architecture" and lack of coherent perspective as the crowd seems literally to exceed the confines of the two-dimensional picture-space.

The last altar is decorated with an altarpiece by Sebastiano Ricci, San Francesco di Paola Raising the Dead Child.

Cross the canal behind the scuola and take Calle S Pantalon which leads into a square.

San Pantalon (🔢, CV) – Despite its unfinished façade (1668-86), this church recalls others in Venice such as San Marcuola and San Lorenzo.

Its main interest, however is its interior ornamented with an undisputed masterpiece by **Fumiani** (1643-1710) comprising 60 canvas ceiling panels illustrating *The Martyrdom and Glory of St Pantaleon★*, executed between 1684 and 1704, and restored with the assistance of the American Committee to Rescue Italian Art (1970-71). The work is a *tour de force* of perspective projecting the nave high into the sky.

The presbytery decoration is by the same artist, often referred to as *"fumoso"* (meaning smoky) owing to his predilection for dark colours, so characteristic of a period tormented by the ever presence of death. To the left of the high altar, the small Sacro Chiodo Chapel dedicated to a relic of the True Cross, houses the *Paradise* (1444) by Antonio Vivarini (c 1420-84).

In the third chapel on the right is a work by **Veronese** (1528-88), *San Bernardino*; in the one following, the second chapel, is his notable *St Pantaleon Healing the Sick Child* (1587) – the *Execution* and *Miracle of St Pantaleon* are by Palma il Giovane (1544-1628).

Return to San Rocco to take Salizzada S Rocco and Calle Large Prima to Campo S Tomà.

Campo S Tomà (🔢, DV) – This lovely square with its simple, now deconsecrated church dates back to the 10C; it was remodelled, however, in 1742. Straight ahead is the **Scuola dei Calegheri**, the guild of cobblers, which acquired the palazzo in the 15C.

To reach Goldoni's house, keep to the left side of the church and cross the bridge over Rio S Tomà.

Casa di Goldoni 🕐 (🔢, DV) – It was in this palazzo, its fine, small courtyard complete with its well and staircase, that the famous playwright **Carlo Goldoni** (1707-93) was born. Home now to the Institute for Theatrical Studies Casa Goldoni, the library boasts a number of documents on the life and works of the Venetian comedy writer *(see Introduction – Literature in Venice)*, playbills and original costumes.

St Pantaleon (died c 305)

Pantaleon was born to a pagan father and Christian mother. According to legend, he was reconciled to Christianity while employed as a physician at the court of Emperor Galerius at Nicodemia and denounced during the persecutions prescribed by Diocletian in 303. His cult was popularised in the Eastern Church, notably during the Middle Ages when he was honoured as one of the patron saints of physicians: his name, appropriately enough, means "the All-Merciful".

To continue to Campo S Polo the easiest way is to just follow the flow of people. Cross the bridge over Rio di S Polo and follow along the right side of the church.

Campo San Polo (🔢, DU) – Still today, this large open space provides a venue for many cultural and tourist events (open-air cinema, carnival celebrations etc) thereby maintaining an age-long historical tradition of ceremonies and games of various sorts, such as bull-baiting *(see PIAZZA SAN MARCO – Museo Correr)*. Two *palazzi* overlook this splendid piazza shaped like an amphitheatre: the high Gothic-style **Palazzo Soranzo** (nos 2169 and 2170), and nearby, the Baroque **Palazzo Tiepolo Maffetti** with its distinctive head of Hercules over the portal. It is strange to think that both these palazzi overhung the water right up until the second-half of the 18C. At the opposite corner is Sanmicheli's 16C **Palazzo Corner Mocenigo**, now the seat of the Guardia di Finanza (Financial Police).

San Polo (🔢, DUV) – The façade of this ancient church, whose origins are rooted in the 9C, was rebuilt between the 14C and 15C. Now hemmed in by houses, the church preserves its main rose window and an ornate side door decorated with organic carving from the turn of the 14C as a testimony to the late-Gothic style. Subsequent restoration in the 19C has unfortunately destroyed the harmony of the original.

The interior, vaulted with a ship's keel roof, accommodates over the first altar on the right an *Assumption of the Virgin* and to its left a *Last Supper* by **Tintoretto** (1518-94). In this second piece, an intimate interior scene full of domestic details that betray a simple way of life is charged with the poignancy of the moment.

Over the second altar on the left, the *Virgin Appearing to St John of Nepomuk* is by Giambattista Tiepolo (1696-1770), whereas the *14 Stations of the Cross* in the Oratory of the Crucifix are by his son Giandomenico (1727-1804).

The chapel on the left preserves the Betrothal of the Virgin and Angels by Veronese (1528-88).

For those wishing to continue into neighbouring districts, turn to the sections on I CARMINI and RIALTO.

"When I went to Venice – my dream became my address."
*Marcel Proust – **Letter to Madame Strauss***

SAN ZACCARIA ★★

(⑨, GX)
Vaporetto: S Zaccaria

San Zaccaria is a stone's throw from St Mark's so there are numerous restaurants, *pizzerie*, souvenir and *passementerie* shops in the area. As the distance from the church increases, so the number of tourists thins out and the atmosphere settles, although never to the point of being deserted, as local colour returns and Venice becomes more congenial to its inhabitants. At its heart, the Campo Santa Maria Formosa and its radiating *calli* pound with every imaginable activity, including its own market. For anyone happy to take a leisurely stroll, it is a good area in which to hunt out shops specialising in typical and characteristic Venetian goods.

For the suggested itinerary allow about two and a half hours.

★★**San Zaccaria** (⑨, GX)
   – This magnificent church is situated in a lively square, behind Riva degli Schiavoni. If coming from Campo S Provolo, one passes through the marble high-Gothic archway with a relief depicting the *Madonna Enthroned with Child and Saints*. Once inside this elegant square, along the left side runs a 15C arcade

> ### If you are hungry...
>
> Why not try the *osteria* **Al Mascaròn** at 5525 Calle Lunga S Maria Formosa.
>
> ### For a snack...
>
> Nearby at 5909 Campo di Sta Marina, is **Dido-vich**; their little *semifreddi* (soft ice-creams) can be most energising and restorative!

beyond which extends a cloister that once harboured the convent cemetery. On the right is the façade of the former convent church with its 13C campanile: note *(on the left)* one of those curious reprimands that one comes across in Venice: in this case, a polite invitation to behave oneself properly! An apt reminder perhaps, addressed to visitors of the famous female convent visited by the doge every Easter Monday.

The original church founded in the 9C, in certain respects, has been incorporated into the new church: its right aisle having been built out of the left aisle of the old church. The present church, dating from the 15C, was built by Gambello (recorded 1458-81) and completed, at his death, by Codussi (c 1440-1504).

San Zaccaria projecting above the rooftops

The splendid white façade, with its three tiers of round-headed windows, niches and semicircular pediment, seems to soar high above the neighbouring houses (it can even be seen from the Doges' Palace, towering above the dense mass of roofs and *altane* "wooden roof terraces". Contrived from a variety of architectural styles, its tall Gothic proportions are cloaked in Renaissance detail. At ground level the lower section is set with square polychrome panels that run horizontally. Above this, a continuous frieze of shell-headed flat niches introduce a vertical element that is then carried through the upper sections, accented first with three windows, then two and finally by a single central oculus. Gently, the Gothic configuration of tall nave and side aisles cede to Codussi's more Classical idiom: projecting piers give way to free-standing paired columns that extend up to a cornice, crowned with free-standing figures – far removed from the statue of *St Zaccarias* by Alessandro Vittoria (1525-1608) above the main door.

The stunning interior is literally covered in paintings: the most important surely being Giovanni Bellini's *Sacra Conversazione* (1505) over the second altar on the left, a work of extraordinary sensitivity and delicate colour harmonies.

On the lower left wall are two panels (1500) by Palma il Giovane (1544-1628): a *Virgin in Glory and Saints* and *St Zacharias in Glory*.

At the end of the right aisle is the **Cappella del Coro** ⊙

Sacra Conversazione

Translated as a Holy Conversation piece, this form of composition unites a central Madonna and Child with particular saints in a single space: an interior scene or landscape. Stylistically, this arrangement developed from the traditional devotional polyptych where saints were separated from the main panel into niches. Here, the figures interact with each other within the same picture plain, as if united in a common cause.

hung with a *Birth of John the Baptist* by Tintoretto (1518-94), a *Flight into Egypt* by Giandomenico Tiepolo (1727-1806), a *Virgin with Putto and Saints* by Palma il Vecchio (c 1480-1528), a pair of organ panels painted by Palma il Giovane, a *Crucifixion* attributed to Van Dyck (1599-1641) and a *Resurrection of Christ with Adam and Eve* by Domenico Tintoretto (c 1560-1635).

In the Cappella d'Oro, also known as the Chapel of St Tarasius, the vault is frescoed by Andrea del Castagno (1423-1457) and Francesco da Faenza (c 1410-c 1450), and the three Gothic polyptychs are by Antonio Vivarini (c 1420-84) and his collaborator (1441-1446/50), Giovanni da Murano. At the foot of the altar are the remains of the mosaic from the apse of the 12C Romanesque-Byzantine chapel. A little further back *(protected by glass)* are the mosaics from the 9C church. Stairs descend into the 10C crypt, submerged in water.

Follow Salizzada S Provolo and proceed straight to the canal; turn left for the Diocesan Museum of Religious Art (see PIAZZA SAN MARCO – Museo Diocesano di Arte Sacra).
Or return to Campo SS Filippo e Giacomo and take Calle della Chiesa, turn left before the canal and follow the water's edge through Campiello Querini and on to Campo Sta Maria Formosa.

Campo Santa Maria Formosa (⑤, GU) – This square might recall the quiet Campo San Giacomo dall'Orio, given their similar semicircular shape and the position of the church: only this square is situated between St Mark's and the Church of Santi Giovanni e Paolo where daily comings and goings of tourists and Venetians alike make this *campo* a busy thoroughfare.

Santa Maria Formosa (⑤, GUV) – The original 7C church to have been built here was dedicated, according to legend, to St Magnus to whom the Madonna appeared in the form of a beautiful, shapely *(formosa)* woman. It was rebuilt by Codussi (c 1440-1504) between 1492 and 1504. It was further embellished with a new main façade in 1604 which in fact fronts a side entrance, and a new canal frontage in 1542, financed by a noble Venetian family, the Cappellos. The 17C campanile retains, above the entrance, a grimacing mask and its original pinnacle – *"A head – huge inhuman and monstrous – leering in bestial degradation, too foul to be either pictured or described, or to be beheld for more than an instant..."* John Ruskin.

The interior, in the form of a Latin cross, includes the chapels of the Scuola dei Bombardieri (mortar founders) which contains a *San Barnaba and Saints* by Palma il Vecchio (c 1480-1528) and that of the Scuola dei Casselleri (trunks and chest makers). Of note in the first chapel on the right is a *Madonna of the Misericordia* by Bartolomeo Vivarini (c 1432-91).

★**Fondazione Querini Stampalia** ⊙ **(⑤, GV)** – The museum may prove particularly interesting to anyone seeking to imbibe the atmosphere of a Venice long disappeared, when, evidently, her life was synonymous with art.

On passing through the main entrance, note on the left the *Madonna di Lepanto* (1571) which once graced the naval ship commanded by Sebastiano Venier.

Exquisite topographical works include *Scenes of Public Life in Venice*★★ by Gabriele Bella (1730-99) and the **series of panels**★★ by Pietro Longhi (1702-85) predominantly devoted to the sacraments and hunting. Look out for the *Boxing Match* after Antonio Stom (1717-39) and *The*

> ### The Abduction of the Maidens
>
> According to a Venetian custom, for the Feast of the Marias, at Candlemas, two girls from each *sestiere* would be married and each would be given a coffer in which to store their dowry. In about 946, the festival was nearly ruined by Slav pirates who kidnapped the maidens and held them to ransom: these were rescued by the **Casselleri**, the artisans who made the bridal chests for the brides. Since then, the doge would visit the Cassellari at Santa Maria Formosa at Candlemas.

Frozen Lagoon by the Fondamenta Nuove by an anonymous 18C Venetian painter. The collection includes works by Giovanni Bellini (c 1426-1516), Palma il Giovane (1544-1628), Luca Giordano (1634-1705), lo Schiavone (c 1503-63), Antonio Canova (1757-1822) – including a clay model for his sculpture of Letizia Ramolino Bonaparte, Palma il Vecchio (c 1480-1528) – Portrait of the Nobleman Francesco Querini, and Giambattista Tiepolo (1696-1770) – Procurator and Sea Captain, member of the Dolfin family.

For those wishing to continue into neighbouring districts, turn to the sections on PIAZZA SAN MARCO, ARSENALE and RIALTO.

"...Since our eyes are educated from childhood on by the objects we see around us, a Venetian painter is bound to see the world as a brighter and gayer place than most people see it. We northerners who spend our lives in a drab and, because of the dirt and the dust, uglier country where even reflected light is subdued, and who have, most of us, to live in cramped rooms — we cannot instinctively develop an eye which looks with such delight at the world."

Goethe – Italian Journey, *8 October 1786*

SAN ZANIPÒLO ★★

SS Giovanni e Paolo
Vaporetto: Fondamenta Nuove, Cimitero

This area is striking not only for its timeless majesty but also because of the broad range of things going on in the district, from the intense business of the *calli* between Campo di SS Giovanni e Paolo and Campo SS Apostoli to the tranquillity of Campo dei Gesuati and the peacefulness of the Fondamenta Nuove. From here, one looks out over the choppy waters of the lagoon and the cemetery of San Michele, the only activity being the passing of the water-buses.

If following the suggested route, allow half a day.

Waiting for the water-bus to the islands...

Have a drink at **Al Giubagiò** *(5039 Fondamenta Nuove)*. If it's cold go inside, otherwise enjoy the sunshine outside where tables have a view over the lagoon. Why not design your own personal bookplate, business card and stationery embossed and printed using traditional methods by **Gianni Basso** at 5306 Calle del Fumo, around the corner from Fondamenta Nuove. If confidence allows, it is well-worth nattering with the affable owner, who without resorting to high-tech computers or other modern paraphernalia, has managed to fulfil various wonderful commissions for patrons at home and abroad, satisfying the most modest to the most extravagantly famous.

Un'osteria?

A quest for a tasty Venetian meal might easily be satisfied by calling upon **Antiche Cantine Ardenghi** *(6369 Calle della Testa)*.

One, nay one hundred pizzas

Try **La Perla** pizzeria *(Rio Terà dei Franceschi)*, just behind Campo SS Apostoli.

Campo di SS Giovanni e Paolo (◧, GU) – Just one look at the square and the activities that seem to go on here – appearing little changed through the ages if compared with Canaletto's painting of *Campo Santi Giovanni e Paolo* – serves to justify its former name, *Campo delle Maravege* (Marvels).

The name *Zanipòlo* is a contraction of the names John and Paul in dialect,

---

The Condottiere

Bartolomeo Colleoni (1400-76) was one of many mercenary soldiers engaged by the Venetian Republic to defend and acquire her territories. A native of Bergamo, Colleoni served Venice for a long time, with considerable success. He also served Francesco Sforza. Returning to the Republic of Venice, he was relegated to the Malpaga castle where he died. His tomb is housed in the Colleoni Chapel in Bergamo.

---

the two saints to whom it is dedicated. Every one of its constituting elements contribute to the solemn vastness of the whole: the imposing basilica, the deceptive perspectives of the Scuola Grande di San Marco, the bridge over the Rio dei Mendicanti, the great "angular" space, relieved only by a well-head and the equestrian monument to Colleoni.

★★**Equestrian monument to Bartolomeo Colleoni** – The proud gait of the rider, his face set with a wilful expression, contrasts powerfully with the restless disposition of the horse: an inspired combination that is rendered all the more majestic by its base.

The fact that the monument has ended up here in this square might be enough to keep Colleoni perpetually turning in his grave: in his will, he stated that he intended the statue be placed before St Mark's, on the understanding that he implied the Basilica thereof. But when it came to defending its own interests, the Republic was both capable and shrewd. Considering the monument not to be worthy of St Mark's Square, permission was given for it to be set up in a place that at least was associated in name to its intended destination, before the Scuola Grande di San Marco.

The commission for such a major monument was awarded to **Verrocchio** (1435-88) by competition. As the master died before it had been cast, Alessandro Leopardi (1465-1523) was charged with the responsibility for overseeing the project and adding the base, thereby acquiring the epithet *"dal Cavallo"*, meaning "of the horse-fame". The inspiration for the Colleoni monument undoubtedly came from the *Gattamelata* by Donatello (1386-1466) in Padua, which, with the Antique equestrian statue of Marcus Aurelius in Rome, rank amongst the best expressions of the genre.

Ruskin's strong opinion is concisely put: *"The statue of Bartolomeo Colleoni, in the little square beside the church, is certainly one of the noblest works in Italy. I have never seen anything approaching it in animation, in vigour of portraiture, or nobleness of line."*

The decorative **well-head** is attributed to Sansovino (1486-1570) who was also responsible for the side of the Scuola di San Marco that faces onto the canal. Alongside the putti runs the Latin inscription: *Mira silex mirusque latex qui flumina vincit* (The stone may be marvellous, but this water is clearer than that in the river).

★★**Basilica dei Santi Giovanni e Paolo** (◧, GU) – The church was founded by Dominican friars late in the 13C but not consecrated until 1430, as a result, it is said of a vision that appeared to Doge Giacomo Tiepolo in 1226.

It is reminiscent both in style (brick) and size of the Frari. It is, in fact, the largest church in Venice, being 101m/330ft long, 46m/151ft wide at the cross and 55m/180ft tall to the top of the dome. Its particularly solemn atmosphere may in part be inherited from a time when it served to hold the doges' obsequies and subsequent burial.

Front – The façade, which remains incomplete, comprises at ground level of a central pointed arch flanked by three blind arches; above, the width is divided vertically by plain piers rising up to niches on the roof line that accommodate statues of the Dominican Saints *(from left to right)* Thomas Aquinas, Dominic and Peter the Martyr *(see MURANO)*. These in turn are crowned with the eagle, the symbol of St John, the Eternal Father and the lion of St Mark.

N. Bosquet/MICHELIN

Detail of the well in Campo di SS Giovanni e Paolo

On either side of the main portal, designed by Bartolomeo Bon (recorded 1441-64) are the two sarcophagi, inset in the Gothic arches, of the Doges Jacopo (1289) and Lorenzo (1268-75) Tiepolo.

Interior – Described by Sir Hugh Honour as "grandiose", the well-lit lofty nave leads to an apse pierced by slender double lancet Gothic windows. In the form of a Latin cross, the church has three aisles and five apses. Like in the Church of the Frari, huge columns carry great beams which support the arches and the cross vaults.

The internal façade commemorates the **Mocenigo Doges:** *(centre)* Alvise I (1570-77) (**1**); *(left)* Pietro (1474-76) – (**2**) monument by Pietro Lombardo (1435-1515); *(right)* Giovanni (1478-85) – (**3**) monument by Tullio Lombardo (c 1455-1532).

Along the left aisle is the altar to St Jerome (**4**), its statue a work by Alessandro Vittoria (1525-c 1600); the pyramid nearby is in memory of the Bandiera brothers (**5**), supporters of Mazzini's *Young Italy*, who were gunned down in 1844.

At the altar to St Peter Martyr (altarpiece after Titian) is the monument to **Doge Niccolò Marcello** (**6**) by Pietro Lombardo; that to **Doge Tommaso Mocenigo** (1414-23) (**7**) with its great baldachin, is the work (1423) of Niccolò Lamberti and Giovanni di Martino who blended Gothic elements with Venetian and Tuscan Renaissance elements.

Flanking the double arch are two statues *St Peter Martyr* and *St Thomas Aquinas* by Antonio Lombardo (c 1458-1516). Before the sacristy is the Renaissance monument to **Doge Pasquale Malipiero** (1457-62) (**8**) by Pietro Lombardo, although the baldachin is Gothic in style.

San Zanipòlo

The **sacristy** seems to burst with ornate decoration orchestrating a celebration of the Dominican order: the canvas by Leandro da Bassano (1557-1622) depicts *Pope Onorio III Approving the Constitution of the Dominican Order in 1216*, emblazoned with the colours red, white and black. The ceiling, painted by one of Titian's relations Marco Vecellio (1545-1611), shows *The Virgin Sending the Two Founders, Dominic and Francis, to Earth*. The scene of the *Crucifixion with Dominican Saints* at the altar and the *Resurrection* on the right are by Palma il Giovane (1544-1628). To the left of the altar is a painting by Alvise Vivarini (1445-1505) of *Christ Bearing the Cross*: the Redeemer is shown looking back, his questioning expression particularly sad: the tragedy of the scene is effectively heightened by the arid background landscape, dotted with buildings on the horizon.

Just before turning into the transept are three panels of a *Polyptych* (**9**) by Bartolomeo Vivarini (c 1432-91) – St Augustine appears stern, a beatic St Lawrence holds the gridiron on which he was martyred, while St Dominic holds out a lily. The 18C organ was built by Gaetano Callido *(see Introduction – Composers in Venice)*.

In the left transept, above the entrance to the Chapel of the Rosary but below the great clock, is the monument to **Doge Antonio Venier** (1382-1400) attributed to Dalle Masegne (active 14C-15C); to its right, besides the entrance stands the bronze statue of **Sebastiano Venier** (1577-78) the victor at Lepanto *(see Introduction – Over a thousand years of glory: 1571)*.

The **Cappella del Rosario** (Chapel of the Rosary or Lepanto Chapel), was built as a mark of gratitude for the great victory over the Turks. The shrine enclosing the *Madonna del Rosario* was designed by Girolamo Campagna (c 1550-1626). It was severely damaged by a fire in 1867 which, amongst other things, also destroyed canvases by Tintoretto and Titian. These in part have been replaced by **Veronese** (1528-88). The ceiling shows the *Adoration of the Shepherds* – with its harmonious grouping of the shepherd, the ass and the lamb; the *Assumption;* the *Annunciation* – its perspective accented by the angel "falling" from the sky watched by Mary from below; and the *Adoration of the Magi* – in which Joseph is just outside the field of view, reaching forward to grab the column.

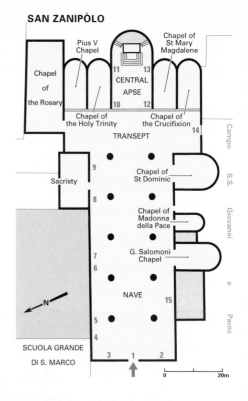

On the walls *(starting from the right wall backing on to the presbytery)* are depicted *St Dominic Saving the Ship-Wrecked with the Rosary* by Padovanino (1588-1649) and a *Last Supper* by Benedetto Caliari (1538-98). In this painting Brother Dominic is portrayed as the apostle in the centre with his arm outstretched while the apostle standing with his hands joined *(right)* is a self-portrait. Opposite the altar, in the *Adoration of the Shepherds*, Veronese has painted himself in the guise of the man standing beyond the column. The Child, his head turned away, is the focus of the attention of the two groups comprising Mary and Joseph on one side and the shepherds with the ox and the ass on the other.

Beyond the apsed chapels on the left, dedicated to St Pius V and the Trinity, respectively, comes the central apse replete with other **funerary monuments**.

Immediately on the left is that of **Doge Marco Corner** (1365-68) (**10**) by Nino Pisano and apprentices – comprising an exquisite *Virgin and Child;* then follows the sepulchre of **Doge Andrea Vendramin** (1476-78) (**11**): a majestic work by Tullio Lombardo ornamented with Classical medallions illustrating mythological figures, and warriors in the niches.

On the right is the funerary monument to **Doge Michele Morosini** (1382) (**12**) from the workshops of Dalle Masegne, surmounted by a Tuscan School mosaic (15C) and framed by an arch; here also is that of **Doge Leonardo Loredan** (1501-21) (**13**) during whose reign the League of Cambrai was formed *(see Introduction – Over a thousand years of glory: 1508)*. Venice *(left)* and the League of Cambrai *(right)* are depicted at the sides of the statue of the doge by Girolamo Campagna (c 1549-c 1626).

Further on, the first apsidal chapel on the right is dedicated to **Mary Magdalene**. The *Four Evangelists* are frescoed by Palma il Giovane; on the right wall is the monument to the **Sea-Captain Vittor Pisani** (1324-80), while on the left is a particularly haunting piece known as *Vanity* or *The Conceited Woman* (17C) depicting a young girl looking at her reflection in a mirror and seeing Death. The sculpture could be a reference to the conversion of a woman in the 14C who became a Dominican after a disturbing experience.

In the adjacent **Cappella del Crocifisso** (Chapel of the Crucifix), the *Grieving Virgin* and *John the Baptist* are by Alessandro Vittoria.

In the right arm of the transept, the **stained glass** (14) will have struck the visitor by its bright and intense colour. The panels are based upon cartoons by Bartolomeo Vivarini, Cima da Conegliano (c 1459-1517) and Girolamo Mocetto (c 1448-1531). At the bottom, the work depicts *(from left to right)* the soldier saints: St Theodore, St John and St Paul – the two Roman martyrs and patrons of the basilica, and St George.

The throne from which the doge watched the ceremonies in the basilica is also in this arm of the transept.

The *Coronation of the Virgin* on the right is by Cima da Conegliano (1459-1517).

The **Cappella di San Domenico** (Chapel of St Dominic), in the right aisle, houses the *Glory of St Dominic* by Piazzetta (1683-1754). Its bold composition is articulated by perspective starting with the friars, taking in the ascending saint, the musician angels and the Virgin, to culminate with the Trinity.

Before the **Cappella della Madonna della Pace** (Chapel of the Madonna of Peace) stands the accomplished and confident **Valier monument** (1705-08), the largest of the Doge monuments. The chapel houses a Byzantine icon and works by Leandro Bassano (1557-1622) *(left wall)*, Aliense *(right wall)* and Palma il Giovane *(vault)*.

In front of the Baroque **Cappella del Beato Giacomo Salomoni** is the tombstone of Ludovico Diedo who died in 1466, a fine example of *niello* engraving. Over the next altar sits an early *Polyptych* (15) by Giovanni Bellini (c 1426-1516) comprising St Vincent Ferrier flanked by St Christopher and St Sebastian. Note the somewhat awkward treatment of the nude, and the characteristically delicate expression of the Child holding on tight to the head of St Christopher, the Archangel Gabriel and the young Madonna. The predella below, illustrates five miracles attributed to St Vincent.

And so to the urn said to contain the skin of Captain Marcantonio Bragadin who was flayed alive by the Turks in 1571 after the surrender of Famagusta *(see Introduction – Over a thousand years of glory: 1571)*.

★**Scuola Grande di San Marco** ⊙ (**5**, GTU) – This ancient **Scuola**, founded in 1260, was transferred here from its original seat in Santa Croce in 1438. Destroyed in the fire of 1485, its reconstruction was entrusted to Pietro Solaro, known as Lombardo (1435-1515) who trained in Florence and worked in Padua before reaching Venice, and his sons Antonio (recorded c 1506-1516) and Tullio (active c 1455-1532), before being completed by Lombardo's arch rival, Mauro Codussi (c 1440-1504), who was responsible for the crowning section of the façade. In certain respects, the Scuola's fate has reverted to the purpose for which it was founded, for at the beginning of the 19C, the building was transformed into a hospital, first for military and now general civic use.

At ground level, the **façade** boasts an effective series of trompe-l'œil panels; two bold lions guard the left entrance and to their right, two groups of figures (by the Lombardo sons) crowd around St Mark healing and baptising Anianus, a cobbler from Alexandria. At roof level, semicircular pediments and ornate statuary crown the elaborate frontage.

Interior – The **Sala dell'Albergo** now accommodates the medical library and several large pictures: two works by Giovanni Mansueti, an artist who was active in Venice between 1485 and c 1526 – *Three Episodes from the Life of St Mark* and *St Mark Raising Anianus (on the left wall)*; one by Palma il Vecchio (c 1480-1528) assisted by Paris Bordone (1500-71) – *St Mark Calming the Storm (opposite the entrance)* and one by Jacopo (1518-94) and Domenico (c 1560-1635) Tintoretto – *The Apparition of St Mark (right wall)*. The entrance-door wall is decorated with *The Martyrdom of St Mark* by Vettor Belliniano (1456-1529).

Note before leaving the room, the lion with the closed Gospel, a conceit alluding to whether Venice, at the time, was at war or at peace *(see I FRARI)*.

The **Sala Capitolare**, also known as the Sala San Marco, has a blue and gold ceiling bearing the symbols of the Scuole. The lion in the centre holds an open Gospel. The large panel behind the altar depicting the *Glorification of St Mark* is the work of Palma il Giovane (1544-1628). Those to each side are by Jacopo and Domenico Tintoretto: the *Arrival of the Ship in Venice* and the *Transportation of the Body of St Mark on the Ship*, as is the painting on the opposite wall showing *St Mark Blessing the Islands in the Lagoon*.

The difference in temperature between the two rooms is particularly noticeable: in addition to the antique medical instruments there are also some valuable 16C texts on display in the Sala Capitolare which have to be kept at a certain temperature. Some of these texts were illustrated by Titian.

Follow Calle Larga Gallina to Campo S Maria Nova, from where the rear of the fine Renaissance Church of Santa Maria dei Miracoli may be contemplated.

★**Santa Maria dei Miracoli** (**4**, FU) – This exquisite church positioned on the edge of a canal, overlooking the small Campo dei Miracoli, recalls the distinctive nature of 14C Tuscan design both in terms of its crisply carved architectural ornament and its marble detailing. The church is the work of Lombardo *(see above)*, erected to house a miracle-working image of the Madonna by Nicolò di Pietro (1409).

In 1489, it was dedicated to the *Immacolata* (the Virgin), the doctrine of the Immaculate Conception having been proclaimed 12 years prior to this. The church, decorated with carefully selected coloured marble and porphyry panels, is often used for weddings.

The **interior**, especially the barrel vault, resembles a casket. Prophets and patriarchs are depicted in the 50 compartments of the coffered ceiling *(best appreciated with the mirror that is provided for this purpose)*.

A flight of steps provide access to the elevated tribune, framed by a balustrade and ornamented with statues by Tullio Lombardo (active in Venice c 1455-1532). The painting by Nicolò di Pietro stands at the main altar.

A Renaissance jewel – Santa Maria dei Miracoli

Cross the bridge into Campiello S Maria Nova, pass before San Cancian and proceed straight on. Take Calle del Manganer in Campiello Cason which leads to the back of the Church of SS Apostoli.

Campo SS Apostoli – *See RIALTO.*

Behind the church, take Rio Terà dei SS Apostoli and carry straight on.

The walk to the vast Campo dei Gesuiti will reveal secluded corners of Venice that are typical of the Cannaregio *sestiere*. This being Venice, simple scenes from everyday life in Campo dei Gesuiti have their own poetic atmosphere.

★**Gesuiti** (◻, FT) – The Jesuit church stands in a peaceful, but rarely completely deserted, square. It is all the more striking for its white marble Baroque façade, decorated with numerous statues, which include a statue of the *Virgin*, to which it is dedicated, over the pediment. The present building was erected between 1715 and 1729 on the site of the ancient Church of Santa Maria dei Crociferi (1150).

The true originality of the building is reinforced on entering: the realism of the white marble curtain, inlaid with green, is so true as to deceive one into believing in the ample drapes in the pulpit and the folds of carpet tumbling down from the high altar.

The sumptuous effect is enhanced by the white and gold stucco of the ceiling, the two central sections of which are by Francesco Fontebasso (1709-69).

Over the first altar on the left sits *The Martyrdom of St Lawrence* by Titian (1490-1576), and in the left transept is the *Assumption of the Virgin* by Tintoretto (1518-94).

In the sacristy is a cycle of painting by Palma il Giovane (1544-1628) which, amongst other things, narrates stories from the Bible *(Manna from Heaven)*, of the True Cross *(St Helen Finding the True Cross)*.

Returning down the right aisle, the sculpture of *San Barnaba* in the penultimate chapel is by Morlaiter (1699-1781) whilst *Tobias, the Archangel Rafael and Custodian Angels* is painted by Palma il Giovane.

Oratorio dei Crociferi ◷ (◻, FT) – In 1150, grouped around Campo dei Gesuiti were the church, monastery and hospice run by the Crutched Friars *(Fratres Cruciferi)*, an Order of mendicant friars that were eventually suppressed in 1656. The hospital also served as a refuge for those who had fought in the Crusades. In 1414, it was transformed into a hospice for 12 destitute old ladies.

Much of its decoration was undertaken between 1583 and 1592 by Palma il Giovane (1544-1628). The subject treated focuses on the history of the Crutched Friars and their hospital in Venice, on the purpose of the Oratory as the hospice chapel, and the liturgical nature of the Oratory. On the end wall is *Christ in Glory Blessing Doge Renier Zen, his Wife and the Procurators of St Mark's, Some of the Crutched Friars and the Women of the Hospice* – **Doge Renier Zen** (1253-68) having been a principal benefactor of the hospital of Santa Maria dei Crociferi.

On either side of the altar, two paintings depict the Foundation of the Order by Pope Cleto (76-88) and its Affirmation by Pope Paul IV (1555-59). The three canvases on the left wall depict scenes from the life of **Pasquale Cicogna**, Procurator of St Mark's and Doge (1585-95). Above the doors are represented *The Flagellation* and *The Dead Christ.* In homage to the Virgin, to whom the chapel is dedicated, the ceiling has been decorated with the *Assumption.*

Continue towards the lagoon.

Fondamenta Nuove (**4**, **5**, FHT) – Visitors will quickly get to know this long jetty because it is from here that the water-buses *(vaporetti)* depart for the Islands of San Michele, Murano, Burano and Torcello. The Fondamenta Nuove which runs alongside the lagoon was constructed at the end of the 16C. A thoroughfare by obligation rather than by design, the Fondamenta offers some respite in the form of bars and news-stands for people waiting for the vaporetto: most useful if awaiting a passage to Torcello for the service is reliably infrequent.

The fact that this corner of Venice provides the only means of conveyance to the outlying islands of the lagoon should not detract from the area's own artistic value, for it is here that Venice's main theatre is to be found, the Teatro Fondamenta Nuove near the Sacca della Misericordia.

Take the vaporetto for the Island of San Michele.

San Michele in Isola (**5**, HS) – San Michele is where Venetians and many of her famous bewitched visitors have chosen to be buried.

On arrival, visitors are greeted by the great white church, designed by Codussi (c 1440-1504), the first Renaissance church in Venice. Its simple façade betrays the ordered structure of the interior. The rational use of features, crowned like the Church of San Zaccaria *(see SAN ZACCARIA)* and rusticated on the ground floor like the Palazzo Ruccellai and Palazzo Medici in Florence, includes a fine doorway, topped with a pediment and a statue of the *Madonna.* Two arched windows frame the central bay with its rose window. Codussi purposefully avoids perfect symmetry and strict geometry by adapting the semicircular upper section. A small indication of the quality of the detailing is inherent in the definition of the shells in the lateral niches: see how the radiating ribs disappear into the shell.

The interior consisting of simple nave and aisles, extends down to a full set of choirstalls, presided over by *St Jerome* carved by the Flemish artist, Juste Le Court (1627-79). The whole is enclosed beneath a sumptuous coffered ceiling. The sacristy ceiling, however, is later in date, painted by Romualdo Mauro (c 1720-68). The **Emiliani Chapel**, on the left flank of the church, is decorated by Guglielmo de' Grigi, known as "il Bergamasco" – the man from Bergamo, who was recorded as working in Venice between c 1515 and 1530.

Cimitero ⊘ (**5**, GHS) – *Ask for a map of the cemetery at the entrance.* Here lie **Ezra Pound** (1885-1972), **Igor Stravinsky** (1882-1971), **Sergei Pavlovich Diaghilev** (1872-1929) and, since June 1997, **Josif Brodskij** (1940-96).

Condemned for his anti-American propaganda, Ezra Pound, the author of the *Cantos* was first interned in a concentration camp and then in an asylum, before spending the last years of his life in Italy. He is buried in the Evangelical section to the left on entering, between the central avenue and the wall, before the intersection of the two paths.

This same Evangelical area contains the grave of Josif Brodskij, a Russian poet and Nobel Prize winner (1987), who drew on the atmosphere of Venice for his work entitled *Watermark:* he lies buried on the right, having turned left at the junction with the paths.

Igor Stravinsky, the Russian composer who took American citizenship and who is remembered for the *Fire Bird, Petrushka* and the *Rite of Spring,* along with his associate Sergei Diaghilev, the émigré founder of the Russian Ballet and major theatrical impresario, are buried in the Greek section, at the end: Stravinsky to the right and Diaghilev to the left.

In the Cemetery of San Michele lies the musician **Luigi Nono** (1924-90) and the great Goldoni actor **Cesco Baseggio** (1897-1971).

"At the eastern corner of San Michele is an old Protestant graveyard of very different temper. It is like a Carolina churchyard, lush, untended and overgrown, shaded by rich gnarled trees with grassy walks and generations of dead leaves... There are many Swiss and Germans in these graves; and many British seamen, who died on their ships in the days when the P & O liners used the port of Venice..."

Jan Morris – Venice

For those wishing to continue into neighbouring districts, turn to the sections on RIALTO and CA' D'ORO.

The outlying islands

BURANO ★★

Burano is the most colourful of the lagoon islands. At the doors and windows of the houses – which seem to have been painted in the brightest colours of the rainbow – women work on their lace pillows while their men see to their fishing nets and boats. Visitors will be hailed with friendly "invitations" from the locals selling *passementerie* (articles bordered in lace) displayed by the "lace-houses".

To follow the suggested route, allow a couple of hours.

On the way to the island

It takes about 45 minutes to get from Fonda-menta Nuova (Line 12) to Burano, the most colourful of the islands. The last stretch of the journey is along the Mazzorbo Canal, an island linked to Burano by a wooden bridge.

The lacemakers' island – Venice has been known for lacemaking since the 16C. The practice was first established in the palaces as a domestic activity, to be supervised by the noble ladies, before spreading to the hospitals and women's institutions where residents were obliged to take up the occupation.

Traditional production depended on the combined use of the needle and bobbin, and proliferated until the second half of the 17C, when demand was threatened by competition from France where Colbert had instituted an industry employing Venetian lacemakers. At last, in the 18C, the Venetian authorities were forced to make some counter moves to halt the continued exodus of lacemakers; certain manufacturers such as **Raniere e Gabrieli** were granted preferential privileges and traditional methods were compromised allowing for a simpler, bobbin-only technique to be used. Between the 18C and 19C, however, demand dwindled until eventually the production of lace for clothing was discontinued.

By the second decade of the 19C there were two lace factories – one in Venice and one on Burano – while needle-point continued as a private, domestic pastime. To safeguard designs and practices, a school was set up in 1872 and charged with the organisation and education of the lacemakers, and their production.

The most colourful of the lagoon islands

Ch. Boisvieux

G. Guitot/DIAF

From the vaporetto landing-stage the way is obvious, indeed almost obligatory: follow Via Galuppi into the square dominated by a statue of the renowned musician from Burano, Baldassare Galuppi.

San Martino – Piazza Baldassare Galuppi is somewhat overshadowed by the austere façade of the 16C Church of St Martin and its 18C campanile which leans 1.85m/6ft 1in, built by Andrea Tirali (c 1637-1737).

Inside, however, is a *Crucifixion* by **Tiepolo** (1696-1770) *(left aisle)* and, on the left of the presbytery, a great sarcophagus around which a miracle is said to have happened. According to legend, this heavy stone sepulchre was thrown up by the sea on to the island of Burano; at first, no-one was able to drag it ashore, no-one that is, until at last a group of local children came along and were assisted in their attempt by the intervention of three saints: Alban, Dominic and Orso whose remains were contained therein. The miracle is further explained in a painting, the *Miracle of the Children and the Urn,* attributed to **Alessandro Zanchi** (1631-1722).

The inhabitants of Burano also attribute the fact that they were miraculously spared from the ravages of the plague in 1630 to the divine intervention of their patrons (the island of Torcello was also saved). The skeletons of the three Saints today lie in the altar below the sarcophagus.

An *Adoration of the Shepherds* by **Francesco Fontebasso** (1709-69) is in the right aisle.

Museo del Consorzio Merletti di Burano ⊘ – Also off the square is the Museum of the Consortium of Burano Lacemakers which displays its important collection of collars, napkins, parasols, bedspreads, centre-pieces, handkerchiefs and lace edgings.

BURANO

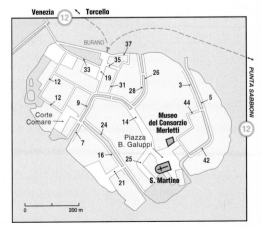

Practical demonstrations by expert lacemakers are also given and the procedures illustrated include the way designs are drafted onto green paper – the most relaxing to the eye; warping; guipure; Venetian point; Burano point; scalloping – known as *punto in aria* meaning stitches of air; unhooking and pressing.

For those wishing to continue into neighbouring districts, turn to the sections on TORCELLO and SAN FRANCESCO del DESERTO.

"Il Buranello"

Baldassare Galuppi (1706-85) acted as choir master at the Ospedale dei Mendicanti *(see Introduction – Composers in Venice: Ospedali)* and the music master for St Mark's Chapel. Besides his contribution to the religious choral tradition, he is associated with the development of comic opera, having composed music to accompany 20 libretti by Goldoni, including *Il Filosofo di Campagna*. Instrumentally, Galuppi sonatas for the harpsichord have recently surged in popularity on account of his hitherto unorthodox tempi and rhythm, notably in the faster movements.

"The men throughout the islands of Venice are almost as handsome as the women; I have never seen so many good-looking rascals. At Burano and Chioggia they sit mending their nets, or lounge at the street corners, where conversation is always high-pitched, or clamour to you to take a boat..."

Henry James – Italian Hours

CHIOGGIA

Strictly speaking, Chioggia is not one of the lagoon islands, resting as it does on two parallel islands, linked to *terrafirma* by a long bridge.

Although there is a Venetian quality about the place, with its double-arched windows and other architectural detail, the atmosphere is different. The traffic – on foot, by sea and by car – is constant; so frenetic, indeed, is the apparent urgency with which all local matters of marine and fishing business are dealt with that the temporary visitor might miss the opportunity of noticing the particular physiognomy of the *Chioggiotti* (the inhabitants of Chioggia). Maybe their traits were more markedly obvious in the past when, according to Lorenzetti, the men from this corner of the lagoon were described as *"very unusual... among the most expert and intrepid mariners in the Adriatic, both courageous and robust...their faces burnt by the sun and furrowed with deep lines"*, and the women were, *"beautiful and olive-skinned, expert lacemakers..."*.

For a leisurely walk around Chioggia allow a couple of hours.

A step back into the past – One of the channels of the Brenta delta was, in Antiquity, called *Fossa Clodia*, from which Clodia, Chioggia's former name, derives. In the 1C BC the Romans transformed it into a commercial harbour.

The problems began in the 9C following the destruction implemented by Charlemagne's son Pepin. Between the 11C and 12C, the saltpans constituted a major source of income to Chioggia, which then succumbed to further devastation between 1378 and 1381 when it became the field of battle between the rival factions Genoa and Venice. The Serenissima was victorious, but Chioggia was annihilated.

Getting to Chioggia

Visitors doing a tour of the neighbouring area, perhaps after a visit to the Brenta villas, will find it easy to get to Chioggia by taking SS 309 which has beautiful views over the Venetian lagoon.
Alternatively, a coach service operates every 30min from Piazzale Roma to Chioggia-Sottomarina. Average journey time: 1hr.

If in doubt...

Ask at the **Ufficio Informazioni di Sottomarina** (Information Office), Lungomare Adriatico, ☎ 041/40 10 68.

Rebuilding began and continued over the ensuing century. Venice intended that Chioggia should be reinforced as a defence post for the lagoon. The town grew up as close to the sea as possible, configured from these early times around Corso del Popolo and the Canale della Vena. Economic development was halted: when the Brenta was diverted, the harbour gradually silted up, excluding large vessels.

The canal that was dug separating the islet from the mainland served to consolidate defences. From the 16C fishing began to supercede the importance of the saltpans as the main industry. In the 20C Chioggia's isolation was in part breached by the building of the bridge carrying the Romea road.

A saunter round Chioggia – The main street, the **Corso del Popolo**, runs parallel to the Canale della Vena – the Fossa Clodia of ancient times, rendered more colourful and lively for its fish market terminating in Piazzetta Vigo. The column bearing a winged lion marks the end of the Fossa Clodia. To cross the canal, walk over the stone bridge, the Ponte Vigo built in 1685.

The corso is dotted with the Duomo and several of the Chioggia churches, among which the Church of **Sant' Andrea** with its 11C Romanesque campanile rising from a square base; **San Giacomo** which was rebuilt in the 18C; **San Francesco delle Muneghette** founded in the 15C but which was rebuilt in the 18C; and the Duomo.

★**Duomo** – The island's principal church, dedicated to Santa Maria Assunta, was founded in the 11C. It was razed to the ground by fire, and so was rebuilt in 1633 by Baldassare Longhena (1598-1682). It is still shadowed by its 14C square bell-tower, although originally, the church would have been orientated on a different axis.

Isola di San Domenico – Extending at the far end of Chioggia, this promontory – reached by following Calle di S Croce, beyond Ponte Vigo – accommodates, in the church, a painting of *Saint Paul* by Carpaccio (c 1465-1526).
The campanile is 13C.

Il LIDO ≙≙

The Lido is Venice's favourite seaside resort. A sophisticated and now slightly decadent place, it is tainted by a legacy left over from Luchino Visconti's *Death in Venice* which was filmed at the Hotel des Bains, and haunted by the curiously disconcerting yet majestic, predominant Hotel Excelsior, so reminiscent in style and sheer boldness of Ludwig of Bavaria's castle in Neuschwanstein.

The Lido also plays host to the Casino and the International Venice Film Festival every September, when film directors, actors and critics meet in Venice, accompanied by the inevitable *entourage* of the so-called international jet set, aspiring beautiful people and gossips.

Getting to the Lido

It is easy to get to the Lido: hop onto line **1**, **82** or **N** from Piazza San Marco and half an hour later, you're there!

For more information

Check out the Lido Tourist Information Centre at 6 Gran Viale Sta Maria Elisabetta, ☎ 041/52 65 721.

It is worth spending a couple of hours on the Lido to explore and soak in all the sights and sounds.

From Santa Maria Elisabetta, there is a bus to Piazzale Bucintoro which leads to Lungomare Guglielmo Marconi. The most prestigious hotels with their colourful beach huts are situated here, along with the Casino and the headquarters of the Cinema Festival.

The Lido beach

T. Zane/MICHELIN

Venice International Film Festival – The first one of its kind, the film festival was inaugurated in 1932 at the Hotel Excelsior on the initiative of Conte Volpi di Misurata and Luciano De Feo, the Secretary General of the International Institute of Cinematographic Art. At the time of its inception, the **Festival of International Cinematographic Art** was more of an exhibition of the art of cinematography than a review, as indicated by its original name, organised to complement the Biennale. Although comedy films were to be excluded, this censorship was not enforced, at least not initially.

Golden Lion Awards – The Festival trophies awarded consist of a sculpted image of the Golden Lion. Particular performances nominated include that of Spencer Tracy for *Dr Jekyll and Mr Hyde* (1941), while the films *Forbidden Games* by René Clément (1952), *Hamlet* with Laurence Olivier and Jean Simmons (1948), *Vaghe Stelle dell'Orsa* by Luchino Visconti (1965) are a few of the golden classics to have carried off the prize.

"Now daily the naked god with cheeks aflame drove his four fire-breathing steeds through heaven's spaces; and with him streamed her strong east wind that fluttered his yellow locks. A sheen, like white satin, lay over all the idly rolling sea's expanse. The sand was burning hot. Awnings of rust-coloured canvas were spanned before the bathing huts, under the ether's quivering silver-blue; one spent the morning hours within the small, sharp square of shadow they purveyed. But evening too was rarely lovely: balsamic with the breath of flowers and shrubs from the nearby park, while overhead the constellations circled their spheres, and the murmuring of the night-girded sea swelled softly up and whispered to the soul. Such nights as these contained the joyful promise of a sunlit morrow, brim-full of sweetly ordered idleness, studded thick with countless precious possibilities."

Thomas Mann – Death in Venice

MURANO ★★

From the water, Murano appears to be walled-in by the long line of furnaces. As soon as visitors step off the vaporetto they are urged to visit the glassworks and even if the commercial aspect of the "invitation" can be irritating, it is nonetheless worth watching the practical side of the various stages and processes, treated scientifically in the Museum of Glass. But Murano is also the island of art. It is therefore a good idea not to get too jaded by the innumerable and tantalising glass shops, before exploring the island's two fine churches dedicated to St Peter Martyr and Saints Mary and Donato.

The suggested route together with recommended visits take about two and a half hours.

Glassworks – By the end of the 13C, glass-making was so widespread in Venice that the threat of devastating fire ravaging the city was ever constant. Three centuries later, the fear still had not abated, bearing in mind the countless little fires that fre-

> ## Getting to Murano
>
> Board line **12**, **13**, **41** or **42** at Fondamenta Nuove or Zattere.

quently broke out as a result of the widespread use of wood and candles. Had these incidents not been contained, it would not have taken much for fire to spread very quickly and with disastrous consequences. So the Grand Council decided to move the glassworks away from the city to Murano – a strategy that would also protect the secrets of the glass-making process.

The ancient history of glass – According to the most authoritative sources, which include Pliny the Elder (AD 23-79), it would be tempting to believe in many of the legends that explain the origins of glass. The most likely theory, however, is rooted in the ancient Orient where potters learnt how to "make" glass from silicon sand when glazing their ceramics by firing them in a kiln. The process was certainly already in widespread use by the time the books of Job and the Proverbs were written as recorded by allusions in the Bible, and commonly practised in Egypt by the fourth millenium BC as small objects found in datable tombs would imply. The colours blue and green were created by the addition of copper and cobalt oxide. The technique for blowing glass however, as favoured by the Romans, came later.

Glass-blowing at Murano

Before its glorious arrival in Venice, glass was produced in Greece and Turkey. In 1203, following the occupation of Constantinople, Venice was secured the "exclusive" collaboration of the immigrant potters in exchange for preferential treatment from the Republic. Not only might they have enjoyed tax benefits and even aspire to become one of the doge's officers, all sorts of misfortunes might befall them if they left Venice – or put more simply, if they refused to return to the city, they were hunted down and killed.

The city's supremacy in glass-making therefore remained uncontested until the end of the 16C, when Colbert, art minister to the French court of Louis XIV (1643-1715), keen to discover the secret of the unrivalled Venetian technique, was happy to divert the services of a treacherous artisan, Giorgio Ballarin, then employed by Agnolo Barovier's studio.

Even today, modern glass creations from Murano are considered to be works of art worthy of prices that escalate from 2 to 50 million Italian lire. Furthermore, a growing interest in comparable pieces within the international antiques trade is undermining the hitherto unchallenged demand for

St Peter Martyr (1205-52)

St Peter of Verona became the third most important Dominican after St Dominic Guzman and St Thomas Aquinas: he was appointed Principal Official Inquisitor for Northern Italy by Pope Gregory IX in 1221. According to legend, he was attacked on the road from Como to Milan by two assassins and received a blow from an axe to his head. Having commended himself and his murderers to God, he inscribed the ground with the words "Credo in Deum" in his own blood before being struck a second time and dying. The most famous representation is that by Fra Angelico in the Convent of St Mark's in Florence. He is the patron saint of Inquisitors.

works by such French artists as Gallé, Lalique and Daum – the main difference being that the Venetian pieces tend to be unsigned and therefore there is always a danger of falling for one of the numerous fakes.

Back to reality and within everyone's budget are the *murrine* which gleam and sparkle with colour, often set into costume jewellery, and the distinctive discs of kaleidoscopic patterns.

The final effect of this unique glass-making technique is achieved by juxtaposing various coloured rods of glass that have been drawn in length and fused when molten. When the composite rods are then sliced cross-wise, one is left with these famous discs.

From the vaporetto *stop at Scalo Colonna, follow the long Fondamenta dei Vetrai and cast a thought for all the glassmakers that have used the thoroughfare in times past and present. Before the canal, on the left, stands the Church of St Peter Martyr.*

San Pietro Martire – Building began in 1363 but the church was only consecrated in 1417. Gravely damaged by fire, it was rebuilt in the Renaissance style before being subjected to further modifications, some of them ill-judged, over the ensuing few hundred years.

The main fabric of the building is brick. A Renaissance main door is surmounted at the front by a large stained-glass window made of *rui*, small circular sections of Murano glass.

Inside, the nave and aisles are apsed and endowed with **paintings★** by illustrious artists: in the left aisle the *Deposition* is by Salviati (c 1520-1575), whereas both *St Agatha in Prison Visited by St Peter and an Angel with a Torch* and *St Jerome* are by Veronese (1528-88). In the right aisle is an altarpiece depicting *John the Baptist and Vincenzo Serena* (patron of the Scuola di San Giovanni dei Battuti of Murano) by the School of Titian; a *Baptism of Christ* attributed to Tintoretto (1518-94); two works by Giovanni Bellini (c 1426-1516) *The Virgin Enthroned between St Mark the Evangelist, Presenting Doge Agostino Barbarigo and St Augustine* and *The Virgin and Eight Saints*; and *St Nicholas, St Lucy and San Carlo Borromeo* by Palma il Giovane (1544-1628).

Once over the Grand Canal, follow the fondamenta on the right to the Murano Glass Museum.

★Museo di Arte Vetraria ⊘ – A visit to the museum in Palazzo Giustinian will particularly appeal to anyone wanting to understand the evolution of glass-making over the centuries.

An archaeological section displays a collection of embalming tools, cups, utensils and necklaces. On the first floor, the physical processes practised by tradition and modern technology involved in glass-making, including coloured glass and *murrine*, are explained with illuminated panels and samples of raw materials. Developments in technique between the 15C and 18C are also defined. The height of artistry attained in the 15C is nobly represented by a wedding cup, traditionally known as the **Barovier Cup**. The museum also houses a collection of modern glass.

Beyond the museum is the Church of SS Maria e Donato.

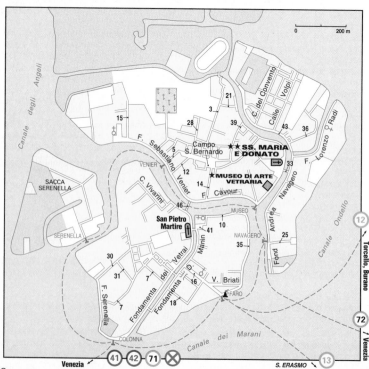

The apse of Santa Maria e San Donato

★★Santa Maria e San Donato – From the outside, it is the apse that is more often remembered in the mind's eye and a thousand times more photographed than the façade which is hidden: unseen that is because it does not face onto the *fondamenta* from which the basilica is normally approached.

The **apse** is a masterpiece of 12C Veneto-Byzantine art, embellished with all kinds of decorative elements. A double series of blind arched openings resting on coupled columns seem to ripple around the semicircular bay. The front façade meanwhile is quite plain.

Founded in the 7C, the original church was dedicated to the Virgin Mary – the incorporation of San Donato dates from the 12C when his body together with what remained of the dragon that he had slain arrived from Cefalonia (the bones of the "dragon" are stored behind the altar). The church was considerably remodelled in the 12C: the mosaic floor was completed in 1141, and extensively restored during the mid 19C.

Inside, five columns with Veneto-Byzantine capitals separate the nave from the aisles, whereas the striking **mosaic floor★★** recalls that of the Basilica of St Mark. Among the profusion of decorative, symbolic and figurative elements, there is one particularly significant section between the second and third columns on the right: this depicts two cockerels bearing a fox, and represents the defeat of Cunning by Vigilance.

Above the apse, a 12C mosaic *Virgin in Prayer* stands alone projected forward by her brilliant gold background.

In the left aisle, is the wooden panel with *San Donato* attributed to Paolo Veneziano (c 1290-1362) and, above the door to the baptistery, a lunette by Lazzaro Bastiani (recorded 1449-1512), depicting the *Virgin and Child with Saints and Donor, John the Almsgiver* (1484).

The wooden ceiling rises like an inverted ship's keel.

For those wishing to continue into neighbouring districts, turn to the section on SAN ZANIPÒLO.

*Help us in our constant task of keeping up-to-date.
Send us your comments and suggestions to
Michelin Tyre PLC
Tourism Department
38 Clarendon Road - WATFORD Herts WD1 1SX
Tel: (01923) 415000/ANG.
Web site: www.michelin-travel.com*

SAN FRANCESCO del DESERTO ★

This little island is ideal for anyone seeking respite from commotion and crowds, particularly in the summer when the islands of the lagoon can get very populous, be it for an hour or two or for longer periods.

A complete tour takes about an hour.

To San Francesco by boat

The island where St Francis landed is still today reached by private boat, departing from Burano – where the canal meets the lagoon as it laps the water's edge in Piazza Galuppi – not far from the front of San Martino. The cost includes the ten minute journey to and from the island and waiting time in between: the guided visit lasts about an hour and is undertaken by a monk – ask the boatman, who will make himself known, about the price.

Visitors arriving for a spiritual rather than touristic sojourn by prior arrangement, will be welcomed off the boat. Information about meditative and contemplative breaks to rediscover the inner self should be sought from the monks on 041/52 86 863.

Monastery – Before St Francis landed on the island on his way back from the Holy Land in 1220, San Francesco del Deserto was known as the *Isola delle due Vigne* (the Island of the two Vines). Its name was changed when a house for Franciscan novitiates was established on the island in 1224. The term *"deserto"* could be a reference to the island left "deserted" when the monks fled from a malaria epidemic.

On four occasions, the monastery played host to Bernardino of Siena who may have paid for the well to be dug to collect water.

Set into a wall in the cloister is a 13C relief of two crossed arms said to be the arm of Christ and the sleeved arm of St Francis.

The tour takes in various paintings depicting the saint arriving on the Island of the two Vines and the miracle of St Francis ordering the birds to be quiet and not to move during prayers.

A panel covers some interesting archaeological remains, including a cistern.

The island's vast **park** overlooks the lagoon and proffers a clear view of Burano. It is particularly beautiful here, almost pastoral in feel, which is unusual for the lagoon islands.

For information on the islands and the sights beyond, turn to the sections on BURANO and TORCELLO.

"It is their (the women on the Lido) custom to sit on the seashore while their husbands are out sea-fishing, and sing these songs (by Tasso) in penetrating tones until, from far out at sea, their men reply, and in this way they converse with each other. Is this not a beautiful custom?"

Goethe – Italian Journey, 7 October 1786

SAN LAZZARO degli ARMENI ★

This island was especially loved by the Romantic poet Lord Byron, as he found the atmosphere lifted his ascetic spirit in times of melancholy. Today, it is no less evocative to visiting travellers.

On arrival by vaporetto, tourists are greeted by charming Armenian monks who will chaperone their charges and introduce them to this memorable island, so green and serene.

The tour takes about an hour.

How to get there

Located near the Lido, it takes about half an hour to get to the Island of San Lazzaro degli Armeni on line 20 from Riva degli Schiavoni (San Zaccaria).

Tours are scheduled to coincide with the *vaporetto* times – the talk begins on landing and continues through the monastery visit. Should you require more time on the island, catch the *vaporetto* that leaves at 2.55pm and check for the departure time of the second return service.

Mechitar (1676-1749)

Named Manug (meaning "child") in honour of the Christ Child, Mechitar the Consoler was born at Sebaste (now Sivas) in Turkey. He was ordained into the Catholic Church in 1696 before settling in Constantinople where he founded a community of Uniat Armenian monks in 1701 on St Benedict's teachings and precepts of monasticism. Two years later, the monks were forced to flee the city and take refuge in Morea, a Venetian territory. The Order was approved by Pope Clement XI in 1711. When Morea was lost to the Turks, the Venetian Republic granted the community the Island of San Lazzaro, a former leper colony. Mechitar's remains are enclosed within the main altar of the church.

The Mechitarists devote themselves to study, education and missionary work and have published a number of important volumes through their printing works in Venice and Vienna. They follow the Armenian liturgy which differs from the Roman Church in attitude to hierarchy (the Armenian Church neither acknowledged the primacy nor the infallibility of the Pope) and their administration of the sacraments.

Monastery – Cross the simple cloister full of flowering plants, kept neat and tidy, to seek out the famous and valuable historical manuscripts that are a testament not only to the Armenian heritage, but also to the kindly Mechitar monks who dedicate themselves to preserving the Armenian culture.

The Armenians and the Mechitar Community – The Armenians are an ancient people whose ancestry has been linked to Noah's Ark which some believe "ran aground" on Mount Ararat, on the Armenian border: a country that extended from the Black Sea to Mesopotamia where the mountains hide the sources of the rivers Tigris and Euphrates. Today the Republic of Armenia is "hemmed in" between Turkey, Georgia, Azerbaijan and Iran.

The country was conquered on several occasions by the Arabs, Turks, Mongols, Tartars, Ottomans and Persians. During the First World War, its people were persecuted by the Turks, almost to the point of extinction, as recorded by the Austrian writer, Franz Werfel (1890-1945) in *Forty Days of Musa Dagh*, an epic tale of Armenian resistance to Turkish invaders. Subsequent diaspora saw the Armenians flee overseas, particularly to the United States.

The buildings ⊙ – The original Romanesque church was built by the Benedictines, who also subsequently remodelled it in the Gothic style. From the 14C, the island served as a leper colony until the last two remaining leprosy sufferers were transferred to Venice (1600s), and it was abandoned.

Life was restored with the arrival of **Mechitar** in 1717 who was given the island by the Venetian Republic. The church was rebuilt. The pavement was lifted, the arches were made into lancet arches and the vaulted ceiling took the form of a starry sky: the monks joke that the sky clouds over during services owing to the large quantities of incense used.

Visitors are then shown the refectory where the monks and the seminarists consume their meals in silence while the Scriptures are read out in Classical Armenian.

On ascending the stairs, note the fine Sienese terracotta relief from 1400 and part of a painting by Palma il Giovane (1544-1628) depicting the *Martyrdom of St Catherine*: the central section of this painting is in St Petersburg.

Armenian stele

T. Zane

Sixth Baron, Lord George Gordon Byron (1788-1824)

Lord Byron was a handsome youth with a colourful personality. After leaving Cambridge, he took his seat in the House of Lords (1809) before embarking on extensive travels to Portugal, Spain, Malta, Greece and the Levant. The experience fired his imagination and he vowed to see Greece freed from Turkish rule. In 1812 *Childe Harold's Pilgrimage* was published securing his reputation as a Romantic poet. However his liaisons with his half-sister and subsequent marriage soon lead to disrepute and restlessness. Byron left England in 1816 for the last time. While in Venice he became enormously attracted to the monastic life at San Lazzaro where he found the spiritual quietude he so yearned and from which he continually transgressed as his passions flourished across the water. He became fascinated with the history and political cause of the Armenian community and set out to learn their language in six months. He collaborated with the scholarly monks to produce and publish an English-Armenian dictionary and grammar book.

Despite being an important centre of Armenian culture, the monastery owns a collection of Flemish tapestries; paintings by Armenian artists; Greek, Phoenician and Assyro-Babylonian artefacts — there is even a 10C BC Egyptian mummy; a huge collection of books in various languages; Armenian ceramics and other diverse objects with exotic provenance or high value. Among the most interesting works of art is a statue by Canova (1757-1822) depicting Napoleon's son, the King of Rome; an Indian papyrus scroll written according to the boustrophedon system which can be read from both the left and the right; *Justice and Peace* by Tiepolo (1696-1770) and the 14C throne of the governors of Delhi (in the room which serves as a reminder of Byron's stay in the monastery).

A highlight of the tour comes with a visit to the archive, a modern circular building containing over 4 000 manuscripts.

He would often swim to San Lazzaro from the Palazzo Mocenigo *(see Il CANAL GRANDE)* for the day before returning home where he continued to work on additional cantos for his *Childe Harold.*

TORCELLO★★

From the landing-stage, a walk along the Fondamenta dei Borgognoni and on by the canal allows a full prospect of the unique lagoon landscape to unfurl. This is especially poignant when there are few tourists. The visitor may get totally smitten like Hemingway who would stay at the Locanda Cipriani and go hunting for ducks: on the other hand, the experience may merely inspire dread as it did for Ruskin who, looking out from the campanile, could only perceive lifeless and melancholic desolation. Either way, intensely evocative it certainly is, ever inspiring strong feelings of one kind. These days Torcello is almost a ghost island where only the stones can speak of its glorious past.

The tour takes about an hour and a half.

Near the **Ponte del Diavolo** which, like Ponte Chiodo in Venice has no parapet *(see CA' D'ORO)* — stands the religious complex of Torcello. It is incredible to think that back in ancient times there would have been thousands of people living here and the glorious history of Venice was merely beginning.

Once upon a time... During the period of barbarian invasions: first the Lombards chased out the Byzantines (6C-8C) and established themselves in Aquileia, Padua, Altinum and Oderzo. The bishop and the inhabitants of Altinum moved to Torcello where, in 639, the

> ### To get to Torcello...
>
> From Fondamenta Nuove, take the same line (**12**) that goes to Burano, which is only minutes away from Torcello.

church and probably the fortifications were built — it is the *torri* (towers) of such fortifications that gave rise to the name of the island. They were not the first inhabitants, however, as the Romans had already discovered the place and records show continual fishing and glass-making activities throughout the 5C and 6C.

Torcello's decline started around the 10C and mirrors the pace of the glorious ascent of Venice. When malaria infested the marshes, Torcello was abandoned by its inhabitants who fled to Venice and Murano. Now there are fewer than 100 inhabitants.

Two ancient churches, a campanile and a museum

The grass, which seems to have got the better of the ancient remains only serves to enhance the evocative suggestion of abandon in the piazza, scattered with various remnants of the past including Roman plinths and the *sedia di Attila* where the bishop or some other potentate would sit. The desolation is the same as that captured in a Romantic Piranesi engraving. In silent testimony to the past are the cathedral, the remains of the baptistery, Santa Fosca and the two Gothic palazzi.

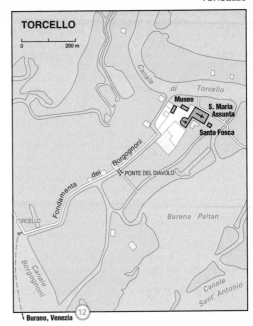

Basilica di Santa Maria Assunta ⊙ –

The cathedral dedicated to the Assumption was erected in 639, as recorded by the ancient **inscription** on the left of the altar which was only "discovered" at the end of the 1800s. It states Imperante Eraclio Augusto e per ordine di Isaacio esarca e patrizio: thereby confirming that the church was built in 639 during the reign of Heraclius, Emperor of Byzantium, at the wishes of Isaac, the Exarch of Ravenna and representative of the Eastern emperor.

In the 9C and 11C, it underwent further modification. Little remains of the 7C baptistery other than fragments of the brick façade, and its many pilasters. The 14C portico supported by the columns and pilasters also serves as a link to Santa Fosca.

Interior – The internal space is divided into nave and aisles by rows of columns and, in stark contrast with the simplicity of structure, the decoration is extraordinarily opulent. The pavement is 11C. The choir, enclosed by Corinthian columns, is separated from the nave by a 15C iconostasis set with fine 11C Byzantine painted panels depicting the Madonna

> ### Wisdom enshrined in the old stones
>
> On Torcello, the route from one building to another could be regarded as a symbolic journey: the baptistery being the Christian synonym for new life, the cathedral representing the duration of a lifetime and Santa Fosca being the burial place for the martyrs – representing death leading to eternal life.

and child flanked by the twelve Apostles with, above, the Crucifixion from the same date. Between the columns nestle delicate Byzantine marble *plutei* carved with semi-symmetrical lions and peacocks. The Roman sarcophagus near the high altar contains the relics of St Heliodorus, the first Bishop of Altinum and friend of St Jerome.

But most striking for their brilliance and quality are the **ancient mosaics**★★: to either side of the apse are represented the *Annunciation* with the the Virgin at her loom, bobbin in hand having just lowered her work basket. The central apse is filled with a 13C *Virgin and Child*. The east facing window represents Christ. The inscription reads: allegory of virtue, Stella Maris or star of the sea, bearer of salvation, Mary and her Son liberates those whom Eve and her husband burdened with sin. Above it lies in its abbreviated Greek form "Mother of God". In accordance with Byzantine iconography, the Virgin is portrayed descending from Heaven. Her left hand holds the hand of Christ, while the child clutches the Sacred Scroll of the Law. Along the arch is written " I am the Lord and Man, image of the Father and of the Mother, from the sinful I am never far but from the repentent I am ever close".

Between the windows are aligned the *Apostles* (12C), walking as if along a bank of reeds, a plant that is typical of the lagoon. Below the window is represented St Heliodorus, a more modern mosaic panel.

Roughly from the same period, in the right apse, *Christ* sits enthroned between *Archangels Michael and Gabriel* (13C-14C) with the *Doctors of the Church* (end 13C) – from right to left: St Augustine, St Ambrose, St Martin and St Gregory the

A Short Pause before the Last Judgement

The Last Judgement is the main subject of the mosaics (13C-14C) at the back of the church. The main elements of the scene, drawn from the Apocalypse, unfold from top to bottom and are divided into two sections: the Judgement below and the Death and Resurrection of Christ above. From the Crucifixion there follows the Descent into Limbo – Christ tramples over many keys and a devil reduced to miniature proportions while determinedly clutching to Adam's hand. Behind is Eve, her hands covered for reasons of propriety; to the right stands John the Baptist who may easily be recognised by his long hair and camel-hair shirt. Beyond rank the prophets, whereas to the left, the two figures with haloes are David and Solomon. At the far edges, the Archangels Michael *(left)* and Gabriel *(right)* stand guard.

Dominating the central section is the *Deisis:* Christ in Glory enclosed within a mandorla, the aura of His divinity, surrounded by the symbols of the Passion. He is flanked by the Virgin and John the Baptist and by two angels. Two more angels support the mandorla from which flows the river of fire down to Hell. Disposed symmetrically around the edge are the Apostles. Those closest to the mandorla include St Peter *(left)* and St Paul *(right)* with the book of his Epistles (here St Paul is included among the twelve Apostles, on a par therefore with San Barnaba).

The lower section recounts the Triumph of the Cross with the spear, the sponge, the crown of thorns and the Book of Life. At the foot of the cross stand Adam and Eve with entreating expressions. The angels' trumpets recall the dead from the bowels of the sea monsters that devoured them (to the right may be seen the victims of the sea, represented as a female allegory with bracelets). Note the angel with the rotulus in his hand: unravelling the sky and the stars that are destined to fall.

Below, the souls are being weighed by St Michael: working to safeguard salvation of those that deserve to be protected from the demons that burden the scale with bags of sins.

To the left are the saved; to the right the damned. It is here that the presumptuous are pushed aside: the seven devils portray the seven deadly sins – Pride, Avarice, Lust, Wrath, Gluttony, Envy, Sloth – which stem from arrogance. The main figure is Lucifer, sitting on Leviathan – the sea-monster described in the Book of Job whose breath sets burning coals ablaze, and flames flash from his mouth, holding the Antichrist.

Below the various punishments are depicted in truly apocalyptic terms: the Proud (kings) are engulfed by fire with Epulonus perhaps asking for a little water; the Lecherous are devoured by the flames of passion; the Gluttons are naked and gnaw at their hands; the Angry are surrounded by water; all that remains of the Covetous are their skulls whose eye-sockets are filled with worms.

Below the rank and file of the Blessed stretches paradise, where the Lagoon reeds grow in profusion. Among them, St Peter with his keys and St Michael may be discerned. Note the angel of the Apocalypse with his wings studded with eyes. To the left, with the cross in his hand, is the repentent thief. Next to him stands a woman, maybe the Madonna, with the chosen who proceed towards Abraham who holds in his arms the Saviour.

In the lunette above the portal is the Virgin, her arms open in a gesture of accommodating mercy. The inscription reads "The Virgin, divine intercessor, purger of all sin".

Great below. Even this mosaic features the same lagoon reeds. The writing spells out "the Godhead is a trinity comprising two beings and one spirit. He covers the earth with grass, extends the sea and lights up the sky." The mosaics of the intersecting vault harbour *Four Angels Bearing the Mystic Lamb* of a type found at Ravenna. From the cornice filled with organic elements emerge the four rivers of the Earthly Paradise, symbolically represented as alternating bundles of lillies, fruiting vines and wheat. The floral mosaic decoration is populated with the same birds and animals (gulls, eagles, lions, bulls and peacocks) as at San Vitale in Ravenna. Those date back to the 7C, whereas these post date them by a short period: for these are also by artists from Ravenna, who came here while the church was being erected.

Campanile ⊙ – At the rear of the basilica stands the old bell-tower (12C). After many years it is now possible once more to reach the top. The climb is easy and the view★★ over the lagoon more than compensates the effort expended.

Santa Fosca – The small church, in the form of a Greek cross, was built between the 11C and 12C. Its octagonal exterior is encircled by open arcading with columns capped by Veneto-Byzantine capitals.

The interior, shrouded in silence, is enclosed below a round wooden roof.

Santa Fosca

Museo di Torcello ⊙ – The collection of artefacts associated with the history of Torcello is displayed on two floors. Interesting pieces, some dating back to the 9C, include capitals, pateras, fragments of mosaic from the neighbouring Cathedral, tablets, a fine mid-15C wooden *Pietà* of the Venetian School, paintings from the Church of St Anthony of Torcello, a work from the Studio of Veronese, books and documents which recount parts of the island's history, pages from the *Mariegola* and fragments of Venetian ceramics.

For those wishing to continue into neighbouring districts, turn to the sections on BURANO and SAN FRANCESCO del DESERTO.

"The light here is in fact a mighty magician and, with all respect to Titian, Veronese and Tintoretto, the greatest artist of them all. ... Sea and sky seem to meet half-way, to blend their tones into a soft iridescence, a lustrous compound of wave and cloud and a hundred nameless local reflections, and then to fling the clear tissue against every object of vision."

Henry James – Italian Hours

I stood in Venice, on the Bridge of Sighs;
A palace and a prison on each hand:
I saw from out the wave her structures rise
As from the stroke of the enchanter's wand:
A thousand years their cloudy wings expand
Around me, and a dying Glory smiles
O'er the far times, when many a subject land
Look'd to the winged Lion's marble piles,
Where Venice sate in state, throned on her hundred Isles!

She looks at sea Cybele, fresh from ocean,
Rising with her tiara of proud towers
At airy distance, with majestic motion,
A ruler of the waters and their powers:
And such she was; – her daughters had their dowers
From spoils of nations, and the exhaustless East
Pour'd in her lap all gems in sparkling showers.
In purple was she robed, and of her feast
Monarchs partook, and deem'd their dignity increased.

In Venice Tasso's echoes are no more,
And silent rows the songless gondolier;
Her palaces are crumbling to the shore,
And music meets not always now the ear;
Those days are gone – but Beauty still is here.
States fall, arts fade – but Nature doth not die,
Nor yet forget how Venice once was dear,
The revel of the earth, the masque of Italy!

Lord Byron, Childe Harold's Pilgrimage, Canto IV

205

Villas
of the Brenta

VILLAS OF THE BRENTA★★

The Brenta Valley is a bucolic stretch of land where the doges elected to have their country houses. Some Venetian families still follow this tradition today. Reflected in the quiet waters of the river, from Padua to the lagoon, these patrician villas possess that air of an exclusive country retreat with literary connotations: an impression that remains true whichever way the visitor might arrive, be it by water, horse, bicycle or car.

<table>
<tr><td>

How to get there

The River Brenta links Padua to Venice by water, but access from either direction is easier by road.
For those coming from the West along the A4, it is advisable to exit at Padova Est. Follow the Noventana road and directions for Stra (SS 11). From Venice-Mestre, follow the signs for Riviera del Brenta and Malcontenta (SS 11).

</td></tr>
</table>

As time passes with the flow of the Brenta... – At the time of the Ancient Romans, the Brenta had only two branches which forked at Ponte di Brenta. Their names – *Medoacus maior* and *Medoacus minor* – have long fallen into disuse. It was on the banks of the *Medoacus minor*, however, that the river's troubled history began. By 1100 the Paduans and the Venetians were already locked in conflict over who should have control of the river's course and the hold on Venice's only other alternate means of access to the lagoon in times of siege.

During the 1500s, in an effort to limit the threat of damage from flooding, subsidiary canals were built. In 1840, after a disastrous flood, work was initiated on redirecting the river to flow into the lagoon at Chioggia but in-filling the delta area proved so difficult that the water was coursed further down to run straight out to the sea, as it does today at Brondolo.

A RIBBON OF COUNTRY HOUSES

Visitors to the Brenta Riviera will doubtless come away with a picture of tranquillity and gaiety that belies the trials and tribulations that have persistently pervaded the centuries: disputes between the Venetians and the Paduans, attempts at snatching the land back from the grasp of the flooding river and the lagoon, the hours of toil exerted by the millstones are all on record.
Today, the Brenta Valley like Venice survives as if by a pact made between nature and architecture.

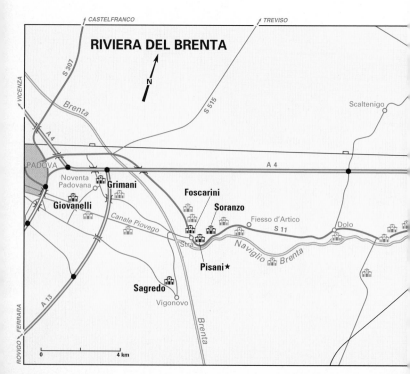

From 1409, with the annexation of Padua, the Republic of Venice was assured of definitive control of the River Brenta and thus started to invest in landed property along its banks. By the beginning of the 16C, opulent villas were being designed and built, set among extensive gardens.

Many find the area oppressive and melancholic as heavy swirling mists and flooding exaggerate the cold and humid atmosphere of the place.

The villas – A villa was intended to provide the landowner with temporary lodgings during his inspection of the running of his farm estate. It would have been erected therefore near the farm, and built on a centralised plan, flanked by *barchesse*.

Before long, the villa's function evolved into being a country home to which the landed gentry could retreat merely on a pretext of supervising their

> ### Barchesse
>
> Up until the end of the 17C, the *barchesse* (from *barca* meaning boat) were the outbuildings of the villa used for storing grain and the boats that had to be "garaged" because it was prohibited to leave them moored along the canal.
>
> Frequently, throughout the 17C, the *barchesse* doubled up as sleeping quarters for use by the extra house-guests invited to the great parties at the villas that might go on for days on end.

tenanted farm. By the 18C country houses were all the rage among the Venetian nobility, who basked in leisure and luxury, while inadvertently singing Venice's swan song.

The preferred holiday periods were the months of June, July, October and November when the balmy evenings might be spent listening to a musical recital or watching a group of players. Few of the many villas can be attributed to specific architects; however, given their artistic quality, it is generally acknowledged that they must have been designed to satisfy highly sophisticated and aesthetically discerning patrons.

Il Burchiello ⊘ – The 18C traveller could choose to journey from Venice to Padua by boat or by carriage. The boat, however, was neither comfortable nor quick and fellow passengers were not always the most salubrious. That is until the *Burchiello* was built in Padua, adapted from the **burchio** that was used in Venice to transport general goods. Passengers were accommodated on benches arranged around tables and protected by a canopy overhead. Further shelter was provided by decorative panels of inlaid wood and attractive drapes against driving rain, biting winds or blinding sunshine. When travelling upstream, the barge was pulled by a yoke of horses.

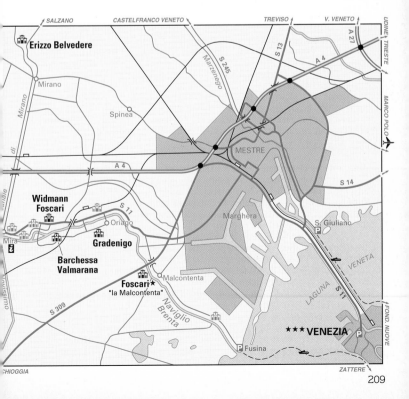

Travelling aboard the *Burchiello* became a pleasure to experience, as warranted by Goethe in his *Italian Journey*, who adds the assurance that one's travelling companions would be *"of good character"* because the Italians would *"be civil even with each other"*. Alas, the legendary vessel did not survive for long: the costly service was suspended when the Republic fell.

What fun they had along the Brenta – Be they nobles or peasants, the Venetians shared the same taste for **farce**. Here, along the banks of the river, where people idled away the time with a good book, puppeteers found an ideal location in which to set up their theatres and animate their characters Brighella, Harlequin, Columbine and Pantaloon. While in the villa gardens, comic plays were staged.

There was certainly no lack of opportunity for having a good time: the numerous **sagre** (feast days) were always a good excuse for throwing a party at which guests could sing and dance the night away in the magnificent villa ballrooms.

As One Nobleman Recalled...

"We went to the main hotel for something to eat and drink and then as night fell we went back to the boats which twinkled with lights. Laughing and singing we headed towards Mira where we were intending to spend the night at the Casino dei Nobili, playing the tables until dawn. But on our way we passed the villa which belonged to the senator, Giambattista Corner. It was bathed in light with torches in the windows, the loggias, near the statues and scattered throughout the garden.

Our orchestra began to play and suddenly another orchestra from the villa joined in. So we disembarked and the master of the household approached us followed by a group of his guests. We started dancing and carried on until dawn but the senator's generosity did not stop there: he invited us to dine with him – me and my fifty companions. The party lasted eight days and during this time senators Corner and Gradenigo each hosted six banquets".

FROM PADUA TO FUSINA, VIA MIRANO

To complete the itinerary given and a full tour of the villas, allow two days.

The first villa on the way from Padua is Villa Foscarini at **Stra**, located in the heart of a part of the Veneto actively involved in the shoe industry, as indicated by the roadside billboards.

Villa Foscarini ⊙ – This villa is named after its most eminent resident, **Marco Foscarini** who was elected doge in 1762.

The *pronao* (projecting columned entrance) might suggest an intervention by Palladio: in reality, the design conformed to the artistic taste in vogue at the time, several decades after Palladio's death. The villa is neo-Classical in style, although modifications were implemented during the course of the 19C. The adjacent *barchessa* is older. The roof is surmounted by four spires reminiscent of the Ponte delle Guglie in Venice *(see GHETTO)*, serving to make the building seem taller.

In the hall of the *barchessa*, frescoed allegorical scenes are set among suggestive *trompe-l'œil* detailing.

On leaving Villa Foscarini behind, the main feature in the landscape is the river along which a succession of villas follow one after another, posted with yellow signs, uninterrupted by any more modest dwellings. In each the distinctive Venetian style is easily recognised in the windows and even the shutters.

★Villa Pisani ⊙ – *The villa is signposted before the car park, which is located about 200m/220yd beyond the entrance.*

Three centuries of European history – The residence of **Alvise Pisani**, elected doge in 1735, comprises a magnificent estate with stables and gardens designed by **Girolamo Frigimelica** (1653-1732) who also submitted plans for the villa which, proving to be too costly, were entrusted to **Francesco Maria Preti** (1701-74).

During the course of the 18C, the villa was progressively endowed with sculpture and paintings but when the Republic fell in 1797, the Pisani family *(see La FENICE - Campo Santo Stefano)* was forced to sell it to Napoleon who, in turn, gave it to his adopted son Eugène Beauharnais, the Viceroy of Italy. Following the Austrian occupation in 1814, Villa Pisani accommodated several other famous figures including Francesco Giuseppe, Maximilian of Austria, Anna Maria of Savoy, Gustav III of Sweden and Carlos IV of Spain. Soon after the unification of Italy, the villa returned to Italian ownership. It now belongs to the State.

First impressions – On sight, the house appears modelled upon a French château. The outside wall, enclosing extensive grounds at the rear, accentuates the horizontal design elements of the façade: the central, projecting Palladian-style bay is charged with decoration, whereas the entrance itself is austerely monumental. Four Atlas figures support the loggia, whereas silhouetted against the sky, statues and pinnacles punctuate the corners of the pediments.

Beyond the entrance opens a gallery supported by columns from which one has a magnificent view over the still water and the Palladian-style stables fronted by their imposing entrance and figures of Zephyr and Flora, sculpted by **Giovanni Bonazza** (1654-1736) and his son Tomaso (c 1696-1775).

Grounds – The great garden designed by Frigimelica extends around a long pond which, although well integrated into the villa's landscape, is a modern addition. It was in fact dug in 1911 by the University of Padua for the purposes of carrying out studies on tidal forces. On the west side is the Belvedere folly, its steps seeming to wrap around two columns.

The east side is the more animated part of the park: the Café-Haus, built on a

> ### Allegorical Painting in the Brenta Villas
> Frequent recourse to allegorical subject matter came in the 17C and 18C from the desire to assert the Venetian taste in "style" – one that was inspired by a *joie de vivre*, a Humanist interest in Classical literature and a predilection for ostentation and luxury. The great battles for the dominion of *terra firma* were now over and Venice was to be celebrated as a proud combatant and conqueror. Now was the time to relish in past glories and to take up the good life.

mound (once occupied by the ice-house) and surrounded by a ditch, was designed as a summer-house for relaxation. Beyond this, on the way out is a gazebo *(access to the upstairs from the side)* from which a wonderful view opens out onto the whole villa nestling in its grounds.

The nearby maze, a common feature in French and Italian Renaissance gardens that rarely survives, will easily inspire images of pretty, if not wholly innocent scenes of blindman's buff: the first participants to find their way out won a place in the lookout-tower from where they could watch the others and shout directions.

Some of the 114 rooms – Villa Pisani has some 114 rooms in honour of Alvise Pisani, the 114th Doge of Venice. This most famous member of the Pisani family lived here from June to October to keep an eye on the grain harvest and the wine production. Climb the stairs off to the left of the entrance, ornamented with wooden statues attributed to Andrea Brustolon (1660-1732), up to the **Sala del Trionfo delle Arti** (The Triumphs of the Arts) named after the ceiling decoration executed by Giovan Battista Crosato (c 1685-1758). The landscapes depicted on the walls are attributed to, among others, Francesco Zuccarelli (1702-88) and Andrea Celesti (1637-1712).

Through into the next room dedicated to Bacchus and frescoed by Jacopo Guarana (1770), it is worth pausing to note the implausible portrayal of an elephant – painted without first-hand knowledge of the real thing *(on the wall through which you have come)*, and look out for the *casone*, a typical peasant dwelling in the Brenta region *(in a panel opposite the windows)*.

Proceeding onwards following the room where Hitler and Mussolini met in 1943, come the Beauharnais suite furnished with a particularly small bed (for it was normal at the time for people to sleep sitting propped up to safeguard against choking on vomit from over-eating!) and the chapel housing an altar by Sansovino (1486-1579) which was brought here by Napoleon when he ordered the Church of San Gimignano in St Mark's in Venice to be demolished *(see PIAZZA SAN MARCO)*. But the most interesting room is undoubtedly the **Salone delle Feste** or "Party Room", in which the most sumptuous balls imaginable were held. The long minstrels' gallery running down the walls of this vast room was where the orchestra would play. The striking fresco was the last to be painted by Tiepolo (1696-1770) in Italy and represents *The Glory of the Pisani Family Surrounded by the Arts and Sciences*. Look out for Tiepolo's "signature", the parrot *(in the right corner, where the wall through which you have come meets the ceiling)*, and the figure who seems to twitch his leg as he looks down from the wall on the way out.

Further down the river – At **Fiesso** (derived from *flexus*), where the Medoacus divides in two, stood one of the grandest villas of the riviera, the Villa Grimani, which was destroyed in the 19C.

Proceeding along SS 11, the **Villa Soranzo** is particularly famous for the façade frescos painted by Benedetto Caliari (1538-98), brother of Paolo who was better known as Veronese. A fine example of *trompe-l'œil*, these depict a balustrade with monochrome characters peeping out from the niches among the inevitable mythological figures.

The cacophony of... mills, caulkers and markets – In nearby **Dolo** there is a building which used to serve as a boatyard: the basin filled from the 17C sluice is visible. The 16C mill is still in operation on the river, although nowadays it is powered by electricity. These aged reminders might nudge the imagination of today's visitors in picturing what it was like in Goldoni's day when Dolo was renowned far and wide for the noise made by the sluice, and described by the playwright, as well as the working sounds of the boatyard, the mills and the grain markets.

A little deviation or a distraction – At Mira, follow the directions to Mirano *(7km/4mi from Mira)* and the road along the canal. **Mirano**, also known as *Il Musone*, is a satellite of the Brenta Riviera. Although it is not blessed with all the features of the riviera proper, it nevertheless has mills, aligned houses and villas that imply its participation in the Venetian culture that flourished alongside the Brenta.

Anyone wishing for a break from the car and a walk in beautiful grounds should visit the 17C **Villa Erizzo Belvedere**, whose **gardens** are open to the public.

A gentle bend in the Brenta – In a delightful corner of Mira, **Mira Porte**, where the houses are terraced into long lines and the Brenta loops around, there was a lock. Today, the place survives as a small but thriving Veneto town, its piazza ringed with bars serving *crostini al baccalà* (salted cod on toasted bread). By the river is the main regional tourist office *(see Practical Information)*. From here the Villa Widmann Foscari and Barchessa Valmarana can easily be reached on foot *(about 2km/1mi)*.

Villa Widmann Foscari ⊙ – The villa where Goldoni, D'Annunzio, Malipiero and Stravinsky all stayed is an 18C building. A suggestion of its magnificent Rococo interior is to be had from outside, in the entrance and the balconies onto which the windows open. The main draw of this house is undoubtedly its ballroom complete with minstrels' gallery, decked, as is usual, with paintings depicting the apotheosis of the owner's family: the *Glory of the Widmann Family (on the ceiling)* is complemented with mythological subjects *(The Sacrifice of Iphigenia* and *The Rape of Helen)* all by Giuseppe Angeli (1709-98).

Barchessa Valmarana ⊙ – This is all that remains of the 18C Villa Valmarana, which at one time would have been flanked by these two *barchesse (see above)*. The main villa was demolished by the Valmarana family in the 19C in order to avoid paying a wealth tax on luxury goods.

The *barchessa* on the left was divided up between six families who modified the original architectural layout and disposition of relative parts. Yet in every way, this mere outbuilding is truly monumental. Surrounded by an Italianate rose garden, it is fronted with a fine portico of double Doric columns. In the centre, a giant order of pilasters rise to the cornice.

As was the norm, the owner's family are glorified in the central **salone** (Reception Room) ceiling. The fresco, painted in the second half of the 17C is attributed to Michelangelo Schiavoni who is also known as Il Chioggotto, a follower of Tiepolo. The water poured from the urn represents the Brenta, the woman (Ceres) carrying grain on her shoulders symbolises Agriculture which, with Viticulture, constituted the principal industries of the area. The lion is poorly drawn, implying that the artist based his drawing on a traveller's written description rather than any knowledge of real animals or even the lions of St Mark in Venice *(see above: Villa Pisani)*. Conforming with similar decorations elsewhere, in-fill panels are painted with *trompe-l'œil* and above the doors are some curious characters looking out over the balconies.

Barchessa Valmarana

Here the main reception room is situated between the **Sala delle Arti (Room of the Arts)** painted with allegories of Sculpture, Painting, Music and Literature, and the **Sala dei Capricci**, named after the oval *capriccio* panels painted with a gentle landscape, in this case, painted in purple monochrome (a *pastiche*, meanwhile, is drawn from the artist's imagination and mixes Classical architectural elements of Antiquity (columns) with such contemporary features as gondolas).

"... had I but fled towards La Mira, when ambushed at Oriago..." – So begins Jacopo del Cassero's story in Canto V of Dante's *Purgatory*, the story of his death in **Oriago**. In Dante's time, the area was marshy and unhealthy. Before the Republic of Venice was established at the beginning of the 15C, Oriago was situated at the edge of the territory of Padua, Treviso and Venice. As a testament to a troubled past, one of the four columns which, in 1375 signalled the "end" of Oriago, is still here, leaning up against the corner of one of the houses along the river: the column is both striking for its unusual form and ancient appearance.

On the other side of the river, crossed by means of the swing bridge, are the 18C Mocenigo Villa and the Villa Gradenigo.

Villa Gradenigo ⊘ – One of the oldest villas on the Brenta, Villa Gradenigo has a square floorplan which was typical of the 16C.
The frescoes decorating the garden front, despite their poor condition, are still discernable as the work of Benedetto Caliari (1538-98), brother of Paolo known as Il Veronese (1528-88).
Better preserved although not perfect are the frescoes inside. In the 19C the villa was divided into several apartments, and several of the frescoes were irretrievably damaged. At one point in the early 20C, the *palazzo* even served as a laundry, the steam ironically being the *coup de grâce* for the paintings. Today the villa is privately owned.
In the reception room on the ground floor which served as a *portego* – half house, half garden – Benedetto Caliari's murals depict the *Judgement of Muzio Scevola* and the *Wisdom of Alexander the Great* – these, strictly speaking, are not frescoes as such, for the practice of applying pigment to dry plaster is known as painting "a secco". This technique despite giving brighter colours is less durable than if the pigment is set into wet plaster *"affresco"*. The room is further decorated with friezes of festooned flowers and fruit and painted architectural elements which were first introduced into Venetian villa decoration by Veronese.

Continue along SS 11 at the junction, turn right off the Venice road, in the direction of Malcontenta.

★ La Malcontenta ⊘ – The focal point of the little town of Malcontenta is the elegant **Villa Foscari** known as **La Malcontenta**, which overlooks the river at an angle.
It would be amusing to think that the curious epithet referred to a notorious member of the Foscari family being "detained" at the villa against her will and therefore *malcontenta* (unhappy): the true etymology, however, is associated with the controversial excavation of a canal called the *fossa dei malcontenti*, which has lent its name to the area of Malcontenta since 1458.

Since the 16C, the villa has been visited by various illustrious people including Henri III, the King of France; having been used as a military hospital during the First World War, it is now back in the hands of its original owners, the Foscari family, who reside here during the summer.

A house in the country: a taste of Ancient Rome on the Brenta – When Foscari commissioned **Andrea Palladio** (1508-80) to design the villa, the idea was to build a residence in the style of one from Classical Antiquity: a central square fronted by a temple portico facing the Brenta. This projecting entrance, flanked by Ionic columns, gives the house a formal austerity relieved only in part by rustication.
The main rooms are accommodated on the *piano nobile* on the first floor: raised above ground level to avoid the risk of flood damage but also to provide space, enough to contain the kitchens and storage areas.

Palladio and Pythagoras

In designing the Villa Foscari, Palladio borrowed a canon of proportion expounded by Pythagoras' theory on the numerical structure of music and, subsequently, of cosmic harmony. The basic numbers used are 1, 2, 3 and 4: the total of these numbers being 10, a holy number. For Pythagoras, number 10 represented a triangle, the *tetractys*.

The south-facing "back" overlooks the widest part of the garden: it is less formal than the main front, relieved with decorative touches such as the broken pediment, varied window heights and arch motifs that interrupt the horizontal lines of rustication. Note the arched six-part "thermal" window, a feature borrowed straight from Roman baths.

It is, however, the complex and precise calculation of geometrical harmonies that is especially unique to the Villa Foscari, developed by Palladio almost to the point of obsession: with all measurements determined by the number 4 as a unit or as a multiple thereof.

Pastel interior – The floor plan shows a symmetry across the width of the villa – whereas the latin-cross shaped *salone* extending the full length of the house runs at a perpendicular axis. Relative to this main space, tall as well as broad, depend all the subsidiary rooms. Space is further enhanced by the fresco decoration executed by **Giambattista Zelotti** (1526-78), whose style of painting is not dissimilar to Veronese's, complete with painted fluted Doric columns. Zelotti's work however, has a greater abstract quality and a tendency towards Mannerism, according to the fashion in central Italy. Filled with light, the room is crowded with mythological characters painted in colours that have faded with time.

On the vaulted ceiling, the Virtues in the centre are the key to the four oval panels depicting *Astrea Introducing Jupiter to Earthly Pleasures, Two Women Offering Incense to Janus, Jupiter and the Eagle with Mercury, Midas Enthroned with Envy and Discord.*

The lunettes depict the *Bauci Banquet* over the entrance door, *Gods Watching over the Slaying of a Wayfarer* on the right and *Gods Leaving the Guests in their Temple as They Return to Heaven* on the left.

To the northwest of the *salone* is the **Stanza dell'Aurora** (Aurora Room) containing *Harvest:* a beautiful Venetian lady, the legendary Malcontenta, making her entrance, whereas the dependent *studiolo* is dedicated to Bacchus and Venus. To the north-east, *Prometheus Brings to Earth the Fire that was robbed from Heaven* is depicted on the ceiling with, on the walls, *Phaethon Struck Down by Jupiter* and *Caco Stealing Arms from Hercules.* The **Stanza dei Giganti** (Room of the Giants) presents a very different, apocalyptic scene of Giants being crushed by huge boulders: a strange antithesis to the peaceful rural landscape beyond. These frescoes, initiated by **Battista Franco** (1498-1561) and completed by Zelotti, recall the influence of the Mannerist painter-architect Giulio Romano (Palazzo del Tè in Mantua 1532-34).

In the direction of Fusina – After Malcontenta, this peaceful, agricultural area gradually gives way to an urbanised, industrial cityscape: as one gets closer to the lagoon, the profile of the **Porto Marghera** chimneys become sharper on the skyline. The road ends at **Fusina** in a car park, where boats leave for Venice, a logical conclusion to the journey across a landscape fashioned by the discriminating nobility of the Venetian Republic, hundreds of years ago.

"In all the villas and also in some of the city houses I have put a frontispiece on the forward façade where the principal doors are because such frontispieces show the entrance of the house, and add very much to the grandeur and magnificence of the work, the front being thus made more eminent than the other parts."

Andrea Palladio in **Quattro Libri di Architettura.**

Beyond the banks of the Brenta

Noventa Padovana – Take Via Oltre Brenta and Via Noventana out of Stra to Noventa Padovana, which is situated on the banks of the Piovego, the canal that links Padua to the Brenta. There, both the **Villa Grimani** ⊙, a large villa built in the 15C out of the remains of a medieval castle, and **Villa Giovanelli** ⊙ which the patriarchs used as a retreat, are open to visitors.

Vigonovo – *Out of Noventa, after the bridges over the Brenta and the Piovego, turn left for Vigonovo-Saonara. Turn right at the bridge, into Via don Sturzo and Via Sagredo.*
The **Villa Sagredo** ⊙ was once the residence of **Giovanni Sagredo** (1617-82), the son of a member of the Council of Ten, Giovan Francesco Sagredo (1571-1620) and a friend and pupil at the University of Padua of the famous astronomer Galileo Galilei.

Evening falls over the lagoon

Practical
information

Planning your trip

ITALIAN EMBASSIES AND CONSULATES

To obtain further information, contact the nearest Italian embassy or consulate:

Embassies

14 Three Kings' Yard, London W1Y 2EH; ☎ (020) 7312 2200; Fax (020) 7312 2230; emblondon@embitaly.org.uk; www.embitaly.org.uk

1601 Fuller Street, NW Washington, DC 20009; ☎ (202) 328 5500; Fax (202) 462 3605; www.italyemb.org

275 Slater Street, 21st floor, Ottawa, Ontario, K1P 5H9; ☎ (613) 232 2401/2/3; Fax (613) 233 1484; italcomm@trytel.com

Consulates

38 Eaton Place, London SW1X 8AN; ☎ (020) 7235 9371; 09001 600 340 (visa information); Fax (020) 7823 1609.

690 Park Avenue, New York, NY 10021; ☎ (212) 737 9100; Fax (212) 249 4945; italconsny@aol.com; www.italconsulnyc.org

136 Beverley Street, Toronto, Ontario, M5T 1Y5; ☎ (416) 977 1566 (from Canada and USA); (416) 977 2569 (from other countries); (416) 977 1119; consolato.it@toronto.italconsulate.org; www.toronto.italconsulate.org

ITALIAN STATE TOURIST BOARD

The **Ente Nazionale Italiano per il Turismo** (ENIT) has offices at home and abroad – for local tourist information services see below:

UK – 1 Princes Street, London W1R 8AY; ☎ (020) 7408 1254; 0891 600 280 (24hr brochure line, premium rate); Fax (020) 7493 6695; enitlond@globalnet.co.uk; www.enit.it *(office open Mon–Fri, 9am–5pm)*.

USA – Suite 1565, 630 Fifth Avenue, New York, NY 10111; ☎ (212) 245 5095; (212) 245 4822 (brochure line); enitny@italiantourism.com. For Los Angeles, ☎ (310) 820 0098 (brochure line).

Canada – Italian Government Travel Office, 1 Place Ville Marie, Suite 1914, Quebec, H3B 2C3 Montreal; ☎ (514) 866 7667/8 (information office); (514) 392 1429 (brochure line); initaly@ican.net

PASSPORTS AND VISAS

British visitors travelling to Italy must be in possession of a valid national passport. Citizens of other European Union countries only will need a national identity card. In case of loss or theft report to the embassy or consulate and the local police.

Entry visas are required by Australian, New Zealand, Canadian and US citizens (if their intended stay exceeds three months). Apply to the Italian Consulate (visa issued same day; delay if submitted by mail). US citizens may find the booklet **Your Trip Abroad** useful for information on visa requirements, customs regulations, medical care, etc when travelling in Europe – available from the Superintendent of Documents, PO Box 371954, Pittsburgh, PA 15250-7954, ☎ (202) 512 1800; Fax (202) 512 2250; www.access.gpo.gov

CUSTOMS

As of 30 June 1999, those travelling between countries within the European Union can no longer purchase "duty-free" goods. For further information a free leaflet, **Duty Paid**, is available from HM Customs and Excise, Finchley Excise Advice Centre, Berkeley House, 304 Regents Park Road, London N3 2JY, ☎ (020) 7865 4400. The US Customs Service offers a free publication, **Know Before You Go**, for US citizens, ☎ (202) 927 6724; www.customs.gov

HEALTH

As the UK is a member of the European Union, British subjects should obtain **medical form E111** from the Ministry of Social Security, Newcastle-upon-Tyne, or from main post offices, before leaving home.

Separate travel and medical insurance is highly recommended – check with your local travel agent before departure.

DISABLED TRAVELLERS

Many Venetian historic monuments do not have modern lifts or wheelchair facilities: however, ramps are being installed to facilitate movement over bridges etc. Wheelchairs may easily be loaded onto the *vaporetti* but not onto the less stable gondolas. For detailed information contact **RADAR** (Royal Association for Disability and Rehabilitation), 12 City Forum, 250 City Road, London EC1V 8AF ☎ (020) 7250 3222. Details can also be obtained from the **Associazione Italiana per l'Assistenza agli Spastici (AIAS)**, Via Cipro 4/H, 00136 Rome, ☎ 06 38 96 04 or from **AIAS Milano**, Via San Barnaba 29, 20122 Milano, ☎ 02 55 01 75 64; Fax 02 55 01 48 70.

Getting there

BY AIR

Venice is served by many international and domestic flights arriving directly at the **Marco Polo Airport** at Tessera (10km/6mi – 20min), linked to Venice by **ACTV bus** line no 5 to Piazzale Roma (1 500L with six stops) and by **ATVO coach** to Piazzale Roma (5 000L). You can also cross the lagoon to Piazza San Marco (other stops include Murano, Lido, Arsenale and Zattere) by using the river service **ALILAGUNA** (17 000L) or choose to take a water-taxi, which, although more expensive, is much more convenient *(see below)*.

International flights also arrive at **Treviso** (30km/18mi from Venice) which is linked to the railway station by bus and then by train to Venice.

Many airline companies arrange flights to Venice. The following is a brief selection:

Alitalia	4 Portman Square, Marble Arch, London W1H 9PS; ☏ (020) 7486 8432; Fax (020) 7486 8431; www.alitalia.co.uk. Reservations can also be made (by telephone only) on ☏ 08705 448 259. 4-5 Dawson Street, Dublin 2; ☏ (01) 677 5171; Fax (01) 677 3373. 666 Fifth Avenue, New York, NY 10103; ☏ (212) 903 3300; 1 800 223 5730 (reservations from within the USA); Fax (212) 903 3350; www.alitaliausa.com Viale Marchetti 111, 00148 Rome, ☏ 06 65 621; www.alitalia.com
American Airlines	www.aa.com
British Airways	156 Regent Street, London W1; ☏ (020) 7434 4700; 0345 222 111 (reservations outside office hours); Fax (020) 7434 4640 (reservations); www.british-airways.com USA – ☏ (1-800) AIRWAYS. Via Bissolati 54, 00187 Rome; ☏ 06 420 12 440.
Go	☏ 0845 605 4321; www.go-fly.com

BY TRAIN

The main line from Milan via Brescia, Verona, Vicenza and Padua to Trieste passes through Venice. A more luxurious alternative is the Orient Express, founded in 1883, that leaves from London (departing late morning) and stops at a leisurely pace in Paris, Basel, Zurich, Innsbruck, Verona and Venice (arriving in the early evening).

Special concessions (less 30%) are available to rail-users in Italy under the age of 26 and senior citizens over the age of 65 (men) or 60 (women) on presentation of an inter-rail card. Children aged between 4 and 12 travel half-price. Unlimited travel concessions are also available to foreigners in Italy: check for details.

A useful aid to rail travel is the **Thomas Cook European Rail Timetable**, which gives all train schedules and relevant information on touring Europe by rail. Timetables are also available from news-stands in Italy and from the **Italian Tourist Office** in London. Apply to the **Ente Nazionale Italiano per il Turismo (ENIT)**, 1 Princes Street, London W1R 8AY; ☏ (020) 7408 1254; 0891 600 280 (24hr brochure line, premium rate); Fax (020) 7493 6695; enitlond@globalnet.co.uk; www.enit.it *(office open Mon–Fri, 9am–5pm)*.

Venice Simplon-Orient-Express

The advent of a truly comfortable train, designed by the American **George Mortimer Pullman** in 1864, was a turning point in the history of European travel. By the mid-1870s the Pullman trains already had sleeping carriages and parlour cars lit by electric light, as well as a restaurant service. The present Orient-Express was the brain-child of the Belgian **Georges Nagelmackers**, who inaugurated the service on 4 October 1883. In 1906, the group achieved another record-breaking feat: the Simplon tunnel was excavated through the mountains between Switzerland and Italy (12mi/537yd). The route could thereby extend from Milan to Venice and on to Constantinople (56hr from Paris!). The legendary luxury train service ran into financial problems after the Second World War, which eventually forced it to close down in 1977. Its revival is due to an American businessman and train enthusiast **James B Sherwood**, who began his mission by buying two sleeper cars from a Sotheby's auction in Monte Carlo.

The modern Venice Simplon-Orient-Express, launched on 25 May 1982, leaves from London-Victoria southbound for Venice, stopping in Paris, Zurich, St Anton and Innsbruck on Thursdays and Sundays. Northbound trains leave Venice on Wednesdays and Fridays. The full trip takes approximately 32hr and covers a distance of 1 715km/1 065mi. Additional connections with Cologne, Frankfurt, Prague and Dresden are also scheduled. The train and its period features have been restored to their former splendour, including the fine wood panelling, Lalique glass and floral marquetry, Art-Deco-style lamps and turn-of-the-century prints.

For further details contact **Venice Simplon-Orient-Express**, Sea Containers House, 20 Upper Ground, London SE1 9PF, ☏ (020) 7928 6000; 0870 161 5060 (brochure line); Fax (020) 7805 5908.

For tickets, prices and concessions apply to:

Ultima Travel, 424 Chester Road, Little Sutton, South Wirral CH66 3RB ☎ (0151) 339 6171; Fax (0151) 339 9199.
Santa Lucia Station, Venice, ☎ 041 71 55 55 (7am–10pm)

BY COACH

Coach services from Victoria Coach Station, London are organised by Eurolines, 4 Cardiff Road, Luton, Bedfordshire L41 1PP; ☎ 0990 143 219; Fax (01582) 400 694; welcome@eurolinesuk.com; www.eurolines.co.uk. Alternatively consult the nearest National Express office or agent.

BY CAR

Formalities – Nationals of the European Union require a valid **national driving licence**. Nationals of non-EU countries should obtain an **international driving licence**, obtainable in the US from the American Automobile Association, US$18 for members and US$20 for non-members. The AAA can be contacted at AAA National Headquarters, 1000 AAA Drive, Heathrow, FL 32746-5080, ☎ (407) 444 7000. Other documents required include the vehicle's current **log book** and a **green card** for insurance.

Main roads – Venice is situated on the A 4 Torino-Trieste road, reached from the south up the A 13 Bologna to Padua road. Exit at Mestre onto SS 11, over Ponte della Libertà to Piazzale Roma.

Maps – Michelin Tourist & Motoring Atlas Italy and Michelin Maps no 970 Europe (1:3 000 000), no 988 Italy (1:1 000 000) and no 429 North East Italy (1:400 000) will make route planning easier.

Parking – At Piazzale Roma the **ASM garage** (municipal car park) charges a set rate on a daily basis of 30 000L. For further information, ☎ 041 27 227 301/2. Another possibility at Piazzale Roma is the **Garage San Marco**. Depending on the size of your vehicle, you will be charged 27 000L (12hr) and 35 000L (24hr) or 37 000L (12hr) and 48 000L (24hr). Those leaving during the night or during a public holiday will be asked to pay an extra charge of 2 000L. For more details, ☎ 041 523 22 13.
Tronchetto offers parking facilities for cars (25 000L for 24hr, 28 000L for the first 24hr in summer), as well as for camping-cars and caravans (30 000L for 12hr). For further information, ☎ 041 520 75 55.

Remember!

In Italy vehicles drive on the **right-hand side** of the road.
The **minimum driving age** is 18 years.
Seat belts must be worn at the front and back of the vehicle. Drivers must wear **shoes**, carry **spare lights** and a **red triangle** to be displayed in the event of a breakdown or an accident.
Emergency **road-rescue services** are offered by the **Automobile Club Italiano (ACI)**, ☎ 116.
Motorways (*autostrade* – subject to tolls) and dual carriageways (*superstrade*) are indicated by green signs; ordinary roads by blue signs; tourist sights by yellow signs.
Italian **motorway tolls** can be paid for with cash or with the **Viacard**, a magnetic card (50 000L and 100 000L) which is sold in Italy at the entrances and exits of the motorways, in Autogrill restaurants and in the offices of ACI (Automobile Club Italiano).
The following **speed restrictions** are enforced:
50kph/30mph in built-up areas
90-110kph/50-70mph on open country roads
90kph/50mph (600cc) to 130kph/80mph (excess of 1 000cc) on motorways, depending on engine capacity.

Fuel is sold as *super* (4 star), *senza piombo* (unleaded 95 octane), *super plus* or *Euro plus* (unleaded 98 octane) and *gasolio* (diesel). Petrol (US: Gas) stations are usually open from 7am to 7pm. Many close at lunchtime (12.30–3pm), on Sundays and public holidays; many refuse payment by credit-card.

Where to stay

HOTELS, PENSIONI AND GUEST HOUSES

Although Venice has a wide range of accommodation available to those visiting the city, the visitor should be aware that prices can be high and value for money difficult to find. Moreover, the expressions "high season" and "low season" lose all meaning in Venice, which is seen as an ideal holiday destination throughout the year. Strangely enough, the summer period appears to be less popular on account of the hot, damp climate which makes sightseeing extremely tiring. **It is advisable to book as far in advance as possible**.

We have listed below a number of hotels and guest houses located in various parts of the city, classified according to the prices they charge for a **double room**. However, as **these prices are known to vary quite considerably throughout the year**, you are strongly advised to enquire beforehand and check out the rates during the period chosen for your stay. Most prices quoted include breakfast. Hotels are sub-divided into three categories:

– **Budget**: Under 150 000L.
– **Our Selection**: Between 150 000L and 300 000L.
– **Treat Yourself!**: Comfort and charm for a memorable stay – with prices to match!

BUDGET

It is worth noting that a number of establishments run by religious orders take in paying guests at extremely reasonable rates. Their only drawback is the early closing time, usually around 10.30pm.

Istituto San Giuseppe – A stone's throw from St Mark's Square, at no 5402, ☎ 041 52 25 352.

Ostello della Giudecca – Giudecca 86, ☎ 041 52 38 211.

Casa Caburlotto – Santa Croce 316/8 ☎ 041 52 25 930; Fax 041 71 08 55.

Casa Capitanio – Santa Croce 561, ☎ 041 52 23 975.

Casa Cardinal Piazza – Cannaregio 3539/A, ☎ 041 72 13 88; Fax 041 72 02 33.

Casa Murialdo-Circolo ANSPI – Cannaregio 3512, ☎ 041 71 99 33; Fax 041 72 00 02.

Domus Civica – San Polo 3082, ☎ 041 72 11 03 or 041 52 40 416; Fax 041 522 71 39.

Foresteria Valdese – Castello 5170, ☎/Fax 041 52 86 797.

Istituto Santa Giuliana Falconieri- Suore Mantellate – Castello, calle Buccari 10, ☎ 041 52 20 829.

Istituto Solesin – Dorsoduro 624, ☎ 041 52 24 356; Fax 041 52 38 124.

Opera Pia Istituto Ciliota – San Marco 2976, ☎ 041 52 04 888; Fax 041 52 12 730.

Patronato Salesiano Leone XIII – Castello 1281, ☎ 041 24 03 611; Fax 041 52 85 189.

Santa Fosca – Cannaregio 2372, ☎/Fax 041 71 57 75.

Suore Salesie – Dorsoduro 108, ☎ 041 52 23 691.

OUR SELECTION

Pensione La Calcina – Zattere 780, *vaporetto* Zattere, ☎ 041 52 06 466; Fax 041 52 27 045. 29 rooms. Air conditioning. Credit cards accepted.
This *pensione* was built on the exact spot where La Calcina used to stand, an inn where Ruskin sojourned in 1876, the photograph of which still hangs in the entrance. The quality of the service has remained the same since and makes for a highly pleasant stay, whether in the tidy bedrooms, eating in the small dining hall, or relaxing on the roof verandah *(altana)* or the floating terrace overlooking the canal. This fully renovated hotel has two major advantages – its location along Canale della Giudecca and its radiant luminosity, a rare occurrence indeed in the small, narrow streets of Venice.

Hotel Falier – Salizzada San Pantalon 130, *vaporetto* San Tomà, ☎ 041 71 08 82; Fax 041 52 06 554. 19 rooms. Credit cards accepted.
Close to I Frari but away from the bustling town centre, this hotel is a quiet haven of peace with a charming little back garden.

Hotel Paganelli – Riva degli Schiavoni 4182, *vaporetto* San Zaccaria, ☎ 041 52 24 324; Fax 041 52 39 267. 22 rooms. Air conditioning. Credit cards accepted.
A family-run establishment fronting the Bacino di San Marco, which can also be admired from some of the rooms. The other rooms are located in a separate building and afford nice views of Campo San Zaccaria. All are decorated and furnished in the Venetian style.

Hotel Serenissima – Calle Goldoni 4486, *vaporetto* Rialto or San Marco, ☎ 041 52 00 011; Fax 041 52 23 292. 34 rooms. Air conditioning. Credit cards accepted. Restaurant.
Just around the corner from St Mark's Square lies this charming, unpretentious hotel, where the walls are hung with paintings by modern artists.

TREAT YOURSELF!

Hotel Abbazia – Calle Priuli 68, *vaporetto* Ferrovia, ☎ 041 71 73 33; Fax 041 71 79 49. 39 rooms. Air conditioning. Credit cards accepted.

An ideal location for visitors wishing to stay near the station. This hotel once housed a Carmelite monastery and retains many of its original features. The bar is the former refectory complete with pulpit and pews, and the long, austere corridors still seem to echo with the footsteps of robed monks silently reciting their prayers.

Hotel Cipriani – Giudecca, ☎ 041 52 07 744; Fax 041 52 03 930. 12 suites (seven in Palazzo Vendramin) with air conditioning. Credit cards accepted. Garden and pool. Restaurant.

Housed in the Palazzo Vendramin, the Hotel Cipriani is synonymous with elegance and good taste. Even its location in a quiet, secluded spot reflects its impeccable style. The main suite commands a lovely view of St Mark's Square.

Hotel Danieli – Riva degli Schiavoni 4196, *vaporetto* San Zaccaria, ☎ 041 52 26 480; Fax 041 52 00 208. 221 rooms, nine suites with air conditioning. Credit cards accepted. Restaurant.

For many of us, the city of Venice conjures up strong images steeped in nostalgia. Those who have a penchant for the Gothic will appreciate the crumbling *palazzi* and the powerful aesthetics of the city. This Baroque vision verging on decadence is perfectly illustrated by the Hotel Danieli, housed in the Palazzo Dandolo since 1822. Needless to say, the hotel was a favourite place of residence among many Romantic authors and musicians, namely Dickens, Wagner, Balzac, Proust, and Alfred de Musset. More recently, it was patronised by celebrities such as Diana, Princess of Wales.

Hotel Des Bains – Lido, Lungomare Marconi 17, ☎ 041 52 65 921; Fax 041 52 60 113. 190 rooms. Air conditioning. Credit cards accepted. Pool. Restaurant.

Immortalised by Visconti's brilliant film *Death in Venice*, the Hotel des Bains still exudes an air of nostalgia that reigns over the superb private beach that stretches out to sea. This high-class establishment boasts many outstanding features: an imposing neo-Classical façade, a stately salon embellished with Art Nouveau panelling, a lovely verandah, a huge park with a pool and the elegant dining rooms suffused with light. All the rooms have been refurbished and decorated with discreet sophistication. A private shuttle service links St Mark's Square to this legendary hotel, which offers cool comfort during the sweltering days of summer.

Hotel Flora – Calle larga XXII Marzo 2283/A, *vaporetto* San Marco or Santa Maria del Giglio, ☎ 041 52 05 844; Fax 041 52 28 217. 44 rooms. Air conditioning. Credit cards accepted.

Art takes pride of place in this hotel, where visitors will succumb to the turn-of-the-century charm and where careful attention has been lavished on every single detail – the decoration of the rooms, the 1920s staircase and the delightful garden.

Hotel Gritti Palace – Campo San Maria del Giglio 2467, *vaporetto* Santa Maria del Giglio, ☎ 041 79 46 11; Fax 041 52 00 942. 87 rooms. Six suites. Credit cards accepted. Restaurant.

At the Hotel Gritti Palace you will be granted hospitality "fit for a doge", an expression to be taken literally as five centuries ago, this superb *palazzo* housed the private residence of the Doge Gritti. Nowadays, during the celebrated Film Festival, it is graced by the presence of stars who traditionally pose for the press on the "floating pontoon" spanning the Grand Canal, affording superb views of La Salute. Characterised by minute detail and lavish ornamentation, the interior of the hotel pays homage to Venice and the fascination that the lagoon city has always exerted over man.

The **Michelin Red Guide Italia**, updated on a yearly basis, provides a detailed list of hotels and reliable restaurants in Venice.

CAMPING FACILITIES

The more adventurous tourists with a tent, a caravan or a camping car will have no trouble finding a spot among the many **camp sites** dottied along the Cavallino coastline. For details contact **Assocampings**, Via Fausta, Ponte Cavallino, 30013 Cavallino, ☎ 041 65 88 13 or **Consorzio Lido Ca' di Valle**, Corso Italia 10, 30013 Cavallino, ☎ 041 96 81 48.

EATING OUT

The finest restaurants are listed in the **Michelin Red Guide Italia**. For a light meal, a *cicheto* or a *spritz*, choose one of the less formal establishments mentioned in the main text. The following is a recapitulation of these various *osterie*, *trattorie* and *pasticcerie*, listed under their respective neighbourhoods. *For assistance with local dishes, see Introduction: Eating out.*

San Marco

Antica Carbonera *(see RIALTO)*

A la Campana *(see RIALTO)*

Devil's Forest *(see SAN GIORGIO degli SCHIAVONI)*

Ai Do Ladroni *(see RIALTO)*

Caffè Florian *(see PIAZZA SAN MARCO)*

Harry's Bar *(see PIAZZA SAN MARCO)*

Leon Bianco *(see RIALTO)*

Piero e Mauro *(see PIAZZA SAN MARCO)*

Caffè Quadri *(see PIAZZA SAN MARCO)*

Ai Rusteghi *(see RIALTO)*

Al Volto *(see La FENICE and RIALTO)*

Da Zorzi *(see RIALTO)*

Dorsoduro

Il Caffè *(see I CARMINI)*

Cantinone *(see ACCADEMIA)*

Dona Onesta *(see SAN ROCCO)*

Linea d'ombra *(see La SALUTE)*

Da Montin *(see ACCADEMIA)*

Ai Pugni *(see I CARMINI)*

San Trovaso *(see ACCADEMIA)*

Santa Croce

Al Ponte *(see I FRARI)*

Ai Postali *(see I FRARI)*

Vecio Fritoin *(see RIALTO)*

Alla Zucca *(see I FRARI)*

Cannaregio

Algiubagiò *(see SAN ZANIPÒLO)*

Antiche Cantine Ardenghi *(see SAN ZANIPÒLO)*

Alla Bomba *(see CA'D'ORO)*

The Fiddler's Elbow *(see CA'D'ORO)*

Alla Fontana *(see Il GHETTO)*

Gam-Gam *(see Il GHETTO)*

Al Paradiso Perduto *(see CA' D'ORO)*

La Perla *(see SAN ZANIPÒLO)*

Ai Promessi Sposi *(see CA' D'ORO)*

Alla Vedova-Ca' d'Oro *(see CA' D'ORO)*

San Polo

Antico Dolo *(see RIALTO)*

All'Arco *(see RIALTO)*

Ai Nomboli *(see SAN ROCCO)*

Alla Patatina *(see SAN ROCCO)*

Da Pinto *(see RIALTO)*

Vivaldi *(see SAN ROCCO)*

Castello and Sant'Elena

All'Acciugheta *(see SAN GIORGIO degli SCHIAVONI)*

Birreria Forst *(see SAN GIORGIO degli SCHIAVONI)*

Da Dante *(see ARSENALE)*

Didovich *(see SAN ZACCARIA)*

Al Mascaròn *(see SAN ZACCARIA)*

L'Olandese volante *(see RIALTO)*

Dal Pampo *(see SANT'ELENA e SAN PIETRO)*

Rivetta *(see SAN GIORGIO degli SCHIAVONI)*

Da Sergio *(see RIALTO)*

Alle Testiere *(see RIALTO)*

Dai Tosi *(see SANT'ELENA e SAN PIETRO)*

La Giudecca

Harry's Dolci *(see La GIUDECCA)*

LARA PESSINA

Getting around

Venice is served by a water-borne public transport system and it is advisable to remember that the name of a *vaporetto* stop does not necessarily mean that the water-bus will stop outside the monument after which it is named. Bear in mind that traffic on the Grand Canal is often congested and services may sometimes be erratic! Suffice it to say that the least exasperating way of getting around is on foot, even if the climb up and over each bridge is nothing short of exhausting.

VAPORETTO *(see map of vaporetto routes pp 24-25)*

The **water-buses** comprise two kinds of vehicle – the lumbering *vaporetto* and the faster *motoscafo* (motor-boat) for longer distances. A reduced service operates at night: check the timetables on display.

Tickets may be purchased individually or in tens *(un blochetto)* from kiosks at each landing-stage and from shops displaying the ACTV sign: a single ticket costs 6 000L; a return (round trip) is 10 000L; 18 000L *(biglietto turistico)* buys unlimited travel over 24hr; 35 000L buys unlimited travel over 72hr from the start of your first journey; 60 000L buys a pass valid for a week. For further details contact **Azienda del Consorzio**, Trasporti Veneziano, Casella Postale 688, Corte dell'Albero 3880 Venice, ☎ 041 78 01 11; Fax 52 07 135.

Line 1 runs from Piazzale Roma and the railway station, the full length of the Grand Canal (14 stops) to Piazza San Marco and on to the Lido – called the *accelerato*, although in some ways this is the slowest line.

Line 82 follows the same route as Line 1, but makes fewer stops and is therefore quicker. It runs from Tronchetto to Piazzale Roma, Giudecca, San Giorgio, St Mark's and on to the Lido.

The *vaporetto* stop outside the railway station

WATER-TAXIS

Beware of touts out to overcharge the unsuspecting visitor! Look out for authorised motor launches bearing a yellow registration number plate inscribed with the symbol of Venice on the boarding side: it is also worth ensuring that the meter is clearly visible and that charge rates are displayed.

As a guideline, a journey through the city centre lasting up to seven minutes will cost approximately 27 000L, with an additional 500L for every 15 seconds thereafter.

Calling a taxi by phone will incur an additional charge of 8 000L (10 000L if you are outside the town centre), as will journeys carried out between 10pm and 7am (night-rate standard supplement of 8 500L) or on Sundays and public holidays (9 000L). Any luggage item in excess of 50cm/19in wide will be charged an extra 2 200L. You will also have to pay an extra charge if the number of passengers exceeds four: 3100L per person up to 20 passengers.

In cases of suspected fraud, make a note of the taxi number, the time of the journey and request a receipt for the fare paid with details of the journey made. The matter should then be referred to the Tourist Information Service or to the local police for further action. However, there is little recourse if unauthorised boats are used.

Radio Taxi ☎ 041 522 23 03 or 041 72 31 12	**Coop Serenissima** ☎ 041 522 12 65 or 041 522 85 38
Venezia Taxi ☎ 041 72 30 09	**Coop San Marco** ☎ 041 522 23 03 or 041 523 57 75
Piazzale Roma (Santa Chiara) ☎ 041 71 69 22	**Coop Veneziana** ☎ 041 71 61 24
Rialto ☎ 041 523 05 75; 041 72 31 12	**Società Sotoriva** ☎ 041 520 95 86
San Marco (Molo) ☎ 041 522 97 50	**Società Narduzzi Solemar** ☎ 041 520 08 38
Lido ☎ 041 526 00 59	**Società Marco Polo** ☎ 041 96 61 70
Airport (Marco Polo) ☎ 041 541 50 84	**Società Serenissima** ☎ 041 522 42 81

TRAGHETTO

As there are only three bridges spanning the Grand Canal (Scalzi, Rialto and Accademia), the other practical means of crossing from one bank to another is by *traghetto* (700L; 1 000L from San Samuele during exhibitions at Palazzo Grassi) which ferries passengers Venetian-style, standing on two feet, at eight points along the canal (Ferrovia, San Marcuola, Santa Sofia, Riva del Carbon, San Tomà, San Samuele, Santa Maria del Giglio and Dogana – *see II CANAL GRANDE: plan*).

GONDOLA

For a relaxing trip on a gondola, be prepared to spend a great deal more: 50min along the canals and the *rii* will cost you 120 000L (official price excluding musical serenades between 8pm and 8am), which can be shared among up to six passengers. Every additional 25min will be charged an extra 60 000L. Travelling by gondola at night may satisfy your yearning for romance but it will deal a severe blow to your finances: between 8pm and 8am, a 50-minute trip will cost 150 000L, with an extra charge of 75 000L for every further 25min. For details, contact the **Istituzione per la Conservazione della Gondola e la Tutela del Gondoliere** ☎ 041 528 50 75. It is understood, however, that charges are always subject to negotiation. Remember too that you can decide how to reach your destination and ask the gondoliere to follow the route you have chosen.
For those who prefer gliding along canals at their own leisurely pace, **boats** may be hired privately from Brussa, Cannaregio 331, ☎ 041 71 57 87 or 041 720 550.

Whiling away the time

General information

CARNIVAL

To hire costume and disguise outfits contact **Il Prato** ☎ 041 52 03 375, **Nicoloa Atelier**, Cannaregio 5565, ☎ 041 52 07 051 or **Falpalà** ☎ 041 52 25 022.

CHURCHES

The main churches are open 7am–noon and 4–6pm. Visitors should be dressed appropriately: long trousers for men; no bare shoulders or very short skirts for women; those who do not observe these conventions may be refused entry by the Verger or others in authority.
As many of the works of art are positioned high up, it is a good idea to bring a pair of binoculars. Small change (100L, 200L and 500L coins) is useful for activating light time-switches.

ELECTRICITY

The voltage is 220ac, 50 cycles per second; the sockets are for two-pin plugs – so do not forget to take an adaptor for hairdryers etc.

ENTERTAINMENT & LEISURE

As regards entertainment, the magazine **Gazettino** provides a comprehensive coverage of the shows, exhibitions and festivals held in the lagoon city, as well as concerts and recitals in churches (I Frari, Santo Stefano, La Pietà). It also features reviews and articles on leading personalities, and provides information on visiting local sights.

Museums – Most museums do not open on Mondays; on other days many close at 2pm and the ticket offices at 1.30pm. In many museums bags must be left in the cloakroom. Flash photography is not usually permitted.

Theatre – The main theatres for drama, ballet and opera in Venice are **Teatro Goldoni** (calle del Teatro), presenting an interesting season of plays and concerts, ☎ 041 520 54 22; **Teatro Fondamenta Nuove** (Cannaregio 5013) whose programme includes music and dance, ☎ 041 522 44 98; **PalaFenice**, Isola del Tronchetto, used as a temporary venue for performances put on by the **Gran Teatro La Fenice**, which burned down in January 1996 (the list of events can be seen on posters around town, ☎ 041 786 537 from 8am to 2pm); **Teatro a l'Avogaria** (calle Avogaria, 1617 Dorsoduro) ☎ 041 520 61 30.

Beaches – At the seaside there are supervised beaches where a fee is charged for umbrellas, chairs and sunbeds; other beaches free of charge may be less well-tended.

VISUEL

FOREIGN EMBASSIES AND CONSULATES

Australia – Contact the consulate general in Milan (☎ 02 777 04 217) or the Australian embassy in Rome (via Alessandria 215, 00198 Rome; ☎ 06 85 27 21; www.australian-embassy.it).

Canada – Contact the Canadian consulate in Padova (Riviera Ruvvante 25, 36123 Padova; ☎ 049 87 64 833; Fax 049 878 1147) or the Canadian embassy in Rome (via GB de Rossi 27, 00161 Rome; ☎ 06 44 59 81; rome@dfait-maeci.gc.ca).

Ireland – Contact the Irish consulate in Milan (piazza San Pietro gessate 2, 20123 Milano; ☎ 02 55 18 75 69) or the Irish embassy in Rome (piazza di Campitelli 3, 00186 Rome; ☎ 06 69 79 121; Fax 06 67 92 354).

UK – Contact the honourary consulate in Venice (accademia Dorsoduro 1051, 30100 Venezia; ☎ 041 522 7207; 041 522 7408) or out of hours contact the British embassy in Rome (via XX Settembre 80a, Rome; ☎ 06 48 25 441; Fax 06 48 73 324).

USA – Contact the consulate in Milan (via Principe Amedeo 2, Milano; ☎ 02 290 351) or the American embassy in Rome (via Veneto 119a, 00187 Rome; ☎ 06 46 741; Fax 06 48 82 672; www.usis.it).

MONEY

The unit of currency is the **lira** which is issued in notes (100 000L, 50 000L, 20 000L, 10 000L, 5 000L, 2 000L and 1 000L) and in coins (1 000L, 500L, 200L, 100L and 50L). The *gettone*, a brass telephone token, is also considered to be legal tender (200L).

Banks – Banks are usually open Monday to Friday, 8.30am–1.30pm and 2.30–4pm. Some branches open in the city centre and shopping centres on Saturday mornings, but most are closed on Saturdays, Sundays and public holidays. Most hotels will change travellers' cheques. Money can be changed in post offices (except travellers' cheques), money-changing bureaux and at railway stations and airports. Commission is always charged.

Credit cards – Payment by credit card is widespread in shops, hotels and restaurants and also some petrol stations. The **Michelin Red Guide Italia** and the **Michelin Red Guide Europe** indicate which credit cards are accepted at hotels and restaurants. Money may also be withdrawn from a bank but may incur interest pending repayment.

Eurocard – Eurocheques are widely accepted, although the value guaranteed is restricted – it is advisable to check on these rules prior to departure. Money withdrawn from Bancomat machines with a PIN incurs a lesser commission than from a withdrawal transacted over the counter at a bank.

PHARMACIES

A pharmacy *(farmacia)* is identified by a red and white cross. When it is closed it will advertise the names of the pharmacy on duty and a list of doctors on call.

POSTAL SERVICES

In Italy post offices are open from 8.30am to 2pm (noon Sat and last day of the month). The principal post offices are to be found at the Fondaco dei Tedeschi *(see RIALTO)* and off Piazza San Marco, behind the Napoleon Wing by the Correr museum. Letters sent **poste restante** *(fermo posta)* can be collected from the main post office. Stamps are sold in post offices and tobacconists. The rates in Europe are: letters 850L; postcards (a few words only) 750L. Airmail must be weighed at the post office.

PUBLIC HOLIDAYS

Public holidays *(giorni festivi)* include Saturdays and Sundays.
January: 1 (New Year) and 6 (Epiphany)
Easter : Sunday and Monday *(lunedì dell'Angelo)*
April : 25 (St Mark's Day and liberation in 1945)
May: 1
August: 15 (Assumption – *Ferragosto*)
November:1
December: 8 (Immaculate Conception), 25 and 26 (Christmas and St Stephen's day).
A working day is a *giorno feriale*.

SHOPPING

Most shops are open Mon–Sat, 8am–1pm and 3.30–7.30pm.
Italian **sizes** are not the same as other European sizes; for women a British 12 in clothes corresponds to an Italian size 44 and a British 5 in shoes corresponds to an Italian size 37; for men a British 40 in clothes corresponds to an Italian size 50, a British 15 in collar size to an Italian size 38, and a British size 8 in shoes corresponds to an Italian size 42.
Italian **videotapes** tend to be recorded on the **PAL** system.

SPECIAL INTERESTS

A passion for art – Courses are organised for experienced restorers of fine, applied and decorative art. Details from the **Centro Europeo di Formazione degli Artigiani per la Conservazione del Patrimonio Architettonico**, Casella Postale 676, Isola di San Servolo, 30100 Venice, ☎ 041 526 85 46 or 041 526 85 47; Fax 041 27 60 211.

The contemplative approach – If you want to get away from the madding crowd and indulge in silent meditation, the Franciscan community provides a retreat on the island of San Francesco del Deserto. They will arrange to pick you up (only those interested in a spiritual retreat) from Burano in their own boat. For further details, ☎ 041 528 68 63.

The younger generation – **Rolling Venice** is a card costing 5 000L available to young people aged between 14 and 29 which offers over 2 000 discounts applicable to various venues: youth hostels, camp sites, hotels, restaurants, university canteens, museums and shops involved in the scheme, as well as reduced rates for public transport and the International Biennale of Art. You can get the card by turning up at one of the following locations with official identification papers:
– **Agenzia Transalpino** at the Stazione Santa Lucia, ☎ 041 52 41 334 (open Mon–Fri, 8.30am–12.30pm and 3–7pm; Sat mornings only) or at the **Rolling Venice Kiosk** (open July to Sept, daily, 8am–8pm);
– **Assessorato alle politiche giovanili** in San Marco, Corte Contarina 1529, ☎ 041 27 47 645 (open Mon–Fri, 9.30am–1pm; Tues and Thur, 3–5pm);
– **Centro Turistico Studentesco e Giovanile (CTS)** in Dorsoduro 3252, ☎ 041 520 56 60 (open Mon–Fri, 9.30am–1.30pm and 3–7pm);
– **Agenzia Arte e Storia** in Santa Croce, Corte Canal 659, ☎ 041 52 49 232 (open Mon–Fri, 9am–1pm and 3.30–7pm);
– **Associazione Italiana Alberghi per la Gioventù** in San Polo, calle del Castelforte San Rocco 3101, ☎ 041 52 04 414 (open Mon–Sat, 8am–2pm).
Besides the card, you can also buy a guidebook of Venice and a brochure with useful information about the city for an additional 10 000L. 15 000L will buy you the card, a guidebook, a brochure and/or a *Rolling Venice* t-shirt.

TELECOMMUNICATIONS

The state telecommunication system is run by the **Compania Italiana Telecom (CIT)**. Telephone bureaux have banks of public telephones where customers pay for the line at the end of the trunk call *(Fondaco dei Tedeschi)*.
Reduced rates for national calls apply after 6.30pm and between 10pm and 8am for international calls.

Public phones – Public telephone boxes are to be found along streets and in most bars. They may be operated by phone cards *(see below)* and by telephone credit cards. To make a call: lift the receiver, insert payment, await dialling signal, punch in the required number and wait for a reply.

Phone cards – These are sold in denominations of 5 000L, 10 000L or 15 000L *(schede da cinque, dieci, quindici mila lire)* and supplied by CIT offices and post offices as well as tobacconists (*Tabaccaio* sign bearing a white T on a black background).

Useful numbers

Assisted operator service (reverse charge calling)	☎ 15
Directory Enquiries (addresses)	☎ 14 12
International Enquiries	☎ 176
OMNITEL Customer Care	☎ 190
TIM Customer Service	☎ 119
Urgent Calls	☎ 197

Emergency numbers

ACI Emergency Breakdown Service	☎ 116
Carabinieri	☎ 112
Central Police Headquarters, via S. Vitale, 15	☎ 06 46 86
Fire Brigade	☎ 115
Foreign Residents' Bureau, via Genova, 2	☎ 06 46 29 87
General Emergency Services (equivalent of British 999)	☎ 113
Lost Property, via N. Bettoni, 1	☎ 06 58 16 040
Police	☎ 06 67 691

Emergency Health Services

Ambulance - Red Cross	☎ 06 55 10
Emergencies	☎ 118
Farmacia S. Paolo, via Ostiense, 168 (24hr pharmacy)	☎ 06 57 50 143
Permanent Medical Service	☎ 06 58 20 10 30
Policlinico A. Gemelli (hospital), Largo Gemelli, 8	☎ 06 30 151
San Camillo Hospital, Circonvallazione Gianicolense, 87	☎ 06 58 701

Dialling codes – For calls **within Venice**, dial the correspondent's number, including the 041 prefix code for Venice.

For calls to **other towns in Italy**, dial the code for the town or district beginning with an 0, followed by the correspondent's number.

For **international calls** dial 00 followed by the country code:

61 for Australia
1 for Canada
64 for New Zealand
44 for the UK
1 for the USA.

For calls from abroad to Italy, the international code for Italy is 39, the code for Venice is 041 – note that following changes to telephone codes in Italy, you should no longer drop the first 0 of the area code.

TIME

The time in Italy is usually the same as in France, Belgium and Switzerland (one hour ahead of the United Kingdom) and changes during the last weekend in March and October between Summer Time *(ora legale)* and Winter Time *(ora solare)*.

TOURIST INFORMATION

Italian State Tourist Board – *See Practical information: Planning your trip.*

Local Tourist Offices – The **Azienda Promozione Turismo (APT)** and its various branches provide brochures, as well as maps and lists of hotels, youth hostels and camp sites free of charge:

APT Venezia, Dorsoduro Palazzo Balbi, 30123 VENEZIA, Italy, ☎ 041 279 2761; Fax (041) 279 2609; www.regione.veneto.it

Castello 4421, open daily, 8.30am–7pm (2pm in winter), ☎ 041 52 98 711; Fax 52 30 399.

San Marco, calle Ascensione, 71/f, ☎ 041 52 98 711 (at the bottom of Piazza San Marco).

Lido ☎ 041 526 57 21

Airport ☎ 041 54 16 115

For the **Brenta Valley**: 26 Via don Minzoni, Mira Porte, Venice, ☎ 041 42 49 73.

Further reading

ART

Venetian Painting: a Concise History – John Steer (Thames and Hudson 1970)

The Stones of Venice – John Ruskin (Da Capo Press 1985)

Palladio and Palladianism – Robert Tavernor (Thames and Hudson 1991)

Palladio – JS Ackerman, P Dearborn Massar (Illustrator) (Penguin Books 1991)

Palladio's Villas – Paul Holberton (John Murray 1991)

Five Centuries of Music in Venice – HC Robbins Landon, John Julius Norwich (Thames & Hudson 1991)

Ruskin's Venice: The Stones Revisited – Sarah Quill, Alan Windsor (Introduction) (Ashgate Publishing Limited 1999)

HISTORICAL REFERENCE

The Travels of Marco Polo – Marco Polo, R Latham (Trans) (Penguin Books 1965)

A History of Venice – John Julius Norwich (Penguin Books 1983)

The Venetian Empire – Jan Morris (Penguin Books 1990)

Venice Rediscovered – John Pemble (Oxford University Press 1996)

LITERATURE

Italian Journey – Goethe (Penguin Books 1970)

The Aspern Papers – Henry James, Anthony Curtis (Ed) (Penguin Books 1984)

The Wings of the Dove – Henry James, J Bayley (Ed), P Crick (Ed) (Penguin Books 1986)

Stone Virgin – Barry Unsworth (Penguin Books 1986)

The Desire and Pursuit of the Whole – Frederick Rolfe (Da Capo Press 1986)

Territorial Rights: Complete & Unabridged – Muriel Spark, Nigel Hawthorne (Narrator) (Chivers Audio Books 1990)

The Quest for Corvo – AJA Symons (Quartet Books 1993)

Across the River and into the Trees – Ernest Hemingway (Arrow 1994)

Thus Was Adonis Murdered – Sarah Caudwell (Dell Publishing Company 1994)

A Literary Companion to Venice – Ian Littlewood (St Martin's Press 1995)

Dead Lagoon – Michael Dibdin (Faber & Faber 1995)

Death in Venice and Other Stories – Thomas Mann (Minerva 1996)

The Passion – Jeanette Winterson (Vintage 1996)

The Comfort of Strangers – Ian McEwan (Vintage 1997)

Volpone – Ben Johnson [can be found in *Volpone and Other Early Plays* – Ben Jonson, Lorna Hutson (Ed) (Penguin Books 1998)]

The Merchant of Venice – William Shakespeare, Jay L Halio (Ed) (Oxford Paperbacks 1998)

An Italian Journey – Jean Giono, J Cumming (Trans) (Northwestern University Press 1998)

OTHER GUIDES

Ghetto of Venice – Roberta Curiel, Bernard Dov Cooperman (Tauris Parke 1990)

Venice – Ian Littlewood (John Murray 1992)

Companion Guide to Venice – Hugh Honour (Companion Guides 1997)

Venice for Pleasure – JG Links (Pallas Athene 1999)

The Stones of Florence and Venice Observed – Mary McCarthy (Penguin Books 2000)

Calendar of events

6 January	Regata della Befana (Epiphany boat race).
10 days before Lent	Carnival.
March	*Su e zo per i ponti* – a race through the streets and squares of Venice *(see Introduction: Unique to Venice: Bridges)*.
Maundy Thursday	Benediction with fire, when a torch is lit in the atrium of San Marco before being carried in procession around the church, lighting all the candles.
25 April	Feast day of St Mark. Venetian men offer a closed red rosebud to their sweethearts, known in Venetian as a *bòcolo*.
May	The *Vogalonga* consists of a marathon of rowing boats that departs from the area outside San Marco and races around the islands of the lagoon before returning to the Grand Canal and back to San Marco.
Ascension Day	The *Sensa* commemorates the Sposalizio del Mar *(see Introduction: Over a thousand years of glory: 1177)*.
Week of 29 June	Feast days of St Peter and St Paul *(see SANT'ELENA e SAN PIETRO: Feast of San Pietro di Castello)*.
Third Sunday in July	Feast of the Redeemer *(see La GIUDECCA)*.
16 August	St Roch's feast day. At 6pm, a procession leaves the Scuola di San Rocco and slowly proceeds towards church. After celebrating solemn Mass, the faithful return to the Scuola, where a person worthy of distinction is awarded the San Rocco Prize for their dedication and humanitarian work.
First Sunday in September	Historic regatta comprising four different events for the young, for ladies, for the *caorline* (six-man rowing boat originally from Caorle, a small fishing village to the east of Jesolo) and for *gondolini* (small gondolas), followed by a great water-borne procession in costume in the presence of a doge and dogeress. This great celebration recalls the time when Venetians returned home with pomp and circumstance, having spent summer in the countryside.
Third Sunday in September	Fish Festival in Burano: plates of fish and *polenta* are washed down with white wine; the meal is followed by a boat race.
21 November	Feast of the Madonna della Salute *(see La SALUTE)*.

Venice out to watch the historic regatta

Glossary

BASIC VOCABULARY

si/no – yes/no
per favore – please
grazie – thank you
buongiorno – good morning
buona sera – good afternoon/evening
buona notte – good night
arrivederci – goodbye
scusi – excuse me
piccolo/un po' – small/a little
grande – large/big
meno – less

molto – much/very
più – more
basta! – enough!
quando? – when?
perché? – why?
perché – because
con/senza – with/without
l'aeroporto – the airport
la stazione – the station
un biglietto – a ticket
una scheda per il telefono – a telephone card

NUMBERS AND NUMERALS

1	uno	**11**	undici	**30**	trenta
2	due	**12**	dodici	**40**	quaranta
3	tre	**13**	tredici	**50**	cinquanta
4	quattro	**14**	quattordici	**60**	sessanta
5	cinque	**15**	quindici	**70**	settanta
6	sei	**16**	sedici	**80**	ottanta
7	sette	**17**	diciassette	**90**	novanta
8	otto	**18**	diciotto	**100**	cento
9	nove	**19**	diciannove	**1000**	mille
10	dieci	**20**	venti	**2000**	due mila

TIME, DAYS OF THE WEEK AND SEASONS

1.00 – l'una
1.15 – una e un quarto – one fifteen
1.30 – un' ora e mezzo – one thirty
1.45 – l'una e quaranta cinque – one forty-five
mattina – morning
pomeriggio – afternoon
sera – evening
ieri – yesterday
oggi – today
domani – tomorrow
una settimana – a week

lunedì – Monday
martedì – Tuesday
mercoledì – Wednesday
giovedì – Thursday
venerdì – Friday
sabato – Saturday
domenica – Sunday
inverno – winter
primavera – spring
estate – summer
autunno – autumn/fall

FOOD AND DRINK

un piatto – a plate
un coltello – a knife
una forchetta – a fork
un cucchiaio – a spoon
il cibo – food
un piatto vegetariano – a vegetarian dish
un bicchiere – a glass
acqua minerale (gassata) – mineral water (fizzy)
vino rosso – red wine
vino bianco – white wine
una birra (alla spina) – a beer (draught)
carne – meat
manzo/vitello – beef/veal
maiale – pork

agnello – lamb
prosciutto cotto (crudo) – cooked ham (cured)
pollo – chicken
pesce – fish (**pesca** – peach)
uova – eggs (**uva** – grapes)
verdura – green vegetables
burro – butter
formaggio – cheese
un dolce – a dessert
frutta – fruit
zucchero – sugar
sale/pepe – salt/pepper
senape – mustard
olio/aceto – oil/vinegar
si puo visitare? – can one visit?

SHOPPING

un negozio – a shop
la posta – a post office
francobolli – stamps
macellaio – a butcher's
farmacia – a chemist's
sciroppo per la tosse – cough mixture
pastiglie per la gola – throat pastilles
cerotto – sticking plaster
scottato dal sole – sun burn

mal di pancia – stomach-ache
mal di testa – headache
punture di zanzara/ape/vespa – mosquito bite/bee-/wasp-sting
il panificio – a baker's
pane (integrale) – bread (wholemeal)
un supermercato – a supermarket
un giornale – a newspaper
pescivendolo – a fishmonger

SIGHTSEEING AND ORIENTATION

si puo visitare?– can one visit?
chiuso/aperto – closed/open
destra/sinistra – right/left
nord/sud – north/south
est/ovest – east/west
la strada per ...? – the road for ...?
una vista – a view
al primo piano – on the first floor
tirare – pull
spingere – push
bussare – ring (the bell)
le luci – lights

le scale – stairs
l'ascensore – lift
i bagni per uomo/per donna – WC facilities men's/ladies'
una camera singola/doppia/matrimoniale – a single room/with twin beds/double bed
con doccia/con bagno – with shower/bath
un giorno/una notte – one day/night

URBAN SITES

la città – the town
una chiesa – a church
il duomo – the cathedral
una cappella – a chapel
il chiostro – the cloisters
la navata – the nave
il coro – the choir or chancel
il transetto – the transept
la cripta – the crypt
un palazzo – a town house or mansion
una casa – a house
un castello – a castle
un monastero/convento – an abbey/monastery
un cortile – a courtyard
un museo – a museum

una torre – a tower
un campanile – a belfry
una piazza – a square
un giardino – a garden
un parco – a park
una via/strada – a street/road
un ponte – a bridge
un molo – a pier or jetty
un cimitero – a cemetery
la barca – a boat
il motoscafo – motor boat
la spiaggia – the beach
il mare – the sea
pericolo – danger
vietato – prohibited or forbidden

NATURAL SITES

il fiume – the river
un lago – a lake

un belvedere – a viewpoint
un bosco – a wood

ON THE ROAD

l'autostrada – a motorway/highway
la patente – driving licence
un garage – a garage (for repairs)
nel parcheggio – in the car park
benzina – petrol/gas

una gomma – a tyre
le luci – headlights
il parabrezza – the windscreen
il motore – the engine

USEFUL PHRASES

Parla inglese? – Do you speak English?
Non capisco. – I do not understand.
Parli piano per favore. – Please speak slowly.
Dove sono i bagni? – Where are the toilets?
Dov'è...? – Where's ...?
A che ora parte il treno/l'autobus/l'aereo ...? – At what time does the train/bus/plane leave?
A che ora arriva il treno ...? – At what time does the train ... arrive?
Quanto costa? – How much does it cost?
Dove posso comprare un giornale inglese? – Where can I buy an English newspaper?
Dove posso cambiare i miei soldi? – Where can I change my money?
Entri! – Come in!
Posso pagare con una carta di credito? – May I pay with a credit card?

Admission times and charges

The visiting times marked in the text with the **clock-face** ⊘ symbol indicate the normal hours of opening and closing. These are listed here in the same order as they appear in the main text. Sights which have partial or full access for the disabled are indicated by the symbol (&)/&.

Admission times and charges are liable to alteration without prior notice. Due to fluctuations in the cost of living and the constant change in opening times, the information given here (valid for 2000) should merely serve as a guideline. Visitors are advised to phone ahead to confirm opening times.

Please note that museums, churches or other monuments may be closed without prior notice or may refuse admittance during private functions, religious services or special occasions; they may also stop issuing tickets up to an hour before the actual closing time. When **guided tours** are indicated, the departure time for the last tour of the morning or afternoon will once again be prior to the given closing time.

Most tours are conducted by Italian-speaking guides but in some cases the term "guided tour" may cover group visiting with recorded commentaries. Some of the larger and more frequented museums and monuments offer guided tours in other languages. Enquire at the ticket desk or book stalls.

The **admission prices** indicated are for single adults benefiting from no special concession; reductions for children, students, the over 60s and parties should be requested on site and be endorsed with proof of ID. In some cases, admission is free (notably Wed, Sun and public holidays).

Churches and chapels are usually open from 8am–noon and from 2pm–dusk. Notices outside a number of churches formally request visitors to dress in a manner deemed appropriate when entering a place of worship – this excludes sleeveless and low-cut tops, short miniskirts or skimpy shorts and bare feet. Visitors are not admitted during services and so tourists should avoid visiting at that time. As it is the norm for all churches to be open daily, only exceptional conditions are listed here. When visits to museums, churches or other sites are accompanied by a custodian, it is customary to leave a donation. Most of the works of art in Venice are housed in churches; the most famous of these charge an admission of 3 000L. A 15 000L ticket, valid for six days and allowing admission to six churches, is also available.

A

ACCADEMIA

Gallerie dell'Accademia – Open in summer, Tues–Sun, 9am–9pm (11pm Sat, 8pm Sun), Mon 9am–2pm; in winter, Tues–Sat, 9am–7pm, Sun–Mon, 9am–2pm. Closed 1 Jan, 1 May and 25 Dec. 15 000L, no charge (EU nationals under 18 and over 60). ☎ 041 52 22 247.

ARSENALE

Museo Storico Navale – Open Mon–Fri, 8.45am–1.30pm, Sat, 8.45am–1pm. Closed Sun and public holidays and 21 Nov. 3 000L. ☎ 041 52 00 276.

C

CA' D'ORO

Ca' d'Oro: Galleria Franchetti – Open 9am–2pm (last admission 1.30pm). Closed 1 Jan, 1 May and 25 Dec. 6 000L, no charge (EU nationals under 18 and over 60 as well as during National Heritage Week). Guided (1hr) and audio-guided tours available. ☎ 041 52 22 349.

SESTIER DE S. POLO

PONTE S. POLO

S. Grandadam/EXPLORER

Il CANAL GRANDE

Palazzo Vendramin Calergi: Sala Richard Wagner – Guided tour (1hr) in English, Italian, German and French, Sat, 10.30–11.30am by appointment only (telephone or fax) made before noon the previous Fri. Closed at Christmas and Easter. Donations welcome. Apply to Associazione Richard Wagner di Venezia, Palazzo Albrizzi, 4118, 30131 Venezia. ☏ 041 52 32 544; Fax 041 52 45 275.

I CARMINI

Scuola Grande dei Carmini – Open Mon–Sat, 9am–6pm (4pm Oct to Feb), Sun and public holidays, 9am–1pm. 8 000L, 6 000L (reductions). ☏ 041 52 89 420.

San Sebastiano – Open Mon–Sat, 10am–5pm, Sun 3–5pm. 3 000L. ☏ 041 27 50 462; www.chorus-ve.org

Ca' Rezzonico: Museo del Settecento Veneziano – Closed for restoration at the time of going to press. ☏ 041 520 40 36 (Ca' Rezzonico) or ☏ 041 522 56 25 (Museum Administration).

F

La FENICE

Scuola di San Fantin: Ateneo Veneto – Open Mon–Fri by appointment, 10am–noon and 4–6pm. Closed Sat, Sun, holidays, Aug, 21 Nov, 23 Dec to 7 Jan and from Good Fri to the Tues following Easter. Contact Signora Clara Bordignon, 10am–noon, ☏ 041 52 24 459.

Palazzo Fortuny: Museum – The museum is presently closed for renovation work.

Scala del Bovolo – Open Apr to Oct, 10am–6pm (last admission 5.30pm). Closed Nov to Mar. 3 000L. Guided tour available (20min). ☏ 041 27 02 464; www.provincia.venezia.it/assap

I FRARI

I Frari: interior – Open daily, 9am–6pm, Sun and holidays, 3–6pm. 3 000L. Chorus Associazione Chiese di Venezia ☏ 041 27 50 462.

Scuola di San Giovanni Evangelista – Open Sun and Mon, 10am–5pm. 5 000L. ☏ 041 71 82 34.

Natural History Museum – Closed for restoration work at the time of going to press.

G

Il GHETTO

Museo Ebraico and Synagogues – Guided tours only to the synagogues (approx. 1hr) daily (except Sat and Jewish festivals), in English and Italian (also German, French and Spanish by appointment), June to Sept, 10am–7pm, Oct to May, 10am–4.30pm. Closed 1 Jan, 1 May, 25 Dec and Jewish festivals. Possible early Fri closing when 3.30pm visit may be cancelled or shortened. Full tour 12 000L, 9 000L (child); entrance to museum only 5 000L, 3 000L (child). Bar and restaurant. Bookshop. ☏ 041 71 53 59.

Palazzo Labia – Open by appointment only. ☏ 041 52 42 812.

P

PIAZZA SAN MARCO

Basilica di San Marco

Atrium – Guided tours (1hr) of the mosaics, Apr to June and Sept to Oct, daily (except Sat–Sun), at 11am; July and Aug, daily, every 30min from 10.30–11.30am and 2.30–4pm.

Galleria and Museo Marciano – Open 16 May to 29 Sept, 9.45am–5pm, 30 Sept to 15 May, 9.45am–4pm. 3 000L, 1 500L (child). ☏ 041 52 25 205.

Pala d'Oro – Open 16 May to 29 Sept, Mon–Sat, 9.45am–5pm, Sun and holidays, 2–5pm; 30 Sept to 15 May, Mon–Sat, 9.45am–4pm, Sun and holidays, 2–4pm. 3 000L, 1 500L (child). ☏ 041 52 25 205.

Tesoro – Open 16 May to 29 Sept, Mon–Sat, 9.45am–5pm, Sun and holidays, 2–5pm; 30 Sept to 15 May, Mon–Sat, 9.45am–4pm, Sun and holidays, 2–4pm. 4 000L, 2 000L (child). Audio-guided tour (no charge). ☏ 041 52 22 205.

Baptistery – Open Mon–Sat, 9.30am–4.30pm, Sun and holidays, 2–5pm. ☏ 041 52 22 205.

Il Campanile – Lift access from Apr to Oct, 9.30am–6pm; Nov to Mar, 9.30am–4pm. Closed Jan. 8 000L. Bookshop. ☏ 041 52 25 205.

Palazzo Ducale – Open daily, Apr to Oct, 9am–7pm (last admission 5.30pm); Nov to Mar, daily, 9am–5pm (last admission 3.30pm). Closed 1 Jan and 25 Dec. 18 000L, 10 000L (student aged 15-29), 6 000L (child aged 6–14), no charge (child under 6).

Dream time

Audio-guided tours available. Cafeteria. Ticket also entitles holder to entry to the Museo Correr, Museo Archeologico, Biblioteca Nazionale Marciana, Palazzo Mocenigo, Museo Vetrario di Murano and Museo del Merletto di Burano. ☎ 041 52 24 951.

Tour through the palace corridors *(Itinerari segreti)* – Guided tour by appointment only in Italian at 10am and noon (11am instead of noon in summer); in English at 10.30am. Guided tour in French also available by appointment. 24 000L, 14 000L (student aged 15–29), 8 000L (child aged 6–14).

Museo Correr – Same admission times and charges as Palazzo Ducale.

Silver reflections

Biblioteca Marciana – The library premises are included in the ticket valid for the museums in Piazza San Marco, along with the Palazzo Ducale, Museo Correr and Museo Archeologico Nazionale. Open Apr to Oct, 9am–7pm; Nov to Mar, 9am–5pm. The library reading rooms are open Mon–Fri, 9am–7pm and Sat 9am–1.30pm. The library usually closes for two weeks during the month of Aug. For a reader's pass, apply to the Ufficio Orientamento with personal identification. The special collection of prints, maps and ancient manuscripts may be consulted between 9am and 1.30pm.

Museo Archeologico – Open Apr to Oct, 9am–7pm; Nov to Mar, 9am–5pm. Closed 1 Jan and 25 Dec. 18 000L (ticket also valid for other museums in Piazza San Marco), 6 000L (child under 15). Bar. Bookshop. ☎ 041 52 25 978.

Torre dell'Orologio – Closed for restoration work at time of going to press.

Museo Diocesano di Arte Sacra – Open 10.30am–12.30pm. Closed Sun and holidays. No charge. ☎ 041 52 29 166.

R

RIALTO

Ca' Pesaro

Museo d'Arte Orientale – Open daily (except Mon), 9am–2pm. Closed 1 Jan, 1 May and 25 Dec. 4 000L, no charge (under 18 and over 60). ☎ 041 52 41 173.

Galleria Internazionale di Arte Moderna – Temporarily closed for restoration work. For details, ☎ 041 72 11 27.

Museo di Palazzo Mocenigo – Open daily (except Sun), 8.30am–1.30pm. Closed 1 Jan, 1 May and 25 Dec. 8 000L, 5 000L (child aged 14–18), no charge (child under 14 and Italian nationals over 60). ☎ 041 72 17 98.

S

La SALUTE

Collezione Peggy Guggenheim – Open daily (except Tues), 11am–6pm. Closed 25 Dec. 12 000L, 8 000L (student), no charge (child under 10). Audio-guided tour available. Bar and restaurant. ☎ 041 24 05 411.

SAN GIORGIO MAGGIORE

Campanile – Lift access when church is open 9am (10am winter)–noon and 2.30–6pm (4.30pm winter). 3 000L.

Fondazione Giorgio Cini: Biblioteca and chiostri – (&) Guided tour only (45min) in English, Italian and French, by appointment, daily (except Sat–Sun), 9am–5pm (last admission 4pm). Closed public holidays, Shrove Tuesday, 25 Apr, 1 May, the week of 15 Aug, 21 Nov and 24 Dec to 7 Jan. Apply at least one week in advance to the Cini Foundation, Isola di San Giorgio, ☎ 041 52 89 900; www.cini.it

SAN GIORGIO degli SCHIAVONI

Scuola di San Giorgio degli Schiavoni – Open Apr to Oct, Tues–Sat, 9.30am–12.30pm and 3.30–6.30pm, Sun, 9.30am–12.30pm; Nov to Mar, Tues–Sat, 10am–12.30pm and 3–6pm, Sun 10am–12.30pm. Last admission 20min before closing time. Closed holidays during the week, 1 Jan, 1 May, 15 Aug and 25 Dec. May also close without prior warning at the request of the local brotherhood. 5 000L, 3 000L (child under 18). ☎ 041 52 28 828.

San Giorgio dei Greci – Open Mon–Fri (except Tues), 9.30am–1pm and 2–4.30pm (occasionally 3.30pm), Sat, 9.30am–1pm and 3–7pm (occasionally 5pm), Sun and holidays, 9am–1pm. Closed during services (Sat at 5pm, Sun at 9.30am and 10.30am). Guided tours must be booked in advance by applying to Padre Nicola or Padre Policarpo. Donation welcome. For details, ☎ 041 52 39 569, 041 52 85 391 or 041 52 27 016; www.ortodossia.it

Museo di Icone Bizantine-postbizantine – Open Mon–Sat, 9am–12.30pm and 1.30–4.30pm, Sun and holidays, 10am–5pm. 7 000L, 4 000L (child). Bookshop. ☎ 041 52 26 581.

SAN ROCCO

Scuola Grande di San Rocco – Open 28 Mar to 2 Nov, 9am–5.30pm; Nov, 26 Dec to 6 Jan, Carnival week and Mar, 10am–4pm; Dec to Feb, Mon–Fri, 10am–1pm, Sat–Sun and holidays, 10am–4pm (last admission 30min before closing). Closed 1 Jan, Easter and 25 Dec. Audio-guided tour available. 9 000L, 6 000L (student aged 18-26), no charge (child under 18 accompanied by parents, also for all visitors on St Rocco's feast day, 16 Aug). ☎ 041 52 34 864.

Casa di Goldoni – Temporarily closed for restoration work.

SAN ZACCARIA

San Zaccaria: Cappella del Coro – 2 000L.

Fondazione Querini Stampalia – Open Tues–Thur, 10am–1pm and 3–6pm, Fri and Sat, 10am–1pm and 3–10pm (concerts at 5pm and 8.30pm), Sun and holidays, 10am–1pm and 3–6pm. Closed Mon. 12 000L, 8 000L (student and over 60). ☎ 041 27 11 411.

SAN ZANIPÒLO

Scuola Grande di San Marco – It is possible to visit the library daily (except Sun and holidays), 8.30am–1pm. Follow the arrows for Biblioteca di San Marco at the far end of the first room, turn right, go upstairs and ring the bell.

Oratorio dei Crociferi – Open Apr to Oct, Fri, Sat and Sun, 10am–1pm. 3 000L.

San Michele in Isola: Cimitero – Open summer, 7.30am–6pm; winter, 7.30am–4pm.

The outlying islands

BURANO

Museo del Consorzio Merletti di Burano – Open daily (except Tues), Apr to Oct, 10am–5pm; Nov to Mar, 10am–4pm. 8 000L, 5 000L (child). ☏ 041 73 00 34.

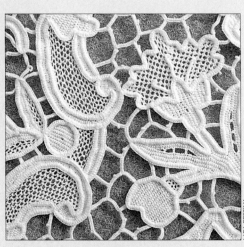

Traditional Burano lace

MURANO

Museo di Arte Vetraria – Open daily (except Wed), in summer, 10am–5pm (last admission 4.30pm), in winter, 10am–4pm (last admission 3.30pm). Closed 1 Jan, 1 May and 25 Dec. Same charges as Palazzo Ducale *(see PIAZZA SAN MARCO)*. For further information, call ☏ 041 73 95 86.

SAN LAZZARO degli ARMENI

Monastery – Guided tours by one of the Armenian monks. 10 000L, 5 000L (child/student). ☏ 041 52 60 104.

TORCELLO

Basilica di Santa Maria Assunta – Open Apr to Oct, 10.30am–5.30pm (last admission 5pm); Nov to Mar, 10am–12.30pm (last admission noon) and 2–5.30pm (last admission 5pm). 5 000L. From Apr to Oct the ticket includes an audio-guided tour in Italian, English, French, German or Spanish. ☏ 041 27 02 464.

Campanile – Guided tour (30min) only in Italian, English, French or German, June to Aug, 10.30am–5.30pm (last admission 5pm); Apr to May, 11.30am–3.30pm (last admission 3pm). Closed Nov to Mar. 3 000L, no charge (child under 6). ☏ 041 27 02 464.

Museum – Open Apr to Sept, daily (except Mon), 10am–12.30pm and 2–5.30pm; Oct to Mar, daily (except Mon), 10.30am–12.30pm and 2–4pm (during this period the archeological section is open Fri, Sat and Sun only). Closed public holidays and 21 Nov. 3 000L. ☏ 041 52 90 589 (office hours) or 041 73 07 61 (museum opening hours); www.provincia.venezia.it/beniculturali

Villas of the Brenta

Il Burchiello – Those wishing to spend a day as an 18C traveller can choose to travel on board the *burchiello*. Although the present-day craft is modern, it follows the same course as it did two centuries ago. It operates between late Mar and late Oct, leaving Padua (Piazzale Boschetti) at 8.15am on Wed, Fri and Sun mornings and arriving in Venice (Piazza San Marco) in the late afternoon, after stopping at Villa Pisani, Villa Widmann Foscari or Barchessa Valmarana and Villa Foscari "La Malcontenta". Departures from Venice (Pontile della Pietà) at 9am on Tues, Thur and Sat. The programme is the same but in reverse order, arriving in Padua in the late afternoon. 120 000L, 70 000L (child aged 6–17), no charge (child under 6). For further details contact New Siamic Express S.r.l., ☏ 049 66 09 44.

Stra

Villa Foscarini – Open Tues–Fri, 9am–noon and 2.30–6pm, Sat–Sun and holidays, 10am–6pm. Closed Mon, Easter, the first three weeks in Aug and from 25 Dec to 31 Jan. 6 000L (includes display of shoes), 4 000L (child and over 60). ☏ 049 98 01 091.

Villa Pisani – Open in summer, 9am–6pm, in winter, 9am–4pm. Closed 1 Jan, 1 May and 25 Dec. 5 000L (gardens only), 10 000L (villa and gardens), no charge (under 18 and over 60, also all visitors during National Heritage Week). ☎ 049 50 20 74.

Mira

Villa Widmann Foscari – Open June to Sept, daily (except Mon), 10am–6pm (7pm Sun and holidays); May and Oct, 10am–5pm (6pm Sun and holidays). ☎ 041 42 41 56 or 041 56 09 350.

Barchessa Valmarana – Open 20 Mar to 3 Nov, daily (except Mon), 9.30am–noon and 2.30–6pm. 8 000L, 4 000L (child). Guided tours in Italian, English, French and German. Bar. Bookshop. ☎ 041 42 66 387.

Oriago

Villa Gradenigo – Open mid-Mar to mid-Nov by appointment only. For details contact the owner Dottore Bellemo. ☎ 041 42 96 31.

Villa Foscari, "La Malcontenta" – Open Apr to mid-Nov, Tues and Sat, 9am–noon. Closed Mon. 12 000L. On other days of the week, by appointment only (15 000L). ☎ 041 52 03 966; fax 041 27 70 204.

Noventa Padovana

Villa Grimani – For details call the villa, ☎ 049 62 52 99.

Villa Giovanelli – By appointment only. For details, ☎ 049 62 50 66.

Vigonovo

Villa Sagredo – By appointment only, Tues–Fri, 6–10pm, Sat-Sun, 2–10pm. Closed Mon, the first two weeks in Jan and for one week around mid-Aug. ☎ 049 50 31 74.

Evening falls over the lagoon

Index

Canale Grande . . . . Building, monument, street or place.
Palladio, Andrea . . . . *Famous or historical figure, term covered by an explanatory note.*

Note: certain sights are listed collectively for easy reference: Campo (square), Canale (canal), Chiesa (church), Chiostro (cloisters), Isola (island), Museo (museum), Palazzo (town house, mansion, palace), Ponte (bridge), Scuola (school), Sestiere (district), Villa (villa).